Cultural Memory
in
the
Present

Mieke Bal and Hent de Vries, Editors

AN ATHEISM THAT IS NOT HUMANIST
EMERGES IN FRENCH THOUGHT

Stefanos Geroulanos

STANFORD UNIVERSITY PRESS

STANFORD, CALIFORNIA

2010

Stanford University Press
Stanford, California

Printed in the United States of America on acid-free, archival-quality paper.

Library of Congress Cataloging-in-Publication Data

Geroulanos, Stefanos, 1979–
    An atheism that is not humanist emerges in French thought / Stefanos
Geroulanos.
        p.   cm. — (Cultural memory in the present)
    Includes bibliographical references and index.
    ISBN 978-0-8047-6298-4 (cloth : alk. paper)
    ISBN 978-0-8047-6299-1 (pbk : alk. paper)
    1. Atheism—France—History—20th century.   2. Humanism—France—
History—20th century.   3. Philosophical anthropology—France—History—
20th century.   4. Philosophy, French—20th century.   I. Title.   II. Series:
Cultural memory in the present.
BL2765.F8G47   2010
128.09'04—dc22

                                                        2009049745

Contents

Acknowledgments

I wrote the original version of this book while at the Humanities Center at Johns Hopkins University in 2005–2007, and then a second, restructured, and longer version after joining New York University's History Department in 2008. I would like to first thank Hent de Vries and Anson Rabinbach for their extraordinary advice and direction throughout. Hent has contributed much of the force and fine-tuning of this book's philosophical voice. Since my undergraduate years, Andy—in equal measure generous, supportive, and critical—has been a wonderful guide to history and its demands on philosophy. At the Humanities Center, Michael Fried, Ruth Leys, Paola Marrati, Neil Hertz, and Richard Macksey, but also Samantha Fenno, Nils Schott, Molly Warnock, and many others showed me trust, critique, encouragement, and friendship; they made my time and study there a singular learning experience. Sam Moyn offered very useful comments on the first complete version of the book, as did Martin Jay on the penultimate draft. I would also like to thank David A. Bell, Peter Gordon, Denis Hollier, Jean-Luc Marion, Jacques Neefs, Molly Nolan, Arkady Plotnitsky, Pamela Reynolds, Jerrold Seigel, Gabrielle Spiegel, and Arnd Wedemeyer, who have, in public or private, been generous in their reading and criticisms of the book's chapters. In Paris, Giuseppe Bianco, Marc Crépon, Michel Déguy, Denis Guénoun, Claude Imbert, Eric Michaud, Frédéric Worms, and the late Stéphane Mosès directed me toward important realizations and research finds; so did Françoise Coblence, who hosted me during no fewer than three research visits and whose amazing hospitality and friendship are very dear to me.

In my research, I have benefited from the help of many librarians and archivists: M. Vasen (EHESS Centre Alexandre Koyré); G. Fau, Fl. de Lussy, and M.-O. Germain (Bibliothèque Nationale); Father R. Bonfils (Archives Jésuites), Cl. Paulhan (IMEC-Wahl); the librarians at the Bibliothèque Littéraire J. Doucet; M. Handzo and S. Waterman at the M. S. Eisenhower Library at Johns Hopkins; and Andrew Lee at NYU's Bobst Library. I have made considerable use of texts from these archives, and I would like to thank Mmes. Béatrice Wahl, Edith Heurgon, and Nina Kousnetzoff, respectively, for allowing me to use and reference materials from the archives of Jean Wahl, the Centre Culturel International de Cerisy, and Alexandre Kojève. A Charlotte W. Newcombe Fellowship from the Woodrow Wilson Foundation in 2005–2006 provided the support for the first draft of the book. I have presented portions of this book during lectures and conferences at the Centre International des Etudes de la Philosophie Française Contemporaine of the Ecole Normale Supérieure, the Centre des Etudes Européennes of the Ecole Nationale d'Administration in Strasbourg, the 2006 American Comparative Literature Association conference, the 2007 Modern Language Association conference, the Comparative Literature Department at the University at Buffalo, the Department of French at Yale University, the History Department at NYU, the Davis Center for Historical Studies at Princeton, and the New York Area Seminar for Intellectual History. I am very grateful to participants at these talks for their criticisms. Fragments of my "An Anthropology of Exit" (*October* 117 [summer 2006]) have been considerably altered for use in Chapter 4; a part of Chapter 6 appeared in my essay "Transparency Thinking Freedom: Maurice Blanchot's *The Most High*" in *MLN* 122, no. 5 (December 2007). At Stanford University Press, I owe a debt to Emily-Jane Cohen who welcomed the book, Tim Roberts who shepherded it through production, and Alex Giardino, who copyedited it. Sona Arutyunyan offered helpful comments at the very last stage of corrections. My thanks also to *The Criterion Collection* for permitting the use of the still from Renoir's *La Règle du jeu* on the book's cover.

I have left for last friends and family who have shown me that this kind of work was worth the effort and can have a future. Chrysanthi Moraiti-Kartali and my late grandmother Sarah Carouso in different ways launched my studies; I am so thankful to them and saddened that Sarah is not here to see this conclusion. My sister Sarra and my late brother Alexis participate, in very different ways, in the thoughts that went into these pages. Joyce Tsai has been a close friend and exacting reader for a decade now. Nicole Jerr has changed the way I think about writing and about the implications of what I have been writing about, with a style and grace that are distinctly hers. Since my arrival in New York, Larry Wolff has been a great friend and mentor, and he has opened worlds for me. Richard Baxstrom and Todd Meyers are comrades, co-conspirators, rare friends: to look back at the writing of this book is both to remember those first years thinking and laughing together and to watch our other conspiracies that are only now beginning to unfold. Throughout my studies and work, my wife Rania has been and is the light and smile of my days and nights; the effort that went into this book would not be worth it if it were not for her brilliance and her elegance and her excitement and her love. Above all, that this work has come to being is a direct consequence of my parents' effort and sacrifices throughout my studies. They supported and guided me without once complaining about or questioning the path I chose and, most importantly, without always understanding what I did and why, and what I sought to achieve. Dedicating this book to them is a very small expression of my love and gratitude.

Baltimore, Paris, Delaportata, New York, 2005–2009

Abbreviations

A   Immanuel Kant, *Anthropology from a Pragmatic Point of View* (The Hague: Nijhoff, 1974).

ALP   Paul Nizan, *Articles littéraires et politiques*, vol. 1: 1923–35, ed. Anne Mathieu (Paris: Joseph K., 2005).

AT   Alexandre Kojève, *L'Athéisme* (Paris: Gallimard, 1998). This is a French translation of an unpublished text originally in Russian. My translations are from the French.

BA   Fonds Kojève 12, "Identité et Réalité dans le Dictionnaire de Pierre Bayle" (unpublished article on Pierre Bayle).

BC   Fonds Kojève 13, "La Critique de la Religion au 17ème siècle: Pierre Bayle" (summer 1937 course on Bayle at the Ecole Pratique des Hautes Etudes).

BN   Georges Bataille, *The Blue of Noon* (New York: Consortium, 2002).

BT   Martin Heidegger, *Being and Time*, trans. Macquarrie and Robinson (New York: Harper and Row, 1962).

DKH   Gwendoline Jarczyk and Pierre-Jean Labarrière, *De Kojève à Hegel: Cent cinquante ans de pensée hégélienne en France* (Paris: Albin Michel, 1996). Translations of Kojève's review of Fessard are from *Interpretation* 19, no. 2 (winter 1991–92): 188–92.

E   Emmanuel Levinas, *On Escape*, trans. Bettina Bergo (Stanford: Stanford University Press, 2003). First published as "De l'évasion," *Recherches philosophiques* V (1935–36): 373–92.

EG   Martin Heidegger, "On the Essence of Ground," in *Pathmarks* (Cambridge: Cambridge University Press, 1998). First published in French as "De la nature de la cause," *Recherches philosophiques* I (1931–32): 83–124.

EH   Jean-Paul Sartre, *L'Existentialisme est un humanisme* (Paris: Nagel, 1970). English translation as "Existentialism Is a Humanism," in *Existentialism from Dostoyevsky to Sartre*, ed. Walter Kaufmann (New York: Meridian Publishing Company, 1989), 287–311.

F   Jean Hyppolite, *Figures de la pensée philosophique*, vol. 1 (Paris: PUF, 1971).

HRP   Bibliothèque Nationale de France, Mss. Occ., Fonds Kojève 10, "La Philosophie religieuse de Hegel" (unpublished notes from the fifth year [1937–38] of Kojève's Hegel course at the Ecole Pratique des Hautes Etudes).

HT   Maurice Merleau-Ponty, *Humanism and Terror* (Boston: Beacon Press, 1969).

ID   Alexandre Kojève, *L'Idée du déterminisme dans la physique classique et dans la physique moderne* (Paris: Biblio-Essais, 1990).

IDPH   "The Idea of Death in the Philosophy of Hegel," in *Hegel and Contemporary Continental Philosophy*, ed. D. K. Keenan (Albany: State University of New York Press, 2004), 27–74.

IE   Georges Bataille, *Inner Experience*, trans. Leslie Anne Boldt (Albany: State University of New York Press, 1988).

IH   Jacques Maritain, *Integral Humanism*, in *The Collected Works of Jacques Maritain XI: Integral Humanism, Freedom in the Modern World, and A Letter on Independence*, ed. Otto Bird (Notre Dame, IN: University of Notre Dame Press, 1996), 141–345.

ILH   Alexandre Kojève, *Introduction à la lecture de Hegel*, 2d ed. (Paris: Gallimard, 1968). Existing translations are from *Introduction to the Reading of Hegel* (Ithaca, NY: Cornell University Press, 1980), and from IDPH.

L   Jean Hyppolite, *Logic and Existence*, trans. Leonard Lawlor and Amit Sen (Albany: State University of New York Press, 1997).

LCr   Thierry Maulnier, *La Crise est dans l'homme* (Paris: Redier [La Revue Française], 1932).

LH   Martin Heidegger, "Letter on 'Humanism,'" in *Pathmarks* (Cambridge: Cambridge University Press, 1998).

MF   André Malraux, *Man's Fate* [*La Condition humaine*], trans. Haakon Chevalier (New York: Vintage, 1990).

MT   Gaston Fessard, *La Main tendue? Le dialogue catholique-communiste est-il possible?* (Paris: Grasset, 1937).

MU   Alexis Carrel, *Man the Unknown* (London/New York: Harper and Brothers, 1935). In French, Paris: Librairie Plan, 1935.

NA   Alexandre Kojève, *La Notion de l'autorité* (Paris: Gallimard, 2004).

NES   Gaston Bachelard, *Le Nouvel esprit scientifique* (Paris: PUF, 1934/1958); English translation, *The New Scientific Spirit* (Boston: Beacon Press, 1984).

NHH   Alexandre Kojève, "Note sur Hegel et Heidegger," *Rue Descartes* 7 (1993): 35–46.

OC   Georges Bataille, *Oeuvres complètes* (Paris: Gallimard, 1969–). Followed by the volume number in roman numerals.

PhP   Maurice Merleau-Ponty, *Phenomenology of Perception*, trans. Colin Smith (New York: Routledge, 1962).

PL   Georges Bataille, *Romans et récits* (Paris: Gallimard [Pleiade], 2004).

RP   *Recherches philosophiques* I–VI (Paris: Bovin, 1932–37).

SNS   Maurice Merleau-Ponty, *Sense and Non-Sense*, trans. Hubert Dreyfus and Patricia Allen Dreyfus (Evanston, IL: Northwestern University Press, 1964).

TE   Jean-Paul Sartre, *La Transcendance de l'ego* (Paris: Vrin, 1965); English translation, *The Transcendence of the Ego* (New York: Noonday Press, 1957). First published in *Recherches philosophiques* VI (1936–37): 85–123.

TW   André Malraux, *The Temptation of the West*, trans. R. Hollander (Chicago: University of Chicago Press, 1992).

U   Jean Hyppolite, "Humanisme et hégélianisme," in *Umanesimo e scienza politica*, ed. Enrico Castelli (Milan: C. Marzorati, 1951).

VC   Jean Wahl, *Vers le concret: Études d'histoire de la philosophie contemporaine* (Paris: Vrin, 1932).

WD   Paul Nizan, *The Watchdogs: Philosophers of the Established Order* (New York: Monthly Review, 1971).

WF   Maurice Blanchot, *The Work of Fire* (Stanford: Stanford University Press, 1995).

All translations from materials not already translated into English are mine. By and large, I have used existing translations so as to ease referencing, but at times I have amended the texts as necessary.

AN ATHEISM THAT IS NOT HUMANIST
EMERGES IN FRENCH THOUGHT

Man Under Erasure: Introduction

I walk among human beings as among the fragments and limbs of human beings! This is what is most frightening to my eyes, that I find mankind in ruins and scattered about as if on a battlefield or a butcher field.

—NIETZSCHE, *Thus Spoke Zarathustra*

But if cows [and horses] and lions had hands / or could draw with their hands and make things as men can make / then horses would draw the forms of gods like horses / cows like cows, and they would make their bodies / similar in shape to those which each had themselves

—XENOPHANES

"Man" is the ideology of dehumanization.

—ADORNO, "THE JARGON OF AUTHENTICITY"

1. Neither Gods Nor Men

From World War I through the 1950s, a philosophical and intellectual revolution in France created a new kind of atheism, demolished the value of humanism, and altered the meaning of "the human" virtually beyond recognition. French thought began in the mid-interwar period to reject central intellectual foundations of nineteenth-century atheism and priorities of inquiries that had forged and sustained conceptions in which man was based on a human "nature" or "essence" that is given or immutable, or served as his own highest being and ideal. Faced with philosophical opposition and political catastrophe, the status of humanism eroded dramatically, taking with it the imagination of a modern humanity based on innate qualities, character, or rights. Once a foundation of knowledge, man was reconceived as a construct of science and technology, religion and history, cultural structure and political fashioning. Once the horizon of existence and thought, the human being became a self-doubting mystery lacking all existential or epistemic certainty other than its own death. Once an ethical criterion and a priority of secular, atheist, and egalitarian commitments, humanism now offered evidence of an imperialism supposedly inherent in modern political projects. Allegedly corrupted by capitalism, humanism appeared to many philosophers and writers as an indefensible foundation of a modernity that needed to be overcome. Through its decline, humanism freed a space for a series of conceptual reorganizations in atheism, in philosophical anthropology, in the understanding of the history of modern thought, and also in a host of problems in contemporary metaphysics and epistemology. The very process of thinking and defining the human imploded a conceptual foundation of modern thought into an unstable category, a figure, even an aporia.

The bulk of this conceptual reorganization took place in the period 1925 to 1950. By the mid-1960s, it had acquired the name "antihumanism" and had become an almost official face of French thought. Yet already by the mid-1930s, a number of very different philosophers and writers had come to recognize their century as an unredeemable era welded by catastrophe, false secular utopias, political hopelessness, and humanist stalemate, and many of them explicitly claimed that an insistence on the ambitions of humanism (as suggested by communism and other political projects) would not ease the suffering. If the nineteenth century was marked by a "Death of God," Man after the era of catastrophe—the age of World War I, the rise of Nazism, Stalinism, World War II, and the immediate postwar period—could no longer claim to fill the void left by God's absence without bringing forth the worst in human history and paradoxically denigrating the dignity of the human subject. Atheist humanism, especially after World War II, could no longer claim to offer a powerful and sufficient ethics for this world. Nor could the persistent conception of this world in terms of the philosophical and political centrality of *Man* (a conception dating to Descartes and proceeding through the tradition of natural law, the Enlightenment, the French Revolution, and nineteenth-century liberalism and Marxism) offer satisfactory alternatives to the economic, material, and political division and ruin of Europe. To approach anew the codes addressing human life and significance, these thinkers developed the case for an atheist ethics not bound by humanism, rejecting Man's prominence as founder and guarantor of knowledge, thought, and ethics, and seeking to offer alternatives to the political and historical impasse they diagnosed.

The political and cultural stakes of this rejection of central premises of post-Enlightenment, liberal, and socialist European thought cannot be overestimated. The emergence and elaboration of "philosophical antihumanism" relied on (and fed into) a set and perhaps even a system of philosophical and political arguments. It became closely linked with a growing mistrust for the utopian and redemptive claims of fascism and communism alike, a contempt for the liberal compromises of the Third Republic, and a broad disappointment with the political engagements of the interwar period. The denigration of France to secondary-power status and the failure of the *résistance* to bring about a more radical change toward socioeconomic equality following the 1944 *libération* contributed further to the mistrust and disappointment. And as a response to this age, the new nonhumanist atheism came to be expressed at different times in existentialist, hyper-ethical, or cynical terms, in nondoctrinaire socialist, reactionary, ultramodernist, or even downright antipolitical principles.

Studying the range of these positions and the way this range was coupled with a precise philosophical and theological transformation that grounded and formed it, this book proposes to reconstruct the emergence of an atheism disengaged from humanism during the second quarter of the twentieth century. It approaches this philosophical, intellectual, and theological problem in its historical and institutional context, in order to show the theoretical reformulations, the political and strategic implications, and above all the resonance of this new atheism and its philosophical world. My argument is that the shift away from classical atheism and humanism should be understood in terms of a synthesis of three parallel and interconnected movements, movements in which very different thinkers with divergent aims and arguments participate. The development, during the 1930s and 1940s, of *an atheism that would not be humanist*—that is to say an atheism mistrustful of secular, egalitarian, and transformative commitments—is the first and central change described here. But it is also a development echoed by and expressed in two others: the emergence of a *negative philosophical anthropology*, and the post-1918 elaboration of *critiques of humanism.* Each of these three movements has its own history, its conceptual development, its sphere of import—and from the viewpoint of their respective discourses, each seems to encompass the others, to offer a space for their emergence.

2. Atheism Beyond the Death of God

Atheism is traditionally identified with secularism and humanism. To make up for the absence of God *in res hominem*, nineteenth-century thinkers from Feuerbach and Comte through Marx and Proudhon, Wagner and Nietzsche linked their atheism with positive ethico-philosophical arguments or projects that claimed to provide for man, as highest being, the modes and possibility of a good life and proper society. Feuerbach famously proclaimed, in *The Essence of Christianity,* that God was but a projection of human nature onto the heavens, indeed nothing more and nothing less than man's representation of his own essence.[1] Yet more explicitly, Feuerbach opened the *Principles of the Philosophy of the Future* with the famous statement, "The task of the modern era was the realization and humanization of God—the transformation and dissolution of theology into anthropology."[2] In France, Auguste Comte tied his positivist project for science and knowledge to a "religion of humanity," a metaphysical and world-historical vision originating in Saint-Simon's utopian socialism and offering an explicitly religious atheism replete with its own catechism, theory of knowledge, and sociological implications.[3] Pierre-Joseph Proudhon used *humanisme* in the later 1840s in a fashion that has been identified recently as an early appearance in France of the term in its modern, and nowadays quotidian, sense.[4]

By the conclusion of the Dreyfus Affair, distance from Catholicism and conservatism (in philosophy, literature, and the political domain) indicated a political engagement that could be identified as humanist; by the 1910s, more importantly, liberalism, "humanism, and idealism" had become moral and political expectations of the secular education projects that the Third Republic supported.[5] *Humanism,* in this broad sense, became what could reach, reveal, and cultivate the proper and ethical *humanum* of man. It turned this edification of man into the core of ethics, and man himself into the irreducible, perfectible bearer and guarantor of dignity, equality, and freedom.

In the aftermath of World War I, this idea of a humanism that suffices as a project, as a mode of life, or as an ethical ground comes to be rejected. Atheism's subsequent antihumanist turn, is perhaps best described by the formulation *an atheism that is not humanist,* which I borrow from an expression of Emmanuel Levinas:

Contemporary thought holds the surprise for us of an atheism that is not humanist. The gods are dead or withdrawn from the world; concrete, even rational man does not contain the universe. In all those books that go beyond metaphysics we witness the exaltation of an obedience and a faithfulness that are not obedience or faithfulness *to* anyone.[6]

The tendency that Levinas points to, this "surprising" disengagement of atheism from humanist hopes, this refusal to direct obedience or faithfulness at someone—Man or God—grounds the far-reaching transformation that occurs across Western European thought from the 1920s onward. Behind this development lay, to a considerable degree, World War I—and even more so World War II. The first war forced philosophers—as it did artists and poets—to address the possibility, fact, and effect of such unprecedented carnage at the heart of a Europe identified with progress and the supposed pinnacle of modernity, opening up an apocalyptic imagination and by and large destroying the cultural optimism that had marked the turn of the twentieth century.[7] In France, a number of young and later prominent philosophers and literary figures identified atheism, the "death of God," and the philosophical enterprise itself, *not* with secularism *but* with the collapse of a unified and virtuous figure of Western man, and with a sense of entrapment in a hostile and dangerous world. Rather than see man's modern control of nature as a sign of liberation, they found in WWI and in the rise of fascism and Stalinism evidence of a devastating failure of individual Man (and Man the species) to come to terms with the world he inhabited so as to offer a ground for ethics, knowledge, and hope. For example, in his early writings on atheism and his famous 1930s lectures on Hegel, Alexandre Kojève distanced himself from the more programmatic aspects of Feuerbach's overcoming of religion and sounded instead a somber note, seeing his times as imprisoning the human being (which had usurped God's place) in a vicious circle marked by violence and the impossibility of further change—almost a "cosmic catastrophe" as he would later put it. Like Kojève, many contemporaries rejected the (communist, democratic, or fascist) options offered by the political world, treating these as ideologies equivalent to religions and reconceiving atheism as a way out of any and all ideological systems. For example, his student and friend Georges Bataille, offering a reading of Nietzsche attuned to this sense of spiritual/political devastation, wrote that "Nietzsche revealed this primordial fact: that once the bourgeoisie had killed God, the immediate result would be catastrophic confusion, emptiness, and even a sinister impoverishment."[8]

In these claims we find a series of theological questions mixed with a mistrust of political hopes and utopias.[9] Indeed, efforts toward the new atheism doubled as reformulations of the theologico-political domain—a new atheist political theology, a new relation of man (and the political domain) to the interrogation (and refusal) of the divine. This may at first appear surprising, given that religion would seem to have little ground in common with a radical antifoundationalism seeking to understand the modern condition not even by crying out "Neither Gods nor Masters!" but rather by whispering "neither God, nor Man. . . . " Yet this non- or antihumanist atheism configured both its secularist competitors and itself as engagements with religion and the divine. For it, theological shadows lurked in the history of modern thought, in concepts and ontological arrangements that ground notions of man, and even in political movements that flaunted their secular credentials. Hence the new atheism's fundamental opposition to the traditional atheist dismissals of religion as obsolete, as overcome by a combination of scientific teleology and social egalitarianism that supposedly aimed toward man's self-perfection *sans* God. Instead, for philosophers like Koyré, Kojève, Bataille, and Heidegger, secular humanisms tend toward religion (and specifically toward a naturalized Christianity). This is especially so because they are attached to ideological claims (and hence grow into what Raymond Aron in July 1944 called "secular religions") and also because they tend to replace God with man, history, a political messianism, the Nation, or the State, frequently pushing under the rug religious problems and questions.[10] Even the new efforts toward an atheism divested of humanist and ideological premises consciously maintain the theological and specifically Christian premise, structure, and/or history of certain questions, to the extent of critically rethinking problems of *anthropotheism*, of *transcendence*, of *finitude,* and so on. Nonhumanist atheism's determined opposition to foundational concepts of man, knowledge, and truth thus contributed to both a diagnosis of religion within humanism, and a self-diagnosis that revealed a dependency on Christian and theological motifs yet did not discredit its atheist credentials and politics. Kojève specifically saw the atheist's inability to think a *voie vers Dieu* as a major failure of atheism in general, which he used to develop a broad revision of "anthropotheism"—the divinization of man that Feuerbach, Comte, Wagner, and others had announced as a necessary consequence of modern self-consciousness and that Nietzsche had located in the Overman's replacement of the dead God and the diseased bourgeois man. A triumph of anthropotheism (in which Kojève thought Hegel's history was culminating) in fact denigrated man to a part of nature, to a content sacred animal wasted in the abyss of a futureless presence.[11] The 1930s critics of classical transcendence made no lesser claims regarding the effects of their philosophical work: Wahl, Koyré, Sartre, Bataille, and Levinas all came to treat the end of classical transcendence as a philosophically necessary and valuable gesture that nevertheless bore with it existential and religious catastrophes—for them, the disenchantment of the world was, politically speaking, a death knell for man. The entrapment of man in immanence had the particular effect of calling up as necessary an escape from the overdetermined world of politics and anthropotheist secularization—an escape that was nevertheless all but impossible.

No less significant to the development of a new political theology was a critique of 1920s idealism (which led to the critique of transcendence in the first place). In the 1920s, atheist humanism remained closely identified with idealist arguments about the capacity of the human mind to transcend and objectively pattern the things that compose the world around it. The new atheism rose with transformations in contemporary philosophy of science, with the reintroduction of Hegel around 1930, and with the new epistemological questions that guided the contemporary reception of German phenomenology. The introduction of scientific and phenomenological innovations brought about new debates over the notion of reality, which resulted in a philosophical rejection of subjectivist idealism—and the variety of atheism and political hope that this idealism bore with it.[12] To the point, the human subject was posited anew as thrown into its world, as finite, and above all as marked by its perennially unsuccessful attempt to come to terms with this world—a world that it plays a part in forming but cannot fully comprehend.[13] Because the world exceeds man, man forces himself onto the world and seeks to map it according to the picture he has formed of it. Yet, philosophers such as Wahl, Koyré, and Kojève argued, this attempt fails to offer a harmonious knowledge of the universe either in scientific terms (notably through the quantum critique of determinism), or in theological or existential ones. This *antifoundational realism* radically reorganized the terms of the philosophical discussion of atheism and the capacity of human knowledge. It stressed that man exists in a reality that is not only void of classical transcendence but also far greater and more complicated than he could understand. At the same time, this reality cannot be treated as simply independent of human consiousness: reality is always "human reality"—per the famous early French rendition of Martin Heidegger's *Dasein*.[14] This critique essentially destroyed the progressivist, teleological, and utopian hopes nineteenth-century atheism had associated with science as an objective representation, and it suggested the humanism of early twentieth-century idealists, realists, and positivists to be theoretically obsolete, scientifically false, and ethically disastrous.[15] In this context, Kojève, Sartre, and Bataille specifically sought an atheism for which the human subject did not simply "overcome" religion and institute a divine humanity that dominates this otherwise godless universe, but instead remained lost in a world without God, constructing gods over and over—whether in religions or in ideologies—and striving to understand this realm that exceeds it.

After 1945, the effort to escape from "secular religions" and subjectivist or voluntarist atheisms intensified. With the destruction left behind by World War II, as well as with the failure of humanism to even mitigate the violence, this atheist critique of transcendence, progress, and utopia turned into an ethical question of whether humanism places an excessive burden on man, drawing up paradises whose construction produces, rather than banishes, human suffering, and whose arrival cannot guarantee the (moral as well as political) harmony it promises. What was also troubling was that the might and violence of ideologies relied on definitions of humanity that made this violence entirely plausible, rational, and for their partisans, almost necessary.[16] Such violence now delegitimated ideologies (including communism and colonialism) in which those defined as men could live with their decency and justice guaranteed regardless of what happened in the name of their humanity.

Particularly significant in this context was Jean-Paul Sartre's shift from an antihumanist ambivalence much informed by 1930s developments in the 1943 *Being and Nothingness* to an adamant defense of a specific kind of minimal humanist commitment in his postwar writing. In his October 1945 lecture "Existentialism Is a Humanism," Sartre called for a new atheist humanism that would allow each man to be suspicious of the failures, religious implications, and violence of any humanism.[17]

One may understand by humanism a theory which upholds man as the end-in-itself and as the supreme value. . . . That kind of humanism is absurd . . . an existentialist will never take man as the end, since man is still to be determined. And we have no right to believe that humanity is something to which we could set up a cult, after the manner of Auguste Comte. The cult of humanity ends in Comtian humanism, shut in on itself, and—this must be said—in Fascism. We do not want a humanism like that. But there is another sense of the word. . . . There is no other universe except the human universe, the universe of human subjectivity. This relation of transcendence as constitutive of man (not in the sense that God is transcendent, but in the sense of self-surpassing) with subjectivity (in such a sense that man is not shut up in himself but forever present in a human universe)—it is this that we call existential humanism. (EH 90–93 / 309–10)

Yet Sartre's turn met with detractors not only among Marxists, Catholics, and the political center—as is well known. Instead, his minimal "existential humanism" was accused by several of Sartre's contemporaries of palliating (and hence contributing to) the very worldview he was criticizing. If his existentialism seemed to bear out the 1930s phenomenological claim that the failure of foundations and of man's status in the universe ultimately called up a new ethical command, most intellectuals who had been instrumental in setting up antifoundational realism nevertheless refused his call for man to decide and to commit politically: this would bind the new atheism to political humanisms and old metaphysical commitments. Instead, at stake for them was a persistent effort to produce new categories unbound by any sense that "there is no other universe except the human universe, the universe of human subjectivity"—by any sense that man is at the center of his world. To the extent that historians and philosophers treat these social and theologico-political problems as formative of a certain Western secular project, the recoil that characterizes the 1930s and 1940s speaks precisely of the movement toward a different political theology. Two more important aspects complicate further the stakes of the new atheism.

First, the atheist recoil from humanism mirrored to a considerable degree the Catholic critique of humanism—indeed at a time when progressive Catholics were turning to embrace a particular kind of "humanism" all the while rejecting secular humanism itself. Just as Catholicism had argued in criticizing secularism, humanity could not ground and fully explain the world it exists in. Pascal, in a classic French reference on the travails of the human condition, had made this very point at the beginning of his *Pensées*, opposing the "Wretchedness of man without God" with the "Happiness of man with God."[18] Ever since Joseph de Maistre, Catholic philosophers had argued vehemently that in an "enlightened" world deprived of God, men find themselves not only abandoned in a desperate, irredeemable situation but also deprived of genuine equality, hope, and ethical standards and obligations.[19] Atheism could not possibly be respectful to human beings, as no claims of respect for man could ever undo the harm carried out through the banishing of God. Yet while contemporary Christian personalism and the "new theology" looked to God to unite humanity and ground the dignity of the individual, this generation of atheist thinkers rejected this alternative as well.[20] Thus the Catholic and Counter-Enlightenment charge against atheism—that the human being (as imagined by secularism) cannot be grounded in itself, and is hence incapable of redemption and incapable of fully comprehending the world through its limited faculties—was now paradoxically imported into atheism, but without Christian promises.[21]

Second, a definitive aspect of the new atheist political theology— and perhaps the best description of its critique of classical atheism—is that it specifically targeted what philosophers like Kojève, Bataille, Sartre, and Koyré (not to mention Heidegger and Theodor W. Adorno) thought of as its mysticism of progress, self-perfection, and history. For them, atheism led, despite itself, to a dehumanization of man—indeed a dehumanization that humanism could not recognize or admit. Against this mysticism, they played with a series of other, no less mystical figures that lies only barely under their texts' surface, particularly in their anti-utopian and antiprogressivist claims and that found expression in the later literature of Maurice Blanchot (*The Last Man* and especially *The Most High*), in Georges Bataille's *Summa Atheologica*, in Albert Camus's *The Myth of Sisyphus*, in Beckett's *Molloy* and *Endgame*. Similarly, the revision of anthropotheism, the figuration of finitude, the critique of dreams of transparency, the effort to replace transcendence with excess or escape—all these figures persist, indeed with a certain mystical background or emphasis that can be felt even in the very effort involved in undoing the possibility of un-self-conscious humanist mysticism.[22] It is in this sense that the effort to overcome atheist anthropocentrism opens to religious and theological problems and questions that now come to coexist with its more radical overturning of both Christianity and atheism.

The abandoning of humanism in atheist thought could thus portray man through a dual figure: weak, mysterious, nonsovereign on the one hand, and on the other, a totalitarian Moloch trying unsuccessfully to portray himself as God, to dominate nature and other men.[23] At stake in this double critique was not a nihilism that, unsatisfied with the "death of God," wished to dispense with socialist hope or "human rights."[24] Instead, the goal groomed in the interwar period was the questioning of the secular Europe that, blasphemously raising the human subject to all-powerful status, had brought itself to the point of techno-scientific apocalypse and to a waste of hope in the self and in the rhetoric of equality and humanism.[25] If modern political movements had failed to improve on God's failures, then their intellectual aridity had to be interpreted in terms that could release philosophy and politics from the rigid, wishful image of man as a good subject and worthy goal in himself.[26] In this sense as well, the atheism that emerges during the interwar period bleeds into concepts of the human, particularly "negative" ones.

3. "Negative" Philosophical Anthropology

The second major dimension of philosophical antihumanism is its contribution to—and conceptual dependence on—the gradual elaboration of a *negative philosophical anthropology*. Negative anthropology, by and large an internal philosophical and theological problematic, attempts a generalized interpretation of man in terms that place unified notions of the human in suspension and deny that it owns or controls his own specificity and particularity. I understand negative anthropology by reference to two histories and traditions: that of negative theology, and that of the modern determinations of "the human."

First, negative anthropology mirrors the principal claim and inspiration of negative theology—the denial to man of positive knowledge of divine nature and the refusal to him of affirmations concerning this nature. By the start of the 1950s—the endpoint of the present study—most philosophers (including figures involved in politics and humanist commitments) rejected the very possibility of an irreducible or given *human nature*, of a *natural man*, or of something in man that is *essentially* or *fundamentally human* and that forms the core of human existence, interaction, creativity, and so forth. Not only could man no longer pose as the crux, end, or foundation of philosophical enterprise, but also the very possibility of conceiving the specificity of man's humanity had come into doubt. Accordingly, what I call negative anthropology is a withdrawal from the possibility of first defining what is specifically human to human beings, their relations, and their self-conceptions, or of treating the worlds of phenomena, practical action, society, existence, and thought as (mental or real) constructs of human subjectivity.[27] Against conceptions of nature and the world deemed anthropocentric and subjectivist, negative anthropology reformulates the question of man, locating him in—and redefining him through—conceptual systems led by notions (such as Being, reality, society, or language) posited as more fundamental than him and as imperative to understanding him. Thus approached, negative anthropology emerges out of two intermingling problematics: (1) the interrogation of man in terms that redefine him by granting priority to other aspects of thought, existence, and so forth (which is to say to define him "negatively" vis-à-vis these aspects); and (2) the problematization of human subjectivity, or—among phenomenologists—of the determination of the human as subject.

Second, negative anthropology offers a broad response to efforts to determine human nature and to define "what is human" since the early

Enlightenment. Participating in a long tradition of treatises on human nature, on the qualities of man, his rights, aspects, and so on, Denis Diderot writes in the article "L'Homme" of the *Encyclopédie*: "Man—masc. sing.—is a sensing, reflecting, thinking being, which freely traverses the surface of the earth, which appears at the head of all other animals over which it reigns, which lives in society, which has invented the sciences and the arts, which has its own notions of good and evil, which gives itself masters, which makes its own laws, etc." The definition is exemplary not only of the anthropocentrism that emerged with modern thought but also of efforts in the eighteenth and nineteenth centuries that sought to address the character or summarize the qualities, faculties, or aspects of the human, frequently offering a hierarchy and linking the human to a privileged one among them—to reason, understanding, sensation, the passions, consciousness, the intellect, and so on.[28] Similarly, in the famous article "Encyclopédie," Diderot writes, "Why do we not introduce man into our work the way he is placed in the universe? Why do we not make him a common center? Is there some point in infinite space from which we can to greater advantage draw the immense lines we propose to stretch to all other points? What a lively and sweet reaction it would create from all beings to man and from man to all meanings."[29] What changes with the advent of negative anthropology is that this kind of definition becomes not just problematic but irrelevant. Qualities attributed to man in Diderot's definition no longer really belong to him: man is no longer to be talked about as the frame for thought, or as the masculine singular of a sensing, reflecting, thinking being, or as "the common center." He can no longer claim to be capable of scientifically understanding the entire world. To the extent that man may still be a sensing, reflecting, thinking being, negative anthropology would counter that these are not properties that simply belong to, or are at play with the fact of his humanity—which is, after all, what is in question here.

A second significant contrast is to Kant who, in his *Logic*, famously founded the three core questions guiding his critical project—*What do I know? What may I hope for? What ought I do?*—on a fourth, *What is man?*[30] Kant thus situated the problem of man at the base of his entire philosophy, and retroactively re-interpreted the three *Critiques* as aiming to address and offer a path toward answering the basic anthropological question.[31] This stance is bolstered further when read together with the opening of the *Anthropology from a Pragmatic Point of View*, where Kant declared man (in words that would later motivate and be echoed by Feuerbach and the early Marx) as his own ultimate end.[32] *Humanism* could then be defined as the mobilization of a foundationalist concept of man. The thinkers considered here treated the concept of man by voiding it of foundationalism, arguing in this way against Kant, against the Platonic-Christian idea that man possesses an eternal soul, against the tradition of identifying man with a certain feature, aspect, or property that embodies or expresses his nature, against the Feuerbachian-Marxist approach that sees Man as his own goal, and above all against the idea of a human nature that is given, foundational, single, or readily available.[33]

Already in the 1930s, partisans of a negative approach to philosophical anthropology would announce a "death of man"—a trope and theme whose intellectual force and significance would not relent until the 1980s. The texts that are today most credited with offering such an understanding of man are Heidegger's 1947 "Letter on 'Humanism,'" Alexandre Kojève's second note on "the end of history," written in 1961 and published in 1968, Louis Althusser's contributions to the humanist controversy in Marxism, Michel Foucault's concluding chapter to his 1966 *Les Mots et les choses* (*The Order of Things*), and Jacques Derrida's 1968 talk "The Ends of Man."[34] To the 1960s as an explicit and even victorious moment of negative anthropology's coming of age, and in order to show the dependence of these texts on a series of elaborations dating to the 1930s, I add two earlier and far less-known stages. The first, in the 1930s, is marked above all by Alexandre Koyré's influence on the philosophy of religion and science, Martin Heidegger's first philosophical inroads into France, Alexandre Kojève's 1930s anthropology—based on a semi-Hegelian and semi-Husserlian definition of man as *pure negation*—and the critique on transcendence in the 1930s by Georges Bataille, Jean-Paul Sartre, and Emmanuel Levinas. In these cases, a crucial desideratum is the rejection of man as a given core, promise, and goal of thought, and the reconceptualization of themes that advanced an anti-anthropocentric, frequently existentialist entrapment of man in his world. The second, and more radical, stage follows with Maurice Merleau-Ponty's theorization of violence and history, Heidegger's critique of humanism, and Jean Hyppolite's post-1945 writings on history, Hegel, and language. At the heart of this second stage is the foregrounding of the dependency of "the human" on philosophical and historical categories that it had itself formerly been seen as grounding.

In a sense, the rise of negative anthropology was more far-reaching than the critiques of humanism in which it was often couched (and to which I will return), and at times even rendered humanism irrelevant. Consider, for example, Merleau-Ponty's late 1940s *endorsement* of a certain humanism—which is thoroughly permeated by a critique of his "elders'" philosophical anthropologies. In the early twentieth century,

human nature had truth and justice for attributes, as other species have fins or wings. . . . Even those of us today who are taking up the word 'humanism' again no longer maintain the same shameless humanism of our elders. What is perhaps proper to our time is to disassociate humanism from the idea of a humanity fully guaranteed by natural law and not only reconcile consciousness of human values and consciousness of the infrastructures which keep them in existence, but insist upon their inseparability.[35]

To argue for this humanism, Merleau-Ponty rejects the philosophical premises on which the elders' humanism was based: natural law, first of all, but also the guarantee that human consciousness identifies itself with certain "values" and certain (political and social) infrastructures. And he argues that there is no transparent and perfect mapping of a "consciousness of human values" and a "consciousness of the infrastructures that keep them in existence." The most that can be hoped for is a *reconciliation*—the very project he sets as "proper to our time": an effort to stitch together components of a theory of man whose compatibility and indeed inseparability "our elders" had thought to be assured, but which "today" is torn apart.[36]

Central to efforts to dismantle "human nature" (such as Merleau-Ponty's) was the critique of subjectivity, which developed together with the import of phenomenology. As Heidegger's thought became central to the emergence of French antisubjectivism already in the mid-1930s, its basic critique of anthropology offers an exemplar of the trends toward negative anthropology.[37] One of the definitive aspects of the French reading of Heidegger, both in the early epistemological/anti-anthropocentric interpretation of the 1930s and in the postwar antihumanist one, is an emphasis on the relationship between Heidegger's concept of *Dasein* and the attempt to locate man and the subject within an ontological horizon that precedes and contextualizes the Cartesian *cogito* and delegitimates philosophical reliance on it. To the extent that French thinkers appropriated elements of Heidegger's critique of Western thought since Plato, they specifically used it to target the prevalent figure of man as independent observer, actor, and interpreter of the world. In his 1927 *Being and Time*, Heidegger approached the existent we usually call man as *Dasein*, stripping its shared element down to its *being-there*. Here, *Dasein* at once subsumes and displaces the humanity of man: it rejects the problematic, inherent in German idealism but also in Cartesian thought in general, of the I as an absolute, independent subject that approaches a world largely separate from it, by

i. finding the individual being as always being-there (*Dasein*), in the world, sharing the fundamental structures of its *Dasein* with other beings (other beings-there);

ii. treating thought and experience as always engaged with the world and dependent on moods and structures that elaborate our familiarity with the world into an interpretation of it, and

iii. postulating the *entirety* of subjective experience as shared in Being-with-others—that is to say, denying its subjectivity and individuality.

In this context, the humanity of man is an important aspect of *Dasein*, but it is neither separate from the problematic of *Dasein* per se, nor more basic than or capable of surpassing its "ontic" determination and moving toward an ontico-ontological one. Moreover, as *Dasein*, the human being is always beside itself, ek-static; only when *Dasein* comes face-to-face with the possibility of its death does its Being become authentically its own. Heidegger (and his interpreters from Kojève through Sartre, Hyppolite, Derrida, and Nancy) emphasizes instead that *Dasein* is (among other things) human, yet the humanity of *Dasein* remains and must be understood as derivative of both its ontic and ontological status.

In his 1947 "Letter on 'Humanism,'" Heidegger adjusted and radicalized his critique of the human subject (and of humanism in general) and offered an expression that in France would acquire the status of a slogan: "We are not on a plane where there are only men, but on one where there is principally Being."[38] Philosophers participating in the second wave of Heidegger's reception—which continued well into the 1970s—paid particular attention to this double critique of the "human" "subject," famously rejecting the earlier French translation of Heidegger's term *Dasein* as *réalité humaine* (human reality), stressing their distance from the 1930s antifoundationalist and realist approach and echoing Heidegger who (somewhat excessively) deemed this earlier wave of readership "anthropological." Yet, well beyond the late 1940s debate, one core argument is inescapable: for Heidegger, it is not man who possesses *Dasein*; it is *Dasein* that contains and makes possible the derivative problem of the human. Heidegger's case, and that of his French readers, is exemplary of the way in which the question of man becomes displaced and rendered subservient to other forms of questioning and would become a privileged locus of efforts to dismantle and rethink the anthropological problem.[39]

Through (and because of) the several different pursuits (including Heidegger's) that sought this destabilization and displacement of the human, this last came to be approached and understood only in terms of *results* or even *side-effects* of an analysis of language, existence, history, and the phenomena man encounters in his surrounding milieus. That is to say: man finds himself thrown in the world of phenomena and life; he is not grounded in some transcendental fashion (Heidegger, Kojève, Malraux, Sartre, Beaufret). As such a situated consciousness, man is, above all, finite; as a scientific observer, man believes himself to find genuine truths but only manages to confirm to himself his own metaphysical presuppositions and cannot claim to be capable of fully describing or understanding nature (Bachelard, Kojève, Koyré, Wahl). In language, he is an interpreter, conduit, and enunciator of signs and symbols that form part of greater systems independent of his individual will, choices, and existence (the Saussurians, Merleau-Ponty, the later Heidegger); historically, he is constructed and operates within cultural, religious, and philosophical limits imposed on him (Koyré, Bachelard, Merleau-Ponty). In each of these systems, he does not grant meaning to reality, language, history, being, and society; he finds his own role and status produced and located by the way they construct his interaction with the world and with other beings. These systems are not consequences of Man's creative activity, desire, or will; they are not figures of his difference from an animal. They are domains in which he finds himself and to which he reacts. They are what grants meaning to "his" experience, to each of "his" forms, thoughts, modes, and conceptual expressions. As a result, the question "What is man?" cannot be given a lasting, comprehensive, transcendental answer. In this sense, the human in man comes to mean less and less: we can only know what he is not, what others and other things are, what his approach to them can reveal.

4. A Short History of the Critiques of Humanism

What we usually refer to today as "French antihumanism" is the most pronounced and politically visible aspect of this emergence of the new, nonhumanist atheism, and the negative philosophical anthropology, namely, the assault on contemporary humanisms: on the legacies and utopian hopes of the Enlightenment, on a liberal-bourgeois thinking grounded in human rights and individual autonomy, on Marxist humanism with its critique of liberalism and its expectations of a superior humanity.[40] Those rejecting humanism saw it as impotent in its defense of man, as ideological and imperious, above all as expressing and (concurrently) masking a hypocritical bourgeois egalitarianism that amounted to disdain for those suffering or underprivileged. Bred by the violence of World War I, and later compounded by the catastrophes of the Soviet experiment, World War II, and Auschwitz, such oppositions to humanism were responses to a long-standing tradition of intellectual dissatisfaction with the political culture of the Republic. They reinforced—and were reinforced by—a continued attempt to reconstitute the intellectual horizon away from an optimistic belief in a march toward human perfection and social harmony. To this worldview, the thinkers I consider here contrasted a harsher one, in which humanism had become little more than a generic ideology justifying political tactics whose commitment to such a march were at best dubious. In considering these critiques as an ideologico-political force, an expression of atheism and of transformations in philosophical anthropology, we move away from both (a) the all-too-easy dismissal of these philosophical arguments as internalist debates and instead toward their arsenal in the public domain, and (b) the notion that antihumanism was merely a response to political fields and problems.

As a target of these critiques, what exactly was humanism? It is notoriously difficult to provide an adequate definition that encompasses the different philosophical and historical developments referred to by the word; it is necessary that we keep in mind here the fact that critics of humanism rarely suggested that their target was an insufficiency in a single tradition (even less a single author), but instead used the term in a general sense. Very roughly speaking, then, the historian can keep in mind several primary constellations that the term can refer to and that are usually seen in positive light: Christian humanism, Renaissance educational humanism (founded on a return to ancient Greek models), Humboldt's reconceptualization of the latter in nineteenth-century Germany, Enlightenment humanism from Montesquieu through Rousseau and Condorcet, nineteenth-century liberal humanism (frequently based on natural law, autonomy over one's own body and mind, and human rights), and socialist humanisms. The quotidian, secular use of "humanism" in modern France refers largely to the tradition that begins with Montesquieu's construction of the legal subject and the *Encyclopédie*'s attack on theological knowledge, and culminates in

(a) the elaboration of an egalitarian defense of the human subject, the advocacy of a *libre arbitre* and of his "natural and inalienable" rights in postrevolutionary liberalism; and

(b) the utopian socialist tradition (later taken over by Marxism), which involved efforts to move society and political culture toward socially and personally harmonious ends.[41]

Political and social humanism, with its commitment to contractarian social theory, its respect for free will, and its trust in human virtue and perfectibility, is at once a consequence and a constitutive dimension of this spirit that has surrounded humanism since the mid-1800s. Even more than the Enlightenment itself—during which the question of rights, for example, arose rather late and to no clear consensus—it was the legacy and even the myth of the *Lumières* that in the century following 1789 reconceived an often-ambiguous political theory as a one-way street of egalitarianism.[42] The nineteenth-century construction of modern humanism thus paid particular attention to the sociopolitical goals of a "human nature" conceived as good and perfectible, and as a result humanism was largely associated with a left-leaning, often democratic, but certainly utopian sociopolitical mentality.[43] This attention to human nature and to the progress of human history also removed this breed of humanism from the Renaissance and

Humboldtian tenet of a return to ancient Greek culture qua apex of human civilization. The philosophies of figures as different as P.-J. Proudhon, Jules Michelet, and Henri de Saint-Simon mixed individual and specific projects with broad humanist themes of a political, spiritual, and educational perfectibility of man. While at the same time, and coming on the heels of Feuerbach's atheist anthropology, Marx's dictum that "man is the highest being for man" offered one of the clearest, and by the 1930s most influential, expressions of this attitude.[44]

The aforementioned difficulty of sifting through humanisms with the aim of distinguishing one's object of study, one's target, or one's exact intellectual adherence, often led writers to attempt broader and simpler definitions—some of which had wide-ranging consequences and considerable disregard for the historical details and ambiguities of the rise of humanism. During the 1930s, a strategy widespread among politically engaged intellectuals was to regard *all* claims to humanism except their own as misguided and violent, reject them en masse, and then counter their supposed failure via a definition that usually amounted to a condensed and exciting summa of their political hopes and arguments. Such attitudes came to characterize even the most systematic of philosophical reactions—whether because humanisms appeared to be advocating notions of man, worldviews, and political engagements that seemed unsalvageable, or also because philosophers sought to present their thought as standing above (and being capable of dissecting) extant political divisions and debates. In his "Letter on 'Humanism'" arguing that humanism was but an insufficient guard for the human being, Heidegger identified it with the entire development of philosophy since Roman times, not only because humanism relied conceptually on the tradition he subsumed under the rubric of "metaphysics," but also because it found its horizons and limitations through metaphysics.[45] As a consequence, human dignity was merely a prisoner of the limited ways in which metaphysics had envisioned it. Consciously writing for a post-*libération* French audience, Heidegger famously rebuked humanism as a synonym of the nihilisms that he believed had reduced Europe to a wasteland: "You ask, *comment redonner un sens au mot 'Humanisme?'* . . . I wonder whether that is necessary. Or is the damage caused by all such terms still not sufficiently obvious?"[46] Forty years later, responding to the 1980s rise of French "neohumanism" and its attack on deconstruction, and echoing Heidegger as much as Jacques Derrida and Theodor Adorno, the philosopher Jean-Luc Nancy went even further, arguing that humanism is not just an ideology (that is to say, "a thinking that does not critique, nor even think its provenance from and proper relation to reality"), but indeed *the* machine par excellence through which a community produces meaning for itself.[47] For Nancy, humanism postulates a meaning for man and identifies this meaning with *the system that produces meaning* in the community, with the "we" through which this community speaks. Thus humanism becomes the community's very raison d'être, validating the community's presuppositions, as well as legitimating its own deployment.[48] Whatever its specific rights and wrongs, every humanism is fundamentally bound to the community's self-regulation; it is thus arbitrary, auto-productive, and all but tautological.

If such are among the most famous definitions of "antihumanism," they are by no means the only ones, and their force in the French context itself relies on the very development of antihumanism in the broader history that emerges out of left- and right-leaning critiques of Enlightenment and socialist humanisms around the turn of the century and culminates in the crisis of humanism articulated from the 1930s through the 1970s. In this sense, while the critiques of humanism rested in part on a frequent redefinition of its meaning, their history suggests a more complex interplay, political involvement, and philosophical consequence. My approach to the critiques of humanism offers at once an archaeology of the antihumanism of the 1960s, a history of the drastic changes of predicament toward humanism from the 1920s through the 1950s—the visible element of antihumanism's development—and a general picture of the intellectual and political premises of the collapse of the humanist imagination.

From the turn of the twentieth century onward, republican humanism was frequently linked in France to the perceived toothlessness and intellectual weaknesses of the Third Republic, as well as to its success in justifying and promoting a specifically secular bourgeois culture reviled by both conservatives and socialists. One could trace earlier crises of humanism and questions back to the Terror, to the nineteenth-century Counter-Enlightenment (notably Joseph de Maistre), the 1871 Commune or the Dreyfus Affair—but after World War I, the crisis begins in earnest, as both the Left and the Right (and not only the conservative Catholic

Right associated with Action Française, whose anti-Dreyfusard claims
had so mocked humanism) started to reject the bourgeois individualism
that, for them, formed the political core of the later Third Republic.[49] The
Right attacked the Republic's association with the legacy of the French
Revolution, its lack of emphasis on national community, and its antiroyal-
ism. To many conservatives, liberalism and individualism helped destroy
the possibility of a genuine community to which man could turn in his
search for meaning in modernity.[50] Among Catholics in particular, who
had long sought to strip atheism of its claim to a radical respect for universal humanity, this emerged as a central theological claim and cultural
strategy.[51] Yet the Left also loudly rejected a parliamentary/capitalist humanism as insufficiently welcoming of genuine social equality and incapable of overcoming royalist and Catholic reaction. The major secular
objections to modern individualism and parliamentarianism, dating to
the work and early influence of Georges Sorel, Gustave Le Bon, Maurice Barrès, Charles Maurras, and others, became widely expressed at this
point.[52] Moreover, the 1920s and, more pronouncedly, the 1930s marked a
break in the optimist teleological conception of history that ensued from
the liberal and socialist positions, and even though France was hardly a
Spenglerian hotbed, this prewar optimism was largely gone in the doubt
about Western civilization and its pretenses.

These arguments exacerbated an existing double crisis.[53] On the
one hand, every political movement rejected bourgeois humanism as insufficient, egotistical, and corrupt, illustrating this rejection with ample
"evidence" furnished by the Dreyfus Affair, occasional political scandals,
the too slow or too fast pace of modernization, and so forth.[54] On the
other hand, each among these philosophies and political stances claimed
for itself a privileged access to the dignity of man, an alternative humanism superior to the false humanisms of its opponents. Criticizing the
philosophers of the Republic, for example, the communist Paul Nizan
wrote in 1931, "On the one hand, we have the idealistic philosophers who
promulgate truths concerning Man; and, on the other hand, we have a
map showing the incidence of tuberculosis in Paris, a map which tells us
how men are dying."[55] The attack is typical, particularly in that it exemplifies the structure of a rejection of mainstream thought and policy for not
taking into account and hence devaluing and rejecting the goals of one's

anthropo-theologico-political commitment. Catholics, Communists, nonconformists, even fascists asserted their own humanism and rejected *all* alternatives. As the republican and idealist bearers of the humanist legacy were but reluctant enforcers of its liberal egalitarianism, they effectively contributed to skepticism toward it by linking it to flaws and problems of modernity. Attempts to appropriate the humanist mantle led to a discrediting of both humanism and the traditional philosophical anthropologies that had accounted for its meaning.

This cultural manicheanism that disregards the political center as intellectually irrelevant continued well into the 1960s.[56] The postwar period, with its different political and intellectual landscape, also marked a significant transformation of these critiques. The wreckage of WWII, and especially the recognition in the period 1945–48 that this wreckage affected the Western world as a whole, its history and tradition, added credibility to the argument that Man could not find meaning either in faith or in his own knowledge and construction of the world.[57] Postwar Catholic critics of atheist humanism became especially influential—Henri de Lubac eventually became a cardinal after yielding much influence in the 1960s, Jacques Maritain and Gabriel Marcel enjoyed substantial followings, and even Pope Paul VI came to emphasize a conception of humanity based on "theocentric humanism" that invoked an openness and respect toward those outside Christianity for the first time. But more importantly for the early postwar period, the discrediting of the nationalist Right and its politics of the will, the short-term achievement of the Parti Communiste Français in identifying itself with humanism, the popular success of existentialism as a dive into the depths of human solitude and suffering, and the return of human rights discourse (which led to much rethinking on the meaning of Europe and to the signing of the Universal Declaration of Human Rights) transformed the intellectual landscape. Like existentialism and the Western Marxist tradition, human rights came to operate as a "humanism from below" and opposed generic and top-down humanisms—a response not only to the perception that the interwar period and World War II had radically undermined the self-evidence of liberal idealism in Europe, but also to the perceived need to limit, by legal means, the monopoly of violence that states held over their individual subjects as well as the states' justification of their practices on the basis of claims of *nature* or *history*.[58] Such a need was also urgent for the West, given the persistent communist assaults on its claims to humanism.[59] At this point, some of the aforementioned thinkers came to unhesitatingly link the target of their critiques of epistemological and philosophical anthropocentrism with the humanist stalemate and with utopian failure. The principal victors of the war, the United States and the Soviet Union, made easy targets for critics of the insufficiency of humanism, particularly insofar as each presented itself as embodying the hero in this humanist manicheanism. The West was routinely denounced for its "fear" of social qua human equality—that is, its anti-communism—for its use of the atom bomb and for its colonial past and present.[60] And with the USSR losing its grasp on the humanist mantle because of revelations concerning the Moscow Trials and Soviet life, and with the abandoning of intellectual utopianism, internal Marxist debates came to also feature antihumanist approaches to questions of everyday life, cultural transformation, and the possibility of genuine humanism in history. For many intellectuals, the superpowers' loss of humanist legitimacy further discredited the idea itself. Here, the persistence of the Marxist argument that within the course of history, humanism was but an ideological position that legitimates violence but genuine humanism had to be postponed to the time following the end of all conflict and the rise of genuine Communist society at once served to de-legitimate the West and met itself with considerable skepticism.[61]

So what matures in the postwar period is a willingness among many intellectuals to reject both the limitations of the dominant politico-anthropological systems and the forms and limits of political engagement allowed them by the ideologically charged national and international sphere. I do not mean to argue here that antihumanism was the driving force or the secret heart of intellectual movements and philosophies, nor do I claim that it was a single movement, concept, idea, or trend; rather, it is what emerged from, shaped, and configured a major matrix of concerns. Again, the problem with secular humanist utopias was not that they simply could not be achieved, nor even that they demanded the breaking of a few eggs. It was that their forging of a New Man through the mobilization of a specific a priori definition of man required both Man's divinization and Man's purge—a cleansing precisely masked by their humanist promises and elegies. Essentialist definitions of man had led, this argument goes, to biologistic, scientistic, political, religious, and/or moralist projects that, as much as they lay claim on universality, prioritize themselves over any such universality. Rather than forging respect for man through their intervention or dream, these ideologies could continue to disguise a politics of the will as a universalism.[62] If in the 1930s anti-individualism had led to antirepublican sentiment, after the war this turned into a strict opposition to utopian promises of all stripes—a tendency that often became plainly antipolitical.[63] Moreover, in line with both the destabilizations of classical concepts (of, for example, *truth* and *metaphysics*) and the apparent decline or delimiting of the Newtonian, Cartesian, and Comtean anthropocentrism, the philosophico-political effort to overcome the perceived limitations of Western metaphysical thought (for which Nietzsche, Heidegger, and others had led the way) now took on particular urgency, an urgency felt in political, educational, and theatrical contexts. The problem of negative anthropology may seem a particular philosophical debate and concern, but critiques of humanism implicitly encompassed and deployed it. In other words, antihumanism became more than a position reflective of one's political stance and status, part and parcel of an antiredemptive, antimoralist, and antimessianist worldview.[64]

Many tropes would thus parallel the directly political critique of humanism. The attack on positivist and realist science and Kantian idealism; the advent of Hegelianism and Heideggerianism; the broad appeal and interests of Beckett, Ionesco, Camus, even Sartre, and later Genet and the *nouveau roman*; the more specialized appeal of Bataille, Queneau, and Blanchot; the expressions of anticolonial sentiment from Malraux's *The Conquerors* through Tran Duc Thao's arguments on decolonization and Sartre's preface to Franz Fanon's *The Wretched of the Earth*; the treatment of linguistics and anthropology as sciences; the internal debates in French Marxism that distanced nondoctrinaire thinkers from the possibility of genuine revolution and led to the gradual abandon of the proletariat as the force of history; and finally the eruption of structuralism: all these intellectual moments involved, *at some stage of their argument*, the recognition that what claimed humanism for itself was but a corrupt and hypocritical system that was disintegrating. Not infrequently, partisans of different antihumanisms struggled with each other by declaring their adversaries or competitors to remain too tied to humanism: Sartre accused Bataille;

Heidegger, Blanchot, Bataille, Hyppolite, and Jean Beaufret all attacked Sartre; Merleau-Ponty criticized both liberals and the French Communist Party; Foucault would disavow his earlier Marxism and (like Levi-Strauss) reject Sartre; Derrida would criticize Heidegger and Sartre alike. This all came on the heels of the exclusivist and minimal humanisms of the 1930s and the postwar period respectively, and it built on the antihumanist climate—at once distinguishing each of these thinkers' projects and investments from this more general climate and emphasizing the overall trend. Similarly, the proliferation of tropes dooming contemporary man to an existence without meaning or future, such as the "last man" (Nietzsche, Camus, Blanchot) the "death of Man" (Malraux, Kojève, Blanchot, Foucault), the suspension of man (Hyppolite), the "devirilization of man" (Kojève, Bataille, Queneau), and the "terror" (Marlaux, Bataille, Kojève, Merleau-Ponty), all emphasize the limitation and obsolescence of a world where humanism has become destructive, but in which there are no alternatives. It is important to underscore the sheer breadth of positions occupied by critics of humanism by the mid-1950s. They range from Catholic intellectuals (including Gabriel Marcel, Henri de Lubac, and Teilhard de Chardin), to Marxists (Maurice Merleau-Ponty, Kostas Axelos, Louis Althusser), to epistemologists (Georges Canguilhem, Fernand Braudel, Alexandre Koyré), to phenomenologists and Hegelians. In France even those, like Merleau-Ponty or Levinas, who after 1945 claimed their projects to be radically humanist rejected existing and popular humanisms as unreliable.[65] As Merleau-Ponty noted, these "humanists" had clearly disavowed the hopes and assurances of what, before WWI was being fantasized as humanism: the belief that a New Man, social harmony and equality, and the march of progress were always attainable and desirable.[66]

Structure and Method

This book is organized in two parts, each structured around an introduction and four chapters. In interweaving the three broad histories considered here, each has a temporal and theoretical focus. Part One addresses the 1930s emergence of a phenomenologically inflected, antifoundational realist critique of transcendence that leads to the adoption of atheist and anti-anthropocentric anthropology and derails the progressivist and idealist paradigm. Part Two focuses on the postwar radicalization of the antihumanist attitude, the competition between different antihumanisms, and the establishment across philosophical systems of negative anthropology.

Part One centers on the period 1926–39: to frame the discussion of the political and philosophical stakes of 1930s critiques of "bourgeois humanism," the section opens with André Malraux's 1926 critique of Western man in his *The Temptation of the West*—perhaps the first major post-1918 critique of humanism—and then turns to consider the philosophical and political targets of most critiques of humanism during the 1930s, namely, the philosophical and educational idealism dominant in the Third Republic, and its best defender, the philosopher Léon Brunschvicg. This sets the stage for four chapters that address the radical stakes involved not only in the political and institutional critiques of this humanism but also—and especially—the undoing of idealism's philosophical anthropology and its understanding of transcendence and reality.

In Chapter 1, "The Anthropology of Antifoundational Realism," I present the radical transformation of French thought in the early 1930s, and I argue that the anthropological (and anti-anthropocentric) impulse originated principally in new approaches in the philosophy of science and the import of German phenomenology. These changes, which found an institutional home in the circle of émigrés around the historian of science and religion Alexandre Koyré, the journal *Recherches philosophiques*, and the Ecole Pratique des Hautes Etudes, radically altered the perceived relationship between the human subject and the world in which this subject finds itself, reducing man from his rationalist and idealist apex as supreme being and rational ruler of nature to a subject fundamentally trapped in modern reality. Two moments of this development are as crucial as they are misunderstood. First, the combined effect of phenomenology and quantum-physics epistemology in the early work of, among others, Alexandre Kojève and Jean Wahl, which produced an *antifoundational realism* and provided an epistemological ground out of which a new anthropology could emerge. Second, through a parallel reading of Alexandre Koyré's early-1930s foundation of modern science in metaphysics and Martin Heidegger's 1930 treatment of "world" I foreground the two influential thinkers' mistrust of transcendental and naturalist claims and show their shared vision of the modern human condition as based on an oppressed metaphysical foundation and past that modern rationalism and science have systematically sought to undo and failed to improve.

But antifoundational realism was not merely a matter for philosophers; it offered a response to a political and cultural situation. Chapter 2, "No Humanism Except Mine!" presents the political and intellectual crisis of humanism in the interwar period by centering on contemporary attacks leveled against "bourgeois humanism" by Communists, Catholics, and nonconformists. Such attacks did not result in an overcoming of humanism per se, but they brought about a fragmentation of the humanist imagination in that each of them claimed for itself a fundamental concept of man that offered him a dignity that no ideological alternative could access. Worthy of emphasis here is the contrast of the "old" secular humanism of academic philosophy to the "new" humanisms emerging in the interwar period—Catholic, Communist, and nonconformist. Against the conventional argument that would treat advocates of the mainstream Third-Republic Left as humanists and the critics of the regime as antidemocratic political adventurers, I argue that *all* of these factions were characterized above all by their competing searches for a New Man who would be compatible with their ideologies and unburdened by what they perceived as the weakness of the Third Republic and the flaws and violence of political alternatives. In this battleground of humanisms, the imaginary of secular humanism was undermined, allowing the shared doubts about the possibility of humanism and the anthropocentric foundations of modernity to take hold. It is thanks to these reactions that new philosophical and political anthropologies acquired a strong philosophical voice, if not yet a distinct political argument as well.

Crucial among these new voices was Alexandre Kojève's 1930s atheist anthropology, which is the subject of Chapter 3. Kojève has long been read as the most influential Hegelian philosopher of this period; however, the reasons behind the power of his work remain misunderstood. Utilizing recently published and unknown materials from Kojève's archive, and highlighting Kojève's divergence from both Catholic and Marxist accounts of the modern human condition, this chapter moves through a series of short studies of Kojève's treatments of *negation, homogeneity*, and *modern anthropology*, culminating in a reevaluation of his claim that *anthropothe-*

ism leads to a death of man at the end of history. This reading allows us to understand Kojève's cardinal place in the theological and philosophical construction of French antihumanism.

Chapter 4, "Inventions of Antihumanism (1935)," approaches the maturation of the early phenomenological attack on transcendence and classical humanism as this took place in writings of Emmanuel Levinas, Georges Bataille, and Jean-Paul Sartre in the period 1935–36. These authors worried about the reality in which man finds himself trapped as a result of the demise of transcendence. As a result, and despite their very different philosophical and political projects, Bataille, Sartre, and Levinas *all* opposed humanism as a misguided ideology that assumed the positing of Man as a transcendentally grounded subject and failed to understand the implications of violence and human finitude. Moreover, all three attempted to escape from the prisonlike limits of this immanent world, emphasizing at once the impossibility of overcoming or displacing it, and the necessity of rejecting its construction of humanist illusions. This argument offers ciphers of a multitude of negative anthropologies, all of which share the claim that the humanity of the human cannot be identified with what the individual is or what he shares with others, but precisely with what he can never be, can never determine, and can never subjugate himself to. Thanks to the adaptability of the phenomenological critique of transcendence, atheism came to be thought as no longer demanding a replacement of human transcendence (deemed wrong) for classical divine transcendence (deemed long outdated), and alternatives to humanism could be proposed.

This second part considers the forceful rise of antihumanism in the period 1943 to 1954. The crucial postwar development was the tearing of the humanist mantle that followed the 1944 *libération*, after the *résistance* had temporarily succeeded in bringing back a sense of humanist accord against Nazism. From the failure of the left-wing of the *résistance* to effect a social revolution or at least substantially affect postwar society arose a fragmented legacy in which the principal claimants to genuine humanism—namely, Marxism and existentialism—involved themselves in an intellectual war through which they undermined not only each other's claims but also the very survival of humanism in the political and intellectual legacy of the resistance and the postwar intellectual Left. Already by late 1946, André Malraux was asking anew—and with specific emphasis on the recent experience of the war, whether European man was dead. By 1947, philosophical debates around the humanist problem—some of them visible and controversial—indicated the presence of a competition between different negative anthropologies, a radicalization of the doubts regarding secular and utopian atheism, and an accumulation of critiques of humanism. The first three chapters of this section aim to show the aftermath of the resistance, the very different elaborations of critiques of humanism in the immediate postwar period, and their parallel *and compounding* treatments of philosophical anthropology and atheism. The final chapter addresses the convergence and consolidation of these critiques around a nonhumanist and negative anthropology.

If the first part of the book aims step-by-step for the development and opening of a new anti-anthropocentric atheism, the second part describes a quickly compounding situation in which different antihumanisms at once contrasted and compounded each other. Chapters 5–7, especially, mark parallel developments in philosophy and literature and could almost be read in interchangeable order.

Chapter 5, "After the Resistance (1): Being and the Demise of Philosophical Anthropology," addresses Heidegger's "Letter on 'Humanism,'" which sought to overcome humanism by arguing for the derivativeness of man from other concepts or categories, notably Being and language (logos). It opens with a discussion of Sartre's "Existentialism Is a Humanism," notably his ambivalent endorsement and advocacy of an existential humanism against other contemporary humanisms. In discussing the critiques aimed at Sartre's transformation of phenomenology into a moral and political anthropology (critiques from the very 1930s thinkers out of whom his own thought had developed), the chapter seeks to show the ambiguity inherent in Sartre's endorsement of an anthropocentric humanism against the 1930s anti-anthropocentric tendencies in philosophy. Heidegger's "Letter," which was addressed to and received by French readers, offered not only the most famous of these critiques of Sartre—and a particularly forceful critique of humanism—but also, and more importantly, the central argument in favor of a negative anthropology. To address Heidegger's theorization of the human in relation to Being and logos, I will attend successively to the philosophical and intellectual-historical context of Heidegger's French readership, the argument of the "Letter" in regard to the problem and traditions of humanism and the then-contemporary context, and, in a close reading of his text, Heidegger's forceful advocacy of negative anthropology.

Chapter 6 turns to examine Maurice Blanchot's understanding of freedom and atheism in terms of a committed antifoundationalism with neither claims to transcendence nor hopes of secular redemption. Blanchot's writings of the immediate postwar period constitute perhaps the most explicit theorization of atheism against secular, rationalist humanism. Radicalizing Kojève's approach to atheism and leaving aside questions of anthropotheism and progress in a review and critique of Henri de Lubac's 1946 book *The Drama of Atheist Humanism*, Blanchot adopted de Lubac's critiques of humanist atheism by reading Nietzsche precisely as a critic of such atheism. My main concern in this chapter is, however, Blanchot's theory of freedom as it emerges from this review and is elaborated in the famous essay "Literature and the Right to Death." Here, Blanchot codes many of the concerns dominant in the early postwar period into an argument on the all-or-nothing stakes of freedom, its relationship to death, and its refusal of a normal life such as that offered by an "Old Regime."

If Blanchot's postwar theory of freedom tended toward a formal rethinking of atheism and action, Maurice Merleau-Ponty's offered instead a theory of terror's unavoidability and a phenomenological theory of historical engagement. Chapter 7, "After the Resistance (2): Merleau-Ponty, Communism, Terror, and the Demise of Philosophical Anthropology," addresses the relationship between the involvement of existentialism and communism in his *Humanism and Terror*, with its consideration of the dependence of the engaged actor on historical contingency and violence, and its demand that a proper humanist outcome to this violence justify his engagement. Rather little attention has been paid to the links between *Humanism and Terror* and Merleau-Ponty's phenomenology; this chapter seeks to explain how Merleau-Ponty's mistrust of forms of given meaning, together with his demand that political action lead to a world of harmonious human relations unmarred by violence—especially invisible yet structural violence—led him to a qualified, fragile, and even pessimistic endorsement of communism. The chapter thus seeks to further the political problem raised by the decline of humanism—a topic of much concern to Malraux, Sartre, and in a different sense Heidegger.

Chapter 8, "Man in Suspension: Jean Hyppolite on History, Being, and Language," completes the course of the book's second part by examining Jean Hyppolite's elaboration of a negative anthropology in his engagements with humanism, historicist Hegelianism, Being, and language. The examination of Hyppolite's work at this point foregrounds the transformation, force, and systematization of antihumanism at the close of the early postwar period; Hyppolite's own address of humanist problems, which led him to a sense of "ambiguity," was especially forceful as a consolidation (indeed an academic consolidation) of the various recent approaches toward the problem of man; moving from a historicist toward an ontological interpretation of man's dependence on other categories (history, being, and logos), Hyppolite completed the antisubjectivist trend of early postwar French thought and established the currents toward negative anthropology (from Kojève and through to Heidegger and Merleau-Ponty) into a specific argument that would frame the philosophical bases of 1950s and 1960s antihumanism across the human sciences, but also in political and much religious thought.

In closing this introduction—a quick note on method. As pulling together every critique of humanism would be neither possible nor methodologically useful, I have sought to balance forms of historical and philosophical analysis, using different approaches for different problems. Thus what follows includes historical sections (in the introduction to each part of the book as well as in Chapter 2), approaches to problems in the history of science and epistemology (notably in Chapter 1 and, less so, in Chapter 3), institutions and intellectuals (in the two part introductions, as well as sections of Chapters 1, 2, and 5), literature (in the introduction to Part One and in Chapters 4 and 6), engagements with Christianity (in Chapters 2, 3, and 6), and phenomenology (throughout). By working on different sorts of moments—at times diachronically, at times by centering on specific texts, moments, or intellectual events, at times emphasizing philosophical analysis and at others cultural history—I hope to address a number of different historiographical questions, such as, How does one trace something like a transformation of atheism? Could philosophical projects as different as the ones considered here be seen to participate in such a transformation? How does such a transformation bring to life the midcentury political *critiques of humanism*, and how does it affect, and get shaped by, frequently unsystematic and even quotidian contemporary conceptions of "the human"? If the problem of "antihumanism" is of methodological interest because it involves a change in something that is not simply a political stance among intellectuals, nor a specific concept or philosophical movement, but instead a precondition of thought, a rather fluid matrix of ideas, a philosophical attitude, then how does one write about something as nebulous as this, keeping together the different strands—political, theological, philosophical?

PART I

THE 1930S

Introduction: Bourgeois Humanism and a First Death of Man

1. The Death of Man (1926)?

In the coda of his 1926 *The Temptation of the West*, the young André Malraux raised a question that would acquire major importance in his literary and political-philosophical life. If European Man was the heart of a culture and a system of thought, and if this culture and system of thought were rotten from the inside, did this mean that man was in fact *dead*? In the course of his intellectual career, Malraux would time and again invoke this question only to turn around and find a solution for it in the political or metaphysical causes he championed. In his most famous novel, the 1933 *La Condition humaine*, his characters could offer an alternative to bourgeois individualism only through commitment to a justice based on a quasi-Marxist notion of human dignity.[1] In the 1942 *The Walnut Trees of Altenburg*, Malraux suggested that the survival of the human spirit depended on the uprooted, cultured, and powerless individual who struggled against the nation-driven, science-executed destruction wrought by modern warfare: having watched this spirit triumph in the late nineteenth century, Europe witnessed its internal collapse in the years leading to World War I.[2] In his 1946 UNESCO lecture "Man and the Culture of Art," Malraux warned that the death of man could now be averted only through a recognition of the heroism of the *résistance* and a turn to the "human creativity" to be found in art.[3] On each of these occasions, Malraux first raised the specter of a death of man and then justified his political and his literary-metaphysical pursuits as the only possible escape from this doom.

The Temptation of the West presents the bleakest expression of this line of questioning. Rather than seek a way out of the feared decline, Malraux announces it as the central tragedy of his time. In the text, the claim of the death of man comes from the European character A. D. who is corresponding, during the course of a trip to China, with Ling, an Asian aristocrat visiting Europe. Throughout the epistolary exchange, A. D. has contrasted the China that consumes him with an individualist Europe that he declares arid and morally bankrupt and that he fears has lost its essence (TW 76, 92). Ling invariably takes up A. D.'s comments as invitations to express his criticism of Europe (in contrast to a China in decline) as a civilization based on an absurd core, increasingly foreign to itself, perhaps even doomed from the start (TW 98). A. D. in turn responds to Ling's criticisms of European culture by outdoing them—announcing, after the death of God, a death of Man: "Our thought is falling in ruins. . . . In order to destroy God, and after having destroyed Him, Western intellect has abolished all which might have stood in the path of Man: having reached the limit of its efforts, it finds only death . . . Europe, great cemetery where only dead conquerors sleep, whose sadness is deepened by the pride taken in their illustrious names—you leave me with only a naked horizon and the mirror of solitude's old master, despair" (TW 120–21). The device of having A. D. address, from outside the West, a non-Westerner in the West, allows Malraux to provide a critique that would not easily fall to political categorization, all the while claiming the knowledge of an insider and enjoying the analytical clarity of distance. Reflecting Malraux's own stay in Indochina and his hostility toward French colonialism, A. D. offers an exemplar of contemporary dissatisfaction, mixing critiques by both Left and Right of the culture of bourgeois democracy and the course of European humanism.[4] The epistolary form then foregrounds and radicalizes the content of this critique: it places the reader in the double bind offered by two figures who claim *both* expertise in *and* cool-headed distance from the essence of Europe. We are thus cornered between two options: Ling's, which doubts the depth of Europe's culture, declaring it absurd and self-contradictory (TW 40), and A. D.'s, which instead considers modernity's problem to be Europe's "success" in turning

its promises into a world bereft of transcendence, future, and life.[5] Within
the epistolary frame, A. D.'s letters take priority: their critique of Europe is
far lengthier and better developed; indeed, they present the most systematic argument of the book. But more importantly, the persistence of their
critique, together with their formal priority, forces the reader to occupy
a place at once identical and different to Ling's. As Ling is supposedly
the one receiving the letters, the (French) reader is identified with this
"foreigner" sympathetic to A. D.'s critique. But the reader is denied the
comfortable distance from which Ling responds—his retreat to a much-
touted "Asian wisdom"—thus further closing the trap set up by A. D.'s account of Europe's decline. This double mechanism, at once identificatory
and distancing, leads to A. D's announcement of the death of Man that,
placed at the very end of the epistolary exchange, is granted the role of a
conclusion, or even a solution, an agreement between the characters that
privileges A. D.'s pessimism while turning the book's earlier core dilemmas and form into a preparation of this concluding declaration.

Malraux's diagnosis echoes Friedrich Nietzsche and especially Os-
wald Spengler; however, its terms cannot be appreciated simply by reference to these precursors, as Malraux is addressing a cultural situation
quite different from the "conservative revolution" that came to champion
Spengler's pessimism concerning European culture in Weimar Germany.[6]
In France, Spengler's verdict was widely considered by left-wing writers
(Malraux had already identified himself with the intellectual Left) as an
insider's perspective to the decay of the bourgeois world.[7] On the Right,
Spengler's positions were partly prefigured by the Counter-Enlightenment
since Joseph de Maistre, and by conservatives since Maurice Barrès and
the early years of Charles Maurras. Conservatism gave them a home, but it
put them in contrast to a political program and language that not only di-
luted Spengler's specific diagnosis but mobilized tooth and nail against its
consequences.[8] The novelty for France of *The Temptation of the West* was
Malraux's transformation of a traditionally right-wing analysis of cultural
decline into a vaguely leftist censure of the political establishment and the
course of secular culture. His philosophical terms resist easy appropriation
by political projects: they lack the program and aims of contemporary
socialism, and they clearly target the conservative rhetoric of safeguarding
the Nation, the Church, and the family that (re)establish them as pil-

lars of a France opposed to the Third Republic. Malraux's accusation is instead better read as an early symptom of a spreading metapolitical willingness in the Parisian intellectual scene to confront the perceived failure of the Third Republic. Rather than lead to a world marked by equality and freedom, rather than signal the triumph of Western Spirit, European humanism had overcome religious submission only to lead to the "great cemetery" of World War I and to the "despair" of the 1920s. In a political culture marked by the war, as well as by increasing political divisions, this was a movement aiming at a general rejection of the status quo, and thus, it located the human precisely in what this culture was destroying.

During the decade that followed *The Temptation of the West*, French intellectuals became obsessed with denouncing bourgeois humanism and announcing possible ways out of its supposedly destructive implications. Since the late nineteenth century, the Dreyfus Affair and the reorganization of secular education had divided intellectuals and the public between a faction that looked to Boulangism and the royalist past, and another that emphasized republican commitment as the progressive defense of the achievements of the Republic. But by the late 1920s and 1930s, the claim to "progressive politics" was no longer in the hands of a cosmopolitan attachment to the Republic, which faced a number of questions regarding its humanist commitment. Was social idealism sufficient as an advocate of the amelioration of conditions of the working class? Was a classical cosmopolitanism, the belief in Kant's "citizen of the world" for example, a genuine model for commitment, rather than an outdated illusion? Were these dimensions of modern humanism even really compatible?

2. "Bourgeois" Humanism and Academic Idealism

Who identified themselves with the Third Republic's humanism after the Great War? This question opens one of the most complex problems of interwar France and the rise of fascist and Communist thought. Before moving to consider the philosophical and political challenges to "humanism," it is worth addressing in some detail what this humanism itself aimed at.

Central to the humanism expressed by the Third Republic itself was a commitment to republicanism, to Dreyfusardism, to the parliamentary institutions and generally to the liberal and Enlightenment ideal of the Third Republic's educational system.[9] However, such a commitment can be misleading, as it did not by itself express contentment with the Republic's humanist ideals—both because these often remained vague and because political tendencies sought to reclaim some of these ideals against any given government's perceived failures.[10] Moreover, the long tradition of antirepublican sentiment, and the broadening of the attacks on the Republic in the 1930s, have identified the Republic somewhat too easily with "humanism" regardless of what this humanism meant.

It would be more accurate to say that the most substantial and sustained identification of humanist commitment with a philosophy of liberal/cosmopolitan humanism was exemplified in the world of Parisian academic philosophy which, by the 1920s, had become a bastion of secular France, distancing itself from contemporary cultural problems to the benefit of an idealist conception of man's future and an identification with Enlightenment ideals of secular equality and education.[11] The rallying point of these philosophers—their intellectual coming-of-age—had been the Dreyfus Affair: it enhanced their profound commitment to republican values, and it also identified their intellectual enemies in the radical Left and Right. The defense and reinstatement of Dreyfus, with its victory of Right over Wrong, reflected for them precisely the ethics of egalitarian cosmopolitanism that the secular Center and Left had sought and continued to seek.

Between 1914 and 1930, the image of French academic thought changed rather little. All of its "stars" had risen to prominence before 1920.[12] Institutionally, philosophy was centered on the Société française de philosophie (French Society of Philosophy, Sfp) and the *Revue de métaphysique et de morale* (1902). The Sfp held regular meetings and talks by Parisian and international figures and mostly advanced a mixture of idealist rational criticism (the French version of Neo-Kantianism), intellectualism, and sociological Durkheimianism. These trends are clearly expressed by the period's major dramatis personae. Emile Boutroux, after two decades of major influence in neocriticist idealism, died in 1921. Léon Brunschvicg, who worked extensively on mathematics, was the principal Kantian at the Sorbonne and the most important university philosopher:

he held considerable power in the Parisian academy and in the examination system, which he directed very consciously toward the advancement
of humanist education. Alain was a Kant-influenced cosmopolitan who
dominated philosophical education of students preparing for the Ecole
Normale Supérieure; many of his students became well known as left-wing
intellectuals in the 1930s (he himself also played a minor role in French
antifascism). The leader of the Sfp was Xavier Léon (also a Kantian), who
had helped organize it since its inception in 1886. Henri Bergson, who was
enormously well known, had occupied a position at the Collège de France
since the turn of the century and had provided the only major alternative
to Kantianism (given especially the decline of spiritualism), a philosophical system that also spoke to protoexistential concerns. Yet by the interwar
period, debates on his thought were no longer principally academic, while
the influence of his cosmopolitanism did not really reach far beyond his
role in the cadre of the League of Nations. But, with the exception of
Bergson, and even though intellectualism and spiritualism still held some
sway, neocriticism (begun by Charles Renouvier and furthered by Boutroux, Brunschvicg, Jules Lachelier, and others) was turning itself into the
intellectual and institutional center of French thought.[13]

Kantianism was crucial to the drafting of the educational system
along goals akin to the late Enlightenment, nineteenth-century positivist
science, and political idealism. Though debate on the politics and effec-
tiveness of the reforms continued until the end of the Third Republic, the
reorganization of education in the 1870s (especially the *Loi Ferry*) and at
the turn of the century propelled traditions of philosophy that emphasized
the democratic ideals of the Republic, while providing a haven for scientific thought originating in debates surrounding the positivist tradition,
and largely removing theology from the academic mainstream.[14] It is especially important, in this context, to emphasize the force and acceptance
of Kant's own understanding of Man's role in thought and society.

As noted already, Kant approached the question of man in two distinct though related ways that remained central to the neocriticist project.
First, in his 1798 *Anthropology from a Pragmatic Point of View*, Kant held
that anthropology is the complete description of man, and he proceeded
to consider it from a "pragmatic point of view," which, for Kant, treats
Man as his own final end.[15] Man can construe a *character* for himself, for

his species, or for the society he lives in, providing it with inherent qualities and diversity and seeking through it his happiness. The political goal, throughout, is to render man a "citizen of the world."[16] Moreover, in his *Logic* of 1800, Kant specifically presented the question "What is Man?" as *the* fundamental question for philosophy: while placing it alongside his three critical questions, he proceeded to argue that it *encompasses* them and that an answer to the question of man can only be sought through the critical project.[17]

With the centrality if not dominance of neocriticism in academic philosophy, and with the peak of this trend in the 1920s, Kant's dual approach to the anthropological question served as indispensable ground for the intellectual trust in a mild and tempered utopian rationalism. This position maintained the foundational role of philosophy in contemporary society and in cultural approaches to modern man. Intellectually, it protected the philosopher from competition by scientism and by the human sciences; culturally, it sheltered idealism from the brunt of everyday politics.[18] The idealism of Kant's Third Republic afterlife was reinforced by the debate between rationalist philosophers and realist scientists on science's approach toward nature, reality, and objects, and the belief that, as an interpreter of nature, human consciousness was relatively independent.

The significance of these arguments is most evident in the work of Léon Brunschvicg. For Brunschvicg, Western humanism is the basis of European culture and thought, and its rise is tied closely to the rise and legacy of metaphysics—which Brunschvicg organized in terms of a progress through great philosophical systems: "Pascal [. . .] posed the problem of man's religion in a three-dimensional humanity, where *the plane of naturalist critique, the plane of the philosophy of spirit* and *the plane of supernatural revelation* encounter each other without confounding one another. Now over the past three centuries, this *triple* humanity has been *our Western humanity* . . . it consecrates the definition of *Western humanism.*"[19] This passage attests to Brunschvicg's identification of Western humanism with the legacy of metaphysics and the Kantian anthropological demand. The "three-dimensional" definition of humanity (and especially of Western humanism) corresponds precisely to the Kantian anthropological foundation of the three questions in the *Critique of Pure Reason* and the *Logic*: What can I know? (naturalist critique); What ought I do?

(rational psychology/ethics—in Brunschvicg's Pascal, the problem of the mind); and What can I hope for? (rational theology—here, the problem of revelation). Brunschvicg treats the three dimensions of the definition as the basic trends of the progress of the mind to absolute self-consciousness.[20] At the same time, he uses the rhetoric of "humanity," of "our Western humanity," and of "Western humanism" as the achievement of a history that, since Descartes, has been the vector, shepherd, and promise of the self-perfecting course of the West. Not only does Brunschvicg thus affirm progressivist Kantian humanism, but he also recognizes it as the logic par excellence of modern history and humanity, at once the indisputable telos of the modern West and the progressive coming-to-pass of its spirit.[21]

Why does Brunschvicg emphasize humanism's metaphysical and historical right-of-way? In his philosophical work, idealism is presented as having overcome both the "failure of realism" and the "anthropomorphic excesses of naturalism"—for him the twin philosophical origins and insufficient expressions of contemporary hermeneutics.[22] Against any attempt to assert the reality of nature and consider the mind through its understanding of the truths of this reality (as in contemporary science), or to fall back on treating nature as an expression of human thought (by which he means intellectualism), Brunschvicg sees Kant's critical thought as a system capable of synthesizing *even post-Kantian advances in mathematical physics*, precisely because within Kant's thought a mathematic ideality serves the priority of the rational living intellect over the data this finds in the world.[23] He proceeds to argue that in modern science and thought, mathematical reason mirrors critical idealism's trend toward the *complete, rational* comprehension of man's world—and, *by extension*, toward the triumph of an optimistic cosmopolitanism at once fundamentally conscious and convinced of its own truth.[24] Because truth and the Absolute are always inherent in or immanent to the mind, and because man cannot exit his mind in order to examine himself and the world objectively, there can be no conception of consciousness and humanity that diverges from this identification of critical idealism, its movement, and its politics.

The political and social aspects of this argument appear in Brunschvicg's occasional articles in terms of a much more polemical defense of humanism. One could even suggest that this defense goes so far as to border on a utopian parody of the humanist hopes of neocriticism: "Anxious reflections by the European on Europe betray a poor state of intellectual health; they stop him from doing his task, to dedicate himself to thinking well, and thus, following Western Reason—which is Reason itself—to bring forth from true science (as a Plato and a Spinoza sought) the purity of religious sentiment, and to chase away the materialist imaginations that are perhaps not the substance of Oriental speculations, but are definitely and in any case what the West has always received from the East."[25] Brunschvicg makes three remarkable points here. First, there can be no doubt as to the truth and value of Western Reason: anxious reflection on Europe expresses—worse, "betrays"—nothing less than intellectual sickness. Without commitment and faith in Western Reason, European modernity faces a defeat at the hands of materialism (which, combined here with the "Oriental threat," points to Soviet Communism). Second, in this critique of materialism, Brunschvicg links "the progress of true science" (that is, against crude, materialist, or realist science) to "the purity" of religious sentiment (that is, a nondogmatic Christian thought). And finally, his seemingly offhand identification of "Western Reason" with "reason *tout court*" again defends the rational humanist apparatus that he is advocating in this argument for its continuity, irreducibility, and perfection.[26] One sees here the reemergence of the tripartite definition of man through rational psychology, naturalist critique, and rational theology.

Two further contexts are especially useful in clarifying Brunschvicg's position: first, the idealism/realism debate, and second, the question of political implication. First, the philosophical debate between idealism and realism was of pivotal significance in Brunschvicg's time, when, by and large, philosophers and scientists shared the classic dualist distinction of mind from world. The problem of truth was largely identified with this distinction: Does truth lie in a reality, as argued by scientistic (that is, realist) positions, or in the mind and spirit of man, as argued by the neocriticists and intellectualists?[27] Brunschvicg took the latter side and left no doubt that because truth is immanent to a transcendental consciousness, not only is the structure of the mind responsible for man's relation to the phenomenal world, but even that the Western mind *in general* was, fundamentally, the bearer of truth in and against the modern age. In this respect, his idealism was sweeping, and Brunschvicg clearly aimed it as a philosophical defense against the critiques of idealism that came from developments in physics and chemistry. When speaking of "the progress of true science," Brunschvicg specifically wished this science to be understood in terms drafted by mathematics and mathematical physics because in this context it could be ruled by Kant's pure reason. Despite realist critiques of his positions, Brunschvicg would largely defend his idealism in matters of science until the end of the 1920s; with the advent of quantum physics and the arrival of phenomenology at the turn of the 1930s, Brunschvicg's idealism would find itself challenged anew from both an anti-idealist perspective and a perspective based on physicists' claims proper.

Second, Brunschvicg's lack of any doubt in humanism reflects a culturally conservative position insofar as it suggests a lack of sociopolitical interest. His idealism may translate (as it did) to contemporary educational policy, but it hardly made for convincing social policy, and it clearly evaded the political or engaged intellectual realm. One could even say that Brunschvicg's position resembled, to an extent, Julien Benda's famous exhortation of eternal values over urgent political needs in *La Trahison des clercs* (*Treason of the Intellectuals*); his contempt for a humanism that would be guided by material concerns plays well with Benda's overall argument. Indeed, in his own conclusion, Benda himself excoriated the demolition of ideals in favor of an "integral realism" that allowed philosophers to turn themselves into "directors of the modern conscience" and to raise man to the status of God. Such a humanity, Benda despondently wrote, would be "unified in one immense army, one immense factory, would be aware only of heroisms, disciplines, inventions, would denounce all free and disinterested activity, would long cease to situate the good outside the real world, would have no God but its desires. . . . "[28] Ideals needed to be defended, kept on a plane of their own: but what idealism's antipolitical strategy meant was that neocriticism could not claim monopoly over the more socially engaged legacy of the Enlightenment and liberal thought; what it resulted in was a vulnerability vis-à-vis the oft-repeated charges of academic abstraction and irrelevance.[29]

The critique of social irrelevance would often parallel, and indeed expand on, the critique of excessive idealism. For example, when, after a lecture at the Société française de philosophie in 1921, Brunschvicg was questioned on the problem of others, he reduced it to a matter of mental representations in the subject's mind.[30] Once again, this position followed from the immanence of the absolute in consciousness, particularly once this was combined with his notion that exiting the self so as to interpret oneself is not possible.[31] As a result, any understanding of the other has to pass through consciousness. Yet his questioner (André Cresson, a long-time friend) retorted that no one in the room seemed prepared to accept being reduced to a representation in Brunschvicg's mind. In this retort, Cresson acted as if he were revealing to Brunschvicg what the narrator of Proust's *Du coté de chez Swann* had discovered while still a child, namely that he was wrong to have imagined "that the brains of other people were lifeless and submissive receptacles with no power of specific reaction to any stimulus that might be applied to them."[32] Cresson accused Brunschvicg of a subjectivism so radical as to be not only theoretically indefensible but also (in political terms) easily interpretable as solipsism.[33]

A rejection of the most powerful academic thinker as obsessed with a selfish defense of a detached egotistical humanism was not too far away, as we shall soon see.[34] The 1930s decline of this generation's influence, which had severe consequences for the "old" humanism, can be traced to three main problems. First, it was due in part to the physical wane of thinkers of rather advanced age and to the lack of immediate, faithful successors. Several figures central to the organization of the Sfp died during the 1930s, and Brunschvicg and Bergson died during World War II.[35] Having already written most of their major philosophical works, these thinkers produced considerably less work during the 1928–40 period. Moreover, the Sfp already gave the impression of a rather old crowd: invitations abroad were extended only to famous thinkers (John Dewey, Ernst Cassirer, Edmund Husserl), and most French speakers were also well established. Except for infrequent political lectures concerning the international scene or the politics of education, the climate in discussions was usually calm, with participants comprising a fairly stable group around Brunschvicg, Léon, Bouglé, Elie Halévy, André Lalande, Etienne Gilson, and Maurice Blondel. After its organization of the Ninth International Philosophy Conference on Descartes, and Xavier Léon's 1936 death, the Sfp itself declined in organization, holding no major conferences and far fewer lectures than before.[36] This turn accentuated the already existing image of a group closed in on itself.

A second problem was fundamentally philosophical and concerned the philosophical self-enclosing of neocriticism around a number of specific debates that were becoming obsolete.[37] New work cited them less often, while in the 1930s, philosophy journal citations tended (among French thinkers) toward the works of Bergson, the psychologist Pierre Janet, the anthropologist Lucien Lévy-Brühl, and the philosopher of science Emile Meyerson.[38] The obsession with Kantianism was also sidelining shifts and debates that had been influencing European thought elsewhere in the last thirty years or so—Russell, Nietzsche, Freud, Husserl, or Marx. This became all the more evident by the time of the famous 1929 Davos debate between the rising star Martin Heidegger and the Neo-Kantian Ernst Cassirer, which was pertinent in the French context because French idealism became vulnerable to the very charge leveled at German Neo-Kantians. Proud of its pronounced distance from the social-political space, slowly weakening on both political and philosophical fronts, it seemed to not have understood World War I as necessitating a reconceptualization of the relationship between man and world in such a manner as to affect both the way in which the human subject perceives and interacts with the world and its vulnerability and constructedness in the world.

Third, neocriticism became a target for both a younger generation of philosophers and of political critics of the Third Republic. The following chapters aim to address the ways in which this younger philosophical generation rejected the philosophical and scientific premises of idealism and developed an alternative and postidealist conception of "human reality" (Chapter 1), as well as the political context in which idealist humanism weakened in a very public fashion and political alternatives to it developed and struggled against each other under the banners of Communism, Catholicism, and nonconformism during the 1930s (Chapter 2).[39] These philosophical and political movements set the stage for a reintroduction of Alexandre Kojève's thought as an atheist and negative anthropology (Chapter 3) and for the critiques of transcendence, humanism, and political stalemate by Emmanuel Levinas, Jean-Paul Sartre, and Georges Bataille (Chapter 4). With the weakening of the idealist humanism that dominated academic philosophy thus begins a new atheism, and with it, the course of philosophical antihumanism.

1

The Anthropology of
Antifoundational Realism:
Philosophy of Science,
Phenomenology, and "Human
Reality" in France, 1928–1934

In 1928, the Japanese philosopher and former Heidegger student Count Shuzo Kuki spent a few months in Paris, gave a number of public lectures, and met the young Jean-Paul Sartre.[1] Kuki was the first to tell Sartre about Husserl and Heidegger, years before Raymond Aron pointed to his martini glass, suggested to the startled Jean-Paul that phenomenology would change his life, and proposed that he read Emmanuel Levinas's *Theory of Intuition in Husserl's Phenomenology.*[2] Unimpressed by the figureheads of French thought that he and Sartre discussed, Kuki delivered his final public lecture on the "General Characteristics of French Philosophy," offering a biting reduction of its modern development to four traits: (i) *inner observation*; (ii) an *alliance with positivism*; (iii) a *fundamental metaphysical*—essentially Cartesian-*dualism*; and (iv) a *"striving to be social."*[3] For Kuki, these traits exemplified contemporary French thought as represented by the established group of philosophers—Henri Bergson, Léon Brunschvicg, Celestin Bouglé, Emile Meyerson, and others—and indicated a distinctly national philosophical labor. Contrasting that labor to the work of German theologian-philosophers he himself was trained by—particularly Martin Heidegger and Karl Jaspers—Kuki suggested that "French" philosophy was the offspring of scientific and scientistic thought. Thus, it was limited to the concept of science it emerged from, and it was at a loss when dealing with questions concerning the status of man in modernity, questions it answered by imposing an antiquated, optimistic, and teleological conception of Man to avoid existential and theological issues that exceeded its scientism.[4] If there is something rude or coarse about Kuki's caricature of "French philosophy," it nevertheless resonated, somewhat like Ling's letters to A. D., among young philosophers who were simply more polite and more systematic in rejecting the dominant themes than Kuki in contemporary idealism. Alongside the powerful Kantian and rationalist glorification of Man, the issues presented by Kuki as limitations of French philosophy were seen in these years to be raising new demands in *philosophical anthropology*, that is, in the thematization of Man as a properly philosophical problem rather than merely a self-sufficient and self-evident ideal or ground of thought, knowledge, and existence.

If we can retrospectively see Kuki's intervention as symptomatic of a broader philosophical change, there is a second, similarly suggestive event worth noting here. In 1929, Léon Brunschvicg, Emmanuel Levinas, Maurice de Gandillac, and Jean Cavaillès attended the debate *What Is Man?* between Martin Heidegger and the Neo-Kantian thinker Ernst Cassirer in Davos, Switzerland.[5] Heidegger's *Kant and the Problem of Metaphysics*, published earlier that year, had challenged the "official" reading of Kant by the two major German Neo-Kantian schools and had extended Heidegger's project of a rethinking of philosophy out of ontological premises.[6] The Davos debate featured a series of lectures by the two thinkers as well as direct debate on the contemporary importance of the Kantian tradition. Crucial to the debate were the limits of anthropocentrism, which both Cassirer and Heidegger rejected: there, Heidegger's originality and harshness. This was a critique not only of Cassirer but, for the French context, of Brunschvicg's neocriticism as well, and it succeeded in setting the stage for later philosophical developments and disagreements.[7] For younger thinkers, among them Emmanuel Levinas (who had worked under Husserl after studying in Strasbourg), Heidegger "so successfully trounced Cassirer . . . that the mantle of leading German philosopher was unofficially bestowed upon him there."[8] During and after the conference,

Levinas celebrated in Heidegger's triumph "the end of a particular kind of humanism."[9] A year later, attempting to recuperate the "profundity" he acknowledged in Heidegger's argument, Brunschvicg (who openly supported Cassirer) reduced it to a testament to the power and self-transformative potential of Kantianism.[10] In 1934, de Gandillac paralleled Cassirer's compliant comportment toward Heidegger with "the succumbing of the German people to the Führer's magnetism."[11] In other words, the debate highlighted divisions not only in Germany but also in France, divisions that served as ciphers for an alternative to Kantianism's association with the old, conventional, secular humanism. How do we understand the range, breadth, and anthropological focus of these two occasions? What do they suggest about the ensuing transformations in French thought? As Kuki's lectures and French participation in the Davos debate retrospectively indicate, French philosophy was entering a period of transformation, shedding its Kantian past and moving toward a counter to the established anthropocentric idealism of the period.[12]

In the French context, the 1930s constituted a philosophical event that altered both the borders and the strategies of philosophical argumentation, and that also formed a new philosophical background for much better known movements. The attack on man as at once *ideal* and *ground* in the thought of the 1920s is clearest in (i) phenomenological and epistemological arguments directed against scientific positivism and neocriticism, and (ii) the dismissal of man's standing as a privileged observer of nature and causality. The corollary of these critiques was an overturning of the classical transcendental juxtaposition of subject to object, which in turn led to what I will call *antifoundational realism*, a kind of philosophical "realism" that denies man any kind of transcendental separation *from* the reality he finds himself in, attributes to him a contribution to this reality, and forces him to accept his powerlessness to radically change— or escape from—it. Philosophical anthropology was radically shaken by these developments: as the philosophical 1930s challenged the dominant subjectivism, scientific expectations, and rationalist commitments, they plunged idealist humanism into an *anti-anthropocentric* turmoil. The question of man lost the foundational answer it had found in neocriticism and became a central target for skepticism.

Institutionally and culturally speaking, this transformation was effected largely by an intellectual milieu centered on the Ecole Pratique des Hautes Etudes, the Russian philosopher Alexandre Koyré who taught there, and the journal *Recherches philosophiques* that he cofounded. *Recherches philosophiques* was especially important, as it acted as a publishing home for many of the philosophical developments of the 1930s (both this chapter and Chapter 4 rely largely on materials published in *Recherches philosophiques*). Philosophically speaking, two major moments in the introduction of phenomenology and the new philosophy of science were crucial to the overcoming of Neo-Kantian anthropology: first, there were the transformations in epistemology occasioned by the discovery of uncertainty in quantum physics and the arrival of German phenomenology, which rendered obsolete Kantian idealism and the debate between *realism* and *rationalism* that had dominated French epistemology and philosophy of science in recent times. In the hands of Jean Wahl, Gaston Bachelard, and Alexandre Kojève, the critique of scientific determinism in quantum physics combined with the phenomenological critique of idealism, leading to *antifoundational realism*. Antifoundational realism undermined existing idealism/realism distinctions, and it specifically rejected the conception of Man as an all-powerful observer, transcendental to nature and the world, aiming toward the perfection of his consciousness and control of modern life. Because antifoundational realism expressly posited a dual reality constituted by both *subject* and *world*, and because it centered on the failure of the former to come to terms with the latter, the picture of man that it suggested was one of a being struggling with and forcing itself on the world it exists in, a world that does not quite ground Man's knowledge of it and forbids him any transcendental perspective on it. Second, during the 1930s, the thinking of Alexandre Koyré and Martin Heidegger expressed the problem posed by man's grounding in modernity. On top of his institutional involvements, Koyré played a major philosophical role for his generation, particularly through his presentation of modern thought and science as conditioned by their metaphysical and religious premises. Similarly, Heidegger's approach to transcendence in his "On the Essence of Ground" (the second of his essays published in French translation) helped overturn the existing perception of the human being as transcending the world, so as to center on man's "casting" of this world—and rounds out the part played by antifoundational realism and Koyré's study of man in modernity.

Perhaps the most appropriate term for a description of the place of man, following the antifoundational and realist tendencies of the early 1930s is that of *human reality*. Marking the codependence of the two terms—the impossibility of a reality pure of any human interaction and the lack of transcendental or absolute status for the human—human reality encompasses the push against idealism and the effort to explain the limitations of the human, its decentering and emptying out in reality. In "human reality," the human loses its separation from this reality and becomes enmeshed with it; at the same time, reality is designated as decidedly human, and not real by itself. But "human reality" has a further force in 1930s thought because in tune with Alexandre Kojève's use of the term to translate Heidegger's *Dasein* in his early, unpublished work, his collaborator and student Henri Corbin used it, apparently with Heidegger's approval, in his translation of early essays that appeared in 1938. Subsequently, Sartre also used this translation in *Being and Nothingness*, though it quickly declined in the early postwar period.[13] Since then, "human reality" as a term has received a plethora of harsh criticisms—"poor," "anthropologizing," "monstrous," even "execrable."[14] These criticisms are perhaps deserved insofar as it humanized and concretized a term used by Heidegger to denote the "thereness" of the human being and its disclosure of Being, but neither its humanity nor its reality (both of which are, for Heidegger, derivative). Nevertheless, the function of "human reality" in the context of the French 1930s, and as a designator of *Dasein*, adjusts what "human reality" might otherwise mean: with Corbin's translation, it now means *Dasein*, that is, it largely names "human reality" the pure thereness, nonideality, and existence that is indicated by *Dasein*, and thus adjusts both "human" and "reality." It thereby allies the human, in its emptiness, with a reality distinctly dependent on it and pulls away "the human" from the foundationalism and idealism to which it was formerly tied and for which "human reality" would later unhistorically be criticized.

1. Institutions and the Generational Rift

The antihumanism of *human reality* is closely tied to the impetus for change of philosophical approach that came from figures who were only tentatively linked to the Parisian philosophical establishment and tradition. These young philosophers taught either outside of Paris (Jean Wahl until 1936, Georges Canguilhem), at the Ecole Pratique des Hautes Etudes (Alexandre Koyré, Henri Corbin, Alexandre Kojève, Gaston Bachelard), or simply outside the French university altogether (Gabriel Marcel, Emmanuel Levinas, Jean-Paul Sartre, Bernhard Groethuysen). Though many had studied in part under "the mandarins," these studies did not form the core of their work, and their expressions of gratitude to the elders are not indicative of philosophical loyalty. Most important are the groups comprising in part of young émigrés, most of whom were from the Soviet Union and had studied in Germany.[15] Among these "visitors" were Emmanuel Levinas, Alexandre Koyré (originally Koyrànsky), Georges Gurvitch, Alexandre Kojève (originally Koschewnikow), and Rachel Bespaloff—not to mention German thinkers like Bernhard Groethuysen and, later, Walter Benjamin.[16] As foreigners and exiles, not only did they enjoy a heightened personal aura, but their foreign education (like Kuki's) clashed with the priorities of French philosophy and provided an alternative to the more traditional French resolutions of philosophical problems. Moreover, their rebellion against neocriticism can be understood somewhat in tandem with that of nonacademic groups seeking a *renouvellement* of philosophy: early French Freudians (the circle of psychoanalysts around Marie Bonaparte and also the surrealists), literary Nietzschean circles (among them Gide's circle and the Collège de Sociologie), Marxist philosophers (like the Philosophies group that included Paul Nizan), and other émigré groups (for example, around Boris Souvarine and *La Critique sociale*).[17] Like them, the philosophical outsiders of interest here largely identified the official liberal humanism and failures of the Third Republic with what they perceived as contemporary philosophical stagnation. The effort to reinvigorate philosophy was thus akin to these often heavily politicized movements, though its attention to epistemological and ontological questions (and the relationship of these to the question of Man) formed a more specific base that cannot really be identified with political tendencies, and indeed often fled precisely their "humanism."

(a) Alexandre Koyré

The work of Alexandre Koyré sits at the center of the 1930s philosophical attempt to reconceive the scientific and theological origins of modernity and the relationship of these origins to a present that oppresses their ambiguities, that claims freedom from its history, and that professes direct access to transcendental truths. Koyré is now known in France and the United States primarily for his work on the history and philosophy of science, especially his influential 1956 lectures at Johns Hopkins, published as *From the Closed World to the Infinite Universe*, and his work on Galileo and Newton.[18] His intellectual-historical formation began with an early interest in mathematics and phenomenology and a turn, during the late 1910s, toward the history of religious thought. No less than Emile Durkheim or Marcel Mauss, and certainly much more than Léon Shestov or the authors linked to the Collège de Sociologie, Koyré provided an intellectual basis for the belief that modernity was based on a metaphysical, religious, and even tragic origin that it oppressed and substituted through a profane humanist claim to transcendence. A prolific writer and teacher already from the early years of his Parisian stay, Koyré is significant here less because of the radicalism of his conceptions and more because of the systematic and erudite fashion in which he presented his positions as achievements of careful modern scholarship. Koyré also played a major institutional role in the reorganization of French thought by operating as an organizational core for varying attempts to move beyond Kantianism. During the early 1930s, Koyré identified these attempts with the introduction of phenomenology in France; besides his position as director of *Recherches philosophiques*, he published and introduced the first translations of Heidegger in French, and he extensively reviewed phenomenological works in *Recherches philosophiques*.[19] On the centenary of Hegel's death, he devoted three essays to him and taught a course at the Ecole Pratique des Hautes Etudes on Hegel's Jena writings. Koyré's exceptional presence in French thought of the period can be seen in his influential participation in these two milieux.

(b) Recherches philosophiques

From 1931 through 1937, *Recherches philosophiques* hosted some of the most significant contemporary debates in French philosophy. That the journal is forgotten today is surprising: it comprised six issues and more than three thousand pages and was perhaps the most significant of its time, featuring studies on metaphysics, phenomenology, philosophy of science, early existentialism, and comparative religion in a way unmatched by other scholarly publications or institutions. It combined these in a synthesis that prefigured existentialism.[20] *Recherches philosophiques* was specifically geared toward alternatives to the dominant philosophical establishment, including, from the very beginning, translations and reviews of phenomenological essays and books, discussions of the history of specific sciences and philosophical movements elsewhere in Europe, and broad bibliographical essays on new publications in France and abroad. Due to their outsider status, many of the younger 1930s philosophers had trouble publishing in the more official reviews, such as the *Revue philosophique* or the *Revue de métaphysique et de morale*; *Recherches philosophiques* filled this gap, offering a voice to young philosophers and contributing to the orientation of their research.

Despite proclaiming openness to established philosophical positions, the most significant and systematic advances of *Recherches philosophiques* concerned the phenomenological approach of the questions of man, transcendence, and time, as well as a convergence of religious/existential questions with the modern history and philosophy of the sciences.[21] Indeed, the programmatic opening section of the first issue of *Recherches philosophiques*, called "Present Tendencies in Metaphysics," turned to both new philosophy and new science, by including Jean Wahl's introduction to *Vers le concret*, Heidegger's essay "On the Essence of Ground," an essay by the Bergsonian Jean Baruzi on the languages of mysticism, and Gaston Bachelard's essay "Noumène et métaphysique." What these essays share is a critique of both classical realism and Kantian idealism; Wahl and Bachelard also converge by their attention to new scientific claims, while Baruzi and Wahl speak to the contemporary resonance of the problem of mysticism.[22]

The philosophy of science section—directed first by Albert Spaier (until his 1934 death) and then by Gaston Bachelard—became especially important for the review. *Recherches philosophiques* regularly dedicated a third of its space to studies of scientific questions, epistemology, and recent research.[23] Studies on contemporary science and their philosophical implications became a crucial feature, not least because this was the first time since the 1890s that a philosophical journal set up science, its truth, and its legitimacy as basic philosophical matter. Moreover, *Recherches philosophiques* linked philosophy of science with phenomenological issues.[24] On this last point, its role in advancing phenomenology was considerable—in a sense, it formed the center of interest in Husserl, Scheler, Heidegger, and Nicolai Hartmann during the 1930s. Besides the publication of Heidegger's "De la nature de la cause," and important articles by Jean Wahl, Gabriel Marcel, Eugène Minkowski, and others, it regularly included reviews of works on phenomenology (often written by Kojève, occasionally in a biting though accessible manner), and crucial essays by Emmanuel Levinas, Georges Bataille, Jean-Paul Sartre, and others who came to link phenomenology with early existentialism.[25] Alongside (as well as *in*) the phenomenological texts we find a number of protoexistentialist sketches and essays; significant contributors here, apart from its editors and those already mentioned, include Leo Strauss, Roger Caillois, Raymond Aron, Bernard Groethuysen, Georges Dumézil, and Karl Löwith: a whole generation whose influence quickly extended far beyond the review's limits.

(c) The Ecole Pratique des Hautes Etudes

The second central site for new intellectual currents was the Ecole Pratique des Hautes Etudes (EPHE), which allowed for a system of teaching that was unlike that of most other Parisian institutions for advanced education, particularly with regard to the study of philosophy, history, and religion. Professors at the EPHE, besides Koyré himself (and Kojève), included Emile Benveniste, Marcel Mauss (who taught his famous course on "The Gift" in 1929 there), Georges Dumezil, and Gaston Bachelard—who were already influential or would become so in the early postwar period. Like Koyré and Henri-Charles Puech, many of the figures who were involved in *Recherches philosophiques* or who were attempting to draft an original (and usually an anti-Neo-Kantian) philosophical project were also teachers or participants at EPHE courses in the 1930s.

The group around Koyré and Kojève reveals much about the circumstances of courses at the EPHE. In a presentation of the status and significance of the EPHE, Alexandre Koyré wrote of his satisfaction with the independence of its Fifth Section in which he taught (the department on "religious sciences"), an independence he credited to the Ecole's distance from religious institutions and from dogmatic theology. Koyré considered it the only place where a historical and philosophical study of religion uninhibited by church or state was possible—arguing that in this, it fully achieved the goal of its founding in the late nineteenth century.[26]

The teaching was aimed at students who were older and more intellectually mature—often taking courses even after completing their doctorates and often continuing studies they had started abroad. Moreover, attendance, the format of the courses, and relations between students and professors were strikingly different to French standards: informal and often quite personal. In Koyré's courses, students regularly included Kojève, Bataille, Henri Corbin (historian of Islamic thought and Heidegger translator), Czech phenomenologist Jan Patocka, Eric Weil, Raymond Queneau, and other occasional participants, such as Emmanuel Levinas.[27] Many of them, Corbin reports, would continue their discussions after Koyré's (and later Kojève's) seminars at the Café d'Harcourt in the Place de la Sorbonne, often extending the seminar for hours; most of these participants would continue to constitute a group well into the late 1930s.[28] Kojève, who taught his famous course on Hegel from 1933 through 1939, was younger than almost all of his "students"—a rotating group that included Raymond Aron, Maurice Merleau-Ponty, Gaston Fessard, Georges Bataille, Raymond Queneau, Henri Corbin, Jacques Lacan, Emmanuel Levinas, Eric Weil, and Koyré himself. In characteristic style, Kojève later boasted that while at the EPHE he had introduced smoking in the French classroom: regardless of its silliness, this claim speaks volumes about the teaching climate at the EPHE.[29] Finally, as can be seen from the content of *Recherches philosophiques*, these teachers and students often published their work together, which suggests that we speak of them as a specific milieu. Their connection to each other is furthered if one also notes the proximity of *Recherches philosophiques* and the EPHE to other institutions, such as the journal *Bifur*, the journal *Mésures* organized by Bernard Groethuysen, and Groethuysen's famous collection "Bibliothèque des idées" at Gallimard.[30] The contrast to the Ecole Normale Supérieure, for example, which remained rigidly structured well into the 1960s, could not be more startling.[31]

2. Realism at the Dusk of Modern Science:
Phenomenology and Quanta in Paris

Beyond cultural, biographical, and institutional factors, two major philosophical appropriations opened the transformation of the philosophical landscape in the turn of the 1930s: *phenomenology*, particularly Heidegger's, and *quantum physics*, particularly of the Copenhagen School, which was perceived as effecting a scientific revolution. Today, given Heidegger's critique of the aspirations of science, Husserl's *Crisis of the European Sciences*, and the routine rejection of phenomenology's possible utility for scientists, the combination of phenomenology and theoretical physics may appear forced. Yet of particular significance in the French context was their shared hostility to any imagination of a reality transparent to the mind—and these were tied from their earliest French appearances, in particular Edmund Husserl's lectures, which became known as the *Cartesian Meditations,* at the Société française de philosophie in 1928. In introducing Husserl, Pierre Duhem cited Hermann Weyl and Werner Heisenberg so as to testify to Husserl's philosophical significance. "[The very evocation of] Hermann Weyl's name, of the homage he pays you . . . when he writes: 'The precise articulation of these thoughts follows closely from Husserl,' and also the beautiful works of Heisenberg say a lot about what science owes you."[32]

The fundamentally epistemological novelty of these two movements, and the question of their role in philosophical treatments of realism were felt throughout the early 1930s, most visibly in works on the history and philosophy of science by Koyré and Bachelard, and most importantly in the turn to a new realism by Jean Wahl and Alexandre Kojève. What is interesting and new here is the *complementarity* of quantum physics and phenomenology, which forms the ground of antifoundational realism.

(a) Quantum Physics as an Overcoming of the Old Rationalism/Realism Debate

To explain antifoundational realism, one must begin with the question of quantum physics. The perception that the relationship between philosophy and science had broken down in the mid- to late nineteenth century was a problem widely considered already from the late 1910s, a problem that led to considerable debate on the priority of each of the two over the other. Most contemporary philosophers by and large worked out this "breakdown" into a debate between rationalism (allied to neocriticism and the claim that science proceeds from the reasoning human mind and encompasses the world as it may be understood) and realism (here claiming that science seeks to comprehend a grand world external to man and proceeds from the real data provided by this world). With its 1931–32 issue, *Recherches philosophiques* signaled the need of a philosophical reconsideration of such categories in light of new scientific findings. The rise of quantum physics from Planck and Einstein to de Broglie and Heisenberg (received seriously by philosophical milieux in Paris in the late twenties) accentuated and gave a particular character to this debate. To appreciate the gravity of this development, suffice it to note that during 1929 alone, several *series* of lectures on quanta were given in Paris by figures no lesser than Paul Langevin, Werner Heisenberg, Max Born, and Louis de Broglie, but also by Hendrik Kramers and Enrico Fermi.[33]

The physical or scientific significance of relativity and quanta aside, philosophical reactions to quantum mechanics diverged even as they came to shape a veritable obsession. Certain thinkers, like Brunschvicg and the scientist and philosopher Paul Langevin, rejected the radical claims and implications of the Copenhagen interpretation of quanta, implying (with Einstein) that Heisenberg's uncertain universe was but an aberration that would soon be corrected. In the philosophical and epistemological work of Meyerson, Kojève, and Bachelard, however, the role of quantum mechanics suggested the possibility of a sort of reconciliation between philosophy, mathematics, and physics, not to mention a far-reaching need to overcome existing concepts.[34] In the early thirties, each of these three authors wrote on the problem of determinism and the impact of quanta, namely, *Réel et déterminisme dans la physique quantique* (Meyerson, 1933), *L'Idée du déterminisme dans la physique classique et dans la physique moderne* (Kojève, 1932), and *Le Nouvel Esprit Scientifique* (Bachelard, 1934).[35] Both Kojève and Bachelard clearly emphasized the idea that physics called for and facilitated a new scene for philosophy, and they explicitly criticized Meyerson for his "antiquated" understanding of realism.[36]

As is well known, the radical novelty of the Bohr-Heisenberg interpretation in the late 1920s relied on the *complementarity* and *uncertainty* principles.[37] The complementarity principle holds that it is impossible to provide adequate calculations of the movement and actions of electrons without using both *wave* and *particle* computations. Simply put, there is an irresolvable contradiction between the wave and particle images that the atom provides the physicist.[38] To understand the atom, the physicist needs to complement wave computations with particle ones. But for Bachelard, Kojève, Koyré, and other contemporaries, the philosophical novelty of quanta rested with the uncertainty principle and its development beyond the claims of complementarity. *Uncertainty* holds that in the study of electrons, the physicist cannot concurrently determine both their location and speed but will *necessarily* err on either of these computations. To locate and gauge the moving electron, the physicist needs to shoot photons at it, photons whose energy necessarily impacts the electron's movement and speed (NES 122 / 122). Consequently, the observer/physicist becomes involved in the experiment, but *also* becomes incapable of predicting what the electron under observation will do next with this newly acquired energy. The result of this is that the determinist foundation of post-Newtonian physics—that such a movement must be fully observable—can no longer be sustained. By extension, as the observer's participation cannot be disengaged from the system under observation, and as the very process of observation relies on the *interaction* between observer and world, the Cartesian and modern construction of nature and space is wrong to postulate the thinking, calculating observer (and his tools of study) as strictly independent and separable from the objects and world of his study. Differently put, any positive knowledge of nature necessitates the observer's fundamental interaction with nature itself. The scientistic and positivist hopes that nature would one day become fully transparent to the human mind suddenly run aground on a major problem behind this transparency: there is no transcendental observer capable of understanding a pure nature distinct from him, and there is also no intellectual process that can determine what lies beyond this observer's reach.[39]

How did quantum physics come to acquire such powerful status and offer a philosophical paradigm shift? Both Bachelard and Kojève reacted to these developments with considerable philosophical excitement. Bachelard's call for a new realism is limited by his lack of philosophical, metascientific rigor, but his work nonetheless makes clear the insufficiency of the old notions of "reality" as well as the potential of quantum physics. In Kojève's *L'Idée du déterminisme*, the connection of science (and the philosophy underlying it) to phenomenology, and the anthropological potential of this connection, are far clearer: while quantum physics provides the impetus (thereby straining his own Neo-Kantian education), phenomenology provides an engine for the philosophical effects of quanta.

Bachelard's *The New Scientific Spirit* extended his late 1920s efforts toward a refutation of science as an objective and unified conception of *reality*—itself conceived as a world purely independent of the mind and reconstructed in terms of an oblique correspondence between the rational and the real. Having already suggested that Einstein's theory of relativity indicated a "collapse" of the Kantian *noumenon,* Bachelard here extended this interpretation to non-Euclidian geometry, Reichenbachian indeterminism, and, above all, Heisenberg's uncertainty principle.[40] Bachelard specified that the Copenhagen interpretation of quantum physics (whose arrival "has put everything into question again" [NES 122/122; trans. mine]), imposes a conception of science that overcomes "elementary" realism (NES 130/130) and suggests the possibility of a reconciliation of the rationalism/realism contrast and an overcoming of its meaning and consequences (NES 130/130). "Physics has no doubt maintained, in its language at any rate, a more or less realistic flavor, but is it indeed true that this obscure residue of realism actually lends weight to the concepts of physics and influences the goals of research?" (NES 131/131). For Bachelard, this did not mean that science could just do away with reality. Instead, the thinking on which science and its advances were grounded had to be cleansed of Cartesian domination: "the partiality in favor of subjective experience" and its consequence, the "progressive objectification" of the world (NES 169/167). For Bachelard (as for Koyré) this effectively implied the end of the classical, antiempiricist mathematization of nature that was characteristic of modern science.[41] Given this much, the scientist could now imagine a realism of an entirely different order—one limited to the possible *actualizations of his thought* ("the realization of the rational" [NES 4–5, 13/4, 13]). Coextensive to this argument was, as mentioned already, the abandoning of the Kantian *thing-in-itself* for an entirely other kind of *noumenon:* "The 'reality' to which this realism corresponds is not transferred into the realm of the unknowable thing-in-itself. It has a noumenal richness of quite another order. The *thing-in-itself* is a noumenon by exclusion of phenomena, whereas scientific reality, I would argue, consists in a noumenal context suitable for defining axes of experimentation" (NES 5/5–6).[42] Real according to this definition is what, in the world, is possible to prove, acknowledge, acquiesce to, experiment on. This is a totality largely distinct from the intentionality of the individual or scientific mind, but nevertheless one that the individual still encounters and interacts with—a reality limited to possible actualizations of thought. The contrast Bachelard makes is not between *phenomena* and *noumena*, but between *a mind* and *a world that could be called "real" only by way of a limited contrast to the mind's perception and interpretation of it*. This reality "is thus reason confirmed," in other words what is available. Still, it is difficult to avoid a sense that while Bachelard provides a new contrast, he does not really step beyond a certain rationalism. "Reason confirmed": such a reality is not strictly speaking indeterminable from the scientist's point of view. Similarly, "the realization of the rational" receives no better or more elaborate definition than that "science conjures up a world, by means not of magic immanent in reality but of rational impulse immanent in mind. . . . Scientific work makes rational entities real, in the full sense of the word" (NES 13/13). Even if we grant Bachelard's unwillingness to work in primarily philosophical terms (and his critique of epistemologists like Meyerson for departing from strictly scientific language), his usage of philosophical terms (such as *noumenon*) leaves them subdued to a rather hasty scientific explanation. For Bachelard, in other words, the reduction of the world to phenomena "with a noumenal richness of their own" successfully highlights the contrast of mind and world and limits this "world" to what the mind can relate to, but does not quite break out of this reduction to scientific immanence to consider the forms and limitations of man's engagements. Bachelard's hesitation to organize the philosophical terms of his approach to quantum physics limits the novelty of his interpretation.

Even more than in Bachelard's work, quantum physics played a central role in the philosophical formation of the then twenty-eight-year-old Alexandre Kojève. Kojève had escaped the USSR and studied in Berlin and Heidelberg under Neo-Kantian thinkers and Karl Jaspers, and then in 1926 he arrived in Paris and extensively studied Weyl, Cantor, and de Broglie. Kojève lauded the Copenhagen interpretation for overturning Newtonian determinism and thus transforming the conception of the physical world from a "determinist" into a "statistical" one.[43] Extending this argument in *L'Idée du déterminisme* (that served as his second PhD thesis, directed by Koyré), he opposed the realism of classical physics with the far more complex "realism" that follows from Heisenberg's uncertainty.[44]

In modern physics, we must distinguish between two kinds of realism that coincided in classical physics, which did not distinguish sufficiently between gnoseological, mathematical, physical and biological subjects and, consequently, the worlds that are attached to them. First, metaphysical realism, which considers the physical world as a *sui generis* reality, independent from the gnoseological and psychological subjects. Then, the properly physical realism, which opposes, inside this world, the subject to the object [*for him the observing and observed systems respectively, as suggested by Heisenberg*—S. G.]—both of which are real in relation to each other and situated on the same ontological plan. (ID 286)

The interaction of observing and observed systems in the milieu of a world is central to Kojève's argument because it reconfigures the philosophical conception of the subject-object relationship. If classical physics was fundamentally realist (ID 278), then modern physics contradistinguished the reality of the observing system from that of the observed, basically showing that there is no such thing as a pure, external reality, that the Kantian in-itself was no philosophical given but an irrelevant metaphysical fantasy (ID 283).[45] Kojève clarifies the distinction between physical and philosophical subjects thus:

Modern physics [is not] any more "idealist," more "subjectivist," more "phenomenalist" in the positivist sense than classical physics was. On one hand, the observed system is no less real than the observing system, and *it is independent from the latter as regards its being;* their interaction is itself also real. On the other hand, the totality formed by the two interacting systems is certainly real and "objective," in the sense that it exists independently as much of the empirical subject (the experimenter in the flesh) as from the gnoseological "knowing subject." (ID 283; italics mine)

If he restricts his attention to the relation between observing and observed systems, Kojève finds the two to be equally real and ontologically independent from each other. He seeks, moreover, to separate this "whole" constructed by the interaction of the two systems from experience in general, insofar as he refuses to efface the independence of the observed system from the empirical subject. Yet this distinction does not serve (here or in the earlier passage) to doubt the far-reaching significance of this new realism; instead, it allows the physical realism to be "real and 'objective,'" and thus (i) amplifies the independence *of the being of* the observed system from the observing system (hence from the epistemological and empirical subject), and (ii) nevertheless does not deny that the epistemological and empirical subject is itself dependent to a degree on the observed system (given that the observing system is part of the empirical subject and the interaction of the observing/observed systems is real). In other words, the observed system is ontologically distinct from the observing one; both are real and irreducible to each other; the relation between their realities is irreducible.[46]

The contrast between the observing and observed systems has fundamental implications for philosophical knowledge and subjectivity (both in a physical and in a metaphysical sense) because it raises the possibility of new differences between subject and world, and, in the philosophical context, of separate and complementary ontologies: an *ontological dualism* based on one *anthropological* ontology and a *separate* one for the world and the things experienced by man.[47] Kojève accordingly criticized the ontological monism and mind/reality contrast of most modern philosophers, arguing that their opposition between subject and object was simplistic and too radical, and the way in which the subject "knows" the object even more troubling. He effectively discarded Husserl's "Parisian Lectures"— the *Cartesian Meditations*—as obsolete and symptomatic of the way in which knowledge and the epistemological subject is treated by "die ganze abendländische Philosophie," chided Brunschvicg for not realizing that science had changed dramatically since the turn of the century, and elaborately opposed any inclusion of electron mechanics or Einstein's relativity in the new, "modern" science (ID 33–34).[48] Still, Kojève did leave a way out of this philosophical failure. In his writing, he offered a parallel between this epistemological-cum-ontological attempt to substantiate and explain the new realism of quantum physics and Heidegger's treatment of *Dasein* and his rethinking of *world* and *reality*. In Heideggerian phenomenology Kojève found the possibility of interpreting the successes and limitations of physics, allowing a fusion of the two to provide a significant philosophical critique of the limitations of each. While Bachelard lacked a properly philosophical language to allow him to speak for the philosophical implications of quanta, Kojève utilized phenomenology as just that language. Jean Wahl drew more or less the same conclusions from atomic physics, whose testimony to science's "recognition of its limits" he appreciated: a call to a new philosophical realism, a legitimation of phenomenological treatments of knowledge, and a revelation of the limits of subjective knowledge (and by extension of consciousness).[49]

(b) The First Wave of Heidegger's French Reception and the Languages of Realism

Contrary to what is often argued, Heidegger's first French readers did not turn to his work because it offered them an anthropology; nor did they, until Sartre's time, construct an anthropology out of it. While they did read him in a fashion that could be treated as anthropological, at the same time they used *Being and Time* to ruin the anthropological argumentation of the "old guard." The oft-repeated reproach that his French readers reduced his fundamental ontology to an anthropology forgets that this interpretation was initiated and utilized by Heidegger himself on strategically valuable occasions; moreover, it ignores the dismantling of philosophical anthropology from its Neo-Kantian peak to the atheist realism under discussion here. Concerned with occasional German critiques of his early work as anthropocentric, or as buried under the shadow of Scheler, Husserl, or even Jaspers, Heidegger specifically displaced the attention paid by French thinkers to Division I, Part I of *Sein und Zeit*, and the anti-anthropocentric emphasis of their critique of idealism.[50] He adopted the reproach that his readers were being anthropological on three occasions specifically designed to press a strict reading of his work and a disciple-like following. In a 1937 letter to Jean Wahl, he criticized the latter's presentation of *Sein und Zeit* as an *Existenzphilosophie* that bordered on anthropology.[51] His famous 1946 "Letter on 'Humanism'" to Jean Beaufret, the retort to Sartre's *Existentialism Is a Humanism* talk at the Club Maintenant, also emphasized the perils of a humanist and anthropologist reading of his work.[52] Finally, in a letter to Hannah Arendt, Heidegger specifically criticized Kojève for being limited to anthropology, in the same paragraph where he praised Kojève's Hegel lectures as a zenith of French thought.[53] The argument has been further perpetuated by philosophers invested in projects related to the limits of man (for example, Jacques Derrida) and others interested in identifying a certain Heideggerian orthodoxy (for example, Jean Beaufret, Luc Ferry, and Alain Renaut)—whether to distinguish themselves *in* it or *from* it—and also by *all* the historians writing on the encounter between Heidegger and French thought: for them, fidelity to Heidegger appeared only after 1945, while the 1930s generation remained tied to its subjectivist and anthropological reading.[54] Good reasons exist for this argument—most significantly the subjectivist radicalization of Heidegger's *Existenzphilosophie* by Sartre, and *perhaps* the rendering of *Dasein* as *réalité humaine* by Corbin—but it does not by itself suffice to explain the early readings.[55]

I want to suggest a different interpretation. As exiles, foreigners, and travelers helped bring phenomenology to intellectuals both in and outside of the academic establishment in France, the status accorded to Husserl and Heidegger was that of providing a step beyond Bergson and the Neo-Kantians, introducing a different form of philosophy that connected ontology to epistemology in a way that was sensitive to both the philosophical and the scientific limitations of Bergsonism and neocriticism.[56] This first generation of readers never accepted Heidegger's thought as marking the limits of their philosophical horizon, but instead considered it as a ground for their thought and also as a kind of evolving argument they could engage with in dialogue, that is, one whose ends and arguments could be furthered or criticized. What Heidegger offered was a way of dealing with the world and objects in it that allowed achievements in epistemology and philosophy of science to not go amiss and to be possible to expand into a philosophical outlook on existence.

Conversely, the methodological transformation of the philosophy of science already suggested above paved the way for the import and philosophical legitimation of phenomenology, primarily Heidegger and Husserl's, but also (a case that is less known) Scheler's.[57] Specifically with regard to Bachelard's attempt to reconstruct conceptions of the *noumenon* and Wahl's search for a concrete basis of existence, Heidegger's 1927 *Being and Time* provided a new way of conceiving (a) the meaning and limitations of *noumena*—which it radically undermined—and (b) the question of (the lack of) a foundation to human existence.[58] Like Georges Gurvitch, who wrote the first text in French on Heidegger in 1929, Wahl, Levinas, Koyré, and Kojève *all* emphasized his phenomenological *and existential* systematization of man's comportment in the world, which they then proceeded to use in their own projects.[59] In addition to the antifoundational realist critique of philosophical and scientific Cartesianism and idealism, phenomenology facilitated, for example, an atheist interplay between a threatened (Kierkegaardian) subjectivity and a totalizing world from which they could not escape and which they could not understand (a point that extends to the question of Hegel's notion of historical totality). In this context, rather than use Heidegger to anthropologize phenomenology, *French philosophers used him for a dethroning and emptying out of existing anthropology and a denigration of man from his earlier status of an ideal.*

Kojève's reading of Heidegger highlights many of these points by tying Heidegger's thought, explicitly, to his reading of Heisenberg. Already in 1929, Kojève had written that philosophers from Descartes to Husserl mistakenly thought that an ontology of the subject served as an absolute grounding for science's aims.[60] In an elaborate 1936 note on Hegel and Heidegger, Kojève emphasized that Heidegger's prime philosophical contribution was his undoing of ontological monism—which, he wrote, marked the "grandiose yet complete failure" of Hegel's own ontology.[61] The same praise of Heidegger's "ontological dualism" marks one of the important notes to his *Introduction à la lecture de Hegel*, as well as the concluding lecture of the seminar, where Kojève interprets the end of history as the death of man.[62] *Yet, to mark this new dualism, Kojève did not utilize (or even refer to) Heidegger's famous and readily available ontological difference between beings and Being.* Rather, subsuming the ontological difference in *Dasein,* he contrasts *Dasein (être-la)* to *Vorhandensein (être-donné) in its totality,* and he interprets the latter as *nature,* as Hegel's *in-itself,* as *world* in Heidegger's "On the Essence of Ground"—the world which *is not* but which "worlds" (EG 126), or also simply as "the world that is given me."[63] Kojève appropriates these in his own term *le donné* (the given), man's "sphere of action."[64] It should be noted here that, in his attempt to see *le donné* as ontologically significant, Kojève uses *Vorhanden-sein* instead of Heidegger's own term *Vorhanden-heit* (for Heidegger, worldly objects do not "have" Being). Kojève writes, "The novelty is the resolute acceptance of *ontological dualism*, of the essential and irreducibly ontological difference between the human being (*Dasein*) and natural being (*Vorhandensein*)" (NHH 37). Kojève identifies Heidegger's *Dasein* with Heisenberg's observing system and *Vorhandensein* with the observed system. Consider the following two quotes (the first of which I have already cited and will repeat here for emphasis):

Modern physics [is not] any more "idealist," more "subjectivist," more "phenomenalist" in the positivist sense than classical physics was. . . . The observed system is no less real than the observing system, and *it is independent from the latter as regards its being*; their interaction is itself also real. (ID 283; italics mine)

. . . the human being (*Dasein*) is essentially a being-in-the-world (*In-der-Welt-sein*); . . . the world (*Welt*) of man differs from nature (*Natur, Vorhandensein*) in an essential way, by the fact that it is modified—or, at least, as revealed and considered to be modifiable. . . . (NHH 37)

In and by these parallels, Kojève clearly echoes Heidegger's discussion of the worldhood of the world and his suspension of the "existence" of any objective reality distinct from *Dasein*'s world (BT §14–18, §43; EG 368n17). For Heidegger, the world is bound up with the understanding (ontological or preontological) through which *Dasein* discloses it: "The question of whether there is a world at all and whether its Being can be proved, makes no sense if it is raised by *Dasein* as being-in-the-world; and who else would raise it?" (BT §43a: 202 / 246–47). Moreover:

When *Dasein* does not exist, 'independence' 'is' not either, nor 'is' the 'in-itself.' In such a case this sort of thing can be neither understood nor not understood. In such a case even entities within the world can neither be discovered nor lie hidden. In such a case it cannot be said that entities are, nor can it be said that they are not. But *now*, as long as there is an understanding of Being and therefore an understanding of presence-at-hand, it can indeed be said that *in this case* entities will still continue to be. (BT §43c: 212 / 255)

In rejecting classical realism and the skeptical question, Heidegger emphasizes (i) that everything that is or can be real for *Dasein* is already part of its world ("even the Real can only be discovered on the basis of a world which has already been disclosed" [BT §43a: 203 / 247]), and (ii) that the reality of *Dasein*, of the world, and of entities that *Dasein* encounters and interprets in the world is never in question—but is, once again, disclosed by *Dasein's* understanding of Being and its comportment as/through care.

Along with *Dasein* as Being-in-the-World, entities within-the-world have in each case already been disclosed. This existential-ontological assertion seems to accord with the thesis of *realism* that the external world is Really present-at-hand. Insofar as this existential assertion does not deny that entities within-the-world are present-at-hand, it agrees . . . with the thesis of realism in its results. But it differs in principle from every kind of realism; for realism holds that the Reality of the "world" not only needs to be proved but also is capable of proof. In the existential assertion both of these positions are directly negated. But what distinguishes this assertion from realism altogether is the fact that in realism there is a lack of ontological understanding. Indeed realism tries to explain Reality ontically by Real connections of interaction between things that are real. (BT §43a: 207 / 251)

Like Koyré and Wahl (who understood these arguments as denials of man's capacity to ever come to terms with, or fully understand, his world), Kojève accepts this position; he writes, "The world of man differs from nature in an essential way," and he underlines that the sheer presence of a *Befindlichkeit* (existential disposition) transforms nature into world (NHH 37–39).[65] What this means, for Kojève, is that the existence of man transforms something like nature qua pure exteriority into a given world man always finds himself in interaction with and continually transforms. If such a nature exists, it does so only in the absence of man, but given man's presence in and interactions in it, such an imaginary nature is immediately turned into a world or reality that man operates in and with, a world that no longer holds anything *in itself.* This is his realism: "Whoever says 'Realism,' says ontological dualism" (ILH 432). Contesting, like Bachelard (NES 130, 176–77 / 130–31, 174–75), "the metaphysical realism that considers the world as a sui generis reality," Kojève de facto defends Heidegger's own kind of "realism" in his construction of this dual reality of observing/ observed systems (ID 323). A sui generis reality that cannot be interpreted and thereby changed is a metaphysical fantasy, but a reality constituted through and by man's interaction with objects allows, for Kojève, a nonmetaphysical, properly ontological conception that corresponds with post-Heisenbergian science. Against Heidegger, who denied science's capacity to reveal Being, Kojève was particularly concerned with showing that the reality of the world, of a *Sein des Vorhandenen* is validated and shown in the theoretical construction underlying uncertainty and complementarity's treatment of an observed system. Kojève accordingly insists that contemporary physics finds itself on the same level as the phenomenological understanding of the world's reality—and they both stand in contrast to the Cartesian foundations of modern theories of knowledge and truth. If up to this point in modern thought, the thinking subject set itself to revealing the truths contained in a spatio-dimensional nature (whether these truths and this nature were in fact merely in the subject's mind or in an external reality), the realism that Heidegger and Kojève promulgate thinks of the subject as involved and reliant on the object of his/her study, an object constructing and limiting the subject's own involvement with it, and a world that is inconceivable in any strict distinction from this subject.

Thus, in Kojève's writing, the availability of phenomenological and ontological language provided a philosophical basis for such a realism without undermining what he considered the properly scientific import and significance of quanta.[66] This interpretation of realism, as a balance of phenomenological and scientific problems evoked by Kojève (and Bachelard), was furthered by contemporaries, particularly Jean Wahl. As Wahl would later argue in his 1947–48 books, *Poésie Pensée Perception* and *The Philosopher's Way*, the terms of realism changed with the arrival of quantum physics and Heideggerian thought in the late 1920s.

It is not possible that a disruption as radical as the one we have been experiencing would not be accompanied by a reshuffling of forms of thought. . . . Einstein, Planck, Bohr, Heisenberg have destroyed the original conceptions of causality, space and time. . . . To tell the truth, the frames have been shattered; there are no more frames. And the things that were in the frames have also been shattered, and the links (causality, substance) between them as well.[67]

After Planck, Einstein, Bohr, and Heisenberg, "the problem is to see not only how science is possible, but how it is that science cannot go beyond certain limits" (PW 206). Similarly, "the realism of Heidegger, if we can call his philosophy realism (and he would question such a determination), is tinged with his idea of 'being in the world.' Here we no longer find the classical distinction between subject and object. . . . " (PW 209). Aiming, in his own critique of metaphysics, at a new realism, Wahl further suggested (again in accord with Kojève [ID 245, NHH 39–40]) that quantum physics and Heideggerian phenomenology share an opposition to anthropocentrism and anthropomorphism in science and philosophy (PW 207, 320); for him, in their different ways, these "movements" reawakened the problems of liberty and human understanding. These are the questions Wahl set for himself and for modern thought in his 1932 work *Vers le concret*.

(c) To the Concrete! Wahl and Antifoundational Realism

Vers le concret (*Toward the Concrete*) was a remarkably influential work: Jean-Paul Sartre wrote, thirty years later, that it was rare as a "book that enjoyed great success with us."[68] But as philosophical manifestos go, its introduction is rather strange. On the one hand, it clearly aims to demonstrate the insufficiency of "the idealism and optimism" of the 1920s, and to reorient current thinking toward "the rights of the immediate" (VC 3). Priority for him takes (i) the status of the reality and world that the subject finds itself in, and (ii) the persistent and floundering effort of the human being to come to terms with this "pathetic world" (VC 19).[69] Already in its programmatic title, the book echoes, alters, and parodies the Husserlian injunction "To the things themselves!" At stake here is the "concreteness" hidden in experience and the immediacy through which we sense it. Yet, on the other hand, the novelty of the book itself is coated in the polite and very classical rhetoric of an account of certain recent developments in philosophy, indicating a conciliatory tone and a terminology almost seeking to convert philosophers of the 1920s. This inclusive tendency is nowhere clearer than in Wahl's mixture of phenomenological with classical philosophical terminology, through which Wahl disrupts and abuses the terms of classical dualities: the thinkers he discusses, Marcel, James, and Whitehead are thus philosophers of transcendence and immanence, "panpsychism" and "panmaterialism," idealists and realists—yet, strictly speaking, they ascribe to none of these terms. We are thus faced with a double gesture: (i) an attempt to exceed and reground contemporary philosophy on the basis of this new "concrete"—to demonstrate the derivative and insufficient character of transcendental idealism and its incarnation in neocriticism—and (ii) a recuperative move that mutes the novelty of pragmatism, Marcel's protoexistentialism, and Whitehead's discussions of spatiality so as to make them easily recognizable to the uninitiated—

indeed to give the impression that these philosophers simply offer almost expected corrective alternatives.

So what does this new movement, this hesitant new anti-idealism amount to?[70] On this question, Wahl is precise and far-reaching. He denies any existence *whatsoever* to anything the subject cannot interact with (for example, to Kantian *noumena*), and he insists on a series of traits that offer an alternative relation of subject to world: the primacy of the world over the subject; the irreducible participation of the subject in any interpretation of the world, the ultimate failure of its effort to fully rationalize or apply itself to the reality that it *does* disclose and encounter but that clashes with the "eternal ideas" the subject hopes for (VC 12, 17–19). Like most modern realists, Wahl distinguishes between two sorts of realism, a naïve and a properly philosophical one (VC 6–7). The particularity of his distinction lies in his rejection of those realisms for which the interaction between subject and world is contingent and where all reality lies in the world—such as classical materialisms, or a substantialist reality à la Hume or Mill that the subject cannot fully experience (VC 7). Instead, his approach to the concrete begins with, and is enveloped in, this very interaction of man to world; in constructing a philosophical background that shows at once the novelty, the common traits, and the singular aspects of Marcel, James, and Whitehead, Wahl links here a reading of Heidegger with a specific skepticism toward modern science. Phenomenology and quantum physics are not elaborately treated as Wahl's targets in this text, but they offer a privileged mode of entry into his subject.

Wahl presents Heidegger only in footnotes and citations, but addresses him as indispensable for the trends and force of contemporary thought.[71] He then proceeds to evade *both* Heidegger's ontological focus *and* his organization of anthropological and existential problems in the construction of *Dasein* (BT Div. I, Part II). In an analysis that is remarkable in its positioning of Heidegger's thought, Wahl writes:

We will often come to refer to Heidegger. He has been profoundly conscious of many of the aspirations of contemporary thought; his clear consciousness of this obscure ground [*fond*] is joined by his remarkable art of translating in abstract terms his own observations and those of his predecessors—whether these be Kierkegaard, pragmatism, Dilthey or Spengler— . . . he has tried to join to the sentiment of individual existence, such as Kierkegaard had sensed it, the sentiment of our existence in the midst [milieu] of things, as this dawns today in philosophy. (VC 3n–4n).

Wahl's analysis proceeds from the last of these points: "the sentiment of our existence in the midst [*milieu*] of things, as this dawns today in philosophy" (VC 4n). Indeed, *all* of Wahl's subsequent citations utilize a strategy of drawing out of *Being and Time* the discussion of *Dasein*'s comportment in and toward the world, and of presenting this in slightly changed form: the subject's *immediate* encounter with the world (VC 11 n2); the spatial and immanent character of this encounter (VC 6 n2), the interaction that shows and conceptualizes the world as "a world of obstacles and tools" (VC 18 n2), and that offers a conception of reality in terms of resistance (VC 18). If Heidegger weaves together the aspirations of modern thought, this is because of the way in which he establishes the problems of world and of being in the world, and because of the way he interprets the enchainment of the *Dasein* among and by the things the self encounters as resisting it in the world.

The *immediacy and enchainment characteristic of this encounter between subject and world* serves here as a critique of Hegel no less than as a critique of substantialist dualisms, including that of the distinction between subject and object as determined from Descartes to Husserl. For Wahl, the subject finds itself *in* the world, not in *opposition* to it; there is no unavailable and absolutely other, no in-itself (as in Kant), in what the subject encounters. And though the subject does not find itself alone before a worldly object that is simply, directly, and completely comprehensible, the encounter between the two is more or less immediate, in the sense that, out of habit, experience, and so forth, the human subject copes in the world and comports itself toward an object without having to consciously do something, without effort, and without having to overcome a certain radical separation.

Thanks to this emphasis, Wahl is perhaps the first among Heidegger's early readers to emphasize a link between his thought and that of pragmatism: even in its immensity and density, the world as conceived by Heidegger is more or less familiar to the subject that it exceeds; it presents itself above all in occasions where it "resists" the subject, in moments when, by producing obstacles, it becomes a philosophical or existential problem.[72] Here, Wahl echoes implicitly the difference of *Vorhandenheit* and *Zuhandenheit* in Heidegger's *Being and Time*, and he refers explicitly to the way in which Heidegger presents *Dasein* as thrown in the midst of a world, accentuating how *Dasein* is fascinated by this world but also how objects in the world inevitably do not bend to *Dasein's* will (VC 11). By way of this notion of *resistance*, Wahl posits man as having only an imperfect understanding of this world, as forced to a receptivity and a participative relation vis-à-vis the world; the world itself in this sense comes to appear, from the perspective of man, as immense and enchaining.

Wahl accentuates the immediate, spatial, and immanent characters of the reality man finds himself in and seeks to explicate. This accentuation eludes the question of skepticism in suggesting that the concrete, which is always "the pursued" (VC 23), is exactly what one engages with most directly, what one depends on in a fashion too ordinary to understand as a philosophical subject. As for Heidegger, reality for Wahl is never in doubt: reality makes itself evident through its resistance to subjectivity's desires and claims, but it also exists on all occasions where man just ignores it, taking his encounters in it for granted. Moreover, by reading *Being and Time* in a way that insists on the spatial and unmediated character of Being-in-the-world, Wahl comes to think the sentiment of the body in James together with Whitehead's theory of voluminosity (which diverge significantly from each other and which do not necessarily implicate in the same way what Wahl calls a "réceptivité vers la réalité" [VC 13]). Understood in Heideggerian terms, Wahl's interpretation of reality does not differentiate between the *existentiell* understanding of reality and existence (in a sense the sense of reality that one experiences in everyday life) and the *existential* (in that sense the analytical) reconstruction of this reality, therefore critiquing the limits of the philosophical interpretation of the world—and maintaining the need for a "mystical vision" (VC 24–25) in man's access to the world. Wahl thus spatializes and deontologizes Heidegger's treatment of human comportment: his interest concerns the interaction through which the subject remains receptive to the world, always trying to produce reality and marry itself to it, always having a sense of Being and eternal values without ever being able to depend on this sense. What Wahl wants from Heidegger is not so much a *Dasein* as an existent with epistemological powers that are by definition insufficient, a subject always already lost in the spatial reality that its existence reaffirms.[73]

Wahl's attention toward science foregrounds and emphasizes the epistemological dimension of his adjustment of phenomenology. Three pages into his text Wahl uses a peculiar passage to approach and critique perception and scientific inquiry.

Perception fails in its explanation of the world, and . . . it is precisely out of this failure of perception that science is born. In general, we should not make use of perception so as to explain; perception presents, it does not explain. And it is certain than in the domain of explanation, one appeals, first of all, to science. It is not then a matter of closing our eyes to the surprising successes of science that today has become capable of clarifying, in such an admirable way, even the causes of its limitations, but simply to see that it is an instrument of analysis. Now the real is not constructed by analysis; an instrument of analysis can break down the real, but it is improbable that [an instrument of analysis] can show how it is made or even to describe it as it is. (VC 3)

Two comments. First, Wahl uses in this critique the very same terms through which he would later, in *The Philosopher's Way*, identify the importance of atomic physics in the transformation of contemporary science: "Science . . . today has become capable of clarifying . . . even the causes of its limitations."[74] His critique of science resembles the criticism of classical science at the hands of Bohr, Heisenberg, de Broglie, and even more so Bachelard. This is above all because Wahl identifies "contemporary science" with the antisubstantialism of Whitehead and James, for whom "the unknowable does not disappear" despite the success of science in clarifying "even the causes of its limitations."[75] Second, echoing Meyerson's work but also Heisenberg's rejection of pure observation, Wahl argues that perception "presents, it does not explain" while science, "as an instrument of analysis, can break down the real; it is improbable that it could show how [the real] is made or even to describe it as it is." This double critique not only follows Kojève and Bachelard's arguments against rationalist and classical realist conceptions of science, but furthers these through a tone (perfectly clear in this last passage) that is reminiscent of Heidegger's refusal of science as a derivative interpretation of the world with no special access to the immediacy of reality for man.[76] What Wahl is concerned with here is the impossibility of reducing the concrete, especially in its immediacy and immanent appearance, to something that *can be known easily and well (or, perhaps, at all)*. Even though science "shows us the other side of the canvas"

(VC 4), it fails because it cannot fully explain or present the less material aspects of the real, an impossibility Wahl turns back on the subject, so as to determine the latter's receptive *welcome* of (VC 13), *encounter* with (VC 11), *communion* with, and *prehension* of (VC 12) the real. Contemporary science is thus of capital importance in *Vers le concret* because through it Wahl discerns the impossibility of an absolute identification of the concrete, that is also to say of any knowledge, analysis, description, or self-sufficient approach to the concrete. Wahl further criticizes philosophy from the point of view of an experience of reality, utilizing the same terms on which he founds his critique of science: "The concrete will never be a given for the philosopher. It will be the pursued. It is only in the absence of thought that the concrete can reveal itself to us . . . the realism is the limit of dialectics; it is its origin; it is its end, its explanation, and its destruction" (VC 23). If contemporary science has succeeded in recognizing this limitation—in quasi-Socratically acceding the impossibility of perfect knowledge of the real—then it shares with philosophy the same problem, the difficulty of heeding Wahl's injunction *To the Real!* ("vers le reel"), the impossibility of overcoming the limitations of analysis.

As Wahl affirms the acknowledgment of analytic limitations as a scientific success that can be understood by way of Heidegger's ontology—"the sentiment of our existence in the midst of things, as this dawns today in philosophy"—he is obliged, by the end of this programmatic introduction, to turn to the concrete as a "mysterious force." It is clear that he maintains certain reservations and refuses to accept scientific reason as determining of the new realism that he seeks. Nonetheless, despite this quasi-Heideggerian skepticism of science, Wahl's realism agrees in all essentials (and in any case metaphorically) with the impulse and consequences of indeterminism and uncertainty. Later, and again in clear agreement with Kojève (ID 299), Wahl would write that, just as determinist science had not blocked the deployment of nonfatalist theories of human freedom, contemporary science could not serve as an affirmation and legitimation of such theories, and that the sketch of a philosophy of freedom was in fact even more difficult in their aftermath. One finds thus in Wahl's approach of the concrete a problem also available in Heidegger's use of "formal indication," in Levinas, even in the ontology of Walter Benjamin's *Goethes Wahlverwandschaften*: all that reveals and unveils the real, the beautiful, Being, the other, and so forth, all that grants a privileged mode of entry and allows us to understand these, also re-covers and obscures them, limits our access and reproduces their inaccessibility. For Wahl, the same principle can be applied to the authors he considers in *Vers le concret*, Marcel, James, and Whitehead: they furnish us with a way toward the concrete, yet at the same time, this way *cannot* succeed, and the concrete redistances itself once again (though, thanks to these authors, we now comprehend the repetition of this distancing). This epistemological problem leaves Wahl rather troubled, particularly in its evocation of "inaccessibility" (VC 24–25), for and against which he appeals to a "mystical vision" (VC 26), but also to this (more sober than mystical) "negative ontology" (VC 24) that leaves in place the concrete as unknowable yet ineluctable. Accordingly, the concrete is for Wahl what is closest and most necessary to man as well as what is most distant to him.[77] If the prime philosophical result of uncertainty in physics is the affirmation of the impossibility of a perfect knowledge of reality, of a *view from nowhere*, in the hands of Wahl, Bachelard, and Kojève (not to mention Bataille and, in the 1950s, of Maurice Merleau-Ponty and others) this amounts both to an attack on philosophical anthropocentrism, and also to a turn toward a negative anthropology (Wahl speaks of a "negative ontology" [VC 24]): the recognition of a human existence whose only describable aspects are its failures, in this case the failure to concur with reality.[78] An emphasis of this sort permeates Wahl's later work—especially on Kierkegaard—but also that of other authors, like Bataille in his *L'Expérience intérieure* and in fact existentialism itself.

The significance of Wahl's usage and "critique" of science, as well as of his tempered and not entirely committed references to Heidegger, is indicative of the shift that his work embodied, because his conception of a new sort of realism, opposed to classical realism no less than to modern rationalism, follows the contemporary scientific suggestion that science can establish neither a pure reality nor a pure intellectualism, and uses phenomenology in order to codify this achievement in philosophical terms.[79] Instead of a breakdown of the relationship between philosophy and science, what we have in the early 1930s is a temporary ambivalent reconciliation, which in the case of Wahl came to found and justify his subsequent philosophical attention. This is *antifoundational realism*—and it is through it that Wahl and Kojève can treat the real as a philosophical as well as an existential problem, doubting an anthropology that posits man (a) at the base of all interpretation of the world, and (b) as the detached observer and humanist actor in a world he can fully describe and affect to the better.

Despite the acclaim it received, the details of Wahl's realism were by no means unquestioningly shared by his contemporaries; nor was his realism widely seen as providing a sufficient answer to the philosophical problems it opened.[80] What *Vers le concret* did, however, was provide a manifesto that reflected the period's movement toward anti-idealism, a systematic joining of the phenomenological impetus and the epistemological attention of the younger philosophers (from Koyré through to Sartre), clearly delineating a human condition bound by (to use Heidegger's terminology) man's *thrownness* in the world, his inability to postulate himself as exceeding or contrasting to the world so as to fully understand or map out this world.

The centrality of antifoundational realism both in philosophical and intellectual terms follows from this epistemological and existential argument. So does the utility of *human reality* for antifoundational realism: the closure, existence, entrapment that the subject cannot distinguish itself from. Human reality is not just a vague abstraction of the world man traverses and exists in; it is also, and more importantly, a protoexistentialist conception of reality in its oppressive guise. In its positive effort, this new philosophical "realism" that objected to the classical realism for which all truth lay in the exterior real, reflected this sense of a restriction of man's access to absolutes distinct from or transcendental to the world in which man finds himself (for example, an Ego that is transcendental with regard to reality, a Reason that interprets fully, positively, and accurately, and so on). It also marked all subjective access to the surrounding world as borne through the engagement with, the knowledge of, and the commitment to this very world. "Human reality" is therefore caught in a peculiar problem: it lacks any ground in structures extraneous to and distinct from the world, and it cannot itself provide an adequate foundation; it seeks grounding but only finds some sort of it in its interaction with the world; and finally, it wishes, unsuccessfully, to not be limited by ground or the very reality it describes. As a translation of Heidegger's *Dasein*, it may have been inadequate, but it imposed his thought as an escape from existing French thought and emptied out the privileged place and transcendence of "the human" in it, precisely by linking it to this new, limited, and particular notion of "reality."

3. (Beyond) the Metaphysical Foundations of Modern Subjectivity

Insofar as antifoundational realism begins with a disengagement with "classical" claims of science and becomes an ontological, existential, and anthropological issue, it calls for a critical reconsideration of modern science and Enlightenment humanism. The reality that man finds himself in renders impossible and unavailable a transcendence in the classical philosophical sense. Approaching now the relation between the philosophy of science and phenomenology with specific attention to Koyré's and Heidegger's recasting of the problem of transcendence and its modern construction facilitates an understanding of the early 1930s approach to the roots of modern metaphysics. Koyré's critique of modern science's claims to self-sufficiency and Heidegger's reorganization of the concept of ground formed *complementary* attacks that undermined humanist subjectivism and rationalism, reconceptualizing modernity as a specific and excessive humanist project. In their different ways, both Koyré and Heidegger strove to show both the radicalism and insufficiency of modern conceptions of man, reason, science, and metaphysics. By depicting the contemporary human condition as profaned—indeed dehumanized—by subjectivist philosophy and modern science (seeking a transcendence it cannot find or achieve) and by dismantling the transcendental claims of modern science and secular humanism, these reformulations undermined the presumed reach of the modern subject.

From the 1932 translation of Heidegger's 1928 "On the Essence of Ground" in *Recherches philosophiques* and the gradual rise of Alexandre Koyré, French phenomenology became marked by an obsession with, and a radical objection to, classical transcendence, by the subject's (lack of) access to transcendence or reliance on it.[81] What made possible this reconsideration of transcendence were the limitations on man's capacity to operate from an unbiased or "pure" perspective imposed by antifoundational realism. In turn, this dissociation of transcendence from subjective existence became linked with a number of tropes—the philosophical and theological problematization of *death* and time (in Gabriel Marcel, Kojève, Malraux, Bataille, Gaston Fessard, and others), the *homogeneity* of everyday life (in Kojève, surrealism, the Collège de Sociologie, and so on), and the foregrounding of "existence" as a term (Wahl, Sartre). Koyré's engagement with modern science was, however, central to its formulation and implications.

(a) Koyré, Galileo, and the Dehumanization of Modernity

After abandoning his early study of the philosophy of mathematics under Husserl (at Göttingen in 1911), fighting for France in World War I, and participating in the February Revolution and the civil war (on the side of the Whites) in Russia, Alexandre Koyré left the USSR a committed liberal disappointed with the victory of Communism. He returned to Paris, where he continued his intellectual career with a dissertation on *The Idea of God and the Proofs of his Existence in Descartes*, emphasizing the connections between Descartes and scholasticism. Until about 1935, Koyré continued to teach and publish mostly in the history of theology and mysticism: the core of his early corpus includes books on Saint Anselm and Jacob Boehme, an uncompleted manuscript on medieval Jewish thought, essays on (among others) Valentin Weigel, Jakob Boehme, Caspar Schwenckfeld, Paracelsus, Copernicus, and Hegel, translations of Copernicus and Saint Anselm, and elaborate bibliographical essays on medieval and modern philosophy.[82] His early teaching centered around the topic of speculative mysticism in Germany, including discussions of Scheffler, Gichtel, Boehme, Baader, Oetinger, Franck (and their influence on German idealism and romanticism), Comenius, Huss, Wyclef, Bovillus, Russian mystics, and also extending to Nicolas of Cusa and Calvin.[83] Several decades later, his student Henri Corbin would remember him as "a great mystical theosopher," a description rather at odds with our idea of him as a historian of science.[84]

As suggested already, during the early 1930s Koyré also worked extensively to introduce phenomenology in France, both within and beyond the cadre of *Recherches philosophiques*.[85] In the late 1920s he revived his connection to Edmund Husserl, with whom he discussed Galileo.[86] At about the same time, he also started publishing reviews of and works on early modern and modern science, as well as on certain founding concepts of contemporary philosophy of science (reviewing, among other things, work on the importance of quantum physics developed by Werner Heisenberg).[87] Partly influenced by Heidegger, and partly seeing in him confirmation of the validity of new anthropological concerns, Koyré proceeded to refer to Heidegger's work as philosophical anthropology even after Heidegger's "affirmation to the contrary."[88]

The theological, cosmological, and phenomenological research dominates his work until 1933 or so; only from 1933 onward did he turn markedly toward Copernicus, Kepler, Descartes, contemporary science, and above all Galileo, thinkers and scientists on whose work Koyré based his understanding of the religious grounds and implications of modernity and the history of religious thought. Koyré had already taught on Hegel's Jena writings in the context of German religious and mystical thought, and on the Reformation from the perspective of Calvin's reactions to Luther and their relation to popular religious thought.[89] Now, arguing against contemporary progressivism, Koyré explicitly treated Copernicus and Galileo in terms that effectively justify much of the Church reaction to Galileo on the grounds of Galileo's own breach and dismissal of the Aristotelian and Thomist cosmos—a cosmos against which Galileo could not offer a complete alternative.[90] Koyré expressly presented his reinterpretation of Galileo as an extension of the work of Pierre Duhem and Emile Meyerson, yet differences from his predecessors were substantive and readily visible, above all in his reliance on phenomenology and his rejection of the terms and discussions of the old realism/rationalism debate.[91] Some reviews of his work (even by figures positive to recent progress in the history of early modern science) responded harshly against his recontextualization and "justification" of the attacks against Galileo by the Church and academia. Aldo Mieli, director of the Académie internationale d'histoire des sciences in Paris, critiqued Koyré: "His point of view is simplistic, often erroneous, and largely based on the gratuitous affirmations of Galileo's detractors."[92] Pietro Redondi notes (a bit excessively), that "far from going unnoticed, Koyré's studies on Galileo were stigmatised as iconoclastic, amidst a climate of positivistic celebration of Galileo's *Discorsi*."[93]

Koyré's positions concerning Galileo rest on three interconnected problems: (i) a questioning of the process and scientific value of experimentation; (ii) the reconstruction of Galileo's work, influence, and achievement as following largely from his Platonic and anti-Aristotelian position, indeed from his use of Copernicus against the Aristotelians; and (iii) the conception of the modern world as founded on mathematics (echoing Galiléo's claim that nature is written in mathematical language, but here explicitly intended both in terms deriving from astronomy and in more metaphorical, metaphysical terms suggesting an equivalence or reflection of the world in mathematics).[94] Like Gaston Bachelard before (and beside) him, Koyré doubted the purity of results that positivism attributed to experimentation.[95] Koyré linked his name to this doubt, both by way of a failed repetition of the experiment of inclined planes and by his (controversial at that time) doubts regarding Galileo's fabled experiment on the Tower of Pisa.[96] In the latter case, and echoing Ernst Barthel, Koyré argued that not only could the Pisa experiment *not* have taken place physically (as a consequence of air resistance), but that historical research indicates the sources reporting such an experiment to be unreliable and to postdate other, more contemporary, sources. Also, more importantly, that as a consequence of his Platonist trust in mathematics and his a priori logico-mathematical construction of an experiment, Galileo *was aware* that he did not require and could not have made use of such a demonstration.[97] Out of his analysis of these two experiments, Koyré came to argue that an experiment confirms or disconfirms the arrangement of metaphysical (prescientific and scientific) presuppositions, rather than the genuine truth-value or falsehood of their scientific postulates.[98] Koyré's championing of Galileo rests precisely on this critique of experimentation, which he turns into an insistence on the unity between metaphysical and scientific thought.[99]

Koyré imposed this "unity" argument to his striking evaluation that Galileo's academic detractors were not entirely unjustified in their reaction because Galileo's argument had no place in the (Aristotelian) conception of the world these detractors had inherited and helped along; indeed, it disrupted this conception in apparently nihilistic fashion.[100]

The meaning of this reaction [of the university milieux against Galileo] seems to have been poorly known by the historians of physics: Galileo's discoveries turned the scientific system of the entire universe upside down (weakening chemistry as much as astronomy), destroying the very notion of a well-ordered *Cosmos, alleging to have eliminated a theory but not replacing it with another. An allegation that science, throughout the course of its history, has never accepted and continues to not accept.*[101]

Again, scientific discovery either confirms presuppositions or suggests the need to adjust them. It does not work without or beyond them. Metaphysics does not merely work beside or parallel to scientific research, but as its foundation. In his talk at the Descartes conference of 1937, Koyré specifically used Galileo and Descartes to combat the elevation of science to a "system of knowledge" purified of metaphysical assumptions, instead giving primacy to prescientific metaphysical conceptions that are invariably reused in the modern scientific enterprise.

In effect, the historians of philosophy, as much as the historians of science, have the habit of opposing Galileo to Descartes—the scientist to the metaphysician; the scientific prudence of the founder of experimental method who renounced the knowledge of causes to devote himself to the research of laws, to the impertinent apriorism of the philosopher of clear ideas who rejects experience and searches for a global explanation of the real. [§] This traditional and almost universally accepted conception—it has in fact penetrated even textbooks—appears to me as pernicious as it is false. False because it presents the respective positions of Galileo and Descartes under a thoroughly inexact light; pernicious, because from an erroneous interpretation of Galilean (and also Cartesian) epistemology, it derives consequences that are themselves necessarily erroneous both on the historical position of Galileo and Descartes and on the nature and structure of scientific thought in general.[102]

In this context, the specific interest of Galileo's astronomy and Platonist science was that they provided actual physical discoveries that translated into a pre- or metascientific and metaphysical context—at once resting on and "proving" Galileo's Copernican convictions, at once clashing with the dominant Aristotelian ecclesiastical-academic establishment and facilitating Galileo's Platonist hope (and propaganda) for a mathematical model of the universe.[103] In this context, Koyré's grounding of science on metaphysical cosmology emphasizes a largely phenomenological, indeed Heideggerian, approach to truth and assertion, historicizing the Neo-Kantian dream of a space that can be reduced to its mathematical form. On the

one hand, his Galileo seeks to restructure scientific categories such that nature, indeed Being, can be fully deduced from a mathematical-geometri-
cal model (hence, postulating an external world in which the subject finds
itself surrounded).[104] On the other hand, the purity of Galileo's system
is based from the very beginning on metaphysical and religious premises
treated as nonscientific by modern science, which recognizes in the world
only the impression that man has metaphysically formed and which it itself confirms. By assaulting the presuppositions of the science of his time,
Galileo heralds the end of the well-ordered *cosmos*, thus providing an orig-
inator for Koyré's own implicit claim that no absolute ordering can take
place—and that scientific determinisms all remain ultimately bound to a
metaphysical fantasy of such order.

Two major consequences follow from this complex of arguments.
The first is that Koyré furthered the position of Heidegger's critique of
"reality" and Wahl's search for the concrete in (and *as*) man's immediate
interaction with the external world. Modern science, like other systems
of interpretation, does not encounter nature per se, but rather elides
it to conceive a "world" characterized by the forms through which *its
interaction with man becomes intelligible to him.* Koyré's quasi-phenomenological stance thus also shows the importance of Heidegger's "Understanding" (*Verstehen*)—what formally precedes an interpretation and a
truth-statement—and the complex and difficult relation of this to the
world. In doubting the subject-object distinction of a thinking human
observer versus a "pure" nature, in postulating the concrete as encompassed in the interaction of thought and intelligible reality yet forever
evading our attempts to understand it, the philosophical appropriation
of scientific antideterminism foregrounded the impossibility of direct
access to "reality" by the "tools" and data offered by this reality itself.[105]
Koyré argued and pursued this point by demonstrating the reliance of
seemingly pure positive scientific knowledge (including experiments) of
science on the acceptance and reconstruction of metascientific (that is,
metaphysical) systems. For him, the scientist thought the transcendental but could not achieve it: experiments and science supplemented and
compensated for this inability.

Second: Koyré would make explicit the consequence of this line of
argument after the war, when he expressly defined the modern scientific

cosmology from Galileo to Einstein as dehumanized and dehumanizing, marked by notions that specifically strip the universe of human participation and life, while falsely pretending to support the perfection of the human mind.[106] "Modern science broke down the barriers that separated the heavens and the earth. . . . It did this by substituting for our world of quality and sense-perception, the world in which we live, and love, and die, another world—the world of quantity, of reified geometry, a world in which though there is place for everything, there is no place for man."[107] Both the scientific prejudice concerning experimental truth and the mathematization of reality contribute to this position, which predates the war and is joined by an understanding of Koyré's effort to ground science in theology and historical-religious contexts as having *existential* consequences, as working against modern science's claims to self-sufficiency, self-legitimation, and progressivist humanism. In this thoroughly secular interpretation of religious import into science, shared by Koyré's students and friends Bataille, Kojève, and Corbin (and also by Léon Shestov and some of Koyré's teachers, specifically Picavet and Gilson), religion does not come in opposition to systematic scientific progress, nor is it to be relegated to the edges of any rigorous system or hierarchy of *savoir* (as it had been in Diderot and D'Alembert's *Encyclopédie*).[108]

In these criticisms, Koyré took on precisely the rational humanist that believes himself to be constructing (or facilitating the construction of) a pure scientific positivity, to be encountering unmediated transcendental truth *and, at the same time,* to be participating in the development and perfection of the Western mind—a philosopher who treats the world as mappable and sees metaphysical commitments as contrasting, rather than foundational of, his "pure scientific" or philosophical ones.[109] Koyré's scientist, who rather than proving a truth is perpetually seeking to articulate his own metaphysical, religious, and prescientific presuppositions as scientific truths, finds himself trapped in an elaborate construction of a metaphysical/scientific system that he can at best disrupt or further facilitate. What modernity has done, accordingly, is dehumanize our existence in and interpretation of the world, by defining it through a scientific radicalism that represses and indeed obliterates its own religious, tragic, metaphysical, radically heterogeneous dimensions and instead becomes itself a metaphysics—a metaphysics that obliterates man under the pretext of promoting him. This recognition did not entail the possibility or promise of a more human(ist) existence or science; nor did it suggest philosophy's task to be an attempt to retrieve the metaphysical or religious dimension that the humanist hopes of modern science had missed. What Koyré's early work implied was that man had to learn to exist suspended between (i) metaphysical propositions formulating his sense of an objective reality, and (ii) an inhuman model of the universe foregrounding his own power-lessness in it and his desire for its domination and ironing out.

Koyré's historical approach is perhaps the most far-reaching, aca-demically established and influential call for a philosophical and scientific antifoundationalism in the turn of the 1930s. What he did on a philo-sophical, theological, and scientific level, systematically and fervently, was repeated and reflected both in the circle of his students (including Kojève and Bataille) but also further around that circle, notably in the College of Sociology.[110] *Koyré pioneered the attempt to reject science's claims to self-sufficiency and to pull out religious or metaphysical backgrounds from seemingly pure or habitual practices and claims.* For this approach, science represses its metaphysical and psychological origin in order to produce an order that for it has transcendental consequences—a position resembling varying Catholic rejections of modern science, though dismissing the con-sequent favoring of faith in Christianity.[111] This critique of the repression of metaphysics in sixteenth- to twentieth-century science and philosophy refuses the historical and theoretical teleology according to which scien-tific and idealist humanism moves toward an authenticity or transcenden-tal truth. Perhaps even more importantly, it conceives of modern society and thought as at once (i) incapable of overcoming the inauthenticity, homogeneity, or uniformity of bourgeois immanence that joins the total-izing impulse of man dominating nature and seeking to reduce the world to a mathematical formulation, and (ii) incapable of "keeping the lid shut" on violent revivals of religious and metaphysical sentiments that, often lacking a properly religious form of expression, will instead choose no less violent and antibourgeois alternatives.[112] It could be said that Koyré, as an intellectual, also found a certain system of beliefs here: despite his liberalism and his discretion, Corbin notes, Koyré occasionally gave the impression of a total agnosticism, of a "despairing nihilism."[113]

(b) Heidegger's Essence of Ground and the Attack on Transcendence

Like Alexandre Koyré's rethinking of the scientific revolution, the early French translations of Martin Heidegger's work also targeted the Second Copernican Revolution's philosophical *humanization* of scientific thought and secular humanist interpretation of the metaphysical tradition. Of these essays, one has been repeatedly commented upon: Heidegger's 1929 inaugural lecture at the university of Freiburg, "What Is Metaphysics?" translated by Henri Corbin in 1931 and later adjusted to feature the translation of *Dasein* as *réalité humaine* (human reality).[114] Yet the force of Heidegger's influence in French thought and of his contribution to questions of anthropology is based perhaps less on "What Is Metaphysics?" than on a second major essay published in French in 1932, "On the Essence of Ground" (in the opening issue of *Recherches philosophiques* in 1931–32), which extends Heidegger's conception of the world to bear on man's understanding of, and relation to, transcendence.

Before embarking on a reading of "On the Essence of Ground," it is important to point out Heidegger's critique of Kant's favoring of the primacy of anthropology and humanism (which was addressed in the first chapter). In Heidegger's 1929 *Kant and the Problem of Metaphysics*, a book read widely in European (including French) philosophical circles in the aftermath of the Davos debate, Heidegger noted that in terms provided by scholasticism and acknowledged by Kant, Kant's three critical questions (What can I know? What ought I do? What can I hope for?) account for the scholastic category of *metaphysica specialis*. In scholasticism, Heidegger notes, anthropology is contained in rational psychology, itself contained in *metaphysica specialis*. By arguing in his *Logic* that anthropology encompasses and grounds the critical project, Kant transforms it from a problem in a subsection of metaphysics to the very ground of metaphysics as such.[115] For Heidegger, this radical reorganization turns anthropology in Kant into the sole authentic foundation of metaphysics, the sole mode of instituting true philosophy.[116] Heidegger objects to this consequence, reinterpreting it (as he reinterprets Kant's philosophy in general) in such a fashion as to show that it also bears the ciphers for a counterinterpretation emphasizing the primordiality of fundamental ontology. He also acknowledges its broad significance for the Kantian and post-Kantian metaphysical systems, implicitly engaging in a critique of its influential humanist approach to questions of transcendence and reason.

"On the Essence of Ground" extends this reinterpretation to further criticize the priority of humanist metaphysics and its construction of transcendence and (less explicitly) Reason, in a fashion that recalls and complements Koyré's contemporary work. Here, Heidegger (i) links the problems of world, reality, and transcendence; (ii) explicitly formulates those problems with regard to the approach, aims, and ground of *the human* and of *human freedom*, while (iii) criticizing and indeed rejecting the classical approach that sees man as transcending (in the sense of *exceeding* and *structuring*) the reality in which he participates. In the early 1930s, this position formed the first consistent phenomenological critique of the classical conception of transcendence to make it into French publication (RP I, 83–124); it provided perhaps the clearest early critique of not only the Aristotelian and Kantian conceptions of space and world but also the Husserlian transcendental ego that Sartre would also target. Heidegger's critical exposition of Kant cites precisely the aforementioned passage of the latter's *Anthropology from a Pragmatic Point of View* where Kant identifies man as "his own final end" (A 3; EG 119), a characterization to which Heidegger objects. As he remarks in a footnote, the goal of his analysis is to clarify his explanation of *Dasein* so as to ward off the critique that *Being and Time* relies on an *anthropocentric* standpoint. Heidegger points out the impossibility or "delusion" of avoiding a "central standpoint"; more importantly, he argues that *Being and Time* "puts its *entire* effort *solely* into showing that the *essence* of *Dasein* that there stands 'at the center' is ecstatic," that is, "excentric" (EG 371 n66). That is to say, even if Heidegger speaks of what in a quotidian and philosophically unrigorous sense would be called *man*, his argument, "the approach, the *entire thrust* and the *goal* of the development of the problem" explicitly displaces and decenters the traditional identification of man with the existent (*Dasein*) and with its essence as *Being*.

In "On the Essence of Ground" Heidegger repeats this self-distancing from the "metaphysical" interpretation explicitly and at length, by first identifying subjectivity with transcendence and then denying the sufficiency of an analysis that begins with subjectivity, that treats subjectivity as the "essential constitution" of *Dasein*.[117] If at stake was only the characterization of the existent as a subject, then "to be a subject means to be a being in and as transcendence" (EG 108). Instead, Heidegger reverses the meaning of transcendence to indicate *neither* an overcoming of beings, *nor* a separation from reality, *but Dasein's* surpassing of objects, nature, and beings *through its casting or institution of its world.* "Although it exists in the midst of beings and embraced by them, *Dasein* as existing *has always already surpassed nature.* [§] Whatever the beings that have on each particular occasion been surpassed in any *Dasein,* they are not simply a random aggregate; rather, beings, however they may be individually determined and structured, *are surpassed in advance as a whole"* (EG 109; italics mine). What Heidegger calls "projection of world" or "letting the world show itself" involves precisely this "surpassing of nature"; *world* is opposed to the idea of a natural reality qua stage of human experience, a stage that man would, as a privileged being, therefore supposedly exceed. Heidegger's contrasting position closely reflects the problem discussed earlier apropos §43 of *Being and Time*: there is no world (nor a lack of world), no reality, without the *Dasein* that institutes it, and the natural state that might be fantasized as preceding such a projection of world. For things to become real, to be present in *Dasein's* world, involves this fundamental transcendence, this transformation of a chaos into an intelligible whole, a world—this *surpassing of beings as a whole.* In Heidegger's formulation, *Dasein* transcends in that it "always casts the projected world *over* beings" (EG 123).

Like Wahl, Bachelard, Kojève, Koyré, and other contemporaries he influenced, Heidegger here presents world as a scene of reality, a reality that exists independently of *Dasein* yet in its intelligibility *as a reality* is outlined and constituted by *Dasein*: a reality at once *as such* and *for us.* It is only in this way that we understand, acknowledge, and recognize the world and its functioning. "We name world that *toward which Dasein* as such transcends, and shall now determine transcendence as *being-in-the-world"* (EG 109). Insomuch as Heidegger treats *being-in-the-world* as *Dasein's* essence, transcendence can be understood prohibitively (EG 111)—as barring a flight from existence or experience. Yet the same process has a constructive significance, in the sense of Heidegger's treatment of *Dasein* as *world-forming* (*Weltbildend*) (EG 123): *Dasein* not only finds itself thrown into a world; it also forms and erects this world: it surpasses

the "sheer" presence or thereness of entities and grants itself a sort of ontological perspective over them, making their thereness a part of experience.
Transcendence as *Dasein*'s casting of world over beings and things is the
formation of individuality: it is the scene of subjectivity and freedom (EG
126–28).

Heidegger extends this argument through a reading of St. Paul, St.
John, St. Augustine, the scholastics, and especially Kant, on each occasion identifying their conceptions of *world* and *transcendence*, yet also contrasting their identifications to his more explicitly "ontological" one (EG
112–19). In Kant's case, for example, the signification of transcendence as
"surpassing experience" is one which Heidegger specifically terms "ambivalent." Transcendence is for Kant what happens in the overcoming of
the "manifold of appearances" *within* experience; but it is also a "stepping
out of experience" that makes it possible to represent "the possible whole
of all things as the object of an *intuitus originarius*" (EG 119). The contrast
of the transcending subject to the (limiting) world constructs the explicitly human aspect of subjectivity (EG 120). "The concept of world stands,
as it were, between the 'possibility of experience' and the 'transcendental
ideal,' and thus in its core means the totality of the finitude that is *human*
in essence" (EG 119). That is to say, the concept of world lies between
Heidegger's two readings of Kant's idea of transcendence in relation to the
humanity of the human subject, which is determined by way of a delinea-
tion of man's finitude. Heidegger's own version of transcendence takes
constitutive elements of Kant's and adjusts them and, through a process of
reprioritization, contrasts starkly his conceptualization of *world* with the
Kantian one. His citational and interpretative strategy is evident in the
following sentence, where Heidegger forces the priorities of his treatment
of world ("in it beings become manifest *as a whole*" [EG 120–21]) on the
concepts he has so far discussed: "Rather, what is metaphysically essential
in the more or less clearly highlighted meaning of kosmos, *mundus*, world,
lies in the fact that it is directed toward an interpretation of human existence [*Dasein*] *in its relation to beings as a whole*" (EG 121). This *whole* that
Heidegger foregrounds involves a deliberate stress on the totality of experience from which transcendence (in the Aristotelian and second Kantian
sense) emerges. Rather than a general imaginary totality of things and beings, Heidegger's *whole* refers explicitly to the limits of *Dasein*'s interaction

with beings—to being-in-the-world as *Dasein*'s essential constitution, its "ownmost, intrinsic possibility as *Dasein*" (EG 110). Rather than a world in which man seeks to recognize his status as "citizen of the world" (A 3–4, 12, 186; cited in EG 119), for Heidegger *Dasein* institutes world so that it may operate (to put it somewhat too quickly) "for the sake of itself" (EG 122, 125–27). If, moreover, Kant's "whole" is connected to his notion of finitude and treatment of subjective existence—especially in the more quotidian and political senses of the meaning of "world"—Heidegger's own conceptual transformation involves his argument that *Dasein* forms this (real) world *through transcendence*, that it at once negates and negatively overcomes objects and nature (EG 111) and at the same time forms through them a world (EG 121).[118] Transcendence thus becomes a scene for the unveiling and interpretation of the world *as a formation or unfolding of reality:*

> Entry into world is not some process that transpires in those beings that enter it, but is something that happens "with" beings. And such occurrence is the existing of *Dasein*, which as existing transcends. Only if, amid beings in their totality, beings come to be "more in being" in the manner of the temporalizing of *Dasein* are there the hours and days of beings' entry into world. And only if this primordial history, namely, transcendence, occurs, that is, only if beings having the character of being-in-the-world irrupt into beings, is there the possibility of beings manifesting themselves. (EG 123)

In the context that I am describing here, Heidegger's approach constitutes a reversal of the classic meaning of transcendence—from a standpoint that explicitly and intentionally distinguishes "reality" from the "transcendental ideal," to a situation where transcendence involves the very entry of man into coexistence with objects and the world around him. *Dasein*'s transcendence involves not a formal distancing, an escape, or an abstraction, nor a constitution of experience and existence, but the very deployment of a world around that experience. From this world there is no escape, no possibility of genuinely standing back and recognizing the world's limits—as any such "standing back" could still only occur within the "limits" of that world and would merely reveal it to be different than thus far presented or imagined.

This is not to suggest that Koyré's grounding of science on metaphysical principles can be simply translated into Heidegger's conception of transcendence in "On the Essence of Ground." It is, however, to argue that *both* Heidegger (at least in the way he was perceived in France during the early 1930s) *and* Koyré argued the necessity of metaphysical and ontological presuppositions for an understanding of empirical and experimental truth. Where Koyré sought to demonstrate the fundamental role of metaphysics and religion in the construction of any positivity, of any absolute scientific truth, of any claim to access of a pure nature, Heidegger attempted to front transcendence as the basic opening—or institution—of the world before the self, a necessary process or fact of existence that rendered impossible any "nature," conceived as an imaginary world of things prior to any interaction with man and thought, and any overcoming of the world with which man interacts.[119] A result of this is the impossibility of a classical conception of transcendence as well as of classical access to the transcendent, to truth in an absolute sense, indeed, once again, to any "pure" nature.

The difference of scope and positions between Koyré and Heidegger also bolsters the claims and concerns that could be subsumed under the umbrella of *antifoundational realism*. While Koyré undermined the assurance of scientific truth, Heidegger's casting of "world" as *not* centered on *Dasein* but still involving *Dasein's* continual transcendence—its "encoding" of world into entities that manifest themselves "as a whole"—emphasized both the basic need for an interpretive subject and the lack of perfect objectivity or truth of this transcending subject. And while Heidegger emphasized the lack of an *immediate* access to entities and the consequent entrapment of *Dasein* in the world it *transcends* and is grounded in, Koyré emphasized the interplay between metaphysical presuppositions and experimental constructions for any conception of truth. These changes transformed the status of science in contemporary philosophy, rejecting the claim that classical determinist science could be historically and phenomenologically trusted to provide an adequate and faithful portrayal of the world and of man's interaction with it, but also seeking to find, in science, the metaphysical and political truth of modern thought from Descartes to Husserl. Together with Heidegger's critique of classical transcendence and the claims of rationalism, Koyré's reformulation of the history of modern science opened contemporary thought to the argument that man's lack of access to transcendence involved a submission to reality and dependence on an ever-faulty and ever-subjectivist conception of this reality, thus advancing and philosophically grounding anxieties that could be named at once *existentialist* and *antihumanist*.

4. "Human Reality": Conclusions

This chapter has sought to demonstrate the epistemological and phenomenological transformation of French thought in two interdependent philosophical moments of the turn of the 1930s: first, the prioritization of "world" and the construction of a new realism that critiques the observing and intervening human subject; second, the construction of "human reality" in this "world" and the limitation of positive transcendental claims made by the subject, the philosopher, and the scientist. What is interesting is that in these moments, shared concerns brought about a concurrence between philosophers of science and phenomenologists: two (only partly distinct) groups that not only sought to show the failure of the tradition of French thought up to that point but also attempted to construct an altogether different ground and strategy for philosophical exploration. It was the new philosophy of science that effectively legitimated phenomenology as a take on epistemological matters and concurred in its criticism of classical oppositions like subject-object, mind-world, and reason-nature. Phenomenology's rise followed not just from its construction of an alternative to existing idealism, but rather from its extension of the contemporary epistemological critique of modern science beyond the realm of science, to the very questions of man and the subject. With Bachelard, Kojève, and Wahl, phenomenology came to provide a basic antisubjectivist language and philosophical system to underwrite the critique opened by quantum physics.

Philosophy of science and early French phenomenology thus served to construct a different philosophical outlook, based on a series of influential and consequential tenets:

(a)   "World" as a nondeterministic—in Kojève's words, echoing quantum physicists, "statistical"—universe that exceeds man and cannot be understood at all on the basis of correspondences to his mind or reason;

(b)   an end of *progressive* historical and rationalist teleologies—through the abandoning and historicization of philosophical claims to truth, the delegitimation of claims to classical transcendence (also in the political space of Communism and Catholicism), and as we shall see, the introduction of an anti-utopian and nonrationalist Hegelianism;

(c)   the doubling of political critiques of individualism (to which I will return in the next chapter) by a wide-ranging antisubjectivism for which "interiority," "Reason," "the mind," or even "the soul" fail to construct a viable subject or to account for its existence.

These basic reorientations translated into a set of direct attacks on anthropocentrism, into a displacement or denial of man's very capacity to exist as the ground of pure philosophical thought and action. Punctuated by a consistent critique of the subject-object relation (Heidegger, Kojève), a critique of man as transcendental observer and designator (Bachelard, Kojève, Wahl), and an emphasis on man's *failure* to grasp the world in the "natural" way so far attributed to him (Wahl, Heidegger, Koyré), antifoundational realism came to mark man *negatively*, by reference to his failures and to the world's capacity to provide obstacles to his reason and desire. This new conception of man qua being-in-the-world, qua human reality, and also qua observer, foregrounds two problems. Man's "inability" to interpret, exceed, or—by virtue of some access to classical transcendence—displace the force and primacy of the world in which he finds himself, sets him in a losing battle against these obstacles. From here follow the persistent tropes of human existence as a tragedy or labyrinth, or else of man as a Hegelian unhappy consciousness unable to reconcile the restrictions of his tormented mind with the grandeur of Man, God, or the totalities to which man is expected to belong.

Beginning at the margins of the university and the restricted realm of *Recherches philosophiques*, this critique spread to other journals and universities and mixed yet more widely with literary concerns.[120] The elder generation of philosophers was under pressure not only by philosophical arguments but also by critiques posed directly by Communists like Nizan, or more implicitly by Catholics and protoexistentialist literary authors, who found it dry, too technical, and too closely tied to a defense of the Third Republic. Yet the philosophical criticisms were crucial because they emptied the legacy of this Brunschvicgian humanism, abandoning the philosophical anthropology occasioned by the Neo-Kantianism that treated man as his own highest end and highest being. Moreover, following Heidegger's critique of Cassirer, Brunschvicg was in his later years invariably (and often explicitly) criticized by most of the younger philosophers, including Kojève and Koyré, Gabriel Marcel, Sartre, Merleau-Ponty, and Wahl, not to mention Paul Nizan and others not tied to academia.[121] For Koyré and Kojève, Brunschvicg's attempt to rejoin philosophy and physics not only was built on faulty foundations (namely, an overbearing emphasis on the mathematical mapping of the universe) but also failed to understand the radical transformation of modern science that followed the recent innovations of quantum physics and their implications.[122] In subsequent years, their critique would extend far beyond the figures already discussed, putting at stake again and again the failure of Neo-Kantianism to account for the limits of observation, reflection, and action in the world. In 1945 Maurice Merleau-Ponty would present a similar critique of the treatments of *nature* and *the other* by Brunschvicg and Lachelier, citing their idealization of the objective as philosophically misdirected and unfounded, declaring: "Now this philosophy is collapsing before our eyes."[123] (In his own thought, Merleau-Ponty would extend antifoundational realism to questions of psychology and physiology, by echoing Aron Gurwitsch in rethinking the problem of the body and the status of consciousness on Husserlian as well as Gestaltist principles.) At stake in these rejections is Brunschvicg's extreme subjectivism, the treatment of the other, the scientifically minded (but no longer scientifically supported) rationalism, and the historical eschatology claiming a progress of the human spirit toward a self-perfection of man.[124] For the younger generation, this arrogant anthropocentrism destroyed what it proclaimed, neither recognizing the disastrous situation following WWI, nor accepting any philosophical need to react to the connection between disaster and the humanist paradox.

Second, antifoundational realism made possible the French epistemological revolution from Bachelard and Koyré through Cavailles, Canguilhem, and so on. Though French thought is usually charged with having abandoned science either in the mid-nineteenth century or following the arrival of structuralism and its supposed submission to Hegelian-Heideggerian "ends" of philosophy, the effort to interweave philosophy and science in the 1930s begins with the critique of scientific and philosophical determinism in quantum physics, with the historicization of science's claim to truth, and with the phenomenological step beyond rationalism and classical realism.[125]

Antifoundational realism struck a broad intellectual nerve by demonstrating that the modern human condition is based on an oppressed metaphysical foundation and past that modern rationalism and science have systematically sought and failed to overcome; and that the pretenses of idealism to have revealed a transcendence, *belonging to man* and immune to this fundamentally metaphysico-religious origin and base, should be recognized as insufficient and overcome. This demonstration, and the proposal of a "human reality" that contrasted and coimplicated man and world at once trapping the subject in the world and rendering impossible any notion of unmediated, untouchable, noumenal nature, led to a reshuffling of political aims and literary, existential, and philosophical interests of philosophers. The failure of translating mind and interiority into exteriority reflected (and furthered) both the contemporary critique of psychology, as well as the existing literary obsession with the precariousness of existence.

Thus, on the one hand, antifoundational realism provided a foundation for a series of much more visible motifs that led toward existentialism. Many of the famous loci for this change of philosophical perspective (protoexistentialism in Wahl, Marcel, and in literary texts—for example, in Malraux or Queneau; the hopes of Hegelianism in Kojève, Weil, and others; the clash between a giant Hegelian totality and an embattled Kierkegaardian subject; the anthropological or existentialist reading of Husserl and Heidegger, new criticisms of psychology—for example, in Sartre or in Aron Gurwitsch) are expressions, or bearers of this change. But without the transformation of the conceptual framework regarding questions of truth, transcendence, and nature, their force and participation in the overcoming of rationalism remains unclear. The primacy of the interaction between subject and world, the entrapment of the subject in the world, and the impossibility of fully knowing the world provide the properly philosophical basis for an understanding of man's weakness as actor. In many ways, philosophical existentialism follows from the dramatic, tragic accentuation of what I have here described as man's inability to conform to, and to fully understand, reality.

Yet, on the other hand, if antifoundational realism can be taken as a premise of existentialism, its affinity is greater toward its antisubjectivism than toward its reconstruction of an embattled subject in need of asserting itself in the world, as would appear in Sartre and Camus. Its anthropocentrism thus would emerge further in the philosophical critiques of the existentialism of Sartre and Camus as overtly subjectivist (by Heidegger, Bataille, Blanchot, Merleau-Ponty, and implicitly by Beckett and others). It has become a commonplace, particularly in readings of the early reception of Martin Heidegger, to see this rise or return of philosophical anthropology in the 1930s as the cause of an anthropologization of philosophy and a profanation of Heidegger's ontology. But this claim involves a specific misunderstanding of the context of contemporary French thought, where the attack on the humanist emphases of the 1920s resulted in anthropological discussions only in the sense that they rejected the primacy and self-sufficiency of anthropology, its status as at once an ideal, a goal, and a ground of thought and action. Instead, it is a significant paradox that the rise of anthropology and the occasional anthropological emphasis of phenomenology involved precisely the undermining of fundamental claims of humanism and anthropocentrism: what evokes man and discusses him, but rejects the idealism that placed him on a pedestal, that made Man of man, just as it rejects the primacy of the anthropological question in the contemporary discussions of man, cannot be said to strictly anthropologize philosophy.

Bridging the gap between the existentialist and antisubjectivist tendencies is a further complex effect of antifoundational realism and the part played by phenomenology in it. Phenomenology was significant and became popular because it made possible the philosophical treatment of political modernity by permitting philosophers the impression of philosophically standing *a step beyond* the political horizon of the day, seeing both its structure and man's impotence in it. This attack on the "solipsistic" bourgeois humanist thinker rejected the "standing apart" from politics that philosophy had been calling for, but paradoxically involved the philosopher in political modernity in that it allowed him to claim to think a more fundamental structure. In other words, by rejecting the intellectual legitimacy of any political utopianism that would claim priority over the subject, antifoundational realism denied the political ontologies of Communism, Catholicism, and nonconformism that subjugated philosophical thought to the commitment to a theologico-political rejuvenation of man. By contrast, antifoundational realism allowed philosophers to speak of their age politically without really involving themselves in contemporary movements and without claiming a separation between philosophy and politics. Moreover, with the development of "human reality," the fall of the transcendental observer and the undermining of the scientific thinker allowed for the end of a theory of humanist progress—both in the sense of Brunschvicg's teleological perfection of cosmopolitan man and self-perfecting observer, and in a more general or quotidian sense for which modernization and science lead to a concrete improvement of man. Thus the early 1930s produced no new *affirmative* image of man, but rather rejected the place accorded to him up to that point and instead welded a tense new framework that saw man as failing to fill any such place. In this "failure" lies the antihumanist anthropology of the new generation. It is through antifoundational realism that arises a new anti-anthropocentric inquiry: the idea that what counts as human can by no means stand as high or strong as posited by the philosophers of the preceding generation, and that a description of his consciousness and Being should begin by an analysis of its closure, breakdown, and disappointments. The human subject changes from a rational, transcendental first-person singular that speaks, thinks, and desires things and representations radically external and comprehensible to it, to an embattled, emptied out *he* struggling with the forces of reality.

No Humanism Except Mine!
Ideologies of Exclusivist
Universalism and the New Men of
Interwar France

1. The Problem of Exclusivist Humanisms in Interwar France

To understand the radicalism of this new and "antifoundational" realism—not to mention its force in unclenching the humanist hold on French thought, it is necessary to turn now to the political and cultural crisis that shook the foundations of humanism and helped turn it into a nearly meaningless term. That by 1930 humanism was in trouble is attested to by the sheer polysemy of the term, that is to say by the dependence of different "humanisms" on competing political ideologies with very different conceptions of modernity. Indeed, during the interwar period, almost all intellectuals adhered openly to a "humanism"—that is, *to a certain conception and legacy of humanism.* Like centrist politicians and academic philosophers, who supported a cosmopolitan, idealist, progressivist humanism, each major faction that competed for ideological and intellectual power (Communists, Catholics, and nonconformists) had distinct interpretations of the meaning and value of the term. Each claimed to possess the *only* philosophy capable of providing man with the dignity he deserved; each derided "bourgeois individualism" and their political opponents as decadent, as hiding their violent core, or as disrespectful toward the universalism supposedly inherent in their projects. Thus, every claim to humanism emphasized not only the universalism supposedly inherent in it but also the absolute impossibility of arriving at a proper care for man in *any* other way.

In this regard, World War I played a tremendous role. That it involved a drastic transformation of bourgeois European values is widely known.[1] Even the sheer image of men returning from the Great War with amputated limbs and mutilated faces, and the recognition that humanitarian ideals and efforts were overwhelmed and insufficient, eased in a significant change of the image of modern man.[2] Modris Eksteins quotes Marc Boasson, a soldier who, before dying in the war, argued:

> The intellectual and moral regression of the world can be avoided as little as an absolute baseness of thought, which will be enveloped in technical perfection and practical skills encouraging illusion. The misery that will follow the war will bring with it a prodigious industrialization, a multiplication of useful improvements. All human activity will turn toward practical ends. . . . Unbiased culture has had its day. Mankind is giving way to human matériel according to the expression the war has already made familiar. The Renaissance is bankrupt. The German factory is absorbing the world.[3]

The "already made familiar" fear that the individual had been reduced to matériel in turn raised the perception that Man himself needed to be stitched back together.[4] But this restitching was no straightforward operation because the memory of the war continued to hang over its possibilities and hopes: Stephane Audoin-Rouzeau and Annette Becker describe eloquently the "cultural demobilization process" that made it possible for the French to understand by 1925 that the war was no parenthesis that could be closed and by 1930 that it was something preferably rejected rather than described in terms of courage and heroism.[5] By 1930, the perception that secular humanism had failed to withstand the onslaught of the war and was tied to its violence was widespread: the Left blamed nationalism, while the Right blamed republicanism for "holding back" the nation. Indeed, writers from André Gide and Georges Bernanos to Antoine de Saint-Exupéry and Georges Bataille saw a cultural civil war playing itself out as a result of the Great War; many thought an aged, corrupt middle class was playing out its last capitalist vestiges against both fascist and socialist political hopes.[6] So-called bourgeois humanism was perceived as (1) the child of Enlightenment legacies of secular conviction, anthropocentric knowledge, and political liberalism; (2) a memory of 1789 as the overcoming of feudal absolutism, an attempt to define individuals as equal human beings deserving their natural rights and societies as joinings of "*libres arbitres*" willfully limiting their autonomy for ideals of social and cosmopolitan harmony; and (3) the progress of a perfectible human spirit not reducible to the corporeal, material, or even the cultural and traditionally religious dimensions of human life. Regardless of how lofty these ideals might appear when considered out of context, at stake in the interwar public sphere was the perception that in contemporary secular society they reigned politically and intellectually, and thus that in their positivity was reflected the state of modern life. "Bourgeois humanism" was identified with the perceived failures of the political and intellectual world to bring about an egalitarian, spiritual utopia—not to mention its own "failure" to embody a whole array of cherished aspects of modern France, from the Catholic Church to Napoleon to the revolutionary tradition. It was thus often considered too abstract, indefensible, and politically irredeemable, if not downright reactionary: an expression of bourgeois individualism and a figure of all that was wrong with the Third Republic, from its inauguration amidst the fall of Louis-Napoleon III and the Commune, through the Dreyfus Affair, the disaster of World War I, the fascist riots of February 1934, all the way up to the Defeat of 1940.

    In proclaiming itself as the only true humanism, each of the crucial and competing conceptions of humanism—Communist, Catholic, and nonconformist—saw generic "humanism" as intimately tied to the reigning secular/bourgeois culture it rejected but also as a malleable notion that could be recuperated within one's own sociocultural beliefs and aims. Such unilateral adoptions of specific and mutually exclusive humanisms fragmented the humanist legacy and led to a radical mistrust of its universalism and force. The intellectuals to be discussed here belonged to these different, if at times intertwined, traditions to varying degrees: some represented the dogma of their positions, others were less "mainstream" in their faction but remain exemplary in their attempts to understand and expound its humanism.

2. The New Men of the 1930s

A few years after Malraux's 1926 *The Temptation of the West*—which serves here as a first explicit rejection of humanism's failure that refuses to commit to a classic right-wing politics—his rejection of the old political bifurcation of Left and Right had come to be echoed quite broadly. In 1930, Paul Arbousse-Bastide, a young philosophy agrégé, posed a series of fourteen questions on humanism and the humanities to a number of university professors, high school teachers, and intellectuals from various sides of the political spectrum, and he published a collection of their responses in a special issue of the Christian review *Foi et vie*.[7] Arbousse-Bastide's survey was politically tinged and conceptually simplistic: for all its pretense to objectivity, it defined humanism by reducing it to a return to the Greeks (that is, to its Renaissance signification, which was precisely the one that Catholics loved to hate), and it avoided any reference to the Enlightenment or to nineteenth-century liberalism and republicanism—indeed even asking whether it is legitimate to "limit humanism to the Greco-Latin humanities," or if humanism were at all linked to a rationalist and individualist conception of man.[8] Implying that the return to the Greeks sufficed to explain the positive content of humanism gave Catholic respondents free rein to denounce. Jacques Maritain had already claimed that "the great primitive causes of the divisions afflicting us, humanism, Protestantism, rationalism, [are] at the end of their tether," and Arbousse-Bastide's inquiry positioned Maritain where he could summarily advocate a theocentric humanism, a humanism that would be "suspended from Christ's grace."[9] Arbousse-Bastide's approach also put some established non-Catholics (like Léon Brunschvicg and Romain Rolland) in a difficult position—having to agree on the insufficiency of his kind of humanism while trying to defend what a meaningful humanism today would be. Keeping with his understanding of the historical "progress of the scientific mind," Brunschvicg held that to be a "worthy continuator of the Greeks" one had to succeed in being contemporary to one's civilization. He argued for the priority of a modern French philosophical culture attentive to the novelty of Einstein's universe as much as ancient thought would have been to Plato, and he rejected the very thing that Arbousse-Bastide considered humanism *without* rejecting Arbousse-Bastide's survey altogether, just proclaiming himself a "heretic" in matters of "literary hu-

manism." Other contributors, like the nonconformist Denis de Rougemont, emphasized humanism as a form of man's self-overcoming and argued for a nonreligious spiritual renewal that would take into account the
transformations in material and scientific culture.

It is important then to understand Arbousse-Bastide's questionnaire
as symptomatic, not only of the broadly perceived insufficiency of a humanism that would see classicist cultivation as high culture but also of
the sense that humanism needed to be rethought given the priorities of a
technical and scientific modernity. Indeed, by 1932, a number of thinkers
mixing elements of left-wing and right-wing thought and not bound to
major political movements—thinkers that came to be known as nonconformists—had come to argue that humanity needed to be renewed, and
that humanism was incapable of delivering either a sufficient response to
the challenges of modernity or the post-1914 world. The struggle for the
humanist mantle begins around this time, as the nonconformist calls were
paralleled by a continuing rise of the communist and socialist Left and
as a new brand of Catholic thought arose from the ashes left by the Papal interdiction of the Action Française. The dual emphasis on dogmatic
orthodoxy and on the need for a more effective and modern response to
contemporary secularism form the background for the theocentric humanism that Catholics came to espouse. On the other end of the political spectrum, socialism changed rather substantially during the 1930s: the
Left had a major success in the rise of the Popular Front in 1936, but it also
found a new intellectual base in Communism, which not only claimed
a far more radical opposition to bourgeois culture but also, through its
link to the USSR, acquired a position of leadership in antifascism.[10] It has
been suggested that, during the 1930s, with the electoral success of the
Popular Front, and in response to the threat of fascism and the Spanish
Civil War, the antifascist coalition of communists and socialists managed
(to a degree) to take over the humanist mantle.[11] However, *every* political faction of the period made an influential claim to be *the only* faction
promulgating a true humanism, and the antifascist success should not
be overestimated. Sustained by a vibrant Catholic culture and a series of
famous and ideologically consequential conversions, Catholic thought
took a more progressive and modernizing turn, finding a philosophical
movement in personalism. To these two poles, nonconformism formed a

third, and more complex one: it offered—especially for intellectuals not concerned with matters of immediate policy—a new domain of intellectual engagement that, from 1930 on, sought a moral and metapolitical overcoming of the Third Republic. By 1932, a number of nonconformist thinkers had expressed their disaffection with existing notions of the human and humanism, a disaffection epitomized in Thierry Maulnier's *La Crise est dans l'homme* (*The Crisis is in Man*). By 1935, the Soviet Union had moved to a policy of defending "socialist humanism," and in 1936, the year of the Stalin constitution, the Popular Front, and the Spanish Civil War—whose stakes intellectuals replayed throughout Europe—appeared the decade's major work of Catholic humanism, Jacques Maritain's *Integral Humanism*. The squabble between these systems of thought and politics had led to hardened positions and intellectual clashes; for each, humanism had been reduced to the shameless ideology of a bourgeois domination unwittingly pursued by rival political movements and was in need of a realignment no one else could offer.

(a) Communism

The dramatic rise of the French Communist Party (PCF) in the 1933–36 period was capped by a double achievement. The first was the recruitment of a number of well-known and influential literary figures who provided Communism with highly visible intellectual ambassadors and legitimated its claim to an egalitarian universalism backed by a serious political program. The second was a takeover of the utopian socialist imaginary. The PCF announced itself with considerable success as the most committed, radical, and responsible form of radical socialism and antifascism; it also sought to present itself as the bearer of both the revolutionary tradition stretching from 1789 through 1848 and 1870 to 1917 and the egalitarian tradition of French utopian socialism (Saint-Simon, Fourier, Blanqui, Proudhon).[12] Through these political and intellectual moves, the PCF aimed, with the backing of the Soviet Union and the Comintern, to promote the image of a Communist New Man, whose world was supposedly being constructed in the USSR, and who was supposedly winning hearts and minds in Europe through the antifascist cause and the critique of bourgeois society.[13] The 1934 First Soviet Congress of Writers, under the direction of Andrei Zhdanov, identified "socialist humanism" as the doctrine from which literature and art would proceed; a year later, the International Writers' Congress that was held in Paris involved a series of talks that explicitly tried to connect this call for socialist humanism with a critique of Western conceptions of man.[14]

Of theoretical concern in this context is the dual core of Marx's humanism. The first, and more fundamentally political dimension of Communist humanism lay with Marx's economic argument, which favors the material overcoming of bourgeois society for an establishment of genuinely human relations. But with regard to the critique of established humanism from the 1930s on, far more influential was Marx's attack, in his 1843–44 "On the Jewish Question," on what he saw as the "abstraction" of the human and the "egoism" instituted by the 1791 and 1793 versions of the *Declaration of the Rights of Man and Citizen*.[15] If the *Communist Manifesto* and *Capital* lay at the heart of the Communist political project, the assault against natural law and human rights became at least as intellectually influential. The claim to a superior humanism relied on Marxism's dual socioeconomic and critical dimension.

The PCF's policy in the early and mid-1930s utilized these approaches, at once (i) emphasizing the singularity and radical credentials of Communism (mostly at socialism's expense), (ii) trying to direct the antifascist movement and to participate in coalitions with left-wing (including socialist) parties, and (iii) aiming to acquire greater respectability vis-à-vis other political movements.[16] This directed the PCF's participation in the Popular Front movement (and, less so, in the Popular Front government), as well as the policy of *la main tendue*, an outstretched hand "offered" by party leader Maurice Thorez to Catholics on April 17, 1936.[17] Antifascism played a major part in the attempt for a cultural advance, insofar as it used the fascist threat as a deterrent against division within the Left, proclaimed Communist leadership, and directed the funding and political support provided by Moscow.[18]

No less significant than the public policies of the party was the Communist appeal in the literary, intellectual, and philosophical world. After the short-lived *Philosophies* group and the surrealist romance with Communism in the 1920s came the rise of communisant literature.[19] Particularly influential among the fellow travelers that made a major contribution to antifascism were André Gide, Romain Rolland, and André Malraux.[20] If Gide and Rolland's towering positions in French literature gave tremendous prestige to Communism, it was Malraux's *La Condition humaine* (*Man's Fate*—though a literal translation would be *The Human Condition*) that set forth one of the most powerful 1930s *Ur*-myths for French Communist and antifascist thought. It was quickly recognized as one of the most significant and influential novels of contemporary literature (winning the 1934 Prix Goncourt), and both Sergei Eisenstein and Vsevolod Meyerhold tried (and failed) to adapt it into film and theater, respectively.[21] Not only did the book situate Communism in the context of a failed revolt that readers could easily identify with the situation of the contemporary German, Austrian, and Spanish Left, but it also forged the protagonists' involvement in this revolt as coextensive with their belief in individual dignity and commitment to the working classes.[22]

Malraux's obsession with the collapse of European humanism plays a major role in *La Condition humaine*, insofar as the entire range of its principal characters are brought to face their relations to (i) a self bound by death and (ii) a universal other expressed through a hope of social equality and human dignity, a hope originating in a Communist conception of human dignity. Out of this dual engagement arises an ethics in which one's actions transform finitude into a confirmation of both one's commitment to the other and a justification of one's life. Characters' lives become meaningful only through a conscious double commitment: to a self fashioned in the encounter with death and to social justice. Only in this way do they find an alternative to the malaise of bourgeois individualism that, in a 1934 talk in Moscow, Malraux denounced as exhausted.[23] Kyo, the protagonist, expresses this position with the greatest determination and care, almost obsessively seeking to bring it out in the thought of his companions. This is what he is recognized for, notably in a monologue of Old Gisors' (Kyo's father) that comes late in the novel and clearly echoes Malraux's worries regarding commitment as a way to save both oneself and Man in general:

"It is very rare for a man to be able to endure—how shall I say it?—his condition, his fate as a man. . . . " He thought of one of Kyo's ideas: all that men are willing to die for, beyond self-interest, stands more or less obscurely to justify that fate by giving it a foundation in dignity: Christianity for the slave, the nation for the citizen, Communism for the worker. . . . Under his words flowed an obscure and hidden countercurrent of figures: Ch'en and murder, . . . Katov and the Revolution, May and love, himself and opium. . . . Kyo alone, in his eyes, resisted these categories. (MF 238)[24]

Kyo's belief in "human dignity" (MF 302) drives the narrative of the revolt and is contrasted to the less intellectual commitment of the other characters. If it "resists these categories," this is largely because it is sufficiently abstract not to require or impose any definitive political identification, while his practical and strategic work evinces the exact moral concretization and political involvement through which Communism becomes a universal call: a joining of moral praxis with trust in a humanity under attack. To this (clearly crucial) endeavor, the novel opposes alternative political approaches, which it does not reject or ironize—for example, the Catholic priest who once instructed Ch'en; the chief of the Kuo Min Tang military police, König, who on the basis of his own past suffering doubts Kyo's Communist commitment; Clappique and Old Gisors, given to individualism and aestheticism, respectively. Not only do these alternatives put in question the specific politics Kyo supports, but they also set the stakes for his humanist concerns. On the one hand, Kyo's commitment illustrates and balances precisely the only course worth fighting for; on the other, the abstraction of his commitment and his failure to understand and convey a viable political strategy following the capture of Shanghai raises questions concerning the fragility and the potential hopelessness of this kind of humanist engagement. The somber finale following Kyo's and Katov's deaths, where survivors attempt to figure out how to proceed with their lives, casts further doubt on this commitment.

Taking account of this ambiguity, several 1930s commentators emphasized "heroism" as the principal trait of Malraux's Communists, figures that engaged in a struggle whose hopelessness they quickly recognized and that advocated certain abstract (and classically French) ideals of equality and fraternity making their commitment all the more worthy.[25] Malraux's readers interpreted this heroism by way of their own engagements: for Jacques Maritain, Malraux pointed to a spirit of self-sacrifice that was Christian by default; for Paul Nizan, this heroism confirmed the superior ethics of Communism. Colored as it was by Malraux's fellow-traveling engagement (which led to his fighting in the Spanish Civil War), this "heroic humanism" undoubtedly provided a definite political orientation for the book even though *La Condition Humaine* by no means offered unambiguous support of Communism.[26] It is nevertheless important to emphasize that heroism here codes the considerable skepticism presented throughout the book over the politics of *La Condition Humaine*, pointing to reservation over the efficacy and futurity, even the tragedy of all humanism.

A second major presentation of Marxist humanism in the early 1930s, written as a polemical essay, was Paul Nizan's *The Watchdogs* (*Les Chiens de Garde*, 1932), one of the harshest and most explicit attacks on established academic philosophy and its conception of man. A member of the Communist *Philosophies* group in the late 1920s, a philosophy graduate of the Ecole Normale Supérieure, *agrégé* in the same year as Jean-Paul Sartre and Georges Canguilhem, Nizan was an orthodox Communist and Stalinist who lived in Moscow during part of the early 1930s, publishing *Le Journal littéraire,* the French edition of *Literaturnaya Gazeta,* and writing on literature and philosophy in French papers. Shortlisted for the very Prix Goncourt that Malraux won for *Man's Fate,* Nizan praised Malraux's arrangement of solitude, politics, and anxiety: though he found it derivative of Heidegger's *Being and Time,* he appreciated its ability to wrest this arrangement away from Heidegger's "wholehearted embrace" of Nazism.[27]

Nizan's *Watchdogs* is an elaborate meditation on Marx's eleventh of the "Theses on Feuerbach," written in terms of a sarcastic attack against the "blind," "self-satisfied" idealists of his day and directed against the abstraction of things and men into arguments about the in-itself or Man-in-general (WD 7–8). His dual aim is (i) to reject contemporary philosophy's claim to have solved the anthropological problem by positing man's relation to the world in terms of ideals or effective conceptual schemes, and (ii) to sketch an alternative conception of philosophy, following which it would no longer be possible for those "starting out in philosophy" to "content themselves with working against other men" (ALP 119).

Nizan's prose lays claim to both rhetorical and philosophical simplicity—to showing the reality of modern man through "a few simple concepts: a few straightforward and, as it were, rudimentary notions which cannot be emphasized too strongly" (WD 12). This move allows, he claims, for an understanding of the futility of idealist anthropology that, originating in the Plato-to-Kant tradition, dominates modern thought and fails to think man in his material, everyday conditions. Nizan continues:

These commonsense notions tell us that there is no such thing as *Homo faber*, *Homo artifex*, or *Homo sapiens*, *Homo economicus* or *Homo politicus*, *Homo noumenon* or *Homo phenomenon* that there are only those multitudes of "singular" men who are born, who lead particular kinds of lives, who beget children, and who die: the laborer who makes 25 francs a day and the politician who lives in the Villa Saïd, the young lady who takes courses at Villiers and the girl of the Cité Jeanne d'Arc who sleeps in the same room as her parents and brothers, the revolutionary militant and the inspector of the Criminal Investigation Department. Thus, on the one hand, we have the idealistic philosophers who promulgate truths concerning Man; and, on the other hand, we have a map showing the incidence of tuberculosis in Paris, a map which tells us how men are dying. (WD 12)[28]

This brutal "simplicity" serves Nizan's rejection of contemporaries en masse for their belief of working for *Man-in-general* (WD 6–7) and their trust in ideals: "To put it bluntly, Monsieur Bergson and Monsieur Boutroux belong to a family of philosophers of which I am the enemy; but my enmity does not spring from any love for the eternal *telos* of Philosophy-in-itself."[29] If, on the one hand, *The Watchdogs* served as a call for an engaged thought and an attack against the Brunschvicgian philosophical detachment that Nizan saw as produced by a deeply misguided trust in the sufficiency of ideals *in abstracto*, on the other, the positive claims of the book appear largely fragmented.[30] The book makes a distinct argument in favor of a philosophy that would begin from the proletariat that he sees as bearer of truth, toil, and thus humanity. Precisely because he dramatizes himself as a *vox clamantis in deserto*, Nizan offers that this argument suffices by itself as a call for a humanist alternative. That is to say, his humanism follows from an implicit assertion of the philosophical legitimacy of Communism, which, given the urgency of the 1930s economic crisis, and given French philosophers' supposed blindness toward contemporary problems and material conditions, results in an overall intellectual superiority, a philosophical qua moral command.

Nizan's attempt to provide a more concrete response to this humanist problem appears in his address to the International Congress of Writers (Paris, 1935) and is an exemplary argument for "socialist humanism."[31] Set up largely by Moscow's man in Paris Ilya Ehrenburg, the International Congress of Writers (in whose organization both Malraux and Nizan were involved) placed the question of humanism's relations to literature and industry at the top of the agenda and sought to promote the 1934 Congress' "solution" for humanism in the Western European context.[32] Nizan's presentation mixed a critique of Western "conformism" to abstract ideals, an attack on contemporaries unable to understand the priorities of Communism (notably Julien Benda and Jean Guehenno, both of whom also addressed the Congress), and an espousal of Communism's ability to succeed where bourgeois humanism had failed. Arguing that the "mythology" that is humanism had always defined man by referring to his totality and natural perfection, Nizan targeted (i) humanist prudence (which limited its universalism), and (ii) (once again) the isolation from "concrete man." As a result, he claimed, non-Communist proclamations of support for humanity invariably failed to allow for a link between the idealist hopes and the multiplicity of men in need of these hopes—and thus failed its own definition. Communism, Nizan wrote, specifically follows from the demand to fulfill these hopes by negating any division between ideals and material reality: "Man is more than ever impoverished, humiliated, solitary, oppressed, by these powers of finance, politics, justice, and police, that are the reality of what one calls destiny. We see hunger, misery, tortures, we are living the time of wars" (ALP 512). In this regard, Nizan's work offers a useful example of a motif that I would like to call *exclusivist humanism*. Not only does he fully identify a positive notion of humanism with his Communism, but he also claims this Communism to be the only proper universalism, and then he denies alternative approaches as insufficient and thereby harmful. Given his deep conviction in the course of the USSR (ALP 229–30, 501–4), and his active participation in *Le Journal littéraire*, this approach acquires a Manichean character typical of antifascism. This dogmatism remained fundamental to Nizan's thought to the point where any compromise was unacceptable—indeed to the point that he committed suicide following what he saw as the catastrophic betrayal of the Nazi-Soviet pact of August 1939.

(b) Catholicism

In the interwar intellectual world, Catholicism rose anew as a social force and a critic of secular humanism that lay claim to a superior and more fundamental conception of human dignity. Throughout the nineteenth century, the Catholic Church strove to identify secularism with the violence of the 1789 Revolution, a destructive mechanistic science lacking regard for human weakness, and a materialist destruction of the "national community." This approach continued—indeed it hardened in the Action Française during and after the Dreyfus Affair—while the Third Republic managed a far-reaching separation of powers in 1905 and a substantial revamping and de-Christianization of educational policies in the 1870s and early 1900s. But if these stages produced a certain image and culture for Catholicism, the interwar period transformed this image and culture—and the lynchpins of its intellectual life—quite significantly. Much more than in the years preceding the Great War, Catholic writers were forced to address the problem of spiritual anguish in an industrialized world of work and supposedly mindless consumption.[33] Without abandoning either conservatism (with its origins in the Counter-Enlightenment) or anti-Communism, Catholic theologians and philosophers nevertheless reacted to the problem of modernity by engaging with opposing social positions and aimed to convince anew of the pertinence, reach, and goals of Catholicism.[34] While more conservative Catholics continued to be involved with the legacy of Boulangism, the Action Française, anti-Dreyfusardism, and a right-wing axis of Nation/Religion/Family, a "progressivist" effort to bring about a Catholic Renaissance utilized new political and cultural means, a broader acknowledgment of changes in modern society, and somewhat more accepting theologico-political arguments.[35] This new thinking was occasioned in part by a certain post-WWI easing of the prewar secularizing rigor (itself facilitated by the Church's participation in the 1914 "Union sacrée" against Germany), and in part by the stress on social aspects of the dogma: the promise of community, salvation, and stable spiritual personhood as suggested by *personalism*.[36] Especially after the Papal interdiction of the Action Française in 1926, Catholic philosophers like Jacques Maritain, Gabriel Marcel, Emmanuel Mounier, and Henri de Lubac sought to become flagbearers of a humanism at once ancient and new, respectful of the success of science but also capable of tempering its radicalism and fundamentally supportive of human spirit and dignity.[37] While the participation of figures of the Catholic renaissance in Vichy's "National Revolution" tends to suggest a rather linear movement from Boulangism and the Action Française to Vichy, the complex interplay between the more centrist—if not left-leaning—Catholicism and that tradition (which heralded no new humanism, no new conception of society) should not be underestimated.

The fundamental tenet of Catholic humanism in the 1930s was theocentrism, the idea that no conception of human dignity is complete without a recognition of a spiritual and transcendental dimension to human nature, a dimension that necessarily entails (in the sense that it *presupposes*) a recognition of God. Without God, the spiritual dimension of human life and culture finds its hopes unanswered, reduced to an anguished cry that can only lead to violence; atheism, particularly in its utopian hopes, serves only as a destructive imitation of genuine faith. Nicolai Berdyaev put it bluntly: "Where there is no God, there is no man either."[38] "Materialism" (commonly used as shorthand for socialism but also for capitalism) is crude and insufficient because it destroys a human spirit so obviously in need of solace. But so is secular humanism in general because it fails to properly acknowledge that man seeks transcendence and salvation more than he aims to emerge victorious as an individual. Secularism is condemned to reducing spirit to matter and man to a selfish arrogant animal that legitimates its own absurd pretenses to divinity, natural beneficence, and so on. This argument was made over and over in the 1930s, to the point that Catholic humanism appeared to have become part of Catholic social and intellectual policy.[39] In 1937, Henri de Lubac, a Jesuit theologian who would become influential in Vatican II and eventually be appointed a cardinal, opened his discussion of Catholicism's approach to society and humanism as follows:

Integral humanism: The first step would be to show to those who have realized that no end short of humanity deserves absolutely to be loved and sought—and there are many such men in many different camps, even in those which are most exposed to one another—that they are obliged to look higher than the earth in the pursuit of their quest. For a transcendent destiny which presupposes the existence of a transcendent God is essential to the realization of a destiny that is truly collective, that is, to the constitution of this humanity in the concrete.[40]

These two sentences express a number of quiet presuppositions that are exemplary of theocentrism. De Lubac accepts the legitimacy of a quest ultimately targeting the moral improvement and social progress of humanity per se, but he also suggests that humanism does not fit the ideology of the secular-bourgeois political culture that it is meant to encompass. The phrase "No end short of humanity deserves absolutely to be loved and sought" is characteristic of a classic humanist rhetoric that de Lubac and his contemporaries specifically wished to take over and turn on its head, at once emphasizing the legitimacy of this language and challenging the secular, anthropocentric vision to which it was tied. Second, de Lubac immediately identifies the necessity of looking "higher," to a transcendent *destiny*, and hence to a transcendent God as the guarantor of human life. Third, de Lubac's use of the term *integral humanism* explicitly refers to the then-recently published analysis of (and attack on) atheist humanism by Jacques Maritain in his homonymous book and indeed rests largely on the critique of humanism offered there.

By 1935, Jacques Maritain was best known for his research, theorization, and deployment of Thomas Aquinas's thought, which turned him into one of the most influential Catholic philosophers of his time. His *Humanisme intégral* (first translated in English under the even less inconspicuous title *True Humanism*) extended his neothomist project by addressing the "What is man?" question: Maritain argued that "'liberal-bourgeois' humanism is now no more than barren wheat and a starchy bread" (IH 155). His metaphor doubles as a critique of the material emphasis of the Left, and indeed Maritain used the 1934 Writers' Congress, with its sponsorship of socialist humanism, as indicative of Communism's delusion that it could overcome the limitations of humanism (IH 152). Maritain retorted that this unfortunate condition resulted from a "materialized spirituality" that had voided itself of the Catholic beliefs that had originally made its rise possible. Though Western humanism, even at its most anthropocentric, depended heavily on elements it plucked (or inherited) from Christian thought (IH 154), this dependence had depleted itself of meaning in its opposition to the essential dimensions of Catholic thought and culture:[41] "If we consider Western humanism in those of its contemporary forms which appear to be most emancipated from every metaphysics of transcendence, it is easy to see that, if there still remains in them some common conception of human dignity, of liberty and of disinterested values, this is a heritage of ideas and sentiments once Christian but today little loved" (IH 155). Maritain instead defended the centrality of communion in Catholicism and Catholic community, which he grounds on a seemingly irrelevant attack on Jansenism. Though the Jansenist tradition itself was hardly a danger to twentieth-century Catholicism, its distancing (in the seventeenth century) of God from Man and its proximity to Protestantism were especially significant (IH 162).[42] Jansenism's insistence on efficacious grace and rare communion offered a straw man for Maritain to attack through an emphasis on communion as founding a continuous experience of God; it is also relevant that Pascal was frequently cited by philosophers and that Malraux's title for *La Condition humaine* involved a conscious reference to Pascal.[43] Maritain's support for an engaged Catholic culture revolves around a conception of community that would center society around communion and that openly reclaims the contemporary significance of medieval Christendom (Aquinas especially—IH 157–60).[44] With the Renaissance, the Reformation, and Jansenism, the culture in which communion heralded a continued engagement with the divine had been undermined, with the result that the intimate link between God and Man was broken and theology was reduced first to naturalism, then to rationalism (IH 164–66). Rationalism, writes Maritain, is the "absolute humanist theology," that is, anthropocentric theology: with it, the Renaissance gave birth to a "classical humanism" whose "misfortune" was "to have been anthropocentric, and not to have been humanism" (IH 167).

Maritain's claim that Christians needed a "sound philosophy of history" (IH 155) has two major prescriptive consequences. The first identifies "theocentric humanism" with his Thomism and his effort to reconstruct the broken medieval links: it leads to his call for a reconstruction of a community based on communion, out of this premodern, medieval model that would make the community aware of its "luminous" relation to God. Second, given that this kind of community is not exactly an immediate possibility in the contemporary world, the theocentric humanist call takes instead the foreground, at once as a theological prescription and a political strategy. "[Theocentric humanism] recognizes that God is the center of man; it implies the Christian conception of man, sinner and redeemed and the Christian conception of grace and freedom . . . " (IH 169). Like de Lubac, Maritain makes a clear if uncompromising attempt to speak to contemporaries of different political stripes—an attempt that seeks less to convince and more to counter their conceptions of man and take advantage of a general shared conception of bourgeois humanism as self-contradictory and self-undermining. Not only does he approvingly cite Hendrik de Man's antimaterialist critique of Marxism (IH 183–84n), but perhaps more significantly, he opens with an approval of Malraux's "heroic humanism" (IH 152), using *La Condition humaine* as exemplary of the possibilities of a heroic engagement that (presumably finding its pinnacle in Catholic martyrdom) demarcates the limits and radical potential of man. His reference to Marx also echoes and reproduces the Catholic opposition that commends Marx's attention to material causality and need, but rejects his rendition of material causality into the definitive force behind human nature and existence: "barren wheat and starchy bread." This repeated engagement with the contemporary Left, this attempt to criticize its humanist hopes is particularly important: within his new Catholicism, it led to a continued attempt to outdo Marxism by the spiritual and moral evocation, which would become central for (even non-Catholic) nonconformism.

Much more explicit in his engagement with Communism than either de Lubac or Maritain was a today unknown but at the time significant Jesuit philosopher, Gaston Fessard.[45] Well-versed in contemporary philosophy from Maine de Biran to Marx and Heidegger, Fessard was a close friend of Pierre Teilhard de Chardin and Henri de Lubac, and the confessor of Gabriel Marcel.[46] He followed Alexandre Kojève's course on Hegel, which he found fascinating, but he countered to Kojève's reading of Hegel a "Pauline" interpretation of the *Phenomenology of Spirit*.[47] Though, like Maritain and de Lubac, he was not a personalist, Fessard made a strong effort to raise issues in ways attuned to personalist views, and he participated in the spread of priorities with personalist undertones.[48] During the occupation, he would become an important figure in the *résistance*, writing a famous appeal for France to "not lose its soul" to fascist anti-Semitism, *France, prends garde de perdre ton âme!*, as well as a number of theologico-political texts on authority and the figure of the *prince-esclave* (slave-prince) which were heavily influenced by Carl Schmitt's friend/enemy distinction and Kojève's theorization of the master/slave relation in Hegel.[49]

In the mid-1930s, Fessard wrote two oft-reprinted books on international politics and the dialogue between Communist and Catholic thought, *Pax nostra. Examen de conscience international* (1936), and *La Main tendue? Le dialogue Catholique-Communiste est-il possible?* (1937). The second, a collection of essays and letters published in Catholic as well as Communist newspapers, critically addressed (already in its title) the policy of the PCF leader Maurice Thorez that offered an "outstretched hand" to Catholics and suggested that the Communist commitment to atheism "made impossible" any real eye-to-eye exchange. If this conclusion looks like a knee-jerk dogmatic reaction, the argument behind it was far more nuanced: Fessard took considerable pains to address secularism and contemporary politics through a Hegelian and Marxist framework, citing extensively from Marx's *Economic and Philosophical Manuscripts of 1844* and directing these citations against contemporary Communist thought and policy that he thought reduced the social impulse to crude materialism.

La Main tendue? criticizes the Communist theory of history, its implication that Communism is ultimately in control of political progress, and especially its "announcement" of a Communist New Man who would mark a new era in human relations. In an attempt to engage Marxism on its own terms, Fessard above all finds Communism theologically unhistorical. He argues that the essence of this New Man lies with the Communists' proclamation of atheism as an ethics of struggle with utopian potential (MT 100). He then counters with the universalism of Saint Paul, through which he defends not only the fundamental Christian dogma of the Resurrection but, moreover, a universalism that (for him) permits divergence of faith and does not reduce man's transcendent aspects to an economic qua ontological materialism. Paul is specifically important to him because of the famous egalitarianism of Galatians 3:28–29: "There is neither Jew nor Greek, there is neither slave nor free, there is neither male nor female; for you are all one in Christ Jesus. And if you are Christ's, then you are Abraham's offspring, heirs according to promise."[50] On the basis of this vision of equality, Fessard interprets atheism as exclusivist and rejects the Communist promise as failing to appropriately and universally administer a care of the soul, all the while maintaining a hope that a genuine dialogue can occur.[51]

Significant responses to Fessard's argument came from two contemporary authors of interest here. The first was Paul Nizan, who saw in Fessard a spirit open to the egalitarian potential of Communism and willing to engage in dialogue. Nizan acknowledged Fessard's rejection of the "outstretched hand" respectfully, implying in his text that the policy could not possibly work on a dogmatic level, only on a pragmatic one.[52] Nizan's response echoed the political needs of Communism in France—not rejecting Catholicism but still hoping to use dialogue to the party's advantage. A second response came in a review written by Alexandre Kojève, which he sent to Fessard in a letter, after *Recherches philosophiques*, which was to publish it, folded in 1937. Kojève inversely faulted Fessard for coming too close to Communist texts, and thus for leaving the Catholic position far too open.[53]

Leaving aside the differences between Fessard's Paulinianism, de Lubac's "New Theology," and Maritain's Thomism, it is clear that a series of common presuppositions and remarks joins Fessard's argumentation to de Lubac and Maritain's (and, to some extent, to the more liberal faction of Catholic reaction to the "outstretched hand"). Three central aspects of Catholic humanism are worth emphasizing as the core of its engagement. First, the attempt to appropriate "humanism" from a concept of basically anti-Catholic import to a central aspect in Catholic antisecularism; second, the idea of religious anti-anthropocentrism as grounding this humanism in man's fundamental relation to the transcendent and the divine; and finally, the priority of spiritually (religiously) centered community as a necessary cultural and social premise of human interaction. These positions were at the heart of Catholic progressivism in the 1930s and marked a new critical approach to secularism, socialism, and idealist humanism. As critiques of humanism, they persisted well into the postwar period and into Vatican II, thanks to de Lubac and Maritain, but also Jean Lacroix, Gabriel Marcel, and others.

(c) Nonconformism

As an ideological conglomerate of the 1930s and a space for all those who rejected established political categories, nonconformism has traditionally posed considerable puzzles for historians seeking to place it and its arguments in its time. In his book *Neither Right nor Left*, Zeev Sternhell famously identified nonconformism with French fascist ideology, seeing much of the intellectual turmoil of the mid-1930s as underwritten by a series of shifts of socialist intellectuals to the antimaterialist, nationalist Right. The other classic work on nonconformism, Jean-Louis Loubet del

Bayle's *Les Non-conformistes des années trente,* provides a different reading of its attack on established culture, centering on thinkers and milieus that were politically and philosophically very different—for example, journals like *Esprit* and *L'Ordre Nouveau*—but shared the contempt for the political middle and the "traditional" Left and Right. While his effort to largely unify their positive projects perhaps underplays their affinities to fascism, this book has the remarkable merit of showing the antinomian spirit so central to nonconformism regardless of differences between approaches and ideological notions. Both historians show in their ways the sheer difficulty of dealing with a set of thinkers and approaches united principally in their rejection of the status quo and in the fact that so many went on to become proponents of fascism, but not in the variety of radicalism or the range of their commitments to the "nonconformist" umbrella. Following from the approaches of Loubet del Bayle and Sternhell, I want to emphasize certain central ideological aspects of nonconformism and its gradual movement toward an acceptance of fascism.

First: its antinomianism—which is suggested already by a literal reading of the term. In a sense, nonconformists called themselves so (or were identified thus) because they rejected the political projects provided by the range of French parliamentary and quasi-parliamentary politics (including nationalism and Communism).[54] Still, nonconformists routinely culled arguments from established political tendencies, deriding the latter for insufficient commitment and proposing themselves as more capable of defending these arguments.

Second: the (metapolitical) claim of a decay of European thought and culture since the Enlightenment, supported by figures from Malraux to Maritain and from Drieu La Rochelle to Valéry, was central to the nonconformist outlook and supported its belief that out of a radical, morally directed political reorganization could arise a new society and culture. By combining aspects of the traditional Left and Right, nonconformism managed to provide a more complex theory of the decadence of bourgeois man and to address problems from machinism in industry to the hope of bioengineering and to the meaning of Europe. It thus came to serve as an umbrella term for a number of thinkers, some of whom veered toward (or embraced) fascism and others who remained committed to a radical Left, all the while rejecting the political culture in general.[55]

Third: nonconformists emphasized as absolutely urgent the need to reorganize the contemporary understanding of man and society in such a way that the fashioning of a New Man could take place uninhibited by perceived disastrous effects of existing political and economic systems. For nonconformists, man was typically "unknown," "to be found," or "to be constructed anew" (as was argued, for example, by Robert Brasillach, Alexis Carrel, and Marcel Déat). Modern Europe—as they argued, following Spengler—was falling apart, or had already become downright inhuman (Robert Aron, Arnaud Dandieu, Pierre Drieu la Rochelle). This overall spiritual, human, and European decline was the very source of the present political and economic crises (Thierry Maulnier).[56] Though the rejection of humanism was not specific to nonconformists, they were among its most aggressive proponents, openly declaring the death of bourgeois society, the technological and material destruction of the human spirit, and the need for a replacement and without linking these declarations to any existing parliamentary political program.[57] As Loubet Del Bayle argues, they were specifically invested in demonstrating at once the prevalence of a crisis of civilization, the dependence of political, economic, or social aspects of this crisis on the more general crisis of human life, and the consequent call for a moral as much as an economic restructuring of man—for a new humanism.[58]

A new humanism: Thierry Maulnier's 1932 book *La Crise est dans l'homme* (*The Crisis Is in Man*) is characteristic of nonconformist thought not only in that it objected to competing attempts to explain what man is and should be, but also in the way Maulnier argued for a specificity and purity supposedly inherent to his own search. As noted in its title, for Maulnier the crisis was not just in contemporary culture, but in the human condition itself. "It appears that the moment for the resurrection of man has arrived. And we're asking for nothing less than the essentials!" (LCr 242–43). Dismissing the "official philosophy of the Sorbonne" and criticizing writers of *l'après-guerre* for failing to provide an adequate and truly novel understanding of the human, *La Crise est dans l'homme* (one of the first works that could be squarely called nonconformist and especially one of the texts that shows nonconformism's demand for a new humanism to have in large part *preceded* the mid-1930s turn in Communism and Catholicism toward humanism) argued, regarding the widespread call for a New Man, that

Robert Brasillach has concluded that we now need to "find man again." Such a formula cannot displease, not least because one finds oneself too often driven to repeat it. But it is still too general and vague. Man? Still? And where would one locate him? M. Poulaille claims to be searching for him in factories; M. Thérive prefers to pursue him in atrocious accommodations or lugubrious metro platforms. If we do not want to confound ourselves with such fallen shadows, where could we find the essence and possible grandeur? What direction do we take to what has escaped or failed us [*manqué*] the most? [. . .] Every new school claims to be tearing down veils, to be rejecting lies, to be returning to man, nature, truth. (LCr 246–48)

To acknowledge the obsession that this New Man constituted, one need only point a little further, to the titles of journals like *L'Homme nouveau* (*The New Man*) or *L'Homme réel* (*Real Man*) to extend Maulnier's own long list of references—not to mention the dozens of articles in *Esprit*, *L'Ordre nouveau*, and other journals that endlessly explored the possible forms of a new humanism and identified with a radical transformation of contemporary culture.[59] But Maulnier's own position, emphasized in the closing pages of *La Crise est dans l'homme*, was also exemplary of the vagueness and political utility of nonconformist definitions of man: he called for a "return to purity" that one could supposedly recognize in an unmediated fashion and that carried with it none of the decorations that defined well-established ideologies (LCr 252). As Merleau-Ponty would note after the war, this stance rejected "the Maurrassian idea of an immutable human nature which reduces political problems to those of an immutable sociology of order," constructing an alternative at once radically reactionary and very close to socialist critiques of Marxist determinism.[60] Both within Maulnier's own project, which would lead him to become a major figure in French fascist thought and indeed a "fascist critic of fascism," and within nonconformism in general, his at first glance vague "call to purity" attempted to outdo both the conservative search for Great Men that would express the supposed eternal truth of human nature and the Marxist attempt to found action on social class and historical determinism.[61]

For other nonconformists, the call to humanist rebirth took a somewhat different path. During the 1930s, their new humanism became closely connected both to the Belgian socialist Hendrik de Man's critique of Marxism (his attempt to construct a socialism centered on a planned economy), and to a personalism (predominantly propounded by Emmanuel Mounier's journal *Esprit*) that derived from Catholic theocentrism but emphasized less this Catholic origin and more its reconstruction of subjectivity as dependent on social solidarity and community, as well as on a desire for social transformation.[62] It allowed for a conception of the subject that distinctly rejected man's capacity for a clear-cut understanding of the world surrounding it, proposing instead a moral and political rejuvenation of the nation and of contemporary society on the premise of providing the link broken by individualism. Personalism, as is often remarked, was less a well-ordered theory of human existence and more an attempt to react to the perceived ills of both individualist and totalitarian impulses in contemporary politics.[63] By advocating a concept of the person against that of the individual—a person that was conceived in antimaterialist and often communitarian terms, against an individual that allowed precisely the reduction to matériel that Catholics deplored—personalism offered a theory of social balance that accounted for the affirmative, even utopian claims in nonconformist humanism because it served to supplant a directly political ideology with a search for a moral revolution and society.[64] Moreover, personalism provides the central link between Catholicism and nonconformism's occasional "reactionary modernist" nostalgia of a world unbound, above all because of the role of Emmanuel Mounier, the most significant Catholic thinker of the period to participate in a non-Church-based, non-Action Française politics whose miscellany of left- and right-wing politics was a consequence of nonconformism's moral emphasis and eventually resulted in a set of positions whose direct political implications often bordered on fascism.[65]

Mounier's writing in the mid-1930s drew from Maritain's conception of the Renaissance as the historical origin of modernity's troubles as well as on the need for a politics that would facilitate a moral and political transformation of man.[66] His writings, like the general tendencies of *Esprit*, which he directed, stressed personalism's superior humanism by submitting the human to the person's dependence on community, and interpreting the person as fundamentally opposed to the conservatism of "liberal, parliamentary, and plutocratic democracy," to materialist reduction, and to autocratic opportunities of totalitarianism that continued until the late 1930s.[67] As Michel Winock writes, "In December 1938, [*Esprit*] launches an 'appeal for a mass gathering in favor of a personalist democracy', that would place 'at the foundation of all public institutions,' 'the care for the human person.'"[68] In this context, *Esprit* defined man principally in *opposition* to the modernity surrounding him, as an existence "*in this world but not of* it," in a fashion that hoped to potentially result in the overcoming of the crisis of humanism as the review perceived it, but also came very close to a spiritual fascism that accepted the fascist image of man as barely different from the nonconformist one.[69] The complex itinerary of philosophers and personalist nonconformists who presented themselves as fundamentally leftist but whose antimaterialism led them to positions often close to fascism, reflects their concurrent commitments to a tradition harshly critical of secularism and socialism, and to a political project linked to an antibourgeois Left but not to its humanism.

That the political abstraction of personalist principles made nonconformism vulnerable to ideological takeover can perhaps best be described by reference to a work of someone who was not explicitly a nonconformist but whose radicalism expressed personalist and nonconformist concerns, and whose work was broadly read in conservative and nonconformist circles. Indeed, one of the most startling attempts to devise a politics unbound by secular democracy can be found in Alexis Carrel's *Man, the Unknown* (*L'Homme cet inconnu*, 1935), a biologistic and eugenicist work that became an acclaimed international best-seller despite its size and often rambling tone.[70] Carrel was a French physician who worked in the United States and who had won the 1912 Nobel Prize for medicine on the basis of his work on wound suture and organ transplants. *Man, the Unknown* brought to the fore his eugenicism, his claim for biology's capacity to provide a harmonious solution to the problems of modern life and society; according to the historian of science André Pichot, *Man, the Unknown* offered Carrel the aura of a "great humanist."[71] After this book, Carrel continued to write political texts (some with none other than Charles Lindbergh), signed on to Jacques Doriot's collaborationist Parti Populiste Français, and attempted to apply his eugenicism through a 1941 appointment at Vichy as regent of the Fondation Française pour l'Etude des Problèmes Humains.[72] Addressing the potential of eugenics for social engineering, Carrel claimed that biological classes—the biological potentials for individual participation in society and (by extension) for the development of individuality into grandeur—are fundamentally tied to social classes (MU 298). Thus, he argued, an aristocracy of geniuses should provide for humanity's future by distinguishing itself from people of inherent biological lack who composed the proletariat. These ties have been almost severed with the mechanical (that is to say, "base materialist" and "poorly" scientific) construction of modern man (MU 273, 278) and the democratic/egalitarian theorization of his role in society (MU 271–72) since the Renaissance. These had resulted in a fabrication that "infringed upon" and "transgressed against" natural laws (MU 273, 321), facilitating man's capacity to thwart natural selection (MU 268, 272) in a way that allowed the survival of individuals of lower potential and thus facilitated the present crisis, resulting in the moral and spiritual destruction of man (MU 272–73). Yet if technical science and politics brought about the moral, social, and intellectual demise of civilization, eugenics could undo the consequences and provide the necessary re-identification of biological and social classes, a redemptive solution for the political, natural, and moral threats of contemporary life and decadence (MU 298–99).

With its fantasy of putting human engineering to work for a restoration of genuine medieval class society, Carrel's moralist eugenicism may strike us as bizarre. Yet *Man, the Unknown* gave Carrel a humanist reputation and his overall work shared with 1930s nonconformism—especially its more reactionary forms—a series of crucial obsessions:[73] the rejection of democracy (which he extends into, or grounds on, a rejection of equality [MU 271]); the call for an overcoming of the proletariat as a class (MU 298, 302); the fear of technology as it has shaped modern society; the frequent excoriation of the Renaissance as the source of modern decadence (MU 278, 320); and the belief that a radical metapolitical project (in his account, the political restructuring of society on the basis of "voluntary eugenics") would lead to a construction of harmonious socioeconomic relations and could substitute for the inhuman condition that is modernity.[74] Carrel's eugenicist revolution used exactly the vagueness and hopes characteristic of nonconformists, for example Maulnier's "resurrection of man." Despite the various and often obvious differences between their projects and his, his is expressive of the 1930s exhortation for a remaking of man and is central as one of the most institutionally influential programs for eugenics in France. With the movement of nonconformism toward a position often concurring with fascism, the calls for a reconsideration of man often coalesced toward a concept of "total" or "totalitarian man," which would prioritize man's links to society, his individuality, and his tendency toward nonreligious transcendence.

3. Coincidentia Oppositorum

Though the struggle between these different sorts of humanisms came to a head in 1935–38, a fundamental structural similarity can be found in the meaning and significance of exclusivist humanism among Communists, Catholics, and nonconformists. Communists like Nizan and fellow travelers like Malraux argued that the radical intellectual commitment to human dignity necessitated a struggle for equality and material satisfaction that trumped the irrelevant ideals and half-hearted politics of the center, and they criticized the moral emphasis of personalism as hypocritical. Catholics emphasized that the anthropocentrism and materialism of secular humanism amputated the height and thus the core of the human being, its relation to the transcendent God. Nonconformists, meanwhile, viewed modernity as destructive of the classical human condition, but also saw in it a potential opening to a new and more harmonious humanity. For the thinkers in each faction—*even the less orthodox or dogmatic ones*—the individualism, idealism, and secular humanism of the day was fundamentally neglectful if not downright destructive of the presence and needs of the human person, as well as of his relations to society, his uniqueness proper, and even his interiority or spirituality. By opposing classical humanism as an expression of the Third Republic, and by calling for the recuperation of a pure concept of the human capable of overcoming the weakness of modernity and contemporary society, these "new" humanisms worked at once toward the intellectual delegitimization of the Republic itself and also toward social and metapolitical alternatives. Their fragmentation of the humanist imagination, and the close identification between their ideological positions and their claims to true humanism, allowed thinkers to *not* renounce the term and its general meaning as care for man and human dignity, *but instead* adapt, reappropriate, or redefine it in favor of belief in *a certain* man and in *a certain, supposedly properly human* response to modernity. That is not to say that the exclusivist universalism each proclaimed reduced humanism to nothing but a flag or a crest of theologico-political claims and general ideology. It is to say that each movement's thought was invariably its humanism, and humanism could be nothing but the exemplary expression of this thought and its care for man. Echoing Jean-Luc Nancy, we may claim that here humanism became the meaning of the utterance *we*—a self-affirming substantiation of one's adherence to a complex ideology.[75]

This should not suggest that intellectuals' philosophical and political positions were set in stone—for many, these slippery oppositions were necessary to their study of philosophical and ideological positions and continuity.[76] Despite their uncompromising conviction in the terms and strength of their own humanism and their defense of its validity and structure, various intellectuals changed political camps—but because of the structure of the opposition to secular humanism they could maintain or only partly adjust their concepts of man and humanism. The ambiguities of Malraux's "heroic" humanism (both for his own political position and also for his readers' perceptions of the significance of his work), of personalism's adherence to Catholicism and nonconformism, of the popularity of Hendrik de Man, of the hopes of the Communist policy of the "outstretched hand"—all these were not aberrations, but rather exemplars of the deep belief that man needed to be remade and that different philosophies offered certain elements necessary to one's way of understanding the world and the possible cause of this remaking. Christian writers, for example, often treated André Gide's interest in Communism as deriving from his desire for a moral revolution forever betrothed to Catholicism.[77] This tendency had several consequences. In the context of permeable ideological positions, humanism tended to justify the (changing) political engagement of the intellectual, on the grounds of trust in a specific (and of course not fully impermeable) sort of human dignity. The frequently invoked *les extrêmes se touchent* argument indicates both the depth of mistrust toward Third-Republic humanism, as well as the dramatic political implications that were possible *because of* this commitment to radical humanism.[78] Surprisingly to us today, one could be a fascist and a humanist, one could become a fascist *because of* one's humanism—indeed, like Maulnier, without having to refuse universalism in the process.

We should emphasize the anthropocentrism of all these positions (the Catholic one included)—one of the defining features of humanism at the time. As reactions to modernity under the later Third Republic, all three ideological trends expressed at once their opposition to what they perceived as an impossible and failed project central to this modernity; their targeting of the educational system, especially its philosophical face, reflected the loss of conviction in both its force and its claims for everyday life. But the fact that even prominent Catholics tried to usurp the rhetoric of humanism speaks to the centrality of the human being in their religious claims.[79] For *all* these thinkers, the central question was how to bring back to man his proper pride of place in the world, his status as the founding block of life. A more radical form of antihumanism emerged from this rising mistrust for European bourgeois anthropocentrism, but this would have been impossible without the multiple delegitimations of humanism proposed by the nonconformists, Communists, and Catholics. Thanks to that struggle and delegitimation, antihumanism became possible and found a footing, as antifoundational realists and others adopted the political tactic of rejecting alternative intellectual projects, while adding a second negation, this time targeting all these hopes for a New Man.

But, finally, the motif of exclusivist humanism contributed to a wide-ranging sense of mistrust for humanism in a different way as well. For while a kind of humanism may have served as the good face of each ideology, there was always another side: these new humanisms did not come without baggage—indeed often barbaric baggage. The Action Française did not stand too far from Maritain or Fessard—and with the Action Française came royalist reaction and anti-Semitism. Communism also meant Stalinism (of which Nizan was a radical partisan), and there were enough left-wing critics of Communism such as Victor Serge or Boris Souvarine (not to mention even sympathizers like Gide) to highlight worries of Soviet violence. As for the nonconformists, their sheer plurality of voices, political Germanophilia, and often vague or bizarre grand solutions rendered their call for a radically New Man just as suspect. If liberal humanism was not the answer, their alternatives were hardly cleaner. Moreover, certain events—most striking among them the support of the Catholic Church for Franco in the Spanish Civil War, and the 1939 Molotov-Ribbentrop Pact—even helped lead believers to radical disillusionment from humanisms they had supported against their supposedly false competitors. Even fanatics like Nizan had a breaking point—and the case of Nizan's suicide is perhaps exemplary as a moment of a complete disillusionment with the possibility of making politics meaningful in an intellectual culture torn by division and war. In this battleground of exclusivist humanisms, the delegitimation of classical universalism that took place through political emphases thus facilitated the implosion of humanism in general. Each of the intellectual projects described here managed to cast suspicion not only on rival humanisms but also on the humanist impulse in general. Against the perceived corruption and violence of all these approaches, the radical mistrust of humanism allowed a turn toward negative anthropology as well as toward a new, nonhumanist atheism—and it is thanks to these "humanisms" that intellectuals began to flee established political movements. For what good was humanism if it needed to be tied to a utopian project whose violence it could not stem and whose goals, beneficence, and harmonious future it could not guarantee?

Coda

Perhaps the best articulation of this question was offered not by a philosopher but by a filmmaker—Jean Renoir. Toward the end of *La Règle du jeu* (*Rules of the Game*), released right at the start of the phony war of 1939–40 and only two years after his great humanist paean *La Grande illusion*, the character Octave (played by Renoir himself) steps out of the chateau where a group of aristocrats are celebrating the hunt of the day with an impromptu costume ball. By this point, the performances inside have degenerated into a silliness tinged with anti-Semitism, while both hosts and servants are quarrelling over defunct or trivial love affairs—even the austere and dull gamekeeper of the castle is running around the house shooting at a servant whom he correctly if pathetically suspects of poaching his wife. Octave and the Austrian marquise hosting him have escaped this mess and are reminiscing; in an effort to imitate for her her late father, a conductor he much admired, Octave steps outside the building onto the back garden, stands at the top of a grand staircase, pretends to pick up a conductor's baton, and faces the building. There is no audience behind him—only the porch—and no orchestra—only the windowed wall separating him from the party inside. "And just as in a dream . . . ," he says; he raises his hands to begin pretending to conduct, and the audio track goes almost quiet. We see him from far behind, as if about to make a cross of his body with his arms spread wide, then in a medium shot as he stops his imaginary baton in midair. But then, in a sad, hopeless gesture, Renoir's Octave lets his arms drop. He turns to sit down on the steps. As the marquise—seemingly everyone's object of desire—approaches him, he pushes her away. Only moments later he tells her that as an artist he is nothing, only a failure, a parasite kept by his rich friends (meaning by *her*), that all he ever wanted was to have a connection with the public, yet even that hope is now gone. There is no longer any action he can himself bring to conclusion—not even an escape from this world of fakes and pathos, which is precisely what she asks of him as he finally declares his love for her and unhinges the only bond the film has not mocked so far. The hope of musical and artistic success dreamt up by earlier generations is gone; the dream of art leading or contributing to any sort of social harmony, any real "meeting of the hearts," is gone; the musicians are gone, replaced by tweeting mechanical birds and amateur entertainers; and rather than connect with an audience a conductor has to instead contend with a bunch of idiots clowning around out of reach, staggeringly deaf to their responsibilities and to the demands of the present, blind to the promises they themselves have made and the dreams they have expressed.

In the terms offered by the 1930s political scene, *Rules of the Game* cannot but be read as a supremely antihumanist film—one convinced of the hopelessness of France, of the frailty, hypocrisy, and violence in any of the self-affirming humanist projects of the day, and of the weakness, fear, and impossibility of any real change or improvement.

3

Alexandre Kojève's Negative Anthropology, 1931–1939

> . . . the eschatological themes of the "end of history," of the "end of Marxism," of the "end of philosophy," of the "ends of man," of the "last man" and so forth were, in the 1950s, that is, forty years ago, our daily bread. We had this bread of apocalypse in our mouths naturally, already, just as naturally as that which I nicknamed after the fact, in 1980, the "apocalyptic tone in philosophy." [§] What was its consistency? What did it taste like? It was, *on the one hand,* the reading or analysis of those whom we could nickname the *classics of the end.* They formed the canon of the modern apocalypse (end of History, end of Man, end of Philosophy, Hegel, Marx, Nietzsche, Heidegger, with their Kojèvian codicil and the codicils of Kojève himself). It was, *on the other hand and indissociably,* what we had known or what some of us for quite some time no longer hid from concerning totalitarian terror in all the Eastern countries, all the socioeconomic disasters of Soviet bureaucracy, the Stalinism of the past and the neo-Stalinism in process (roughly speaking, from the Moscow trials to the repression in Hungary, to take only these minimal indices). Such was no doubt the element in which what is called deconstruction developed.
>
> —J. DERRIDA, *Specters of Marx*

1. Christomimesis, Theanthropy, and St. Paul

Among the figures Alexandre Kojève attacked in his 1930s course on "Hegel's Religious Philosophy," St. Paul stands alone. Kojève would routinely assault what he perceived as his contemporaries' philosophical incompetence, but Paul was hardly a contemporary, and still Kojève's criticisms of him constitute the harshest passages of his famous *Introduction à la lecture de Hegel.* Paul, Kojève writes, destroys Jesus' ethics of a life of works and reverts to pagan claims on immortality and a Jewish theology of transcendence to put a distant God back in his place.[1] Paul crucifies Jesus a second time and intentionally empties his tomb—*and thus his life*—of meaning, locating truth only in faith in the resurrection (HRP XXV.12 [E.510]).

That these statements are directed against a competing *theist* interpretation of Hegel (advanced by Kojève's Catholic students and premised on a Pauline sublation of Greek philosophy and Jewish monotheism) hardly explains their ferocity.[2] Nor should this attack be downplayed through a comparison of Kojève with one of his main sources of inspiration, Friedrich Nietzsche.[3] Instead, Kojève's critique should be seen as aiming at the heart of his philosophical obsession with the Eastern Orthodox theme of *theanthropy*, which he reinterprets as the instance when after a long historical rise, Man comes to recognize his ontological status as that of a finite God and thus becomes one with nature, with Being. Kojève's account of Paul hinges on a refraction of Jesus through his own antifoundational atheism and the philosophical theology of Vladimir Solovyov, who mediates for Kojève the treatments of Paul by Hegel and Nietzsche.[4] For Kojève, Jesus is Solovyov's paradigmatic *theanthropos* (God-Man): he is the first man to have understood himself as God, and he is also God's *self-revelation* as (nothing other than) Man. Kojève presents this argument as Hegelian: Jesus exists in a community, where he is recognized by his peers as a God (ILH 258–59)—negating (that is, transforming) the world through *grace* and *works.* In a period governed by Roman law and (in a different sense) by a "nihilistic, bourgeois, and atheist" abandon of a heroic past (supposedly expressed in Greek comedy), Jesus embodies the transformation from this social cynicism to a belief in the divine, all-powerful nature of man (ILH 256), and to an attack on the socioreligious status quo and its conception of man. His peers (the Apostles) record and propagate his life as that of an exemplar to humanity. Because of his self-consciousness of existing (that is, acting) as a God, Jesus, who has lived as a Man, dies on the cross as God. The Crucifixion is a scene of divinization as much as a scene of death: it marks the divinization of Jesus as Man and the death of the embodied God. What grants Christianity its universalist promise and singular status in Hegel's conception of history is then this identification of God and Man (ILH 258), indeed the identification of God and Man that occurs in their death.

The core of Kojève's position is double: Man saves himself *in that* he recognizes his own status as (temporally finite) God, that is, as negator and transformer of nature and existence. Kojève presents this mimetic appropriation of Jesus' *theanthropy* as a promise of overcoming the Greek humanist worldview, as the organization of a self-effacing, self-deconstructing Christianity that leads to man's self-consciousness. Yet Paul's intervention misconstrues the force and goals of theanthropy. Paul, lacking direct personal access to God qua embodied and finite negativity, transforms him into a representation through which the Christian believer can place faith in an infinite divine. For Paul, says Kojève, salvation does not come through works and grace, but through a turn to faith and therefore to representation: Jesus represents the divine realm, faith in which implies nonhuman salvation from human misery. In Paul's hands, the mimetic appropriation of theanthropy by other men is rejected for a *faith in faith,* which turns to a God eternal, distant and not readily accessible to the community of the faithful, a God *in* whom one now *believes for* salvation from the cynical Roman/bourgeois culture (ILH 254–55).

The entirety of subsequent Christian theology redeploys this distancing mechanism through which man comes to believe in a representation capable of redeeming him. Only after some eighteen centuries, argues Kojève, does man come to understand the original promise of overcoming human tensions and recognizing himself as God (HRP XX.3 [E.389]). This accession to divinity occurs at the end of human history, is accomplished through the attainment of full self-consciousness of man's finitude and status as a pure *negation* of Being, and it marks the philosophical novelty and political significance of Kojève's interpretation of Hegel. For, in an apparent paradox, as soon as humanity attains said self-consciousness, overcomes the world of violence that is the basis of its history, and accedes to its own divinity, then negation is overcome, and *Man dies*: he is reduced to an animal of "the species homo sapiens" (ILH 436n), a mere "body in human form" (ILH 388n). This, Kojève states, has already taken place.

2. Reintroducing Kojève

Alexandre Kojève escaped from the Soviet Union in his early twenties, studied philosophy and Eastern languages under the Neo-Kantians and Karl Jaspers in Heidelberg, and settled in Paris in the late 1920s where he turned to physics and set theory before meeting Alexandre Koyré and concentrating again on the history of theology and philosophy.[5] Kojève remains best known for his influential 1933–39 course *Hegel's Religious Philosophy* (the title is important) at the Ecole Pratique des Hautes Etudes, a series of 130 lectures attended by a small group of promising, and later very prominent, intellectuals—among them Georges Bataille, Henri Corbin, Jacques Lacan, Emmanuel Levinas, Raymond Aron, Maurice Merleau-Ponty, Raymond Queneau, Eric Weil, and Gaston Fessard.[6] In these lectures Kojève reorganized Hegel's *Phenomenology of Spirit*, prioritizing anthropological tropes and *replacing* Hegel's ontology and philosophy of nature.[7] As is often noted, he offered a radical Heideggerian reading of Hegel that Heidegger himself had failed to propose in his—by comparison tame and faithful—1931 lectures on the *Phenomenology of Spirit*.[8] Kojève's approach is still famous for three points:

(i)   his treatment of the dialectic of Lordship and Bondage (*Phenomenology of Spirit*, chap. IVa), as the presentation of the violent genesis of man through the negation of his fundamental being, that is to say through the master risking his life and the slave achieving self-consciousness by working, hence transforming nature;

(ii) his religious, theological, scientific, and philosophical thematization of time; and

(iii) his obsession with the climax of history around Napoleon (or Stalin, as he liked to provoke in the late 1930s), which concludes man's advent to self-consciousness and results in the effacement of man.

Kojève's contribution to French antihumanism is widely seen as an amalgam of the first and last of these positions. Because Kojève conceives *anthropogenesis* (the hominization of a humanoid beast) and subsequent history as founded in the conflict of opposed desires (ILH 19, 30), and because he sees the end of history as the end of tensions and violence, he justifies historically transformative action that helps Man reach this end. "It is the Terror that ends slavery, the very relation of Master to Slave, and thus also Christianity. Henceforth Man seeks satisfaction on this earth alone, inside a State" (ILH 144).[9] If the peace that history ends with is the judge of history, then, as one commentator put it, "the negativity that made the arrival of the end possible will, in retrospect, be judged moral, regardless of how violent or destructive it is. . . . Even the bloodiest violence or the grossest injustice, if necessary for the eventual completion, will be (or will have been) good."[10] This justification of state violence and revolutionary terror on victims regardless of reason or obvious purpose is often understood as a late 1930s propagation of the USSR (as an intellectual *justification of* the Moscow Trials).[11] It certainly provided a prototype for the argument widely used after WWII by Communists and fellow travelers trying to play down Soviet violence.[12]

I want to present a different picture of Kojève's thought and treatment of violence, by providing an account of themes introduced in his 1930s writings and lectures, which specifically engage his *atheism* and *negative philosophical anthropology*. This helps to explain the implications of the at-first-sight ludicrous diagnosis of a "death of man" (or of the troublesome legitimation of violence in history), and it also suggests a far more complex system on the basis of which Kojève arrived at these conclusions, affected his contemporaries' perception of the modern human condition, and offered an antihumanism. Three issues give direction to Kojève's 1930s writings and help explain his understanding of violence, his rejection of notions of human nature or permanence, and his conception of atheism as a negative anthropology:

(i)   Kojève's *ontological dualism* and his definition of man as a *negation* of *the given*;

(ii) his concept of *homogeneity* and its effect on issues of negation and anthropotheism;

(iii) his interest in the development of a modern anthropology that follows from Judeo-Christian tenets and climaxes in "the end of history."

What I aim to explain is the mixture of ontology, history, and anthropology that sets up Kojève's antihumanism. In many ways, his is an extraordinary case, not only because of the force of his argument but also because of the bizarre persona he acquired over the years. While for some Kojève was a *master thinker*, the political and philosophical complexity of his contribution to existentialism, Hegelianism, and antihumanism has often been disregarded as capricious.[13] That interest in Kojève has languished while the study of most of his contemporaries and students has flourished is in part explained by four interdependent misrepresentations:

(i)   the continuing trust in Raymond Queneau's version of the 1933–39 Hegel lectures: Queneau supplanted Kojève's scripted lectures with his own summaries (which are not always dependable), thus obliterating the bulk of Kojève's elaborate interpretation;

(ii)   the survival of a Kojève myth, elaborated in part by Kojève's own megalomaniacal misrepresentations of his own work, and in part by the Straussian reading of Kojève (by Leo Strauss, Allan Bloom, and even Francis Fukuyama), which sees him as a respectable defender of evil and state violence (as opposed to the "good" Strauss);

(iii) the long archival languishing of a tremendous amount of Kojève's writing, which has aided the image of Kojève as an off-shoot philosopher who lectured extemporaneously and rarely wrote a word: in addition to long essays on modern mathematics, Solovyov, Pierre Bayle, and a 1,000-folio-page manuscript on "Phenomenology, Philosophy, Wisdom," the Kojève archive includes 770 folios of scripted lectures from the Hegel courses and reveals the total lecture script to have amounted to at least 2,682 folios;

(iv)   the widespread interpretation of Kojève as a Marxist thinker, a claim for which there is little evidence.[14]

Thus, while American commentary on Kojève has centered on the Hegel book and his debate with Leo Strauss on tyranny and modernity, French commentary has emphasized the influence of the Hegelian instruction and has tried to demonstrate why Kojève's reading of Hegel was useful but flawed, indeed how it is possible to return *de Kojève à Hegel*.[15] Much further commentary has been unphilosophical, often restricted altogether to the argument on the "struggle for recognition," and (among Kojève's partisans) downright elegiac.[16] No surprise then that Kojève remains a subject of little philosophical scholarship, that he has acquired the tag of "totalitarian philosopher," or that thinkers as different as Richard Rorty, Robert Pippin, and Jacques Derrida have expressed exasperation at his claims and those of his occasional followers.[17] Given this picture, even arguments that hit the mark on much of what is central to Kojève's thought often cannot reconcile this thought with the existing image of Kojève. My argument aims at a reinterpretion of Kojève's Hegel on the basis of archival and recently published material. Focusing the antihumanist question at this material facilitates a reading of Kojève that is more attentive to his original terminology and the tropes and contradictions of his complex early works. It helps explain why Kojève's "confirming rearticulation" of Hegel's thought became so wildly inspiring in its attempt to reconcile an all-encompassing philosophical System with the fraught economic and violent political world in which Kojève found himself. And it shows how and why Kojève, while attempting for a long time to explain humanity's historical ascent toward anthropotheism, toward its own divinization, instead collapsed into a sort of animality upon achieving precisely this divinization— in other words, how the promise of modern thought and history, far from succeeding, instead inverted into mankind's self-erasure.

3. Ontological Dualism, the "Lieutenant of the Nothing," and a Recasting of Hegelian Negation

In the first chapter, I described Kojève's early 1930s attempt to link quantum physics and phenomenology in a critique of Kantianism and in an account of the limitations of the rationalism/realism debate important to 1920s debates on philosophy and science. Like other contemporaries, Kojève saw in Heidegger and Heisenberg a surpassing of both idealism and classical realism. Heisenberg's principle of uncertainty turned the Kantian noumenon on its head by rejecting the postulate of an unknowable in-itself *in* objects encountered by an observer. Instead, it treated external reality per se as independent from the observer and impossible to understand in terms of determinist reason: this reality thus complemented and contrasted that of the observing subject. Kojève saw this same transformation also taking place in a contrast of Heidegger's *Dasein* [*Being-there*: Heidegger's substitute for, and elision of, man and the subject in pre-Heideggerian thought] to *Vorhandensein* [*presence*: the "being" of the world of objects present-at-hand, the world as constituted by *Dasein* as Being-in-the-World].

Kojève thought that this fundamental philosophical and scientific revolution of the 1920s favored a turn toward *ontological dualism* (as opposed to the humanist metaphysical dualism of the past), according to which the very Being of man could and must be contrasted to the Being of the world that man is "given" [*donné*] to interact with.[18] "As for dualist ontology itself, it appears to be the principal philosophical task of the future. Almost nothing has been done yet" (ILH 487n).[19] The establishment of this argument starts with *L'Athéisme* (*Atheism*), a manuscript Kojève penned in Russian in mid-1931 (two years before the Hegel course), which is fundamental to his claim to be constructing a new philosophical system that reaches beyond existing ontology.[20]

Rejecting any direct, unmediated relationship between Being and Man, and introducing instead Heidegger's definition of *Dasein* as Being-in-the-world, Kojève suggests that just as *Dasein* (rendered "*Man*" in the French translation of Kojève's *L'Athéisme*) finds itself always already being-in, in-the-world, in constant interaction with it, this very world cannot be thought to exist fully independently of the *Dasein* to which it is "given," by which it is encountered.[21] Kojève proceeds to explicate being-in-the-world (Man-in-the-world) *through an emphasis of its contrast to this world*—a world which, *together with* Dasein's *own body and self,* is given to *Dasein* (AT 105). The choice of term *given* [*le donné, l'être-donné*] slants Heidegger's "*es gibt*" (usually translated as "there is") toward a subject that is faced with this "givenness that lacks a giver." "The given" is not merely what is present, or available (AT 107, 122); in a sense, it is *everything that is.* As such, Kojève suggests, it supercedes problematic alternatives like "nature" or "world," that carry naturalist, foundationalist, or classical realist implications.[22]

The "given" then has a sense of a situatedness of the human being that conversely also situates the world, corporeality, and consciousness. *Le donné* is all that is given to one, *including oneself as given to one*: "Man is not given to himself in the void, but in a world" (AT 77; italics mine). *Le donné* is antifoundational by definition because it is based on the interaction between man and the world he exists in, and it does not affirm the independent existence of a mind or a reality per se.[23] In this expression and interaction, it appears in such a way as to be impossible for Man to identify either as his nature, or as his absolute other. "Here the given is given simultaneously in two ways, but in such a way that one of its forms may predominate, and gradually pass from power to action: *there is the world, and me in the world—[or] me, and the world around me . . . while the given itself is always given as an interaction between man and the world, that is to say as 'man in the world'*" (AT 105; italics mine). Insofar as *the given* is what *is-there*, what *is*, what *is recognized* by Man *as Being* (AT 71), Man must conversely be identified with the negation of *all* that he is given, including himself. Because there is no eternal nature of man, Man's thoughts and actions involve an interaction with the given *that involves and requires the transformation of the given.*[24] Such a transformation occurs even with Man's thinking because it involves a transformation in the sense of a reinterpretation of the world. Kojève's approach here is unequivocal: the atheist is Man as he rejects transcendence (the very existence of an outside to the *world*). The atheist reduces to *nothing* this possible outside, and defines only (his) world as the field of existence and action (AT 97 et al.). Here appears a basic problem: as Kojève states, idealist atheism fundamentally identifies the speaker with God, therefore founding the world in Man, the subject. An anthropotheism (that is, an understanding of Man as Supreme Being) of this sort is troubling because it amounts to subjectivist solipsism (AT 77) and because it disallows any understanding of the difference between men and things and of the question of the paradoxical for him existence of others (AT 248 n156). The given is thus nothing less than a way out of the argument that the denial of God in a direct "relationship" of Man with God allows Man's self-conception as transcendent God. Kojève treats negation as a form of destruction and transformation of the given. By sheer virtue of the existence in the world of a *Befindlichkeit* (existential disposition), what could imaginably have been a "pure nature" in the absence of a *Befindlichkeit* is directly transformed into a world subject to action, interpretation, and transformation by man. Negation here is (and is intended to be) reminiscent of Hegelian *Aufhebung*, yet Kojève repeatedly discards the Hegelian influence for this "interactive" relationship.[25] (Indeed, in his 1939 commentary on "Lordship and Bondage," Kojève renders "determinate negation" as *suppression dialectique* [dialectical suppression], evading *négation* [ILH 21].) More clearly, negation involves the Heideggerian reconceptualization of transcendence in "On the Essence of Ground"—thanks to which the interaction between *Dasein*'s intention and objects in the world is mediated by transcendence as imposition or revealing of world.[26] The negation of the given, this setting aside of man as a kind of pure intuition or intention that a priori exists only insofar as it is a conception (and transformation) of the self, others, and the world, transforms (creatively negates) the world or Being as this would exist in the absence of this man.[27] Now, if man, as a negation of the given (including of himself), involves the denial of all foundation, then, Kojève concludes in an astonishing formulation, atheist man is "ein nichtiger Mensch, der sich in Nichts gegeben ist, der sich nicht gegeben ist, sich nichtet und vernichtet": "a negating Man, who is given to himself in the Nothing, who is not given to himself, who negates and annihilates himself" (AT 184).

This passage is astounding, not least because it is repeated endlessly during the course of Kojève's Hegel lectures—even in the very last one: "Man is a Nothing that negates itself and maintains itself in (spatial) Being only by negating this Being" (ILH 435, 431). It is also striking for its relentlessness: though Man himself is *also* given (and though he is in the given), man is only what denies this "givenness" [*donation*], and ontologically speaking, what denies it *ad infinitem* and *ad absurdum*, and thus what completely lacks positive definition.[28] Unlike the (Christian) believer, who accepts the fundamental existence of an outside of the world, of Man's aspect (such as the soul) that relates directly to what is "outside," to God, and thus offers man a link to a transcendental "beyond" to the world from which he can recognize and participate in God's transcendence ("Man-outside-the-world" [AT 91–103, 118–21]), the atheist restricts belief to the limits of the homogeneous reality that he understands and within which he exists. Thus the given is the basis of existence and human reality—without this meaning that man himself is founded in it, rather than existing as its continuing negation. Man is thus given as at once homogeneous with the world (AT 104–5, 109) and different from it (AT 107)—the fact of his effect on it and self-distinction from it is that, while the given is by and large static, man is far more distinctly Non-Being, a refusal of Being and its permanence, of any determination of the human provided on biological or cultural grounds (AT 110–11, 184).[29]

Kojève's own later emphatic supplanting of determinate negation (in the strict Hegelian sense) with his own conception of *Man as negation* is directly responsible for his reduction of Hegel and Heidegger to the terms of philosophical anthropology and for his identification of Man with a continuous process of becoming (ILH 431).[30] From the beginning of *Hegel's Religious Philosophy*, Kojève extends the contrast of Man and the given, using the above terminology as if it were simply Hegel's.[31] Kojève's treatment of the given and its negation by man begins, first of all, with Mastery, Man's "historically" first self-identification as an individual, as a Negation of nature in Desire—in Desire qua Desire for the other's Desire—in the willingness to die rather than give up Desire; and second in the Slave's uncompensated work for the Master (ILH 27), which turns him into an individualized I and humanizes him out of the status of "living cadaver" (ILH 22). In the last lectures of 1933–34, Kojève indicates that this approach moves beyond the mere opposition of Master and Slave—and it is this ontologically minded extension that interests me here.

This revealing becoming [*devenir révélateur*] signifies that the Totality implies *human* reality, which is not a *given* eternally identical to itself, but rather a temporally progressive act of self-creation. (ILH 532)[32]

Man in Hegel . . . is the Nothingness (*Nichts*) that annihilates given-Being existing as World, and that nihilates itself (as real historical time or History) in and by that annihilation of the given. (ILH 574)[33]

The same emphasis continues throughout the course (ILH 198) until Kojève's concluding lecture, which famously announces the "end of history," specifically grounding this on a presumed end to the fundamental distinction between Man and given Being. Identifying Man with Hegelian determinate negation, Kojève writes, "Man is thus *Nicht*-sein, *Not*-Being, *Nothing*," to be contrasted to *Being*, static-given-Being. "And this Negativity—that is, this Nothingness nihilating as Time in Space—is what forms the very foundation of specifically human existence—that is, truly active or creative, or historical, individual, and free, existence. This Nothingness, too, is what makes Man a *passerby* in the spatial World: he is born and he dies in it as Man" (ILH 431–32 / IRH 155). If Kojève seriously believed that Hegel's monistic ontology was "a complete if grandiose failure," this postphenomenological dualism served as the core of his own effort, the basis for any understanding of man's modern condition.[34] Its claim and effect is distinct: nature and Being are *given*; man is the core of the *Phenomenology of Spirit*, and the movement of the dialectic from anthropogenesis in chapter IVa ("Lordship and Bondage") through death in chapter VIII ("Absolute Knowledge") is not the history of Reason or the progress of Spirit, but the ascent of Man. It is important to emphasize the difference between Kojève and Hegel on this matter, and the productivity of Kojève's reductive approach to Hegel. Indeed, as philosophers from Jean Hyppolite to Jean-Luc Nancy (to stay with the French context) have shown, the *Phenomenology of Spirit* does not allow for a direct identification of Man with *Aufhebung* (sublation) as Kojève requires. For Kojève (already in *L'Athéisme*) interaction with the given permits largely "homogeneous" modes of being. Differences of matter and substance, of form, qualitative content, and mode of Being of the given, and even of different (if complementary) conceptions of the world (physical, mathematical, and so on [AT 77]) do not much alter the fact of givenness, or the ontological relation of man to the individual beings and objects with which he is faced (AT 105).[35] By contrast, the Thesis in Hegel is not coded as homogeneous, while Hegel's determinate negation cannot be identified with Man and involves what Kojève would undoubtedly consider transcendental leaps in *Seinsmodus*, in *worldview*, in the given. Georges Bataille's notes from the course suggest that Kojève allowed this disagreement with Hegel— a disagreement crucial to the ontological arguments of the two—to become apparent throughout his lectures: "According to Kojève, negativity only in the human being—for Kojève: open Dialectical Schema—for Hegel: closed schema."[36]

4. Homogeneity, Ontological and Social

An extension of this argument, further distancing Kojève from Hegel's concept of determinate negation, involves what Kojève calls *homogeneity*, a strategic idea that limits Man's negation of the given. After discussing homogeneity as a mathematical concept in his as yet unpublished 1929 typescript *Zum Problem einer diskreten 'Welt,'* Kojève introduced it anew in *L'Athéisme* as a question concerning ontology and developed it further in *Hegel's Religious Philosophy*, adding a sociological dimension to this original ontotheological basis. By 1936, Kojève had become convinced that the goal of history in Hegel was the construction of a *homogeneous* universal state, in which men were virtually indistinct from their given environment, where action "produced" few changes in this environment, and where human satisfaction was the norm and any attempts to radical change were by and large nonexistent.[37] Kojève soon came to question the ontologically affirmative style of this sociohistorical teleology, veering between it and a position that if the meaning of history is not known by us, then the universal homogeneous state *is not just* the marker of history's conclusion *but also* the conclusion of humanity as such. By the late 1930s, homogeneity mostly holds this latter, negative connotation, and the end of history no longer involves just the rise of man to universal recognition and satisfaction, that is, to the eradication of tension and hence of negation. Instead, history's end denotes the triumph of homogeneity over negation, the reduction of man to a condition that would be uniform with and indistinct from the world that surrounds him.[38]

So, what is homogeneity? In *L'Athéisme*, the term signifies *immanence, consistency,* and *internal diversity* (AT 126), and it is applied, first of all, to beings and to the world. Something is homogeneous when the differences between its parts are not such as to form self-sufficient totalities of their own, or, simply put, when as such this something is basically the same. Kojève uses it to suggest that the given the atheist finds himself in is a world marked only by immanence, an immanence man unsuccessfully seeks to overcome (AT 95, 106–10, 126–30). "'Man in the World' as 'Man who lives in the world' constitutes a homogeneous whole closed in itself (in its givenness to itself), . . . delimited from all sides by death" (AT 126). Man-in-the-World is *as such* homogeneous insofar as his existence is marked by the lack of transcendence from the world or from himself. He identifies death as the main limit to homogeneous existence because it either marks the radical end of this existence, or suggests for the theist the existence of "l'homme en dehors du monde" (Man-outside-the-world), that is, a beyond premised on a Platonic/Christian, metaphysically dualist conception that postulates the soul to be fundamentally transcendent to man's immanent existence (AT 96, 98, 121, 127). Man-outside-the-world is radically other, or heterogeneous, to Man-in-the-world, in fact no less heterogeneous than death per se and the *nothing* that can be identified with death. This is because Man-outside-the-world demands the existence of an *outside* to the given, because Man-outside-the-world is premised on the irreducible fact of death as radical annihilation of Man-in-the-world—a death that reveals a metaphysical possibility not bound to the world. It is thus not possible to reduce Man-outside-the-world to the limitations of what is homogeneously given to Man-in-the-world (AT 127). That is to say, given the irreducibility of the heterogeneity of death, theism is open to transcendental concepts such as of God, Man, the soul, and so on; these are *given* to the theist, just as death is *given* to the atheist. Atheism is not open to transcendence; it merely postulates human existence to also be immanent to this conception of Man as negation. "In his interaction with the world, man does not step outside these limits, and despite actions he directs or submits to, he remains within the limits of the (spatio-temporal) world and conserves with it the same mode of being. . . . Despite their differences, man and the world participate in the same reality of things, they are homogeneous in their mode of being and joined in their opposition to the nothing" (AT 109). If Man's existence is homogeneous, then the interaction between him and the world expresses the homogeneity of these constituent opposites inasmuch as it is only possible on the grounds of a certain reduction of each to terms provided by the other: "Man and the world participate in the same reality of things." That is to say, the difference between contrasting, homogeneous wholes does not reduce these to each other ("Man and the world are not totally homogeneous" [AT 107]), but it does suggest that the interaction between them largely ignores those parts of each that do not immediately correspond, translate, or apply to the interaction itself. "The given of what may be to 'man in the world' is a certain kind of interaction between him and what is given him. The interaction presupposes and conditions homogeneity; or, rather, homogeneity is there as an interaction that separates and reconnects two separate but connected somethings that do not exist as such beyond the interaction where they are homogeneous" (AT 127). Thus conceived, homogeneity is significant for two reasons. First, it provides a frame for negation. Because interaction between man and world is homogeneous, the ontological difference between the two can never be considered in terms of man relating to, interpreting, or altering this world by even momentarily "stepping out" of his existence and experience. Negation (again unlike sublation) is bound to and by the world. Moreover, it follows from there that the homogeneity of Man-in-the-world, of the given, and of Man's negative interaction with it is distinct from and indeed rejects any a priori validity of a philosophical, religious, or ideological apparatus constructed to explain, coat, or ground this interaction. Here, the postulation of Man-outside-the-world fundamentally alters the metaphysics of human existence by allowing the existence of transcendent values and an idealized representation of man. As he does not see this in Hegel, Kojève declares him an atheist (ILH 538). To put it all too bluntly, there are no absolute values for the atheist, there are no identitarian arguments that can make ontological or metaphysical sense, *there is no figure of Man that can rise to take the place of the God the atheist denies*: the denial of any transcendence other than in death (in other words, other than that of the nothing) is necessarily absolute.

The second reason follows from the first: homogeneity organizes and contextualizes the fundamental ontological dualism that animates Kojève's thought. In the above passages, it is clearly identified as constraining and disrupting the radicalism of the distinction between Man-in-the-world and world: "Homogeneity is there as an interaction that separates and reconnects two somethings that are separate but interlinked" (AT 127). By locating Man (as negation of the given) squarely within the limits of *world*, Man-in-the-world premises negation inasmuch as it rejects any sort of transcendental influence on the world and the given by something fundamentally external to these. As this immanence is saturated by homogeneity, negation is not a process that fundamentally alters the world in toto; it is not a process that alters the world's limits and structure. It is a set of thoughts, intentions, and actions that form, present, and to a limited extent change the world, that do so in a sense as ordinary as it is lasting and significant for the particular Man-in-the-World that is thinking and acting them.

Given this peculiar interpretation of negation, it is no surprise that in some of the most important among his Hegel lectures, Kojève specifically denied that the dialectic formed the core of Hegel's method (ILH 38, 449, 455, 460) and actually argued that Hegel may have been the first nondialectical philosopher (ILH 460), or that Hegel's method was fundamentally speculative and akin to Husserl's phenomenology (ILH 38–39, 57, 449).[39]

Insofar as the structure of Kojève's own notion of negation takes over that of *Aufhebung* in the Hegel lectures, Kojève can be said to distance himself from Hegel's conceptual machine by turning negation into a necessary moment in each "Thesis" that seeks to undo this Thesis: a moment identified with man and undermined by an essentially self-preserving Thesis. In *Hegel's Religious Philosophy*, homogeneity appears only in lectures dealing with the end of History, where it lurks behind Kojève's claim that in Hegel's "Universal Homogeneous State" all men recognize each other (ILH 145). In the last few lectures on Hegel's "Absolute Knowledge," the claim that existence in the posthistorical State has become fully homogeneous has a fundamentally flattening character: it expressly undermines the radical character of ontological dualism by suggesting the reducibility of man to (static, given, *homogeneous*) Being, which is undifferentiated among men, animals, and the inanimate).[40] By a peculiar extension, homogeneity in posthistorical existence (the destruction of tension and undermining of radical negativity) necessarily entails men's *satisfaction* with their condition because it implies that if they were not satisfied, they would continue transforming the world. This issue is of exceptional consequence in Kojève's reading of Hegel. What it means is that, taken to its extreme, homogeneity obliterates any distinction between man/negation, on the one hand, and the given/world, on the other, that is, it is impossible to have any further historical or dialectical movement. The universal homogeneous state, in which all citizens are satisfied, is also the world that no one can manage to overcome. Man is at one with his environment (however "good" it may be). Homogeneity, in this sense synonymous with Heidegger's inauthentic existence, irons away Man's individuality and denies the irreducible singularity of his death, transforming the recognition of each individual by every other into a universal recognition of their satisfied impotence and indifference, and hence rendering invalid any serious rapport with death: men die and live in indifference and inaction. If the above analysis of Man in terms of negation and homogeneity is still formal and by and large ontological, Kojève did proceed, during the later 1930s, to provide it with a more social, historical, and specifically modern face, as well as to rid it of "optimistic" and quasi-utopian expectations.

5. Reason and the Modernity of Philosophical Anthropology: Reactions to Bayle and Fessard

By June 1937, Kojève had completed his translation and commentary of chapters I through VI of Hegel's *Phenomenology of Spirit*, and he was reaching the heart of his interpretation, the chapters "Religion" and "Absolute Knowledge." By that stage, Kojève's deployment of philosophical anthropology out of Hegel's *Phenomenology* had long centered on the relationship between Heidegger's concept of finitude and Hegel's struggle for recognition that Kojève had treated as the instantiation of *anthropogenesis*, the birth of man out of a prehuman consciousness.[41] Yet despite its fame, the Hegel-course with its twenty-plus seminars a year hardly suffices as a description or summary of his mid-1930s activities and thought. After starting the Hegel course, Kojève published extensively on contemporary philosophy and the history of science in several journals, such as *Recherches philosophiques,* the Frankfurt School's *Zeitschrift für Sozialforschung,* the *Revue philosophique* and the *Revue de synthèse*. Together with the Islamologist and Heidegger translator Henri Corbin (with whom Kojève had followed Koyré's courses and also Marcel Mauss's 1929 course on the gift, and who was also his student) he translated Hendrik de Man's *L'Idée socialiste,* a fundamental moment in the Belgian socialist's self-distancing from Marxism.[42] In the summer of 1937, he paused teaching of the Hegel course and turned to two other projects: (i) a long review of two books by Gaston Fessard, a controversial Jesuit student of his Hegel course and himself a translator of Hegel; and (ii) a course and an article on the thought of the seventeenth-century philosopher Pierre Bayle and "the origins of liberalism," which Kojève would later consider crucial to his intellectual output.[43] Two questions originating in the Hegel course permeate and organize Kojève's approach to these projects: *the role of Reason in the rise of Spirit,* and *the existence and details of a specifically modern conception of man*. Kojève's engagement with these thinkers' works radicalizes certain anthropological tropes and abandons a positively teleological Hegelianism for a skepticism toward rational, anthropocentric progress.

(a) Kojève on Reason in Bayle and Fessard (and Hegel)

Until mid-1937, Kojève's treatment of the rise of Spirit to the end of history tended to treat this end as the pinnacle of rational philosophico-historical progress. Largely a "positive" development, this rise leads, Kojève writes, to superior human self-consciousness and to a realization of universal citizenship in a rational, peaceful state (ILH 145–49). He postulates the rationalist ideal of the Enlightenment as an undisputed part of this story, as *a secular marker of Western man's debt to the Judeo-Christian legacy*: only with Hegel (and Napoleon) is this legacy finally overcome (ILH 536–37). Even though Kojève argued for a primacy of anthropological problems over rationalizing themes, and despite his explicit opposition to 1920s rationalism, in the early courses he did not express major qualms about Spirit being fundamentally rational.[44] In the lectures of 1935–36 and 1936–37, Kojève grants three principal themes to Reason: (i) Reason is a par excellence Christian element; (ii) Reason equates (that is, reduces) the *world to one's* rational mind *and overcomes anything that gets in its way*; and (iii) Reason thus reveals, for the Christian, a complete and successful understanding of the given. Under the heading of this quasi-transcendental reason, the world becomes totally rational (ILH 80–82). Accordingly, the 1935–36 lectures on chapter V (Reason) of the *Phenomenology of Spirit* set up the advent of the universal homogeneous state in Hegel as a conclusion of Christianity and a triumph of Reason.[45] In these descriptions, complications posed by Reason are overcome: the rational Intellectual, an embodiment of individuality, seeks to move past the *Tierreich*—the "kingdom of beasts" of intellectuals in the ancien régime—and even becomes aware of the limitations of Reason (for example, as presented in Diderot's *Rameau's Nephe*w).

While working on Bayle, Kojève changes registers altogether. He treats Bayle as a radical rationalist, concerned above all with using Reason to oppose religion as it manifested itself around him. In the Bayle lectures, the core problem appears to be the very *definition* of Reason, its power and its limitations. Kojève treats Bayle's concept of Reason as strictly immanent and antifoundational (BA 7–9): a self-subsisting force suppressed by the Church, yet persistent to the point of undermining itself.[46] Pointing out Reason's dependence on a state tolerating and supporting it, Kojève emphasizes Bayle's distinction of Faith from Reason, of the Church from the Republic of Letters. In order to insist on this distinction as basic to a liberalism founded in tolerance, Kojève praises Bayle's concept of Reason for allowing a resistance to both fascism and communism—in the same way that in the seventeenth century, for Bayle, it had opposed both Catholicism and Protestantism (BC 19). It is the particularity of this concept of Reason, which appears in its radically directionless character, that explains its force. Kojève distinguishes less between Faith and Reason than between two respective and "fundamentally different" conceptions of man. These conceptions parallel, by and large, his contrast of the atheist to the Christian in *L'Athéisme*. The first of these covers decidedly the Faith/Reason opposition; the second allows for a limited notion of reason and a belief in the need for action.

There are, I believe, two essentially different ways of understanding man. For one, the individual is directly and immediately attached to (theoretical or "moral") values that subsist independently of the existence of the individual, of humanity, of the empirical world where men live. This immediate, essentially contemplative, and inactive contact is the properly *human* content of the life of the individual, who consequently, can and must become disinterested in all (natural or historical) empirical conditions of his existence. *For the other* way of seeing (which I read in its radical form), values transcendent to the empirical world do not exist; the life of the individual is limited to his relations with nature and with other men, and—these relations being necessarily active—it is action rather than contemplation that constitutes the *human* content of individual existence—technical action vis-à-vis nature, and moral action vis-à-vis other men. (BC 16–17)

Kojève expressly locates Faith and Reason on the side of the first conception of man—where they serve as values independent of immanent reality. The second conception is a "Weltanschauung *in statu nascendi*" (BC 16): it concerns much more clearly an approach to the question of everyday life in modern society, and it allows a new opposition, between socioreligious *conformism* to a *nonconformist, revolutionary rejection* of the parameters set by society and political culture (BC 17–18). In this worldview, Reason is reduced to a strictly immanent and personal reason ("my" reason). "To escape from embarrassment . . . man had to give up the egoism premising him as rational man. He had to distinguish between his Reason and Reason itself" (BA 9bis). Kojève expressly rejects the modernity of an absolute or quasi-transcendental Reason standing beyond the conflict of individual reasons (a conflict that cannot be overcome [BA 10–12]), and he criticizes Bayle for remaining an exemplary "conformist" intellectual of the Enlightenment, for forcing "reason" to give way to "Reason." "To save his faith in

Reason, he was forced to abandon his clear and perfect trust in the reason that was his" (BA 9bis). Instead, a fully modern concept of reason would accept the primacy, radicalism, and necessary limitations of the desiring, reasoning subject and would allow for a conception of society as the inter-action of desiring, rational individuals. Because Hegel's Reason does *not* go beyond the "first" above conception, Kojève proceeds (in terms that evoke Rosenzweig and Adorno) to explicitly abandon Hegel's Reason for belong-ing to the "first" conception of the world, *for being totalitarian and myth-ological* (BA 9bis).[47] The conclusion is startling: Hegel's Reason is merely an alternative to faith in a conception of Man founded on transcendental values. Instead, Bayle's concept, based in part on his "skeptical positivism" and his objection to any external, divine transcendental Reason, allows us (i) to see the difference between the two concepts, the "totalitarian" and the more limited, "personal" one, and (ii) to note the passage from one to the other and even the second's inability to fully escape from the Judeo-Christian worldview.

This second conception of "Reason" is dissected further in Kojève's review of Gaston Fessard's books *Pax Nostra: examen de conscience inter-national* (1936) and *La Main tendue? Le dialogue catholique-communiste est-il possible?* (1937).[48] In the two books Kojève reviews, Fessard specifi-cally engages in attempts to bridge the divide between Communism and Catholicism, on the grounds of what he perceives as their shared Pauline, internationalist, and egalitarian hopes, writing with the expectation that the terms of this engagement would really be the Catholic ones.

In his review of Fessard, Kojève again speaks of Reason and "my reason" specifically as tools for philosophical thought, implicitly reject-ing the existence and power of a Reason beyond "my" reason (DKH 134/190). Conceding such a Reason would force Kojève to qualify his equation of atheism with the rejection of transcendence and hence per-mit an interpretation of modernity "after Hegel and Marx" founded on Fessard's "Platonism" (DKH 132–33/188–89). More importantly, it would mean conceding to Fessard a *rational* progress of History, with a "defini-tive and absolute" *rational* meaning, and leading to a *rational* end (DKH 134–35/190–91).

I believe this much can be granted to Father Fessard: If history (in its entirety) must have a *meaning*, recourse must be made not only to the Good-God of Plato, but also to be the God-Mediator, to the God-Man of the Christians. Only—who says and who proves to me that history *must* have a meaning—or, more exactly, that it actually has one? Certainly I, like every man, have *wished* it were so. . . . But is this something that *can* be discussed rationally or philosophically? It seemed to me that Father Fessard was addressing my *reason*. (DKH 133–34 / 190; trans. modified)

"My *reason*": unlike "my faith" or my trust in a transcendental Reason, my *reason* may not accept the conviction that there is a given meaning to history (even less that there is a positive meaning to history). We find here one of the principal skeptical corollaries of Kojève's antifoundational atheism: the course of the negations of the given cannot be seen as directed toward an end that is a priori meaningful and "good" for man. The recognition that Reason doesn't validate a progressivist, rationalist teleology of history in Hegel, but is rather a totalizing, reductive conception with Christian resonance, seems to have radicalized Kojève's approach to Hegel's thought during the last two years of the course, in terms of tone if not express argumentation. In the Fessard review, as well as in the article and course on Pierre Bayle, Kojève distinctly objects to the position for which the progress of history is the movement from Christianity to rational thought—a position that he himself had at times supported (ILH 76). Once conceived as a remainder of the sublation of Christianity that turns the intellectual into a *fundamentally conformist* critic of the Enlightenment era, Reason *as an absolute* is now strictly excluded from the modern worldview and allowed only in the form of a highly personal rational realization of the self and the self's thought. In the 1937–38 seminar, Reason is *strictly* identified with the attempt to eradicate "external reality" while the earlier claim that Reason sublates Religion is also displaced by an emphasis on the sublation of theology by anthropology.[49] During the concluding seminar series of 1938–39, Reason plays virtually no role in Kojève's long descriptions of Wisdom.[50] Bataille's 1937–38 notes contain a single comment on Reason: "The Man of Reason is the Slave who believes himself to be free. Intellectual bestiary of imposture."[51] Kojève's most important student (and personal friend) Raymond Aron would use precisely this attack on rationalism in his own thesis *Introduction to the Philosophy of History*, which he defended in late 1938, to argue against all optimist, progressivist rationalism in history.[52] Kojève's rejection of academic rationalism had evolved into a rejection of transcendental reason and of the teleology that would have it dominate history's end.

(b) Kojève's Contrast of Pagan to Christian Anthropology and His Attempt to Construct a Distinctly Modern Philosophical Anthropology

In Kojève's readings of Hegel and Bayle, the move from revealed religion to atheism is first of all an anthropological transformation. In the same way that it affected his interpretation of Reason, Kojève's study of Bayle instigated and colored a fundamental modification of his understanding of the difference between theology and anthropology in the later Hegel lectures, and, above all, of the status of a specifically modern anthropology, in particular (i) its contrast to pagan anthropology, and (ii) its foundation in and ambivalence regarding Christian anthropology. Kojève's reflections again begin from his relentlessly deconstructive identification of *man* with *negation*. Here, Kojève elucidates and complements this identification with specific attention to themes he sees as expressing man in modernity, whom he opposes to the Greek world, and intertwines with the emergence of modernity out of Christianity. In other words, Kojève approaches negation in terms of *freedom, historicity, and individuality* (ILH 38).

First, negation is *freedom* because it is action. Action is a very broad term that comprises all the approaches by man of his world, from the observation/interpretation of the world all the way to an aggressive, violent transformation of the given.[53] During the 1930s, and increasingly concerned with political developments in both the Left and Right, Kojève slowly moved from an approach that emphasizes the more *observational* aspect of human distortion of nature (negation as beginning with *Befindlichkeit* or the presence of an existential disposition) toward the second, more *violent* approach.[54] This culminates in Kojève's rejection of contemplation in favor of action in his "Lordship and Bondage" essay, the book's introduction (ILH 11). Nevertheless, because of its transformative force and its opposition to Being, *action in each of these guises must be conceived as violence against Being, against the world.* Even in the guise its own descriptive other, that is, as discourse, action interprets and transforms the given world—and does so in a fashion that destroys it (ILH 541–42). Action contrasts man to the world that has fully designed and surrounded his simply animal or given dimension: all and any action on his part is confirmation and practice of his freedom.

Involved in negation is also *historicity,* understood primarily as memory. Historicity permits man to remember and know the forms of the given through which he has existed and which he has opposed. In this operation, the options of negation are limited and at the same time concretized—the specificity of their transformative and violent dimensions is clarified. "In remembering the given which he was and which he negated, Man remains 'specifically determined' by its concrete characteristics, while nonetheless being free from it because he has *negated* it" (ILH 504 / IRH 233; translation modified). This concretization through action and memory is crucial to negation and its practice because it carefully adjusts and reapplies, in the context of Hegel, the problematic of homogeneity, at once maintaining and radicalizing it. Kojève here severely limits man's capacities and fantasies of power over nature and others; in a sense, he concretizes negativity.

To these two elements, Kojève adds a third, *individuality* (ILH 155–57, 505, 535–36), which completes the modern anthropological triptych because it actualizes man's awareness of his finitude (ILH 267). Kojève contrasts the pagan tradition of an eternal, nonindividualized self, to modern man, for whom he postulates essential difference and the recognition of human particularity (ILH 506, 535). In the treatment of consciousness of finitude as the only radically individualizing aspect of modern existence, Kojève is at his most Heideggerian. Individuality further opposes homogeneity's imposition of a fundamental identity shared by all men; instead, the express singularity of a human being, a union of the particular and the universal (ILH 155), is central to the consequentiality of negation and the force of anthropotheism: that is, to man's ability to exist in relation to his death and in strict separation from others.

The breakdown and extension of *negation* into *freedom, historicity,* and *individuality* serves Kojève particularly in that it shows the reliance of modern anthropology on its Judeo-Christian foundation and origin. Indeed, though Kojève distinguishes between a Greek and a Judeo-Christian anthropology, he only inconsistently treats "modern" anthropology as having stepped out of its Judeo-Christian foundation. In early 1934, he argues that Hegel subsumes Christian anthropology into his atheist thinking, and transforms it into a consciously philosophical and irreligious argument (ILH 38 passim). At times Kojève presents a need to conserve this foundation and discard the properly religious import of Christianity; on other occasions, he appears willing to suggest that modern anthropology is the direct result of anthropotheist dimensions of Christianity, of Christianity's self-undermining construction of a religious distinction between Man and God. Through this concrete overcoming of Christianity in modern secularism rises the "advent of absolute philosophy" in Hegel, which reveals that *human reality* (also Corbin's term for Heidegger's *Dasein*) is not an eternally self-identical given, but rather an act of temporal, progressive self-construction (ILH 532). Still, at the time Kojève began his course on Bayle, this problem remained unresolved. In the context of his study of Bayle and his review of Fessard, Kojève poses it anew and radicalizes his position. "Does the abandon of *religious* Christianity necessarily signify a relapse into paganism? Can one not overcome religious Christianity and conserve Christian anthropology—which, more or less all of us accept—in abandoning Christian theology, which implies so many at least at first sight insurmountable difficulties, difficulties that Bayle was so concerned with?" (BC 18). Kojève's reading of Bayle distinguishes between two ways of approaching questions of man, which, though mutually exclusive, often coexist and clash in Enlightenment texts (notably in Bayle himself). The first such view, which Kojève associates with paganism and Christianity, addresses the aforementioned opposition of Faith to Reason and marks human submission to theoretical or moral values said to exist independently of the empirical individual. The second follows in the atheist aftermath to Christianity that begins with the early Enlightenment; here, values held to transcend the world do not exist, and two options follow: conformism, on the one hand (Bayle's choice [BC 17 and passim]), and action, on the other. For Kojève here "it is action, not contemplation, that constitutes the human content of individual existence" (BC 16). Action, conceived no longer in terms of a *contemplation* or *conception* of the world, defines man's individuality: conformism means self-subjugation, freedom involves acknowledgment of one's individual existence and action to enforce/express this. The rejection of transcendence, and with it of

Religion, Reason, and so on, directly aims at the assumption of negativity as the basis of modern existence and individuality.

In Kojève's review of Fessard, this ontotheological argument acquires a more distinctly Hegelian character. Here, Kojève specifically engages the second, post-Christian view of man as a sublation of the pagan philosophical and Christian theological views, objecting to Fessard's argument that the central Hegelian move that constructs a modern anthropology is fundamentally Pauline, involving the synthesis of Christian Faith out of the sublation of pagan philosophy and Jewish religion. In one of the rare occasions where he invokes Marx in the 1930s, Kojève objects to Fessard's contrast of Marx's atheism with Hegel's supposedly Christian Spirit.

In transposing Hegel's historical schema, Father Fessard presents (Catholic) Christianity as the *synthesis* of the pagan *thesis* and Jewish *antithesis* and infers from that that any attempt to "go beyond" Christianity in fact leads to a relapse into either the "pagan" attitude of subordination to Nature and to the empirical given in general, or the "Jewish" attitude of eternal and sterile negation. Now all of Hegel's effort, integrally accepted on this point by Marx, tends to prove that the pagan *thesis* and the Judeo-Christian (or "bourgeois") *antithesis* can and must be *aufgehoben,* that is, *suppressed* insofar as they are unilateral and "false" but conserved insofar as they are true and essential, in and by the post-Christian, or what means the same thing, postrevolutionary *synthesis,* which is essentially atheist and areligious. (DKH 132 / 188)

This position further approaches the aforementioned anxiety that motivates the Bayle lectures—namely, of a fall back into paganism. Through the approaches involved in the studies of Bayle and review of Fessard, the problem of "what comes after Christianity?" hence finds a more substantive answer that recognizes the theological and philosophical underpinnings of Christianity and also avoids treating these as myths that ground modern atheism. Kojève's struggle against his Catholic opponent follows from this schema of modernity, which now grounds a stance on radical secular disenchantment. For Kojève, the drama of modernity is the refusal of myths—a refusal that cannot eradicate their role as a sort-of underground of modern life and thought—a position he would also hold in criticizing the College of Sociology.

[Fessard] has at most shown that the idea of a ("definitive" and absolute) goal of history—and consequently of my action within it—necessarily implies, even for

Hegel and Marx, a more or less Judeo-Christian myth. . . . But the misfortune is that a myth which knows itself to be a myth is no longer a "myth," but more or less a "fable," conventional or not. And the misfortune of "modern" man that Hegel and Marx had in view, having *been* more or less modern men themselves, is due precisely to the aptitude for *recognizing* myths as such, and consequently in the incapacity of producing and conserving them as myths which are *believed*. To show to *that* man, by an "existential" interpretation, that Christianity is a requirement of a desire inherent in human nature which it alone can satisfy—is to affirm or awaken in him the suspicion that Christianity, even in its "Hegelian" or "Marxist" transposition, is only a *myth*, or an "ideology," fundamentally sexual, social or something else. (DKH 134–35 / 191)

Once again, Kojève rejects transcendental categories, evoking instead the "essentially atheist and areligious post-Christian synthesis" that, during the subsequent year of his Hegel lectures (1937–38), would become the basis and goal of the overcoming of Religion. In these lectures, Kojève recognizes theology as displaced and idealized anthropology and seeks to explain religious history, particularly the gradual secularization of Christianity into Enlightenment ideology. He thus comes to postulate an end of history that lacks any idealist or paradisial basis: man, bereft of myth and Religion, can only look to action, that is, to violent negation and transformation. The critique of Reason and the attack on "myth" are paramount to Kojève's understanding of modernity insofar as they contextualize the overcoming of theology by anthropology and describe the limitations that man has to face, especially the homogenizing process of secularization and the movement beyond absolute Reason as a step into a reality and society the individual is incapable of controlling. On these premises Kojève radicalizes the free historical individual by emphasizing the motifs of theanthropy and of the *Man of the End of History*, while also undermining any notion that pluralism would determine a state composed of free historical individuals.

6. Anthropotheism/Theanthropy

Against the radical homogenization of modern society, Kojève poses a single figure of human existence as specifically resisting reduction, homogenization, and the disenchantment of modern life and as instead fulfilling the rise of Man ever since his genesis in the struggle for recognition and the Slave's work. This figure is the *theanthropos*, or God-Man. Kojève repeatedly presents it in terms that distinctly recall the Nietzschean Overman, Hegel's Napoleon as embodiment of the World Spirit, the Christ of Hegel's early Jena period and of the "Life of Jesus" (ILH 148).[55] Theanthropy is at once a goal of History and a result of the successful coming to self-consciousness of Man in history; the theanthropos is in full consciousness of himself and his finitude, powerful enough to bring about the end of history and also to stand at this end alone in the full light of Wisdom.

Kojève's approach to the problem of theanthropy comes in large part from his early study of the nineteenth-century Russian thinker Vladimir Solovyov. Central to Solovyov's contribution to Russian Orthodox theology and to the philosophy of religion is his entwining of "Godmanhood" and "Sophia." Godmanhood, as is often noted, is first and foremost a reference to the *dual nature* of Christ as God and Man.[56] It is also a conception of Christian history as a gradual redemptive rise of the individual man to *Sophia*, a state of Wisdom that makes man capable of overcoming the Fall and being fully redeemed.[57] Perhaps echoing an obsession of the Soviet avant-garde, which found in Solovyov's thought a call and partial model for its hopes of engineering the new world, Kojève wrote his dissertation under Karl Jaspers on Solovyov's religious philosophy; in the early 1930s, he published several articles stemming from this dissertation, and in 1932, he prepared a series of lectures that he planned as a course at the Ecole Pratique des Hautes Etudes on Russian theology.[58] Solovyov was so important to Kojève that one might argue that Kojève read Solovyov and nineteenth-century European thought through each other. Even though Kojève struggled with what he perceived as an idealist solipsism in anthropotheism from the very beginning of his philosophical writings (AT 76), his early conceptions of man appear to have adopted the notion of a being perfectible to the point of redemption—the realization of Godmanhood in the individual and in humanity in general. This is evident, for example, in the early lectures on Hegel: Kojève specifically retains the conception of man as a being whose rise to the status of God-man brings about the end of history (ILH 148) and who can already be seen in the very inauguration of theanthropy in the death of Jesus. In this context, the force of the critique of St. Paul becomes evident.

As the exemplary *theanthropos*, Jesus is *not* a figure whose effect on humanity modernity should oppose and scorn, but rather the major figure for imitation and recreation, the universalist promise of an anthropology of lived experience and human perfectibility. By contrast, Paul turns Christ into a *representation* accessed through faith, and therefore reinstates a Judeo-Platonic premise of God other than, and transcendent to, man. Accentuated by "Christianity's reliance on private property," the "Roman juridical person," and "Jewish monotheism," this transformation in the hands of Paul forces a certain distinction of the particular from the universal (ILH 255) by substantializing Spirit in a theological representation (ILH 258).[59] But Jesus, coming after the comedic, nihilistic atheism of late antiquity (ILH 255), had transformed this atheism into the promise of anthropotheism, that is, the promise of raising humanity to the point where its divine status will be obvious to all. "Hegel takes to the letter the Christian myth of the—unique—God who in becoming Man, dies as a God" (HRP XX.3).[60] Because Christ died *as a God*, he announced "la dure parole" (ILH 256), performed, via his own death, the death of God, and laid this last as a base of Christian anthropology.[61] Through his death, God has revealed himself to be Man: Jesus reveals at once the absence of a higher being—as he is the one revered by his disciples as a God—and the need to recognize the death of each man as the death of the only being that breaks with Being (nature, the given) to exist as *negation*.

In this way, Kojève advances not only a rejection of Paul's sublation of pagan philosophy and Jewish theology but also a specific conception of the *theanthropos* as a being to be imitated and achieved. Here, Paul allows Kojève to again take up a certain position of Ludwig Feuerbach's thought all the while destroying its conceptual premises.[62] Although he repeats Feuerbach's classic claim that religion is displaced anthropology (ILH 215), Kojève does so with the specific intention of turning man into a finite, nontranscendent God—using terms of Christian thought and identifying the free historical individual he had described with the *theanthropos*.[63] *By blaming Paul, Kojève maintains a Christomimetic model of recognizing one's lived experience as that of a God and one's finitude as absolute, as the basis of modern atheist Man. Kojève considers the God-Man that concludes history as paradoxically reflective of this promise.* This Christomimetic conception of modern man does not concern the specific ethics of life and works that Kojève sees in Jesus, but rather the conclusion of the free, historical individual. As the latter figure permeates the vicissitudes of Catholic and Protestant theology (the very theology that relies on Paul and moves away from theanthropy) it reappears in the conclusion of Christianity with the evolution from Christian/modern anthropology to the end of man: a process of self-overcoming that has led to the Enlightenment and the humanist impulse of modern atheism. It deals with the premises on which the perfection of human self-consciousness can take place, a free, historical individual *capable of overcoming the weight and violence of history and of producing a free world.* In this way, Jesus, like Man at the end of history, embodies Spirit.

In the 1st Stage [of Section VIIc of the *Phenomenology*] where he speaks of Christ himself, [that is to say] of faith in the incarnation of God, Hegel begins by saying that this idea of theanthropy is the central idea of Christianity, the specific, novel, and essential content of absolute Religion [. . . .] I only want to note that Hegel speaks here of the Christian Spirit, or—if you prefer—of Christ, by utilizing exactly the same terms that served him in the "Preface" to speak of Spirit in general. This fact suffices by itself to show that Hegel's thought is not Christian, but [fundamentally] atheist, that is to say anthropotheist. (HRP XXII.2)[64]

In Kojève's reading of Hegel, it is thanks to this intertwining—and not because he is "Desire" or "violence"—that man comes to genuinely equal negation. He is modern, in the sense of *free, historical,* and *individual,* because he has managed, in and through Hegel's conceptualization, to achieve an identification with God. "Christianity is a 'revealed' Religion because it reveals the identity of God and Man, an identity that we should interpret literally" (ILH 258).[65] "Literally" means that Man *is* God: there is no transcendental figure, and man is finite, inasmuch as he dies, yet he is also free and perfect as a negator of nature, the world, the given. For Kojève, Hegel overcomes the dialectic of a Christian religious approach and an Enlightenment-based philosophical approach, moving toward a modernity that recognizes anthropotheism as an existing condition and historical goal. Here, the promise of theanthropy and of its at once inaugural and exemplary instantiation in the Christian incarnation, is both a promise of radical equality and satisfaction and an attempt to step beyond humanity and history into a modernity of radical self-consciousness and a universal community of Supermen. Modernity is thus the self-overcoming or, to use Jean-Luc Nancy's term, "auto-deconstruction of Christianity."[66] "We know in effect . . . that for Hegel Christianity is not one religion among many, but the [*right*] Religion, in the sense that it is a vanishing Religion in the process of disappearing. . . . Christianity is the vanishing of Religions, of all Religions, of Religion *as such*, of the theme of faith in God . . . in general" (HRP XX.3).[67] There are significant consequences to the argument that Jesus's revelation of theanthropy leads to a self-deconstructing Christianity and ultimately to an atheist anthropotheism. We can start to draw some conclusions by connecting *theanthropy* with other themes considered in this essay. On the one hand, Kojève's description of the overcoming of Christianity by and in atheism at once maintains an important religious motif while claiming that it has been fully voided of its religious content and implications. When Kojève says, echoing but also criticizing Feuerbach (AT 182; ILH 215; NA 54), that Christian theology is a *representation* of anthropology that must be overcome in atheism, he seems to argue in favor of the fulfillment of this anthropology by virtue of its valorization and promise of Man as God (Christ in ILH 256–57). But this position not only transforms the very premises on whose basis Kojève's claims might be read as extending Feuerbach's—notably by refusing Feuerbach's sensualist/materialist interpretation (which influenced Marx)—but also by refusing to think of theology as simply a universe of mythical discourse, a representation that serves as a displacement of anthropology. Instead, Kojève presents the world after the Cross as a world filled with illusion—the illusion of a transcendent God—and bereft of the fundamental promise of Christianity, that is, Man's rise to self-consciousness, to an assumption of the status of absolute yet nontranscendent, limited negator as heralded by Jesus. This could be said to secularize Christianity. However, given that Kojève recognized no difference between myth and religion, a description more appropriate to Kojève's terminology is that his presentation "demythologizes" Christianity—that is, empties it of religious claims—while at the same time radicalizing it. In other words, having already rejected the narratives that would hold Hegelian history to be the culmination of Reason or of Christian Spirit, Kojève was paradoxically and systematically stripping the atheist interpretations of Hegel of their fundamental arguments, instead forcing Christomimetic theanthropy as the guide to man's complete understanding and control of the world, as well as to the redemptive promise of the future. Kojève at once utilized and undermined fundamentally religious categories for describing the human being and its history from the Cross (the death of God) to the end. *In this way, he stripped both religious and secular humanisms of their hopes for ethical-philosophical sufficiency and political progress.* Religious humanism (particularly the Catholic version espoused by Fessard and others, like Jacques Maritain) was impossible because it could not fathom the possibility of human good without a Christian God. Secular humanism could not claim access to absolute conceptions of Man or Reason, nor to materialist or sensualist immanence that could justify and prioritize certain types of action.[68] The only possible claim, for Kojève, was that the peace promised in the advent of perfect self-consciousness had to be achieved in man's attempt to reach theanthropy, even through violent self-transformation and the destruction of transcendental hopes. Atheism thus advocates a promise of the future while denying the priority of any kind of humanist present or ethics. *The acceptance of violence is a necessary extension and conclusion of this argument.*

A second consequence follows, indicating further delicacies and paradoxes in Kojève's argument. *At the same time that anthropotheism makes a promise for the future, it also breaks this promise and inverts its universalism into the shallowest homogeneous existence.* That is the fate of the free, historical individual. Throughout his reading of Hegel, Kojève describes three figures as matching this interpretation of theanthropy, three figures aware of their finitude, dominance of nature, and overcoming of homogeneous existence. One figure, Kojève's Hegelian Sage (that is, Hegel and Kojève themselves) is required to draw out the anthropological meaning of the end of history and the importance of those who bring it about. The other two directly claim for themselves the status of finite Gods. These are (i) the Master and (ii) Napoleon (the Man of the End of History) (ILH 30, 153). Surprisingly perhaps, Kojève associates these two "God-Men" not with Christian works but with exemplary instances of violence and the undoing of a world (the anthropogenetic struggle for recognition and the Revolutionary Terror). The struggle for recognition in which the Master triumphs opens human history by initiating negativity proper. By embracing his finitude and risking death to vanquish the Desire of another, the Master rejects and indeed denies his animal being, thus becoming human (ILH 22). Finally, the Man at the End of History (Napoleon or even Stalin) ends history having become satisfied and successfully shown his power, a power he derives from a repetition of the negative power of the exemplary, original *theanthropos*, Christ. To these figures Kojève contrasts modernity as a process of homogenization and a necessary overcoming, that is to say an eradication, of individuality. This is the central inversion, *the basic sublation,* that occurs in Kojève's Hegelianism, and the most significant marker of his late-1930s "pessimism": the denial of universality to theanthropy opens us to the problem of the end of history. Though in the early lectures theanthropy is supposed to be characteristic of all (inasmuch as they have all risen to the post-Enlightenment state of satisfaction, and so forth), here it can only be seen in the extraordinary, messianic exception of the Napoleonic sovereign. Kojève's more pejorative descriptions of the end of history point precisely to this paradox, where the advent of theanthropy is also the death of negation, that is to say the immersion into Being, the death of Man.

7. "Il n'y aura jamais plus rien de nouveau sur terre": The End of History as Death of Man

The above problems usher in the central question of Kojève's late 1930s work, the idea of the end of history, with its immediate consequence—the inversion of the free historical individuals facing theanthropy, into living dead men. This final discussion of Kojève's 1930s thought aims to point out (i) how history "ends," according to Kojève, and (ii) how this implies a "death of man" and Kojève's resulting endorsement of antihumanism. In the late 1930s, Kojève explains the path to "the end of history" by way of two distinct approaches, each of which consists of *several* underlying narratives. Kojève often mixes their registers and approaches, even using each of these to avoid having to justify another. None of these arguments seem to suffice by themselves to make Kojève's point; as a result, many commentaries on Kojève produce reductive and often indefensible positions.[69] More interestingly, these different approaches closely reflect significant moments and developments in his 1930s thought, therefore providing a complex conclusion to (even at times unrelated) questions he raised.

First main approach: Kojève's first approach follows from the discussion initiated above. Anthropotheism inverts its promise of a concrete identity of man and God, turning man at the end of history into a being similar to Nietzsche's last man, an inauthentic, homogeneous human incapable of existing as a free historical individual and instead surviving as a part of the given, human only in name. This largely *historical* and *anthropological* approach is the consequence of two combined narratives. According to the dominant first narrative, the end of history is the satisfaction of human Desire, in other words, of the form of Negation that accounts for *anthropogenesis* in the struggle for recognition. Kojève emphasizes that after the French Revolution, and having combined elements from both mastery and slavery, all men are *citizens* of a global (or eventually-to-be-global) State, having thereby overcome their status as slaves and destroyed relations of mastery and nonrecognition (ILH 146). In the early stage where he first discusses the end of history, its implication has an air we could today describe as open and pluralistic.[70] The citizens and former slaves are here capable of becoming sovereigns, *chefs d'état*, like Napoleon, forcing their will, particularity, desire, and power on the world (ILH 146). The sovereign Man of the end of history, the Man that ushers it in, is a God: Napoleon, in Kojève's repeated descriptions, is fully satisfied in his vain existence and triumph over others (ILH 145–47). Napoleon is "beyond Evil and Good"—a Schmittian hegemon for whom "there is no universally valid morality, except for others" (ILH 153). As such, he is perfectly satisfied, "Man 'perfected' *by the integration of all of History*": "Napoleon is the revealed God" (ILH 153). By 1937–38, this reading acquires a logical if distinctly pessimistic consequence: if Napoleon is indeed the God-Man, no other can produce historical change, even though according to the 1936–37 lectures these others still "recognize" each other, thereby ending the fundamental historical struggle. We find here both an argument about political messianism, and about its impossibility in the present, its hopelessness. In 1939 Kojève openly argues that men at the end of history are incapable of overcoming their homogeneous reality, of negating nature; they are thus reduced to it. *Beyond the sovereign*, people recognize each other only as "equal in their impotence," to quote Adorno: no longer desiring, no longer negating, satisfied in their potential to rise to the peak of the hegemonic ladder.[71] Man's satisfaction is his succumbing to homogeneity and his end. "Il n'y aura jamais plus rien de nouveau sur terre": *Never again will there be anything new on earth* (ILH 443).

A second narrative runs through this first one, substantially buttressing the above anthropological claims. It concerns the achievement of the French Revolution and the Terror, in particular the revolution's successful realization of Jesus's anthropological promise (equality and the end of slavery), and its demolition of St. Paul's construction, Christian theology. Modern revolutionary action, writes Kojève, is not only the consequence of atheism. It is the actualization of Christianity: through it, the atheist brings about the arrival of Hegel's Science.[72]

In the moment when the ideal is realized, dualism disappears—and with it, Religion and Theism. The ideal is realized in and through revolutionary negating Action (ILH 213).[73]

Three things are significant here. First, the realization of the Christian ideal destroys dualism—in the sense of destroying not just the illusion of transcendence but any work toward it and any rendition of it, and ushering in homogeneity. Second, this realization takes place in the French Revolution (ILH 212)—a moment in the past, decidedly not something that political messianisms could strive for. Third, the result of this realization is the "sublimation" (ILH 213) of Christianity by Hegelian thought. What Hegel's contemporaries ("romantic poets, Schelling, Jacobi, Kant himself" [ILH 211]) saw as the divinization of man, Hegel corrected by demonstrating the impossibility of a divinized man in any sense separated from his reality: that is, by humanizing God. In other words, Hegel understood—or, better, acknowledged—(ILH 211, 213, 214) that transcendence is impossible, that the only possible world in which man can recognize himself is reality as he exists in it. This is the realization that allows man to finally place "an 'equal' sign between human ideals and human reality" (ILH 212) and makes it possible for Hegel to write the *Logic*, recognizing the end of human development, the end of human negation of the given.[74] This conscious humanization of God is also the homogenization of Man, that is, the recognition that Man can no longer transform himself radically and, in accepting reality as it is, brings himself to an end (ILH 220).[75] This second narrative joins Kojève's "historical" plot with a distinctly anti-anthropological end. Because humanity now reaches the achievement of its "full plenitude" (ILH 309), because human reality is now fully free and individual and historical, because in short Christianity has been achieved and indeed *realized*, it is possible to say that *man is no longer distinct from his reality, from the given*. Man therefore no longer exists as a negation of the given, or even distinguishes himself at all. Kojève repeats here the objection to anthropotheism he first voiced in *L'Athéisme*: anthropotheism is a solipsism that fails to recognize the difference between men and things (AT 77, 248 n156). In his success, man has depleted himself. As humanity achieves itself, overcomes the world of violence that is its historical condition, and becomes theanthropy, that is, becomes identified with the eternal, the divine, with *Being*, negation is overcome and *men become indistinct from each other and from nature (that is, homogeneous with each other and with nature)* and are reduced to animals of "the species homo sapiens" (ILH 436n), mere bodies in human form (ILH 388n).

Second main approach: This approach is tied to his ontological and metaphysical analysis of Man as *negation*. In identifying Man with negation and contrasting these with the stasis of the given, the eternally self-same Being, Kojève eventually also identifies Man with *Time*. "Hegel . . . identifies Space with Being . . . a move that is banal and very Cartesian. By contrast, his identification of Time with the Self (personal I), that is to say with Man, is novel" (ILH 431).[76] Not only is Man Time, Kojève continues, but the whole anthropological project can be expressed and explained as a consequence of this equation, that is, in temporal/ontological terms. As if he had already argued through his equation of Man and Time, Kojève proceeds instead to justify the very anthropology he has already elaborated on the basis of this final equation:

This is the Hegelian conception of Man=Action=Negativity. . . . Hegel here opposes the Self (=Time) to Being (=Space). Man, therefore, is *Nicht-sein*, not-Being, Nothingness. To oppose Time to Being is to say that time is nothingness. And there is no doubt that Time must actually be understood as an *annihilation* of Being or Space. But if Man *is* Time, he himself is Nothingness or Annihilation of spatial Being. And we know that for Hegel it is precisely in this annihilation of Being that consists the Negativity which *is* Man, that Action of Fighting and Work by which Man preserves himself in spatial Being while *destroying* it—that is, while transforming it by the creation of hitherto unknown new things into a genuine Past—a nonexistent and consequently nonspatial Past. And this Negativity—that is, this Nothingness nihilating as Time in Space—is what forms the very foundation of specifically human existence—that is, truly active or creative, or historical, individual, and free, existence. This Nothingness, too, is what makes Man a *passerby* in the spatial World: he is born and he dies in it as Man. (ILH 431 / IRH 155)

Set up in Kojève's last lecture series, this point is undermined in the "death of man" passage that concludes the course. The death of man is the end of ontological dualism, of the contrast of Man and Being, of the contrast of Time and Being. Kojève again breaks this argument, this time into three parallel narratives depicting the "death of Man" as an "end of Time."[77]

First, Kojève immediately evokes his support for ontological dualism, this time arguing that "there is thus a Nature without Man: before Man and after him" (ILH 432) insofar as human (i.e., negating, temporal) existence requires such a Nature, or Being, to which it will contrast itself.[78] This Nature (or Being), which is eternal, survives man (ILH 434). History, then, which is human history insofar as it concerns the changes of Spirit and not of Being, can end. Which it does, once man has incorporated himself into nature, once he has achieved anthropotheism and can no longer negate the given or distinguish himself from it. This point is emphasized in Kojève's famous 1946 footnote on the end of history (ILH 434–35) and its 1962 extension (ILH 436–37), but it is also discernable in the above arguments and even in the earlier ones. Just as God cannot for Kojève be Spirit (because he does not negate nature and Being), the Man-God that Man becomes at the conclusion of history has found truth and has become Being. He is therefore a part of nature and a confirmation of the end of ontological dualism, in other words, part of the end of negation, the end of man. In other words, once Man overcomes Time by becoming God (and thus losing finitude from sight), by completing History and succeeding in constructing eternal knowledge in Absolute Knowledge and Discourse, at that point there is no more Time, History is complete, and Man can no longer claim that he is crossing in/through Time. Despite its direct identification with Time and Man and just as in the review of Fessard, Kojève's History does not acquire a distinct meaning or significance—instead, it becomes discernable and understandable only from the vantage point where all meaning is clear and no novelty is possible. Man is now a God bound not by history or Time, but by the nature he has created. He loses the singularity of his death from sight and becomes once again indistinguishable from nature.

Second, Kojève depicts the end of History as the end of Time and Man by turning to Absolute Knowledge, or "Wisdom," as the conclusion of Hegel's philosophy. Absolute Knowledge, as Wisdom, evokes, once again, Solovyov and his concept of *Sophia*. Absolute Knowledge is human Discourse that breaks the limits of time; it occurs at the end of history in the "Sage's" look back in time to recognize the realities of history (that is, in the *Phenomenology of Spirit* as developed by Hegel and redeployed by Kojève). Wisdom is the step beyond philosophy, the completion of philosophy and of philosophy as history (ILH 439). As it is identical with Spirit without at the same time being finite and temporal in the sense that man is finite and temporal, it comes beyond rational human discourse and beyond the moment of madness that Hegel "had to endure" and it recognizes the truth of Being ("The Real is the True," Kojève enjoyed repeating after Hegel [ILH 448]). For these reasons, Absolute Knowledge as Wisdom now recognizes Man's negation as an *error* to be corrected, an error that has been overcome and concluded (ILH 433–34). In his self-achievement at history's end, Man no longer has anything to offer Absolute Knowledge except its articulation (which Hegel and Kojève have achieved). Thus ends individuality (ILH 443) and human action—and, with them, man-centered philosophy.

We have seen that this action, proclaimed at first as the essence (*Wesen*) of man, ends up being effaced, to the profit of purely contemplative thought, which is that of Hegel himself . . . and we have seen that this effacement of action, that is, of true Negativity, signifies an effacement of man (in the Judeo-Christian, modern sense of the term, that is, of ideas of individuality, freedom, and historicity that are the central anthropological categories, and that also are the fundamental ontological categories).[79]

A third version of the metaphysical and temporal end of history would appear three years later in *La Notion de l'autorité*. Kojève suggests here that if 1789 was humanity's break with the "Past" and identification with anthropotheism, then 1848 became its break with the "Future."

The Bourgeoisie, created as a political authority by the "project" of [17]89, does not accept the "project" of [18]48 and the combat. It thus turns from this fateful date not only against the Past [which it eliminated in its revolutionary 1789] but also against the Future. It encloses itself in the Present. It is only thus that it is really present. . . . In the Present, the only real, the Bourgeoisie realizes itself as such:

this is the period of its domination. But a Present without Future or Past is but a "natural" Present, nonhuman, nonhistorical, nonpolitical. The domination of the Bourgeoisie is but a progressive disappearance of political reality as such, that is to say of the power or the authority of the state: life is dominated by its animal aspect, by questions of alimentation and sexuality. (NA 145)

A being incapable of dealing with both past and future, a being locked in an eternal present—this is precisely what Kojève considers to be a *homo sapiens* animal lacking Spirit or Time.[80]

But the Present, deprived of the Past, is not *human,* that is to say historical or political, except to the extent that it implies the Future (otherwise, it is a present of brutes). (NA 143)

As for the Present, it "dehumanizes" itself insofar as it detaches itself from the Future. (NA 158)

No negativity means no more temporality, no more creativity, no more man: a satisfaction with present reality unable to overcome its present condition. It is the loss of the self, and of man, into eternal Being. By and large, Kojève interlaced the above approaches and narratives to an extent that rendered impossible an interpretation of the "end of history" that would explain what causes what, how this and that unfold, why all this would take place in 1806 (or, as he used to say, with Stalin). Nevertheless, the basis of this argument is one: Man effaces himself completely at the moment when he becomes a God, that is to say at the culmination and conclusion of history.

8. Influence: Mastery of Self, a System for Marxism, and the Death of Man

Kojève's interpretation of Hegel, its influence on contemporaries, students, and philosophers in the postwar period and its role in the construction of modern antihumanism can be explained in terms of three complex and interrelated aspects of his work and its aura.

First, Kojève articulated in very influential terms and with very clear consequences the conception of modernity as a clash between a *giant Hegelian totality* and a *threatened Kierkegaardian subject,* a clash that was felt as extremely pertinent following the academic rise of Jean Wahl and his 1936 *Études Kierkegaardiennes*, the protoexistentialism of thinkers like Gabriel Marcel and Georges Bataille, the literary output of Malraux and the early Jean-Paul Sartre, or the new investments in Nietzsche and the early influence of Heidegger.[81] Kojève's rendition of this theme placed considerable stress on the tragic dimension of the negating (thinking and desiring) subject, asserting the reason of this negating desire as definitive of human resistance to homogenization. Yet at the same time, he happily sided with Hegelian totality, asserting that an understanding of the world today requires the understanding and assumption of anthropotheism and therefore the overcoming of this dilemma. Non-"theanthropic" men are therefore condemned to being devoured and quashed by history, either through war and violence during its course, or through the reduction of man to animal at the end of history.

Particularly expressive or revelatory of this problem is Georges Bataille's famous "Letter to X (Lecturer on Hegel)." Its overriding question is how, if things are truly as Kojève describes them and history has ended, Bataille's own life—"or better yet, its aborting, the wound that is my life"—which fails to conform to that kind of a posthistorical world, might be meaningful except as "the absolute refutation of Hegel's philosophy."[82] Such a reaction, which Bataille was not the only one among Kojève's students to express, reflects Kojève's influence on his students and his success in drawing up the premises, or parameters, of problems such as the one described above. That is to say, with his setting up of a powerful position in the Hegelian Sage, and his assumption of that position in his lectures, influence, and disregard for their existential anguish, Kojève came to be identified with the omniscient philosophical Master that he only too happily presented himself as—whether out of charisma, out of his form of expression, or out of his particular slanting of the *Phenomenology*. Kojève's self-conception as a new Hegel watching the end of history not only provided a powerful system through which his students also read Heidegger, Nietzsche, and Kierkegaard, but which also forced them into a trap—a reading of Hegel in which only a successful, complete mental effort to conquer Hegel and become a God-Man could amount to Wisdom as opposed to worthless inauthentic life.[83] Bataille's "Letter to X" shows an awareness that those students who, like Bataille himself in the letter, "failed" in this effort, or who rejected many of his positions ended up caught in his conceptual prison, incapable of overcoming his philosophical constructions in toto, *precisely because they were left unable to get out of Kojève's solution to the "tragic clash" between individual and totality*. If Kojève had a "propagandistic" way of teaching, as has been suggested, this was it: his successful confusion of personal and historical categories that left his listeners unable to step outside of his way of setting forth the problematic *and* its solution at the same time.[84] In this way, Kojève almost single-handedly produced what Vincent Descombes has correctly called a *common language* for post-1930 French thought.[85]

Second, Kojève provided a peculiar system that worked as a foundation for Hegelian Marxism. I have repeatedly suggested that Kojève was not a Marxist, except perhaps in the vaguest sense of the term—someone belonging to the Left and claiming (however ironically) to support the USSR.[86] Kojève appears to have been more of a nonconformist with certain Marxist tendencies—at once deeply critical of Soviet thought and society but also apparently committed to Marxist utopia and concerned with overthrowing all existing concepts and idealizations of man. His opposition to Feuerbach's materialism and sensualism, his translation of *L'Idée socialiste* by Hendrik de Man (a socialist text decidedly opposed to Marxism and fundamental to French nonconformism), his endorsement—in his Bayle lectures—of a militant universalist liberalism opposed to fascism and communism alike, and finally his endorsement of the erasure of man at the end of history, these are all significant signs of a certain distance from or philosophical ignorance of Marxism. Kojève's critical perception of Marxism is evident above all in an aforementioned passage from the Bayle course:

It suffices to replace the words "Protestant" and "Catholic" for the words "Fascist" and "Communist" to see that our situation is very similar to Bayle's. Certainly, Protestantism and Catholicism have nothing to do with Fascism and Communism. But there is the same fact of finding oneself in the presence of two doctrines, proclaiming universalism yet mutually exclusive, and the same attempt to maintain oneself between the two and—despite the principle of [tolerance]—against them. This is why I believe that the study of Bayle's arguments, for which he tried to justify the attitude that he took from *his* world, may contribute to a better comprehension of the attitude, analogous to his, that . . . we could take, in the world that is ours. (BC 19)[87]

Kojève's famous February 1939 interpretation of "Independence and Dependence of Self-Consciousness: Lordship and Bondage," published in
Mésures, which occasioned the Marxist reading of his thought by the use
of an epigraph from Marx (ILH 9) and its claim that "in his nascent state,
man is never simply man[, he] is always, necessarily, and essentially, either
Master or Slave" (ILH 15), does not even acknowledge the Marxist argument that the slave's work leads to his alienation from the objects he produces and lacks any sense of (or hint of political support for) an ethics
centered on the slave's liberation.[88] Moreover, Kojève's reading of Hegel
and his political engagement in the 1930s do not pay dues to contemporary Marxist problems—the question of class struggle, alienation, or the
legitimacy of a dictatorship of the proletariat (which Kojève rejects altogether)—but can be understood as participating in nonconformist debates
instead.[89] As suggested in Kojève's argument favoring quantum indeterminism in the first chapter, Kojève also rejected the possibility of interpreting science through a Marxist lens.[90] Though Kojève liked to think of himself as a "Marxist of the Right" and to be perceived as such after the war by
his former student Maurice Merleau-Ponty, his Hegelian rival Jean Hyppolite, and his friends Leo Strauss and Carl Schmitt, his postwar output
only involves criticisms of the USSR as the "only classical capitalist country of the highly industrialized world . . . , which calls its 19th century capitalism by the name of socialism."[91] With the exception of Merleau-Ponty,
who rejected much of Kojève's interpretation of Hegel and who became a
Marxist for other reasons, none of Kojève's interwar students were, or became, strict Marxists.[92]

Nevertheless, it can still be argued, correctly, that Kojève heavily influenced his contemporaries' perception of Marxism. His Hegelianism is
not so much consistent with Marx as capable of providing a philosophical
system from which a vengeful Marx *might* follow. Indeed, Kojève's eventual use of the term "action" to subsume every transformation of the world
clearly suggested, in the Bayle and early Hegel lectures, that the essence
of man lies with the radical transformation of the world by revolutionary
action. Moreover, his systematization of Hegel, and his endorsement of
the end of history as a universal goal worthy of violence, played a central
role in French philosophical Marxism because it provided the basis for the
common "to make an omelet you need to break some eggs" argument that

justified Soviet state violence. In this regard, Kojève's stance on utopia and political messianism is ambiguous, at once advocating "Revolutionary Action" and showing its result as a reduction of life to living death, a life without deliverance or future, an end of history without a true synthesis. For this position, Kojève needed not only the Hegel-Marx tradition, but, more importantly, Nietzsche's "transvaluation of all values" (and its coding in negation qua revolutionary action), Solovyov's apokatastatic fantasies and the promise of the resulting anthropotheism that concluded human history and violence but also turned man, finally, into pure being—a subject at ease with its (not necessarily harmonious) world.[93] In this way, Kojève systematized the mistrust of the subject of classical humanism in the 1930s into an antihumanist attack on the bourgeois existence of modernity that would form the intellectual background for "any future Marxism." This "quasi-Marxism" added one further dimension to the puzzle of his influence. As Kojève's influence was often perceived as Marxist (especially with Jean-Paul Sartre's engagement with Hegel and Marx in the mid-1940s, but also the rise of Jean Hyppolite and Hyppolite's attempts to distinguish his reading of Hegel from Kojève's), and as it avowedly centered on matters of anthropology, Kojève's reading became known as anthropological, as an anthropologization of the Hegelian system.[94] Kojève's reading was anthropological *only* in the sense that it put subjectivist humanism into radical doubt, destroyed any sense of man's humanity except by reference to *negation* (and reconstructing an anthropology out of this negation), and eventually even erased modern man by denying him both his Judeo-Christian heritage (and the anthropology that ensues from there) and his hopes for a redemptive conclusion to history. In other words, it was anthropological only insofar as it was radically anti-anthropocentric, anti-idealist, and antisubjectivist, insofar as it produced a discourse on man *in* the negative (Man is not part of the given or Being), a discourse of man *as* a negative. Still, this misreading of Kojève's reading of Hegel as Marxist and anthropological aided the vanguard character of Kojève's influence and fame, as well as its radicalism. Because Kojève's reading became known as Marxist and anthropological despite its relentless negation of man, it managed to "damage" or seriously undo anthropology "from within," to structure it around a series of questions bound to lead to the decentering of the subject: Man is Negation born in violence and subjugation. But history is finished, so man is dead.

Finally, thus, and most radically, Kojève influenced his contemporaries (and, yet more, young philosophers of the postwar period) through his conception of the end of history. *Both* his interpretations of the human being in modernity, that is, as a violent, negating (hence, free, historical, individual) being, and as a being desiring the end of violence, its own end *as* man, did away with the idealist politics of early twentieth-century humanism, turning instead to a radically realist, historicist conception of modernity. Here, no less than the force of his argumentation, it was the subsequent *forgetting* of certain among Kojève's contributions or sources of inspiration (for example, Solovyov's anthropotheism) that helped the construction of this radical persona. This forgetting made it impossible to understand the inner workings of Kojève's argument and thus highlighted precisely those parts where Kojève discussed violence and the end of history. Overall, this argument was not *the only* philosophical antihumanism of the interwar and post-WWII periods—nor was it necessarily the strongest. But it was a powerful and well-structured approach that included substantial readings of most major recent German philosophers of interest at the time and a powerful system of modernity with the potential of radically influencing Hegelian Marxism. That man was finished, dead, or that he was pure violence directed against his fellow man: these positions landed Kojève in the pantheon of contemporary thinkers and provided substantial responses to the dilemmas of his contemporaries and followers (from Sartre to Bataille, Lacan, Merleau-Ponty, and so forth). Kojève's antifoundational atheism is the first that assumes the legacy of German idealism and its culmination in Hegel, but it also explicitly expresses itself as opposed to humanism and to any anthropology with a positive, foundational concept of man.

4

Inventions of Antihumanism, 1935: Phenomenology, the Critique of Transcendence, and the Kenosis of Human Subjectivity in Early Existentialism

[Sartre] jeered at all humanistic shibboleths: it was impossible, he thought, to cherish an entity called "Man," or indeed to hate it either.

—SIMONE DE BEAUVOIR, *The Prime of Life*

The night we're entering isn't simply the dark night of John of the Cross, isn't just the empty universe bereft of a helpful God—it's the night of real hunger, of the cold we feel in our rooms, of something that seems glaringly obvious in police stations.

—GEORGES BATAILLE, *On Nietzsche*

1. The End of Classical Transcendence and the Illusions of Modern Humanism

If, in the early 1930s, the phenomenological impetus served to overturn the idealist universe, then by the mid-1930s, younger thinkers had decidedly attached it to harsh rejections of both "humanism" and definitions of "the human." In the period 1934–36, Jean-Paul Sartre, Georges Bataille, and Emmanuel Levinas composed and published original philosophical writings that reflected as much their theoretical and political concerns as their engagement with the new phenomenological limitations placed on man and on man's world. Following—to different degrees— the early development of antifoundational realism, Alexandre Koyré's contestation of scientific claims to positive truth, the Heideggerian rethinking of transcendence that tended toward a perception of reality as radically limiting and indeed trapping man, and the Kojèvian restructuring of atheism and philosophical anthropology, these three authors confirmed the decline of classical notions of transcendence and extended the new "human reality" to bear in particular on the prisonlike hold of the immanent phenomenological world. As a result, Bataille, Sartre, and Levinas _all_ opposed humanism as a misguided, obsolete ideology that required the positing of Man as transcendentally grounded subject and failed to understand the implications of violence, the ground and givenness of human existence, and the limitations of finitude.

A parallel close reading of the refutation of the transcendental ego in Jean-Paul Sartre's "Transcendence of the Ego," the rethinking of subjectivity and sovereignty in Georges Bataille's "The Blue of Noon" and "The Labyrinth," and the imagination of excendence in Emmanuel Levinas's "On Escape" and "Reflections on Hitlerism," can highlight the extent to which their critique of subjectivity and idealism came to offer novel theorizations of sovereignty, political engagement, and the possibility of action in a world beyond transcendence. In Sartre's work, the critique of the classical subject involves a specific attack on Husserl's transcendental ego—the part of the phenomenological existent that exceeds the empirical and immanent dimensions of subjectivity as Husserl had laid them down. Published in _Recherches philosophiques_ in 1937, "The Transcendence of the Ego" ("La Transcendance de l'ego") formulated the clearest and most elaborate opposition to the idea of a transcendental human "I" that forges or independently interprets reality, and it explicitly sought to complete the contemporary philosophical "replunging of man" into the world (TE 86 / 105).[1] Bataille attempted, in the aphorisms in "The Blue of Noon" ("Le Bleu du ciel") and in related essays, to reconsider Man, Being, and sovereignty in such a way as to attack the political and theological illusions of both materialist conceptions of the subject and the belief that transcendence was part of this subject or available to it. His argument that man becomes sovereign when he empties himself of social and ontological determinations of himself takes into account precisely the impossibility of any transcendental origin of the subject and the radical limitation imposed by the world. Emmanuel Levinas's first text of original philosophy, his 1935 "On Escape" ("De l'evasion") not only aimed beyond the neo-Kantian and positivist frameworks but also turned against the new realism emerging from phenomenology and contemporary science, so as to insist on the failures of any philosophy that does not form, in its very foundations, the desire of the subject to evade and escape the life in which it finds itself. "On Escape," also published in *Recherches philosophiques* in 1935–36, right next to Bataille's "The Labyrinth" ("Le Labyrinthe"), specifically attacks the pre-Heideggerian construction of a purely human subject as well as the Heideggerian enclosure of man in a "world," positing escape in a transcendence-less world as necessary yet impossible and seeing the desire to escape as the most profound characteristic of a dying age.

To read together Sartre, Bataille, and Levinas serves a number of purposes—despite the fact that the specific texts considered here were little known, and also despite (or rather *precisely because*) their very different projects (and major later differences). First, reading these essays together lays out the positive stakes of the early import of phenomenology. Second, such a reading shows the similarities in these authors' interpretations of the uncomfortable relationships of the subject to the world—their shared denials of the traditional unity, the irreducible I of Reason, and the foundational status of the subject—and by extension their rejections of an eternal or irreducible human essence and the Kantian and Marxist notion that man is his own highest being and goal.[2] Third, by refiguring the more epistemological treatment of transcendence to be found in antifoundational realism into an explicit breakdown, these texts lie at the limit between a general *Existenzphilosophie* concerned with explaining the status and position of man and an *existentialism* in which positive determinations of subjectivity only serve to oppress the individual existent. Most importantly, they expand this critique of transcendence and of received definitions of the human to provide different determinations of the human that would not accept a positive content.

No less significantly, these philosophical critiques have distinct political consequences. It is fair to say that the three authors shared a general nonconformist contempt toward existing humanisms, as well as toward the state of French politics. *Recherches philosophiques* itself seems to have shared the critiques of existing political philosophies to be found in nonconformism and several interestingly ambivalent figures (for example, Arnaud Dandieu and Denis de Rougemont) published in it. Nevertheless, it lacked a defined and specific political project, and its philosophical opposition to established thought did not suggest a positive alignment with the political claims and alignments of nonconformism itself. Its directors shared none of the political positions that led nonconformism toward fascism. Like *Recherches philosophiques*, which did not publish efforts to retrieve a fundamental essence for man, Sartre, Bataille, and Levinas also opposed the nonconformist hope of refounding man or giving him a new birth in the purity of his nature. Reading Bataille, Levinas, and Sartre together shows the aggressiveness with which they opposed contemporary political considerations of humanism as involving access to transcendence (as posited by Catholicism), to an eternal and retrievable human nature (as posited by personalism, for example), as subsuming a perfectible humanity (for example, as per the neocriticists, such as Brunschvicg), or even as citing man's dependence on "genuinely universal" equality and a totalizing or teleological capture of history (as argued by Communists and some nonconformists). Rejecting these widely received approaches was crucial to the counters offered by each of these three authors. Against a conception of humanity as identified with the transcendental ego (where all that is human would be reduced to my nonempirical "I") Sartre identified "humanity" with the interpersonal realm, with "my" actions as these occur within experience and shared with others. Similarly, Bataille saw "old" conceptions of humanity as homogenizing, as destructive of difference, and as ultimately destructive of the particularity (the internal tumult) of the subject; against that humanity, Bataille sought a conception of subjective sovereignty that arises when the subject is emptied of all determinations imposed on it by the homogenizing political world, when the subject escapes from this world. In his criticisms of contemporary thought and culture, Levinas contemptuously linked existing humanism with a bourgeois drive toward self-sufficiency, which involves the construction of an

I that forgets and oppresses all that is "not-I." Adding to this position, Levinas also attacked any identification of humanity with reality or Being, which for him follows the arrival of Nazism, as well as of Heidegger's thought, whose drive toward Being and whose claims on man reflects the Nazi reduction of man.[3] This shared redefinition of "the human" as following from a weakened and trapped "I" incapable of transcendence, internally divided and emptied of a subjectivity based on the capacity of consciousness to command the world, is fundamental to the move from an *Existenzphilosophie* based on the epistemological and phenomenological antifoundationalism and realism of the 1930s and toward a clearly existentialist questioning of the anxieties and political powerlessness of the subject. By extension, all three authors see their recognition of the fallacy of man's access to transcendence as now locking the subject in a reality that it literally has no power over, an existence it can only hope of overcoming or sidestepping, and hence a fascination, desire, need for what Levinas calls "excendence," or what Bataille treats as sovereignty overcoming the homogenizing determinations of the subject. Levinas's replacement of excendence for (the no longer available) transcendence is not just exemplary but foundational of this new condition, of the atheist existentialist demand for an overcoming of a condition that cannot be overcome—a motif that would find many parallels and echoes in later existentialism. Sartre's attempt to efface the transcendental ego into a social I in order to permit a thinking of man's anxieties and his revolts, man's (to use Levinas's term) being-riveted in the world and to Being, similarly emphasizes the inability of "the me" to escape and presents the hope that such an immersion will permit a thinking of both everyday life and its losses. Each of them thus rejects, refutes, and seeks to overcome humanism as a radically destructive fantasy, which in the name of preserving the self destroys its genuine and fragile selfhood and produces an illusion that is ultimately as violent as it is misconceived.

2. Humanity as the Realm of Intersubjectivity in Sartre's "Transcendence of the Ego"

Explicitly seeking to reduce the human subject to the Husserlian empirical, psychophysical *me*, Sartre's "Transcendence of the Ego" first doubts and reorganizes the necessity and utility of a transcendental *I* or *ego*, and then proceeds to use this doubt to critique subjectivity. The essay, Sartre's first phenomenological one, was written in the aftermath of Sartre's 1932–33 stay in Berlin and was published in *Recherches philosophiques* in 1937, in the same volume that his work on *The Imagination* was reviewed and criticized.[4] The title of the essay is itself polysemic: *transcendence of the ego* could be said to point (1) to Sartre's target (the classical transcendental ego), (2) phenomenological consciousness as a transcendence of this classical ego, or even (3) a performative operation by which Sartre's essay transcends the (transcendent) ego. The title thus replays and emphasizes the complex terrain on which Sartre tries to undermine the ego whose transcendence is philosophically unwarranted—or differently put, to reject the Kantian (transcendent) ego—when he theorizes subjective existence as immanent and largely separated from transcendental consciousness. Implicitly granting Wahl's realism and Heidegger's understanding of *thrownness* and *world*, he denies that the I, the subject, scientist, thinker, or individual can account for consciousness beyond experience.[5] *Contra* the Kantian critical project, whose aim is to establish the conditions of possibility of such consciousness, phenomenology deals with the *fact* of consciousness and therefore is "*a scientific, not a critical study*" (TE 17 / 35).

Sartre's treatment of the transcendental I rejects it as both a formal structure of consciousness (TE 37–39 / 54–55) and the empirical condition of its possibility (TE 26 / 43). Instead, he proposes an alternative approach to the link of consciousness and the empirical self, a breakdown of the classical subject and a rejection of the priority of the "I," such that consciousness will itself remain transcendental, absolute, inhuman, and impersonal, while the subject will exist, reflect, and function only in immanence and society, specified and interacting as a "me" (TE 18–19 / 36). Thus, while consciousness transcends experience, while its capacity for reflection and intuition remains distinct from the empirical world and serves as the agent of the Husserlian *epoché*, the subject, the me who speaks and copes, is fully reduced to empirical reality. Through this determination, the "I" (the ego, as opposed to the "me") can no longer be a connection to transcendence and consciousness, nor even a constituent element of the unity of the subject, but rather is relegated to being the active face of the empirical me in the world (TE 44 / 60). Gone are the claims to a transcendental origin of personality and individuality, as well as the appeals—so dear to neocriticism—to a history of the Western mind that would be formative of the individual. For Sartre, these involve a basic confusion about what is absolute and what is empirical, conflating consciousness, the empirical self, and the I of this self, and mistakenly turning the individual into a form of transcendence evoking and imposing its alleged superiority on the empirical domain. At stake instead is the maintenance of a consciousness as irreducible to the specific I, or even to its general empirical incarnation, its background as a me. Two passages foreground and intertwine Sartre's attention to "the human" in the context of this philosophical antisubjectivism.

The first is an ambiguous note early in the text suggesting that the main direct consequence of the erasure of the transcendental ego is the complete association of the human with the social and the interpersonal: "The I only appears at the level of humanity and is only one aspect of the me, the active aspect" (TE 19/36). This point involves a number of philosophical operations—some of which Sartre initiates himself, some of which he inherits from Husserl and pushes here in a specific direction. What is significant is that Sartre's organization of the relationship between *transcendence, consciousness,* and the *I* specifically defines this last by contrasting it to *both* the realm of transcendence *and* the form and meaning of consciousness, indicating it as a sort of experience of interpersonal, immanent existence. Consciousness cannot survive a philosophical construction that would simply identify it with transcendence through the intervention of the ego (TE 23/40). Such an identification would destroy consciousness in its purity so as to reconstruct a unified subject—and would therefore destroy the transcendental realm as such. We cannot understand or set up phenomenological consciousness by way of a transcendental formalization of the individual I: we would fall back to Kantian idealism. Consciousness is antisubjectivist—it is *with me* but not just *mine.* It is shared, much in the way that in Heidegger the structure of *Dasein* is shared among different beings, and cannot be identified with a single subject. Here, it would be impossible to imagine a shared dimension to reflection that would not fully depend on the reduction of all minds to *my* mind, to the fully empirical construction of minds, to terms of a condition of possibility of consciousness. Thus, consciousness needs to be transcendental per se, but without simply leaving the personal, individual domain to human experience, to human reality. By excising the I from the transcendental field, and by imposing it as the "active" dimension of the subject qua *me*, Sartre posits it as placed and played out in fundamental immanence, which here he calls the "level of humanity." Thus, according to Sartre, the I should be an object for consciousness, a phenomenon for examination (TE 26 / 42) that is not superior to the I of others. Its difference from the unreflected, passive *me*—from my existence amidst things and other people—identifies it with the interpersonal realm.

If the ego is neither able to step out of experience and into some realm radically other than that of experience nor capable of "entering" or constituting the world (something that the sheer existence of an impersonal consciousness does), of constituting its own worldly, experiential presence, then Sartre's "level of humanity" indicates that together with the ego, *humanity* too falls to the stroke of the *epoché*. The I (as a phenomenon in the world) and humanity are what constitutes the unity of the subject's acts; otherwise, in its interaction with the world, a person is present as a me. If humanity is the domain in which the face of the me is the (de-transcendentalized) I, then such "humanity" is neither a transcendental basis for the subject, nor an extension of the transcendental realm, a theater of anthropogenesis that allows man to emerge so as to experience and think objects, nature, and others. Humanity is instead the social and experiential realm that "the me" finds itself in, *with* and *in* which it acts as an I; it is a sort-of totality of subjects and nature conceived as the basis of experience.

The second passage to consider is a famous section of Sartre's conclusion, where he affirms and explicitly defends the phenomenological take on man:

> . . . nothing is more unjust than to call phenomenologists "idealists." On the contrary, for centuries we have not felt in philosophy so realist a current. The phenomenologists have plunged man back into the world; they have given full measure to man's agonies and sufferings, and also to his rebellions. Unfortunately, as long as the *I* remains a structure of absolute consciousness, one will still be able to reproach phenomenology for being an escapist doctrine, for again pulling a part of man out of the world and, in that way, turning our attention from the real problems. (TE 86 / 104–5; translation slightly modified)

This extraordinary concluding passage clearly identifies Sartre's antisubjectivism with what he interprets as phenomenological realism, linking these with his handling of man's anxieties and suffering—and with the lack of a transcendental ego, which up to now strictly separated man from his worldly existence. Responding to objections of "theorists of the extreme Left" TE 85/104—presumably meaning Nizan, his former roommate at the Ecole Normale Supérieure), Sartre echoes antifoundational realism and writes of the "injustice" of treating phenomenology as a new idealism. Sartre is intentionally reductive here, inasmuch as he completely evades the dimension in which phenomenology rejects classical realism and cannot be reduced to it. Even more than Wahl, Sartre ignores (or, more appropriately, renames) Husserl and Heidegger's claim to a distance from realism by referring, in terms of tone and appeal, to the history of philosophy that supposedly tilts so much toward the idealist side as to not only legitimate phenomenology's realist claims but also undermine the "metaphysical materialism" of Marxists. And Sartre momentarily imagines himself a grand purveyor of philosophy, a Hegelian "we" of Absolute Knowledge sensing where his new discovery has already shown its potential: "for centuries we have not felt. . . . " At the same time, he emphasizes the failure of this very fantasy of the philosopher as distanced purveyor: the "real problems" are those of man's anxieties, sufferings, and revolts—none of which can be distanced from the reality-context in which he finds himself, none of which can be relegated to problems of the old transcendental ego. "The phenomenologists have plunged man back into the world; they have given full measure to man's agonies and sufferings and also to his rebellions" (TE 86/105). Up to the 1930s, the very problems of anxiety, suffering, and revolt were not really seen as properly philosophical subjects, but rather as problems of a literary or Pascalian quasi-theological world lying (at best) at the limits of philosophical endeavor. Witness, for example, Emmanuel Levinas's later recollection of the new tensions in French thought as expressed in 1937:

I remember the 1937 Descartes Congress. New philosophical tendencies were already being affirmed: existentialist thought, Catholic thought, Marxist thought. Anguish, death, care, were increasingly popular topics. In the course of one session, Gabriel Marcel launched a fiery attack on those thinkers "deprived of any gift of inner life," blind to God, blind to death. At which point Brunschvicg, . . . with

that air of having no air, said: "I think that the death of Léon Brunschvicg preoccupies Léon Brunschvicg less than the death of Gabriel Marcel preoccupies Gabriel Marcel."[6]

For Sartre, like others, the transformation of such problems into philosophical issues was phenomenology's great gift. By contrast, the "alimenta-
ry" and "digestive" philosophy of Brunschvicg and contemporary rational-
ists ("empirico-criticists," post-Kantians, and others, in any case including
Brochard, Lachelier, and Meyerson) ate up things into thoughts, providing
forced interpretations of the "I think" that amounted to solipsism.[7] This is
why phenomenology helped move philosophy away from a reductive epistemological emphasis of the period, all the while—and for the first time—
permitting an effective understanding of the world surrounding man. It
is interesting that Sartre writes "*re*plongé" [replunged], therefore specifically charging idealism with dragging man and thought away from some
"primordial" connection to reality. Sartre's argument (like the definition
of man it proposes) returns from its momentary self-distancing into the
impersonal "on" of the history of philosophy back into the problems for
which contemporary phenomenology can provide a philosophical basis. It
is, Sartre suggests, in the impossibility of dissociating the *I* from the reality
it is surrounded by that we find man's suffering and anxiety, and against
which we see its revolt. Not only should phenomenology be praised for
turning philosophy toward "reality," but also its novelty and significance
lie in its effort to foreground *and to think* the reality of anxiety, suffering,
and revolt.

Nevertheless, all this could be squandered if phenomenology and
postphenomenological thought were to follow Husserl's later path toward
an elision of the purity of the transcendental consciousness, rather than
accept Sartre's own call to erase even the least link between the two. Sartre
repeats this in the tone of an ethico-political imperative, which is significant because, once again, it prioritizes the demand of keeping man
"in the world" over alternative problems. "Unfortunately, as long as the
I remains a structure of absolute consciousness, one will still be able to
reproach phenomenology for being an escapist doctrine, for again pulling
a part of man out of the world and, in that way, turning our attention
from the real problems" (TE 86 / 105). The significance of "Transcendence
of the Ego" in the context of 1930s thought is thus considerable. Sartre

resolutely defines man as the being that exists in the world and that cannot be torn away from it in order to think the world, or objects per se. His position extends Koyré's argument against the positing of absolutes in science. As noted already, for Koyré, the scientific systematization of such absolutes does *not* ensue from a human capacity to attain transcendence; what claims a transcendental truth is invariably formed on the basis of religious and metaphysical presuppositions and appears truthful only because it confirms them. These "presuppositions" mirror Sartre's passive, unreflected, immanent "me," the site of the above-noted imprisonment of transcendental consciousness in empirical existence. As the passive part of the subject, *the me* more or less absorbs, grounds, and traps this consciousness; it is only through this imprisonment and the subsequent clash between the outside and the me that "real problems" appear and can be seriously considered as problems for philosophy. Here Sartre also comes close to Wahl's emphasis on the world as an obstacle to man, and man as severely limited and incapable of understanding this world: from there arise anxiety, suffering, and revolt.

"The Transcendence of the Ego" is significant for a further reason. Through Sartre's complex intellectual role between phenomenology, psychology, and literature, it brings about a meeting of these realms, particularly phenomenological antifoundational realism, literary protoexistentialism (as in Malraux, Bataille, Queneau, and so on), and the Catholic personalism that led to existentialism—and presents phenomenology as a way out of the impasse to which contemporary political, social, and religious problems had brought idealist philosophy. Again, the reach of Sartre's claim is extensive—consider the following contextualization by Dennis Hollier. Hollier finds in the literature of the 1930s, markedly in Malraux, Caillois, and Sartre, an emptying of the psychical *I*, the first-person singular that speaks, thinks, and desires.[8] This "emptying out" he connects to Politzer, Artaud, and the College of Sociology, seeing in them a concern that specifically elides and rejects humanist sufficiency, imposing a "terrorist lining" to any claim of humanism in early existentialism.

The humanism of a living person is thus coupled with the icy stiffness of a cadaver. The motif of such a conjunction recurs . . . in passages that illustrate—at least for early French existentialism, that of the period between the two world wars—how difficult it is to separate the humanist message of existentialism from its terrorist shadow. The terrorist moment is not merely the starting point; it will always remain the inescapable inner lining of humanist generosity. Here the fellow traveler is no longer the fraternal militant; he is the terrorist aesthete. The constructivism of a communitarian honeymoon will never succeed in completely masking its frigid, inhuman accompaniment: the militant's warm anthropocentrism is defocused, veiled by a Copernican revolution that transforms the decentered planet into an earth without men.[9]

Sartre does not do this *exactly*; he denies the universality of man as a third-person impersonal "*on*" that serves as a history of the mind, a progressive occidental consciousness as humanist teleology. Thereby, consciousness is emptied of worldly content. At the same time, Sartre formalizes the I as the interpersonal active force of the me that provides a specific "body" for consciousness, *while denying such a formalized I any transcendental access or force.* By denying the psychical *I* as a link between man and transcendental consciousness, Sartre empties the relation between them. By denying the ego qua structural connection of the empirical subject to the transcendental realm, Sartre's text echoes Catholic theocentrism's denial of the status of "supreme being" to man, but without consequently seeing man as existing under God. By assuming phenomenology's facilitation of such a critique, Sartre repeats the dismissal of man's standing as observer of nature and a designator of meanings in it and rejects the transcendental juxtaposition of subject to object. The resulting approach to humanity—as a phenomenon (or even an epiphenomenon), separated from consciousness and transcendence and located together with the active I in the realm of intersubjectivity—strips it not only of direct access to truth but also of any identification with the ground of the self (the me), any identification with the existence and thought of the self.

3. Sovereignty, Kenosis, and the Reconstruction of the I (Bataille's *The Blue of Noon*)

After reading Bataille's 1935 manuscript of *The Blue of Noon*, its dedicatee André Masson wrote of his excitement: "At last, a book that has nothing humanist about it."[10] This "nothing humanist about it" is shorthand for a philosophical critique of the human subject that sees this subject as "attaining" sovereignty over itself and the world *only* in moments where great internal tumult undermines its participation in and dependence on an immanent, homogeneous world. That is to say, a human subject becomes sovereign when it empties itself of its social and ontological foundations as human subject. But what is the philosophical and political significance of a claim?[11] What does it say about humanism in the mid-1930s? How does it emerge out of a literary text such as *The Blue of Noon,* and how does it critique other conceptions of sovereignty and subjectivity? How does it identify Bataille's philosophical thought and his interests shortly before the beginning of his work in the Collège de Sociologie?[12]

In *The Blue of Noon*, Bataille sets these questions against a backdrop defined by the intellectual division that dominated the 1930s, the struggle between fascism and antifascism. He acknowledges this backdrop and announces the terms of his opposition to *both* political alternatives in segments of the book that reflect the fascination and revulsion he feels toward them. In the first of these, narrator and protagonist Henri Troppmann finds himself nauseated by the commitment of the character Lazare (Bataille's rendition of Simone Weil) and her stepfather on behalf of the working classes, discouraging it literally as pointless, crypto-religious, and doomed. "'All the same [. . .] if the working classes are screwed, why are you both Communists, or socialists, or whatever?' They stared at me, then glanced at one another. Lazare finally answered [. . .], 'No matter what happens, we must not abandon the downtrodden.' Well of course, she's a Christian. . . . I was beside myself, I was outraged with shame. 'Why *must*? What's the point of it?'" (BN 49; trans. amended). The second passage comes in the coda, when Troppmann is confronted with Nazism, in guises of a handsome Nazi officer he crosses in the street, the swastika-red dress of his companion Dorothea, and the singing of a Hitler Youth boys' choir: the book ends with him confronting in these figures "this catastrophe" of a "rising tide of murder" in which "all things were surely doomed to conflagration, a mingling of flame and thunder, as pale as burning sulphur when it chokes you" (BN 126).[13] Like Bataille, and though he identifies himself as a leftist fellow traveler fascinated by the aesthetics of Nazism, Troppmann scorns both Communism and fascism as theologically unsatisfactory and politically disastrous. Communism is a weak extension of secularized Catholicism, while fascism provides a new way of Being (in Heideggerian anxiety before death) only to attach it to a politics of murder.[14] Troppmann's distance from these alternatives picks up Bataille's political engagement in 1934–35, notably in the group "Que Faire?" whose opening invitation asked, "What do we do against fascism given the insufficiency of communism?"[15] It also moves beyond this participation and toward a philosophical anthropology that rejects competing contemporary humanisms (Catholic, Communist, or fascist) and their conceptions of the self and its relation to the divine, material reality and society.[16]

The connection between Troppmann's political points and Bataille's philosophico-political writings of the period relies on the establishment of an author-narrator-character relation in *The Blue of Noon*'s peculiar "Part One." Part One is a two-page excerpt from a set of aphorisms composed in first-person narration that, after abandoning his attempt to publish the novel in late 1935, Bataille put out as a separate philosophical meditation (also titled "The Blue of Noon") in the journal *Minotaure* and, in 1943, included in his book *Inner Experience*. It thus not only provides something of a "glimpse into Troppmann's mind" but also foregrounds an exceptional identification of Bataille with his character—as both of them enunciate or write this text. For *The Blue of Noon* the book, Bataille squashed this 2-page excerpt, as "Part One," between the 15-page introduction and the 110-page "Part Two," the rest of the book.[17] Yet in content, form, and temporal progression, Part One does not link the introduction to Part Two. Rather than narrate in the past tense, as do these sections, its syntax and mode of address is extradiegetic, direct, set in a formal, timeless, often prognostic present. Only the short middle section of Part One recounts a story, indeed a dreamlike episode that is repeatedly echoed in the rest of the book. Cased between an opening series of paradoxical, despondent aphorisms involving an impossible knowledge ("The ground will give way beneath my feet. I will die in hideous circumstances") and a conclusion marked by a rise out of desperation and into a furious joy incommensurable with the constraints of external reality, this middle section recounts Troppmann's meeting with *the Commander,* a figure of death that terrifies him and lays bare his sexual impotence.[18] In linking Troppmann's observations on his desperate fate to an encounter with a representation of death, the tone of Part One interprets and frames Troppmann's internal tumult. (Troppmann even says in Part One that, ever since meeting the Commander, "I have been doomed to a solitude that I reject and no longer have the heard to endure.") What we find in these observations is a prototype for his desire to disrupt social constraints as it is doubled by his failure to maintain a dignified composure. It is this formalized tumult that, throughout Part Two, leads Troppmann to mood swings from shame to happiness, and back to tears and bodily fits (BN 35). At the end of Part One, wallowing in self-contempt, Troppmann provides the paradigm for his turns from debilitating tumult to sovereign self-control: "Born of disreputable pain, the insolence that persists in spite of everything started growing again: slowly at first, then in a sudden burst that has blinded and transfigured me with a happiness that defies all reason. At this moment I am intoxicated with happiness, drunk with it [. . .] I triumph!" (BN 15–16). This passage, central to Troppmann's philosophical self-depiction, relies on an understanding of sovereignty described in the longer original version of Part One. This longer version links together a series of 1930s themes from Bataille's work, for example his philosophical arguments and his mythology of the "pineal eye" that illustrates the human condition as forever trying to see beyond the horizontal, earthly plane of immanence to which man is bound. While old philosophical and scientific anthropologies failed to understand the restrictions of immanence and the illusory character of transcendence, Bataille suggests that this changes with the 1930s and the newly emerging anthropology. Following in the steps of Kojève and Bachelard, Bataille writes about quantum physics in "Le Labyrinthe," where he criticizes Meyerson's conception of modern science altogether.[19] Moreover, like Sartre's *Transcendence of the Ego*, Bataille's position echoes Jean Wahl's antifoundational realism in that it objects precisely to the Cartesian possibility that man may claim to control more than his embodied and empirical self. More clearly still, Bataille's anthropology follows from Kojève's ontological dualism, and his contrast between *the given world* and *the Being of Man,* which identifies Man with a radical and ultimately nondialectical Negation of this given. Again, for Kojève this Negation does not involve a genuine transcendence or even, strictly speaking, a sublation. Though a negation of the world, man is bound to the homogeneity prompted and forced by immanence. Bataille identifies human existence with (i) a Negation of the social and natural world, a Negation constrained by a homogeneity that recuperates difference for socio-ontological uniformity, and (ii) an insufficiency overwhelmed by the surrounding world. These two positions are central to his antihumanism and his notion of sovereignty.

Let's proceed with the first of the above definitions (Man is constrained negation) and return to the second (Man is insufficiency) later. *If man is truly given in the world, then any transcendence, any radical self-distancing from the world, is impossible; the question is how to recognize the constraints of an intolerable immanence—how to recognize them as constraints.* Bataille accepts from Kojève that man is nothing but (i) the destruction and transformation of the world he finds himself in, and (ii) his self-construction as something beyond nature and beneath religious fantasy. In "The Blue of Noon," the longer version of Part One, Bataille writes: "And just as a negation of Nature turned human life into a transgression and a transcendence that throws all other things back into the nothing, in the same way . . . the negation of all that is above things and men, becomes an order and a law that strips unhappy life of the links that still paralyze its vertiginous movement toward the void."[20] For negation to be genuine, Man must negate even what he has turned into the superhuman, not merely the social, the material, and the natural. The "vertiginous" movement toward the void thus replaces these, just as it echoes Heidegger in destroying the classical transcendental realm. For it, man must accept the context and premise of a stark, prisonlike reality he cannot understand or control, in and against which he needs to operate: "The very movement in which man negates Mother Earth who gave birth to him, opens the path of subjugation. Human beings abandon themselves to petty despair. Human life is represented then as insufficient, as overwhelmed by the sufferings or the deprivations which reduce it to ugly vanity."[21] This double attack—on nature and also on forms of subjugation set up under the guise of divinity—evokes sovereignty and self-sovereignty as a political and philosophical necessity.

Politically read, this attack presents sovereignty as a struggle against the yoke of homogeneity. Given that Man finds himself constrained by immanence, his first concern is with differentiating himself from other men and the immanent world he recognizes around him. Bataille's "heterology" involves a transformation of Kojève's notion of homogeneity. Once again, in Kojève homogeneity is a mostly *mathematical* and *ontological* concept. It concerns the nondifferentiation of interacting agents or aspects of a whole (in the ontological case: the world and man in it). But Bataille sees homogeneity first as a force of social uniformity—a constraint on radical, unstable Negation forced on Man by his appurtenance to structures of stability and similarity. For him, the basic structures of modern subjugation follow from both a political formulation (modern democracy) and a scientific and metaphysical conception (positivist/realist thought and secularization). These systematically destroy any proper experience of the heterogeneous and its derivative forms such as the sacred—what grounds the persistent hopes of surpassing homogeneity, whether in the remnants of religion, or in the new, or (illusory) hopes of transcendence to be found in fascism. Following from his identification of democracy and commercial economy with homogeneity in *The Psychological Structure of Fascism*, Bataille describes society as torn between authority and an anarchy that democracy fends off through adaptation: "In practical terms, the function of the State consists of an interplay of authority and adaptation. The reduction of differences through compromise in parliamentary practice indicates all the possible complexity of the internal activity of adaptation required by homogeneity . . . depending on whether the State is democratic or despotic, the prevailing tendency will be either adaptation or authority" (PSF 139). As in other contemporary essays, Bataille clearly sees these alternatives as amplifying the prison of immanence, as destructive of the possibility of negation. It is against such a Heideggerian-Kojèvian vision of modern homogeneity qua inauthenticity, nondifferentiation, imprisonment, that Bataille's protagonist-narrator of *The Blue of Noon* sets to present himself as different, as irreducible to the homogeneous world of sociality, and indeed as unable to properly function as a subject altogether. The attack on political and social conventions follows from here: if fascism and communism are illusory and contemptible attempts to provide a new experience, then an acceptance of democracy, its political anthropology, and its conventions, is no better. In *The Blue of Noon*, the primacy of adaptation as technique of social formation constitutes an endless source of amusement and contempt for Troppmann: he praises his lover Dorothea/Dirty for rejecting social conventions ("Dorothea" in Greek means "gift of God," or "gift-giving Goddess," which Troppmann inverts into her nickname in English, "Dirty"); he accuses his friendly nemesis Lazare of turning Christianity into a cadaverous socialism; and, from his sick-bed midway through the book, he tries to force a rather strange intimacy on the younger, "peasantlike" Xenie in terms specifically targeting her facile accommodation to intellectual life. These women become attractive and troubling for him precisely when they evoke the heterogeneity of death—that is, when they become identified with "the Commander," the meeting with whom Troppmann recounts in the middle section of Part One.[22] They also reveal, however, that the attack on the sociopolitical homogenizing grip becomes interesting mostly because Troppmann, who carries it out, is not a Nietzschean or Kojèvian Overman, a hero in the face of death, but rather a complete mess. As such, he evokes Emmanuel Levinas's treatment of insomnia and nausea in *On Escape*, and Sartre's thinking of nausea in *Nausea*; Troppmann is also a precursor to Blanchot's characters from Thomas to Henri Sorge—characters who, mired in an experience of "the second night," face at length their own *near*-emptiness.[23] Troppmann's sexual and political impotence, his failure to assert himself, his sense of intellectual *desoeuvrement,* his renunciation of the negation he might represent—all these bring forth a character *at once* devoted to voiding himself of negation and concerned with distinguishing himself from any participation in shared existence, from any form of subjugation on the basis of social expectations or illusions of order. His adoption of this swerve between a falling into the abyss and an ecstatic triumph, between tears and sickness and rapture—this is precisely his turn to sovereignty as a rejection of homogeneity qua subjugation, a refusal to live on the same plane as others. It is further highlighted by the ambiguous aforecited passage on Negation as a double overcoming of nature and the divine, and a supplanting of a life in tumult for them. While in the original manuscript of "The Blue of Noon," in the long original Part One Troppmann calls the need to overcome illusions of transcendence an *order* and a *law*, Bataille's subsequent publication of the same text in *Minotaure* includes one substantial change. It replaces the content of this *order* and *law*—which was to destroy "all that is above things and men"—with "the authority which maintained [human life] in oppression." Here, the radical rejection of such authority opens a space for the search of sovereignty. In *The Blue of Noon*, it is clear that for Troppmann there is nothing above things and men, only perhaps the "sky blue" (*le bleu du ciel*) reflected in the pure force of the SS officer's deep blue eyes, from which Troppmann shies away anxiously.[24] This expression ("all that is above things and men") points precisely to this lack and thus emphasizes Troppmann's persistent rejection of both uniformity and the idols of secular redemption that maintain it in place. By contrast, in the philosophical aphorisms of "The Blue of Noon," the rejection of authority must be made explicit: the "I" through which Bataille (rather than Troppmann) speaks is not bound to a narrative in which it continually rejects Being-with-others for a self-emptying self, and therefore this clarification of the at-once political and subjective revolt locates a source of this oppression and defines this source: the authority that maintains "all that is above things and men" and hence also maintains the oppression of man and human life.

But the social dimension of homogeneity is not all—sovereignty is a fundamentally ontological problematic. At stake in it is not only the clash between a receding self and the surrounding sociopolitical milieu but also a relationship between the I, the world, and Being as the I lives and conceives it. Bataille's 1935 essay "The Labyrinth" (republished in *Inner Experience* as a follow up to "The Blue of Noon") explicitly extends and foregrounds the ontological aspects of this treatment of the limitations of human Being. There, Bataille expressly sees a prisonlike immanence of the world as encompassing man and clashing continually with man's attempts to escape from and negate it. At the same time, Bataille seeks to recover the possibility that man might fleetingly grasp Being on occasions where the tripartite I-world-Being relationship collapses.

To argue this point, "The Labyrinth" turns to the second aforementioned definition of man: Man is insufficient, incapable of claiming wholeness or autarchy. Implicitly founding *insufficiency* on Kojève's understanding of desire, Bataille turns it into an ontological question from which to criticize completeness and the desire for it: "At the basis of human life there exists a principle of insufficiency . . . the sufficiency of each being is endlessly contested by every other. . . . A burst of laughter or expression of repugnance greets each gesture, each sentence or each oversight through which my profound insufficiency is betrayed. . . ."[25] This last sentence turns Kojève's desire for recognition on its head: rather than show the desire as impossible to close off, social existence contests, and imposes itself on, each being's attempt to see itself as a being negat-

ing reality. The implicit target here is Heidegger—specifically his claim
in "On the Essence of Ground" that, because of *Dasein*, beings always
appear manifest as a whole.[26] The critique of subjectivity suggested here
by the insufficiency of the I is precisely a consequence of the rejection
of this *wholeness*: without a tension between "me" and the world, without a proclamation of insufficiency as a crux of human existence, Being
would be nothing more than an immanence that reduces the individual
to shared homogeneous sociality. This is the significance of the narrator's
statement, in Part One of *The Blue of Noon*, that "the exhausted head
where 'I' am has become so fearful, so greedy, that only death can satisfy
it." In other words, if man is indeed defined by his insufficiency, then his
being reveals itself to him when his attempt to grasp and negate the world
in fact shows his imprisonment in it. For Bataille, Being is not something
I have access to, but instead what reveals and is revealed by my inability
to fully exist with others.[27] This "I," unstable and formless and ill-fitting
in Troppmann's anxious head, is a sort of empty and undirected core,
definitive of the particularity of Troppmann's tumult. Only death offers
an absolute escape from this tumultuous I, but the I rejects this death,
choosing the tumult instead, i.e., preferring the condemnation to live in
a "fearful, exhausted and greedy" head, a world-renouncing, unsatisfied,
desiring, insufficient head. It is from here that the I proceeds to narrate
and eventually to announce its triumph in the recognition of happiness
amidst tumult and misery, against both death and political ironing away.
But Bataille continues this definition and delocalization of Being: "Being
in the world is so *uncertain* that I can project it where I want—outside of
me. It is a clumsy man, still incapable of eluding the intrigues of nature,
who locks being in the me. Being in fact is found *nowhere* and it was an
easy game for a sickly malice to discover it to be divine, at the summit of
a pyramid formed by the multitude of beings" (L 366 / 173 / 82). The shift
away from Heidegger is important here: to approach the question of Being
is not merely to pose it but to link it to a flight from self-sufficient "human
reality," a flight from any answer to the question of Being that celebrates
such a reality. Being appears in moments of a breakdown between the I
and the world, when the inability of the I to master the world is revealed:
in tumult, in Troppmann's drunken stupor. As this passage suggests,
Being is "ungraspable" because *both* my insufficiency *and* my excessive

dependence on the prison of immanence turn Being into something impossible to simply place or control.[28] In a sense, Being is what happens when this torn ego clashes with the world—when it can be recognized as chance, political goal, or tumult. It is *thus* that Being reveals man, as Bataille notes in "The Labyrinth" as "only a particle inserted in unstable and entangled wholes" (VE 174): this is how it reveals the I as uncertain and unable to operate as a proper monad, a part of a series, a particle in a homogeneous structure, a *subject*.

These are then the contours of Bataille's definition of sovereignty in the mid-1930s: sovereignty is the recognition of the irreducibility of the I to the immanent reality in which it exists; it is the nonidentification of Being with the I and the world, the recognition of its not-belonging to its representations in the self and the world.[29] *Not* an overcoming of the difference of self and world, but rather an engagement in the continuing play of these failures of correspondence, coherence, and structuration. (It is important to note that this inversion of the depths of depression and loss into a "triumph" does *not* involve a moment of subjectivity proper.) The triumph Troppmann asserts lies in the persistence of the inner self in its tumult, in its failure to either affect or actually escape from the world: its sovereignty *is* the destruction, or rather the emptying out (the *kenosis*) of subjectivity and of man's place in the homogeneous society or world.[30]

Besides the obvious modification of Heideggerian and Kojèvian themes and the attempt to empty out subjectivity for purposes of a hope of sovereignty, what is at stake here? First, Bataille clearly inverts non-conformism's hope for a new foundation of man into an argument that no such foundation can ever properly allow for the sovereignty of the *I* trapped in the world and in politics. Moreover, in this figure of emptying out subjectivity, emptying out Troppmann's self—or more specifically, his head (an empty head that would, by 1937, be replaced by the chopped-off head of *Acéphale*), Bataille emphasizes a further inversion of anthropotheism. In the contrast of Being, subject, and world, at stake is a *kenosis* that can find no resolution in resurrection or a relation to the divine: the God-Man and the Overman reemerge in the self-evacuating too-much-man (Troppmann), and find themselves sovereign only thanks to his complete destruction of self. Bataille in this sense criticizes both Nietzsche and Kojève, in ways that he would make more explicit during the war, and in an implosion of motifs of self-transcendence or Christomimesis in which they had respectively put stock.[31] Third, Bataille's theory of sovereignty has at least three major and noteworthy targets, Rousseau, Mill, and Schmitt, whom Bataille plays against each other. He agrees with Rousseau that politics is founded in a grasp and expression of the general will, but he rejects Rousseau's advocacy of participation in the general will in favor of a self-sovereignty against the mass. Conversely, Bataille, who knew of Schmitt at least since Kojève's lectures of May 1934, rejects Schmitt's idea of sovereignty as existing at the limit where the legal order no longer holds sway (because there is no *real* difference regarding the existence of the subject in the legal order or at its limits), but he agrees that sovereign is he who separates himself from this order (from the general will) and does not fall under its constraints, suggesting that every person decides on an existential "state of exception" vis-à-vis their homogeneous involvement in society.[32] As regards Mill's advocacy of freedom, Bataille clearly distances himself from the famous claim that "over his own body and mind, the individual is sovereign."[33] It is in the resulting notion of an impossible sovereignty, at once so ultrasubjective, so antisubjectivist, and so opposed to humanist involvement that it could not be recuperated by its contemporary social theories, that the core of Bataille's philosophico-political argument is formed.

4. Escape as the Impossible Guarantee of Another Humanity (Phenomenology, Nazism, Levinas)

Emmanuel Levinas's "On Escape" was published in *Recherches philosophiques* next to Georges Bataille's "The Labyrinth" and Karl Löwith's "La Conciliation hégélienne." Read as a reaction to the economic and political instability of France in the mid-1930s, Levinas's text echoes Wahl and Heidegger's insertion of the subject in the midst of a certain reality, as well as Sartre and Bataille's arguments against the self-sufficient, transcendental *I* (E 50). Its radical novelty lies, however, in Levinas's self-distancing from the imperatives of these contemporaries: his express (if not hyperbolic) effort to *escape* from this reality. Politically speaking, both the language and the tone of "On Escape" carry a quasi-romantic, typically nonconformist, even "reactionary modernist" protest against the malaise of bourgeois modernity (E 50)—a demand for flight from a 1930s culture permeated by financial disaster and sociopolitical insecurity.[34] Levinas breaks with both the implications of romanticism and the socialist imagination of an escape from bourgeois modernity in two moves. First, he conceives of (Heideggerian) Being as the proper basis for any serious thinking of escape; second, he radicalizes escape to such a point that it becomes almost empty, directionless—an almost *formal* movement. The force of these moves becomes clearer if they are understood in the dual context marked by the complex movement toward realism and the contemporary rejection of transcendence (E 51). At the same time, the overall connection of escape with "the humanity of man" needs to be read in the specific context of Levinas's recent essay "Reflections on the Philosophy of Hitlerism" ("Quelques réflexions sur la philosophie du hitlérisme").[35] Levinas published that essay in Emmanuel Mounier's journal *Esprit* (he would later refer to the personalist *Esprit* as "a journal representing a progressive, avant-garde Catholicism"); the text, in its assault on Nazi anti-Semitism, reveals differences within nonconformist ranks and speaks to the comfort that Levinas felt publishing in a predominantly Catholic and politically ambiguous journal.[36] As Jacques Rolland has suggested, "Reflections on the Philosophy of Hitlerism" foregrounds themes that shed light on the concluding claim of "On Escape" that "every civilization that accepts being—with the tragic despair it entails and the crimes it justifies—merits the name barbarian" (E 73). Levinas writes in "Reflections on Hitlerism" that "Hitlerism" attacks "the humanity of man" because for Nazism, "the situation to which [man] is riveted [does] not add itself to him, but instead [makes] up the very ground of his being."[37] This statement requires some unpacking. Levinas opposes the reduction of man to the reality in which he finds himself, a reality conceived as the irreducible and inescapable ground and world of his being. That is, he opposes the reduction of man to the material and real conditions of his possibility, his situatedness in the world as conceived in biological, social, and political terms. This situatedness is there; it is a fundamental fact of human existence, experience, and life, but it *cannot* by itself make up and define man's humanity. Reducing man to that situation erases his spirituality, his connection (or possibility of a connection) to anything other than the world surrounding him; in terms more akin to phenomenology and antifoundational realism, situatedness may be said to mistake the Husserlian transcendental reduction for an ontological monism directed by the field of experience and the "natural" composition of entities, or it may be said to essentialize Heidegger's Being.

Thus, by reducing man's humanity to certain constitutive foundations of his reality, Nazism institutionalizes and normalizes ontological violence. Levinas's critique reveals both the priorities and the givens of his position. On the one hand, it implicitly concurs with the contemporary attack on the priority of transcendental idealism, the argument that the human subject *as such* does not have access to transcendence in the Platonic/Cartesian/Enlightenment sense. This "riveting," which Rolland correctly interprets as foregrounding one's corporeal existence (one's inability to get rid of one's body and of the "grounding" in reality that this body offers and enforces), is a different way of admitting the irreducibility of Being-in-the-world. But this should not suggest that it is possible or desirable to equate being-riveted with the limits of subjective existence, to equate the immanence it forces with the humanity of man: being riveted is not equal to existing *in a reality* one cannot overcome or sidestep. Nor is the facticity of riveting equal to the specifics of the situation or reality in which man finds himself. (Here, Levinas seems to be targeting Heidegger as well, whose equation of transcendence in "On the Essence of Ground" with the opening of a world that serves as man's ground may be said to allow for this sort of a reduction.) Indeed, Levinas seems more comfortable with a reading that allows for this situation to be "added on." But how can this "added on" be accounted for? How can man escape the reduction to existence, reality, Being?

Levinas specifically emphasizes, in "Reflections on the Philosophy of Hitlerism" and in "On Escape," the need to reconceive the finitude of Being involved in this being-riveted not in terms of a failure, but rather as the basis for any philosophical move beyond the limitation of "the ground of his being," beyond what would hold one to this ground. Escape from this ground is the heart of "On Escape." Here, Levinas posits Being, whose introduction "already looks like an escape" (E 57), as *the proper ground of escape*, the footing from which escape becomes comprehensible (as a drive and need) and necessary because the strict, transcendental separation of the individual from the world is no longer possible. Indeed, it is only the coming to pass of Heidegger's "philosophy of Being" that makes a genuine escape or "excendence" imaginable, because Being sidesteps the ambiguities of the classical thinking of "freedom," the idealist imagination of transcendence that led to the self-sufficient, "harmonizing" ideal of *being human* advanced by modern bourgeois intellectuals (E 51, 55, 57).[38] As "good" and structurally similar to escape as classical freedom may have appeared, as necessary to the dignity of man as it was, it invariably operated by reference to an "infinite being" (E 51) and tended to produce ideals in which man would posit the evasion and overcoming of ontology all the while inadvertently ontologizing such freedom, evasion, and overcoming. For Levinas, Being marks a philosophical advance because it foregrounds the brutal purity of "what is"—of a certain actuality, or existence, or "reality." But at the same time that it reduces man to this reality, it also makes him (to use terms from earlier discussions) incapable of understanding and overcoming it, locked in it and feeling a general malaise regarding his existence.[39]

In Levinas's interpretation, the Heideggerian infatuation with Being arrests, heightens, and resolves the ambiguity that had been at the heart of Western thought and its conception of man: the tendency to ontologize (E 50), to enforce a harmony between Being and the world (E 50), to see being as what man is given as. In this ambiguity, Western thought has found its limitation, so much so that Heidegger's idea of a Being not limited to mere presence "already looks like an escape" (E 57). It is not, Levinas retorts: just as Nazism displays a demand to transform man into the limited totality of his biological, corporeal being, a biologization and substantialization of the spirit, at once pushing Western bourgeois thought in a specific direction and undermining its ambiguities, Heidegger's thought at once overcomes the illusory and wishful conception of freedom as imagined in the European conception of man and reduces man to Being. This is a harsh reading of *Being and Time* because it interprets Being by identifying it with man's givenness as an ontico-ontological existent and denies the possibility that this existent's ontological questioning can reveal something more than the mere identity of its givenness with the essence of man. Levinas then identifies this grounding with cases where man's riveting to himself becomes clearest and most disturbing—shame and nausea—situations where man is almost reduced to the uglier limitations

or modes of his corporeal presence.[40] The operation, plasticity, and movement of "being riveted" (E 66) specifically demands that man be brought
back to the fact of his being as a ground, to the horror that is his presence
when it is merely malaise, only to realize the impossibility of evading this
being. That is to say, shame and nausea demonstrate the failure of classical
theories of freedom because they show man's inability to escape his condition and situation, to distance and distinguish himself radically from
the reality with which he interacts. They also demonstrate the failure of
contemporary reductions of man to being because these reductions again
miss the brutal, indeed disgusting nature and character of this being. To
return to the language of antifoundational realism, Levinas understands
the "humanity of man" as bound to man's interaction with his world, as
radically constrained by it, yet at the same time as dreaming of escape
from his "being riveted" to it. This, Levinas writes, is hardly the case with
European modernity: modern European humanity identifies itself with
the bourgeois drive toward self-sufficiency and security, with Man's reduction to a conservative and self-preserving existence, but it also maintains
the idealist fantasy of overcoming reality. Levinas rejects both of these
directions, not so much to defend their ideals *a contrario* but in order
to reveal the Nazi assault on European humanity that, for him, follows
from them: if left to these purposes, modern European humanity finds its
target and truth in its own dehumanization, in Nazism.

Levinas conceives escape from these options as *excendence* (E 54):
the subject's movement toward transcendence, carried out on a ground-
less plane of immanence that has already rendered genuine transcendental
foundations or goals unreachable and meaningless. *Excendence* is at once a
movement beyond being *and* a consequence inherent in the basic structure
of Being itself, a revolt against Being necessitated by the very imposition
of Being. In other words, it too demands (at least) a double movement: a
philosophical paradigm shift into Heideggerian ontology and a recognition of this ontology as a prison. It recalls Bataille's occasional emphases
on "exit" and on impossible sovereignty, it involves the impossibility of
an opening of the homogeneous to a proper, absolute heterogeneity. Excendence promises an ideal of happiness, genuine freedom, and human
dignity (E 56) because it provides a contrast to "what is." A total escape
from *what is* is not possible. Yet despite, or indeed *precisely for,* this rea-

son, escape allows for the radical refusal of what is. Levinas radicalizes excendence into a formalization of the insatiable need for an escaping move *through* and *from* the purity of Being: otherwise, however necessary, mere semiempirical, philosophical, literary innovations of escape are inadequate and unsatisfactory. This is to say that escape cannot accept any compromise, and despite (or *precisely because of*) its impossibility it must be maintained as a pure, almost formal move escaping existence and all that it entails.[41]

In its radicalism, in its impossibility and precariousness, the demand for escape *becomes* the human dignity that Levinas imagines in the modern existence of all that is: it is the refusal of the totalitarianism of ontologisms (Heidegger's above all) and the racial biologism of Nazism alike: it identifies the two and recognizes their force as a degree zero of modernity. We thus come full circle to the concluding claim of "On Escape" that "every civilization that accepts being—with the tragic despair it entails and the crimes it justifies—merits the name barbarian" (E 73). The humanity of man cannot be reduced to being—it lies with its rejection by escape.

For all its rejection of what is, and despite the extremely antirealist tone and opening passage, Levinas's escape cannot be identified with idealism. The presumption that the human subject is bound by the reality it finds itself in (in Heideggerian terms its Being-there with all its ontic suppositions and implications) can be found throughout Levinas's argument and indeed is necessary for any excendence—for any conception of an antidote to "being riveted" to one's being. If, as Levinas states, "we must without restriction state, against Parmenides, that non-Being is" (E 71), then Levinas's idealism is a *negative idealism* that marks no more than the hope that a thinking of insufficiency might provide the basis for something beyond what merely is, which at this stage is unclear (and which would only partly be covered by Levinas's own later emphasis on *the other*). "Non-Being is" means that the impossible (for example, escape itself) still is, despite its impossibility and inexistence. As a result, and dodging the terms of the Hegelian/Kojèvian (and later Sartrean) claim that Man becomes (or *is*) Non-Being, Levinas argues that the precariousness of escape, the subject's desire for and need of it are precisely what marks its human dignity—not its belonging to an ideology or its trust in Man's self-perfection or eschatological triumph. All these are totalitarian fantasies that still engulf man, that still make up his being, and that, if anything, obscure his escape. A "negative" idealism is then the trace of humanity and subjectivity in a world that exceeds and undoes them; escape is the movement, the operation toward a consciousness of this humanity: "Escape is the need to get out of oneself, that is, *to break that most radical and unalterably binding of chains, the fact that the I is oneself*" (E 55). The need to transcend the ego and the world that this ego works with and through which it is riveted to itself is the need that shows man to be more than what he is, more than merely the ground, more than what Hitlerism reduces him to. Not merely accepting human reality, Levinas attacks its annihilation of subjectivity by instead equating humanity with the excess and evasion of such subjectivity and reality, an excess and evasion as necessary as it is impossible.

5. The Disproportion of Man: Negative Anthropology and Ciphers of Existentialism

It is difficult to see the three authors as participating in the same project—even their use of identical or similar terms betrays very different goals and (in retrospect) different projects. But in their different philosophical languages and aims, Bataille, Sartre, and Levinas stake out positions that bear substantial commonalities. All three radicalize the dismissal of transcendental subjectivity; all three dismantle, divide, and void the human subject of the idea that it can be defined as human by the reduction to a certain content, empirical or not; all three come to redefine humanity in such a way as to rid it of any foundational claim. Thus, their efforts further tendencies begun with antifoundational realism in the early 1930s, but their questions and approaches provide ciphers of a more existentialist kind of questioning—a questioning that begins from the anxieties of this divided and even trapped subject—and at the same time attack more explicitly the perceived failure of humanism and existing conceptions of humanity. In many ways, these philosophical contributions lie at the very limits of the 1930s political imagination: none participate in an explicit or clear political project, and each of them denounces, in its way, the very possibility of even starting such a (*humanist*) project. This position is original, and it appears linked to the impetus, formal claims, and consequences of phenomenology.

It is significant to mark out the debt of these writers to contemporary thought. I have already indicated certain links to Kojève, Wahl, and *Recherches philosophiques*. Second, they complemented and extended the conception of science and modernity advanced by Koyré, especially his critique of the modern take on transcendence. What Sartre, Bataille, and Levinas treat as a philosophical illusion (that man and the ego appear on a transcendental level) was described by Koyré as a veritable history of an illusion—that of the "occidental consciousness," formed from Descartes's scepticism through Kant's pure reason and continuing to the present. If Koyré's history of science rejected the scientist's hopes to a pure, correct interpretation of reality and trapped him in a world dominated by the metaphysical legacy he partakes of, a world voided of transcendental truths, limited by the uniformity and homogeneity of scientific immanence, and moving toward a dehumanization and emptying out of human reality, Koyré's position is reflected in these authors' refusal of classical transcendence (in its contrast to immanence and experience). This refusal, in Sartre and Levinas, constitutes a rethinking of modernity's theological-metaphysical basis such that a dedicated antifoundationalism, hesitant to admit any firm basis for man's interpretation of the world and willing to point to his failure to do so, would displace the apparently dominant subjectivist idealism.

Sartre, Levinas, and Bataille also built on Heidegger's reconsideration of transcendence, which specifically posits the latter not as an escape from the limits of existence or a view *into* existence from outside, but rather as *Dasein*'s "projection" of a meaningful world over the meaningless chaos it would otherwise find itself faced with—its recognition of a shared manifestation of the beings and things it reveals and that reveal themselves to it. If Heidegger's "On the Essence of Ground" moved transcendence away from the Kantian interpretation and into a theory of casting a world out of objects and interpreted nature (and hence into a formal theory of existence as ground and freedom), then these texts from 1934–35 complete the movement against classical transcendence, by aiming at radically different directions while evincing the exact same intellectual-historical constraints. The antifoundational realism that began with Jean Wahl's search for the concrete *in* the interaction of man with exteriority finds its pinnacle and limit in Levinas's expression of a need for an evasion of and exit from the overbearing reality marked through and through by man's being and also in Sartre's double unwillingness—to grant any content to transcendental consciousness, or even to allow for a direct link between transcendence and the human ego. In other words, the Heideggerian problematization of transcendence and the philosophical imagination of an (a priori impossible) exit or escape from human reality are the two sides of the coin of 1930s philosophical anthropology at the limit. On the one hand, man's transcendent foundation is no more, and consciousness is empty of all and any worldly content. On the other, the problematics of *escape* and *sovereignty* foreground the impossibility of any genuine "stepping out" of reality and its structures, and imposes the survival of such a *beyond* as a domain that is formally as well as existentially necessary, even if it is strictly speaking inaccessible.

Furthermore, Bataille and Levinas both appear to echo the Hegelian, or rather Kojèvian conception of Being as equal to the given which man, qua negation, must always deny. The collusion of the Heideggerian and Hegelian theorizations of Being appears in critical terms in both authors—critical in that both emphasize the impossibility of overcoming one's being, or givenness, together with the absolute need to reject (ontologically and politically) the stagnation, tutelage, and violence they associate with the present, the given, and being. I don't wish to suggest that Bataille and Levinas use Hegel to overcome Heidegger. Rather, in their positive conceptions of man as a negation (Non-Being, sovereignty) that is incapable of transcendence proper and is also ever-unwilling to accept the world and the present situation, they appeal for a highly similar rejection of being that utilizes negation and its limits.

We are thus faced with a double conception of humanity in each of these three authors—conceptions as political as they are philosophical. Sartre, Bataille, and Levinas reject emphatically the humanist ideas that praised man as an ideal or as a ground of existence and thought. In the texts under consideration here, this "old" notion of man is identified explicitly with a conception of subjectivity that must be discarded together with traditional philosophy: it is a guarantee of a false totality, and transcendental unity of the subject that can no longer be maintained and is even politically undesirable. Moreover, the transformation in the premises and conditions of possibility of political thought that can follow from these claims is of the order of nothing less than a veritable revolution. For Levinas and Sartre, man is *by no means* an adequate foundation for the existence and the understanding of reality—he has no special access to it and cannot be seen as transcending the totality (or even the various different parts) of this reality. Sartre's dissociation of transcendental consciousness from the I as the active part of the self specifically targets the subject qua unity of I-humanity-transcendence. Levinas attacks both the idealism that trusts too quickly in freedom and fails to understand the priority of a reality that engulfs and entraps man, as well as any political ontology that would fail to understand that man cannot be simply his givenness and ground. In his attack on "all that is above things and men," on all "authority that maintained [human life] in oppression," in his use of tumult as a limit by contrast to which the homogeneity of existence reveals itself, Bataille implicitly concurs that the modern imperative is one of undoing a conception of humanity that would distinguish it in some way from the brutal and ugly reality of its existence and from its effort to overcome, to exit from, this condition.

Modern humanity, it turns out in Sartre's, Bataille's, and Levinas's arguments has paradoxically dehumanized itself, has reduced itself to a way of understanding the world whose humanism leads to its own submission to this world. By failing to properly understand the limitations and illusions imposed by its interaction with reality, modern humanism has led to Nazism. The corollary of such a claim is that *only phenomenology, buttressed and contextualized by a philosophical understanding of the rise of modernity, can reopen the question of man in such a way as to allow both his fall from the delusional idealist pinnacle, and a solid philosophical reinterpretation of his theo-political situation in modernity*. Thus, these essays complete the early phenomenological disfiguring of classical man, the destruction of the trust in a teleological occidental consciousness and its progress to humanist perfection, and the attack on claims of philosophical and scientific absolute or even positive knowledge.

Each of the three authors further provided a site that could be interpreted as a positive concept of the human—but they do so only while marking it out as basically impossible (Levinas's escape, Bataille's sovereignty), or they use it to complement the breakup of human subjectivity. Because of the terms of his rejection of Nazism (as a violent political reduction of man to his biological givenness), and because of his reliance on *excendence* as a demonstration of the insufficiency of realism, Levinas can be said to identify the humanity of man with escape, with the movement of the subject that is at once impossible and irreducible. Sartre's new site for humanity is defined by the *I* as activity of the *me* within the realm of intersubjectivity—humanity is to be found therein, that is, as a phenomenon or corollary of the breakdown of transcendence that can maintain neither itself nor the I as premises of thought, consciousness, and action. Sartre refuses to give further content to the specificity or even the humanity of this humanity. Bataille's argument (which may be thought in existentialist terms) allows Troppmann to step toward the destruction, or more appropriately the *kenosis* of a human subject as a specific unity or particle of society that performs, behaves, and acts in the world. The outrageous claim that such an emptied, chaotic subject should be sovereign and should thus show the other necessary part of humanity (not just the homogeneous and homogenizing one) in and because of its rejection of the world and negation of its own purpose and understanding of Being was an expression of contempt for the political alternatives of the 1930s, for the homogeneity these alternatives arise from, and for the false sovereignty they fantasize. All of this marks at once the radicalism and antihumanism of Bataille's novel.

In other words, all three authors provide this "new" idea of the human with a formal status but no real "content"—at most a content conceived by way of opposition. The dismantling of the subject, its entrapment in "reality" leads at once to a need for escaping and overcoming this reality and a formal demonstration of this impossibility. In all three writers, the human appears anew precisely in the limits between reality and man's effort for self-determination and autonomy in it. It is this sense of a man trapped in a world beyond his control and crudely attempting to rationalize and dominate this world that dominates the loss of faith in humanism. The human subject falls from a rational, transcendental first-person singular that speaks, thinks, and desires things and representations radically external and comprehensible to it, to an embattled, emptied out *he* struggling with the forces of reality and unsuccessfully fantasizing the possibility of a new transcendental distancing from the world.

6. Coda

The 1943 appearance of Jean-Paul Sartre's *Being and Nothingness* produced a revolution in French thought by almost single-handedly creating the movement that would become internationally famous under the name of existentialism. Sartre's work also brought together a lot of different strands of 1930s thought and elaborated a theory of freedom largely commensurate with the critiques of humanism that he and his contemporaries had formulated in the 1930s. The almost Bataillean tone of Sartre's famous phrase "man is useless passion" deserves a juxtaposition with a few sentences in which Bataille, whose *Inner Experience* Sartre excoriated in a scathing review, proceeded to present man in terms that bring to a similar conclusion the move away from humanism and affirmative anthropology these thinkers had pursued in the 1930s:

> If man's an occurrence, what occurs isn't the answer to a question—it's the occurrence of a question. We ask questions and can't close a wound opened by hopeless questioning in us: "*Who am I? What am I?*"
>
> I am—man is—a calling into question of what we are, of individual being wherever it is—a limitless calling into question, or being, insofar as it becomes self-questioning. . . .
>
> Each occurrence (each individual being) is the outcry of a questioning, an affirmation of a randomness or contingency. But man's more than this: there's questioning in us and it's not just the kind of questioning that there is in stars (or microorganic life). We conjugate all the modes of questioning in the forms of our consciousness, finally becoming (reducing ourselves to) a questioning that doesn't have an answer.[42]

Bataille's interpretation of man as "a questioning that doesn't have an answer" directs to a radical conclusion the claim, shared with Sartre and Levinas during the mid-1930s, that any "new" idea of the human can have a formal status but no real content, definitive expression, or exact determination. Sartre's subsequent emphasis on the precedence of existence over essence argues much the same thing—as does, to a degree, the very careful reformulation of the human in Levinas's work from the late 1940s through the early 1960s, away from a Kantian imperative and instead toward an experience of the other and especially of the face of the other. This convergence of position among three major writers whose post-1945 paths would use some of the same language and sources of philosophical inspiration and yet would differ so dramatically in the desiderata of their arguments and the moral philosophies is not worthy of note simply for itself. It is also a testament to the influence and force of a questioning put in motion by antifoundational realism and pursued, in radically different forms, and with divergent results, for decades to come.

PART II

THE POSTWAR DECADE

Introduction: The Humanist
Mantle, Restored and Retorn

At the Sorbonne on November 4, 1946, during a lecture in a UNES-CO-organized conference aimed at clarifying what kind of politico-philosophical approach to humanism UNESCO should adopt, André Malraux, by then broadly respected for his part in the resistance, returned to his old question: Is Man dead?[1] "At the end of the nineteenth century, Nietzsche's voice took up anew the ancient phrase overheard on the archipelago, 'God is dead!' and gave back to this phrase its tragic accent. What this meant was clear: it meant that one now awaited the royalty of man. The problem posed for us today is to know, *yes or no*, if, in the old land of Europe, man is dead."[2] Malraux spent much of his lecture arguing in favor of a rebirth of France and Europe out of the ashes of war—a rebirth he premised on the success of the resistance and the legacy of European art he sought to revitalize at the time.[3] Yet he carefully kept his question of the "death of man" in the foreground.

It is not at all certain that the European is dead, but it is certain that he is abandoned, that he himself is abandoning his values and . . . prepares himself for death in the same way that any ruling class or any ancient Empire chooses to die from the moment when it is no longer determined to live.[4]

A certain humanism is possible, but—and we must say this well and clearly—it is a tragic humanism.[5]

This tragic humanism, evocative of his 1930s books like *Man's Fate*, but even more of his pessimistic 1943 *Walnut Trees of Altenburg*, speaks to a widespread recognition of the force and destruction of war and is particularly significant in the immediate context of the talk.[6] Through it, Malraux was implicitly responding to an earlier argument presented at the conference, namely Julian Huxley's notion of a "nonpolitical" philosophy of humanity on which Huxley, as director of UNESCO, hoped the organization would be based.[7] Huxley had staked UNESCO's general philosophy on "a universal scientific humanism, unifying the different aspects of human life, and inspired by evolution." But Malraux criticized both the "scientific" premise and the use in unifying material and spiritual aspects of human life.[8] His (by no means Nietzschean) evocation of "tragedy" speaks of a tragedy of science and technology that far from marking the progress of man had led to technologies of war. It also expresses his—and not only his—mistrust of any ideological project that would uncritically evoke a universalist humanism after World War II, even if this evocation aimed at a defense of the individual from violence. Insofar as he believed that art could lead a resurrection of European culture from its ashes, his effort was among the less aggressive efforts to emphasize the "death of man" Malraux once again feared. In posing this question again in late 1946, and given his massive political capital at the time, Malraux found himself addressing a much broader series of controversies concerning humanism than when he first turned this question into a premise for political action in the 1920s. Through his timing, Malraux signaled the end of a short-lived humanist reconciliation and stood literally at the cusp of a new exposion of antihumanism, one that would be much more far-reaching than its 1930s progenitor.

Following the occupation of France in 1940, the situation concerning humanism changed dramatically. While the Vichy regime advanced its "National Revolution," the resistance transformed the prewar fragmentation of the humanist imaginary by casting the struggle it was engaged in as aimed not just at the restoration of France proper but also the vanquishing of Nazi barbarism.[9] The certainty that opposing the occupation meant struggling against inhumanity was omnipresent in partisan journals (like *Franc-Tireur, Combat, Mouvement de libération nationale*—and even in the names of such journals as *L'Homme libre*), in mimeographed calls to resistance, in works of literature, and even in a number of *Declarations of the Rights of Man* that were offered throughout the war years.[10] As the historian François Furet would later write, reinvoking this resistance versus barbarism duality, World War II "constituted an event both too gigantic and too universal not to have a simple meaning that could also be universal."[11] By 1943, the *maquisard* and Free French struggle against National Socialism and Vichy was coded in terms of a redemptive and universalist message of patriotic humanism. With Léon Blum's "rehabilitation of French democracy" at the Riom trial, and with the hopes that a social revolution would accompany the end of German occupation and the Soviet advance in Eastern Europe, the *Maquis* belief in the emergence of a fundamentally French egalitarianism and in the overcoming of recent political failures managed to bridge many of the utopian, religious, and political oppositions that had defined the late interwar period.[12] Further emphasizing the failure of the Third Republic and the expectation of change toward a more genuine democracy, a complex mixture of beliefs in national unity, social welfare, and the construction of a New Europe spread to link socialists to Catholic partisans to De Gaulle's *France Libre*.[13]

With the enthusiasm that prevailed after the *libération*, this trust in a reconciliation of humanisms and in the need for a shared humanity continued until the early months of 1946, by which time mounting disappointments had become definitive.[14] Until then, few could agree with Georges Bataille's despondent October 1944 diagnosis of fascism as "the fact of human beings," not just of insane barbarians, and of fascist violence as mobilizing "an essential part of Man."[15] Instead, for most intellectuals, "the human" could only stand in contrast to the fascist disaster because the legacy of the resistance provided a self-conception that was not just national or sociopolitical, but *moral*. This political morality is what drove resistance hopes for the social terms of the peace still in the making, for the role of France in a new European and world scene, and for the ethical and political role of individuals, intellectuals, and leaders in the French order. The humanist excitement that followed the success of the *résistance* was as extraordinary for intellectuals as it was philosophically complicated. Exemplary of this excitement is Francis Ponge's 1943 poem "Notes on Man," with its announcement that "Man is the future of man."[16] In its confidence in the future, this stanza bears the political certainty of a slogan that covers over substantive differences of belief and political aim in order to mark the claim to a humanism born in wartime as a continuing necessity. The publication of Ponge's poem in the first issue of Jean-Paul

Sartre and Maurice Merleau-Ponty's journal *Les Temps modernes* (in October 1945) emphasized thus that a commitment dating to 1941, which had justified a struggle for man that appeared impossible to achieve, was still at stake and needed to continue despite the resistance triumph.

The difficulties that gradually came to divide the political realm were paralleled by, if not directly expressed in, a growing intellectual recognition of complexities covered over by claims such as Ponge's. Indeed, the years of occupation, often coded in terms of violence and suffering, remained significant after 1944 precisely because the ideas embraced by the resistance could not be easily turned into political goals in a democracy, just as the resistance itself had difficulty in accepting the institutional framework and political offerings of the Fourth Republic.[17] The switch from a cause supposedly benefiting all of humanity to a victory muddled by new micropolitics brought about among intellectuals a dual attitude. On the one hand, they treated the war as a caesura and highlighted the distance from the prewar era; on the other, they gradually turned differences and political oppositions into new fights and a rising disappointment over humanism per se. This dual attitude, which emerges in 1945, deserves close attention.

Exemplary of an emphasis on the distance of 1945 from 1939 was Merleau-Ponty's first essay for *Les Temps modernes*, which unequivocally termed the present time a new world already through its very title, "La Guerre a eu lieu" ("The War Has Taken Place"). Merleau-Ponty explained this assertion by noting that, before the war, "we had secretly resolved to know nothing of violence and unhappiness because we were living in a country too happy and too weak to envisage them" (SNS 139). By contrast, the war had demonstrated the ineluctability of violence in human life and had come to offer a picture of the need to remember this violence when thinking of the political options men were faced with. This perception was often described in terms of a historical model: the pre-WWI period was an era in which the world was "in order"; the Great War and the interwar era at once showed the ugly side and failed illusion of that "order." To quote Bataille:

Everything was self-evident in my childhood: a civilized man was clearly a being of reason; history, as the emergence, stage by stage, of a civilized humanity, was the slow but sure establishment of reason. Those who still experienced the war of

1914 as children could not imagine the bonhomie that reigned before. It was believed then that the world was well made as it was, that is to say that reason had triumphed over violence. That was the common idea of conservatives and liberals. The former thought that changes risked reintroducing disorder, while the latter—radicals and moderate socialists—that it was necessary to eliminate violence little by little. What remained of oppression was not founded on reason.[18]

In such a model, which Merleau-Ponty largely shared, the last war annihilated any hopes that the crisis of World War I could be overcome; it confirmed the end of rational man and highlighted the post-1945 era as one for which neither progress nor any kind of universal bonhomie could be expected without radical changes—which weren't themselves forthcoming. In the first years after 1944, when the direction of Western Europe remained much in doubt and the weight of the recent wars dissimulated for intellectuals the possibility of expansion and progress, such narratives of violence dominating over reason underwrote a sense of Europe as a geopolitical and philosophical entity coming to a close. Recognizing this is crucial to understanding a series of significant problems regarding humanism's loss of place in the modern world.

One such problem is the rise of human rights discourse from 1942 through the signing of the Universal Declaration of Human Rights in 1948, particularly the effort to move away from teleological theories of man's self-perfection and natural benevolence, and to advocate a humanism "from below" based on the need to provide a framework for a basic defense of human beings as individuals.[19] Nevertheless, human rights left many intellectuals unconvinced precisely because they were seen as characteristic of the 1789–1914 period, as bourgeois tools that did not fully address the recent memory of the resistance as a necessarily violent practice or the complexity of state-group-individual relations; the Catholic and conservative efforts to appropriate the rhetoric, humanism, and politics of rights also contributed to this.[20] These ambiguities can also be seen in the political sphere: in France, the First Constituent Assembly sought in early 1946 to draft a "Declaration on Human Rights" that would be accepted by referendum together with a constitution for the Fourth Republic. Such a declaration was only achieved thanks to ideological compromises, but it was also quickly abandoned—without replacement—by the Second Constituent Assembly in the following summer.[21] Human rights were perhaps a good way to establish some sort of basic humanist principles, but they were neither a guaranteed solution nor a broadly shared middle ground. Other intellectuals worked hard to advance human rights—most notably, the jurist René Cassin, who had designed the Charter of de Gaulle's Free French forces, was a major force in the United Nations Committee on Human Rights, and as of 1947, was a frequent French delegate to the United Nations and UNESCO. Cassin became a Nobel laureate in 1968 for his work on human rights. But in the French context human rights seemed at best a compromise and by no means an achievement.

Second, several international conferences on "modern" or "European" man took place across Europe during the early postwar period, notably at the Rencontres Internationales de Genève and at the Société Européenne de la Culture, but also under the aegis of UNESCO (which organized the aforementioned 1946 Sorbonne conference in which Malraux, Aragon, and Huxley spoke). The Rencontres Internationales de Genève forum would broach the subject of European humanism repeatedly, in 1946 (on the European spirit today), in 1949 (calling for a "new humanism"), in 1950 (on the rights of the mind), in 1951 (on the knowledge of man in the twentieth century), and in 1952 (on man in relation to science).[22] Such conferences would persist in the 1950s and 1960s, something that testifies to the continuing political and intellectual pertinence of the questions involved, the lack of any obvious answer, and the force of Western European efforts to resolve them.[23]

A third consequence of this caesura with the pre-WWII period was the consecration of a number of influential older intellectuals (for example, Léon Blum, Jean Paulhan, André Gide, and even Malraux) as "great humanists"—in the sense of towering bearers of French culture who had fought for egalitarian and universal ideals. This may seem like a secondary effect, but because it identifies humanist culture with the passing of great figures forceful in the past, it is not. In a world marked above all by the poverty and destruction wrought by World War II, these "humanists" were seen as irreplaceable because so few were left, because they pointed back to a pre-1918 world supposedly marked by Dreyfusardism and *civilisation*, and because their embodiment of a politically uncompromised French humanist culture offered both an image of a continuity in French culture and a conviction that this continuity was coming to an end.

If, then, rationalism and humanism seemed more easily identified with the past, the fast development of fissures in the temporary humanist reconciliation was no less crucial. In the context of post-*résistance* humanism, the principal division that ensued from these changes was between Communists (who claimed that true humanism followed from class struggle and the reality of postrevolutionary human relations) and anti-Communists (who over time became increasingly critical of the Soviet Union, namely, its international policy and its violence).[24] This division gets much more complicated once the question of the resistance legacy is raised.[25] First of all, the privileges and cultural capital accorded to the resistance, together with the frequent public evocation of its success and importance were unpopular among those who had endured Vichy and the occupation without openly participating in the resistance struggle (not to mention Vichy's supporters who were trying to make their way quietly in a new era). By contrast, those who had been active members of the resistance were faced with the problem of figuring out how to incorporate this past experience of violence in peacetime, or (differently put) how they could possibly celebrate and cherish memories of war. With the slow process of reconstruction under way, many former *résistants* were unwilling to accept that what they had fought for was merely this reconstruction, and many refused to recognize any present intellectual and political struggle as commanding the same contrast between good and evil as the one in which they had acted. Many *résistants*, like Merleau-Ponty, Sartre, Eric Weil, not to mention a large contingent of Communists and fellow travelers, shared a belief in the ineluctability of violence within human struggle and were unwilling to accept moral philosophies for which violence—the violence they had suffered, fought, and even inflicted—was merely an aberration. Many had also to deal with the problem of the USSR, onto which they projected the memory of the resistance, but whose brutal repression and Eastern bloc dominance left them powerless against antitotalitarian accusers.[26] For these overlapping groups, the rejection of simplistic humanisms was a corollary of their rejection of positive ideas of human nature and the effort to disengage from the political hopes on offer. This is where the Communist/anti-Communist divide became significant. For those suspicious of Communism (for example, Malraux or Raymond Aron), Soviet power and totalitarianism had grown to take over the shadow left behind by fascism. Meanwhile, a series of best-sellers and intellectual affairs concerning Soviet violence from the 1945 translation of Arthur Koestler's *Darkness at Noon* to Victor Kravchenko's 1947 *I Chose Freedom* and David Rousset's 1948 turn of attention from Nazism to the Soviet Union, heightened mistrust toward the USSR and its profession of humanism.[27] But to Marxists and fellow travelers, who had established their humanist credentials already since a mid-1930s commitment to antifascism, the strategic success of the USSR in the European war and the solid PCF electoral outcome after the liberation granted such intellectual popularity and force to their case for the dependence of human relations on an overcoming of capitalism that they did not hesitate to associate any and all intellectual opponents with fascism—with an ideology "as brutal" or "as threatening to the interests of all humanity" as fascism.

By late 1946, the breakup of the Union Nationale and the Mouvement de Libération Nationale (a breakup that Malraux enthusiastically supported and that framed his return to the question of man's survival) had left the political arena divided over problems of humanism and violence. With the passing of any possibility for a "third way" (a move toward a radically new democracy and toward a politics not bound to the USA/USSR divide) and with early cracks showing in the legacy and memory of the resistance already in mid-1945, new competition and new languages of political criticism emerged.[28] The folding of several influential journals that had emerged from the resistance and had contributed to its philosophical priorities (for example, *Fontaine* or *Confluences*) played a part in the deepening of intellectual divisions. The failure of radical social hopes, which by late 1946 had been compounded by questions concerning the experience of violence in World War II and the apparent return of a relatively weak republic often dominated by urgent economic questions as much as by political squabbling between Communists and Gaullists, added to the mistrust of new humanisms. Here, the tenor of the 1930s conflict of exclusivist humanisms reemerged. Intellectuals who in the 1930s had already rejected political alternatives had little reason to expect from them any real improvement in human relations, especially after a second (and far more brutal) European War, the return of a capitalism mixed with impoverishment and destruction, and the decline of France as a European and colonial power.

Here it is fair to say that with the old Right defeated, Communists captured the humanist mantle and sought to direct it against the revelations of Soviet violence.[29] In contrast to everyday life in a still-unreconstructed and impoverished France, they proposed a world guided by the concretization of abstract ideals, by social and material equality, by the end to all fascism in the completion of the revolution. Because of their contempt of democratic politics, the Communists' decimation of competing claims to humanism became even more influential than Communism itself, particularly in the expectation that human rights and liberal notions of equality could sufficiently provide for genuinely human relations. Thus, if Communists successfully wore—at least for a couple of years— the humanist mantle, emphasizing the role of an impersonal history that moves toward genuine human relations and heightening their criticisms of competing movements, this is not to suggest that their practical and domestic politics were as intellectually significant as the critical dimension of Communist humanism. Merleau-Ponty's rejection of liberalism is exemplary of the breadth and depth of mistrust for political solutions and offers again an exemplary formulation:

Democratic optimism allows that, in a State where the rights of man are guaranteed, no liberty any longer encroaches on any other, and the coexistence of men as autonomous and reasonable subjects is assured. This is to suppose that violence appears only episodically in human history, that economic relationships in particular tend of themselves to effect harmony and justice and, finally, that the structure of the human and natural world is rational. We know today that formal equality of rights and political liberty mask rather than eliminate relationships based on force. And the political problem is then to institute social structures and real relationships among men such that liberty, equality, and right become effective. The weakness of democratic thinking is that it is less political than moral, since it poses no problem of social structure and considers the conditions for the exercise of justice to be given with humanity.[30]

The mistrust of democratic solutions was central to the intellectual Left's rejection of liberal humanism and participated also in the disregard for idealism.[31] As Tony Judt argues, it was also characteristic of the near-universal rejection of the idea that justice could or should be universal.[32] This went beyond Communism proper: for many, it expressed the failure of politics (Communist politics included) to provide for an improvement in real living conditions. After 1948, when it became increasingly clear that Communism was not on the way to fulfilling its promises, the Marxist critique of the language of rights and democratic optimism backfired on Communism as well, leaving many intellectuals disillusioned with political promises altogether.

Competing with Marxist humanism—and indeed very influential—was also Catholic humanism, which remained theocentric and sought, especially in the decades that followed, to be identified with the turn to individual rights that would dominate the 1948 Universal Declaration of Human Rights. Leading Catholic intellectuals from Maritain and de Lubac to Marcel and Berdyaev all insisted on the need for both human rights and the placement of God above man in the human order of things.

But the major new philosophical humanist alternative to Marxism, born in the resistance, heavily indebted to antifoundational realism, and rising in popularity, was existentialism. Thanks to Sartre's effort to set it on powerful political ground, existentialism became involved in a dialogue (often one-sided) with Marxism and advanced a democratic socialism consistent with the Marxist critique of democracy, as well as a moral demand founded on a Hegelian-Marxist conception of the universal.[33] This had become increasingly necessary in 1945, as Communist attacks on existentialism's success multiplied.[34] Sartre's moral philosophy of action and responsibility had *not* been fundamentally humanist in his early work: like *The Transcendence of the Ego*, his 1938 novel *Nausea* had denied the validity and utility of humanism. His major 1943 work *Being and Nothingness* sought to utilize elements of the transformation of French thought in the 1930s so as to establish a new conception of subjectivity that took into account this sense of entrapment in the world and the demand for a need to act not reduced to humanism but still reflected in the ethics of the resistance. Sartre's advocates often highlighted his opposition to humanism as a conviction in the improvement of the human condition and in a belief in a fundamental human essence or nature (expressed most famously in the dicta "Existence precedes essence" and "Man is useless passion"). But with Sartre's political effort, expressed at the height of popular humanist hopes in October 1945 in his lecture "L'Existentialisme est un humanisme" (Existentialism Is a Humanism) and—still later—in his call to engaged literature in "Qu'est-ce que la littérature ?" (What Is Literature?), these oppositions softened.[35] Sartre began to approach the humanist problem in an ambiguous fashion, expressly seeking to partake in a politics that was radically left-wing, indeed unorthodox Marxist, without completely succumbing to Marxism's erasure of the individual in favor of class politics.[36]

Thus by late 1946 mistrust of the rhetorics of humanism became the political starting point for philosophical searches of a new conception of man that would reject his priority and could explain why and how man could have been revealed to be so precarious, violent, and incapable of constructing a better world. It is significant then that Malraux's UNESCO lecture on "Man and the Culture of Art" is contemporary to Heidegger's composition of the "Letter on 'Humanism,'" to the appearance of Merleau-Ponty's *Humanism and Terror* as a four-part essay in *Les Temps modernes* (October 1946–January 1947), the publication of Kojève's *Introduction à la lecture de Hegel* (an abbreviated form of his Hegel seminar), and Maurice Blanchot's composition of his seminal literary essay "Literature and the Right to Death." These works facilitated a new engagement with the possibility of antihumanism. Their authors, fully aware of the complexities of the postwar context, radicalized the anti-anthropocentrism of the 1930s to allow for what they conceived as more genuine, fundamental conceptions of man. As, for many of them, neither Marxism nor existentialism adequately covered the 1930s critiques directed toward idealism and humanism, the need for a rethinking of humanism came to transform conceptions that had become popular in the late 1930s and especially the later wartime period—of human entrapment in the world, of the limitations of transcendence—into premises for a radically negative understanding of man.

At stake in the four chapters that follow in this second part of the book is the postwar negotiation of antihumanism, the establishment of a philosophical and political negative anthropology premised on a radicalization of phenomenological approaches of the 1930s, but also on a wariness of political utopias, and a turn toward language and being. These offer a competition between different philosophical and political positions in the effort to provide a theory of humanity that would suffice as a recognition of the failure of humanism and for an anthropological ontology that would be more fundamental than humanism could allow.

What takes place during this period is less a continuation or radicalization of the 1930s effort to undermine idealism, notions of transcendence, or man as given, natural, or essential, than the establishment and organization of a satisfactory antihumanism. Which is to say that at stake in the course of early postwar thought is the insistent questioning of the place of man in the world and in thought that results in an affirmation of a negative anthropology, the modification of atheism to move beyond or outside of secular humanism, and the critique of humanisms deemed to be too facile, anthropocentric, or idealistic. In each of the major texts to be considered in the four chapters that follow, Sartre's "Existentialism Is a Humanism," Heidegger's "Letter on 'Humanism,'" Blanchot's "Literature and the Right to Death," Merleau-Ponty's *Humanism and Terror*, and Hyppolite's writings around 1950, each author makes a sustained effort to address these questions and to criticize alternative approaches to them. As *critiques*, these texts affect the intellectual landscape sketched out in Part One in two forceful ways. First, they reframe, radicalize, and move beyond the anti-anthropocentrist trends of the 1930s, suggesting antifoundational realism to have been too subjectivist, critiquing Kojève's "end of history," and furthering the sense of entrapment in "reality" suggested by the early Levinas, Sartre, and Bataille (and thus the chapters that follow address intellectuals' *antihumanist* critiques of Kojève and of the early existentialism of Sartre and Bataille). The postwar emphasis on anti-anthropocentrism thus distances negative anthropology and antihumanism from the very existentialism that in the 1930s they had helped spawn. Second, these texts target the dominant humanisms of the period and at once build on and compete with each other (in a movement we could title "No Antihumanism Except Mine!"). In this vein, the following chapters address both the political positions philosophers (notably Sartre and Merleau-Ponty) assumed in defense of the anthropological element of their thought, and the more formal or ontological emphasis of others (Heidegger, Blanchot, and Hyppolite). The discussion that follows suggests how these positions not only rejected other, ostensibly more classical "humanisms" but, in combination, also managed to hone the broader anthropological and atheological argument that each of them sought in different terms. Not least at stake in this compounding argument that follows is the question of modernity and historical existence—the question of the present time and of the hopes that could be associated with subjective existence, the "end of metaphysics" and the possibility of over-coming the historical determination of the post-1945 era, the nostalgia for a better era coupled with the demands of modernity and the possibilities of novelty and critical thought. The different arguments by Heidegger, Sartre, Blanchot, Merleau-Ponty, and Hyppolite thus negotiate a number of terms and problems, among them freedom, history, action, modernity, violence, at the same time as they address the legacy of the resistance, the possibility of politics in a world that can no longer depend on the certitude of progress or human harmony, the geopolitical division of a communist East from a capitalist West that was perceived as leaving Western Europe to hang in the balance, and the survival of man in an atheist universe. It is this last, the meaning of atheist life in the modern world, that underlies and in many respects frames the arguments that follow.

5

After the Resistance (1): Engagement, Being, and the Demise of Philosophical Anthropology

Phenomenology triumphed in the early postwar era. The most significant journal of the period, *Les Temps modernes*, was formed and directed by two phenomenologists, Jean-Paul Sartre and Maurice Merleau-Ponty; Georges Bataille's and Eric Weil's competitor, *Critique*, depended at least as much as *Les Temps modernes* on the influence of phenomenology. Histories of existentialism, which emerged quickly because of the popularity of Sartre, Camus, and Beauvoir, invariably constructed the genealogy of contemporary thought by reference to Husserl, Heidegger, and Hegel. The latter's influence was tied in turn to the rise of Kojève's intellectual fame and Jean Hyppolite's academic career. But phenomenology also quickly turned against the existentialist vogue. Together with many young thinkers who came of age during and right after the war, and who objected to existentialism's growing attachment to Marxism, virtually all philosophers who had participated in a quasi-phenomenological and anti-idealist overcoming of the "old" humanisms expressed their general agreement with certain existentialist premises but came out in opposition to the humanization of existentialism in Sartre's work after *Being and Noth-*

ingness and especially in the 1945 lecture "Existentialism Is a Humanism" and the essay "What Is Literature?" Koyré, Kojève, Wahl, Bataille, Heidegger, Levinas—*all* these contemporaries argued against Sartre's effort to turn the phenomenological impulse, political ambiguity, and anti-utopian imaginary of their 1930s thought into a humanism essentially allied to the Soviet Union and fueled by a political anthropology of the dignity of human existence.[1] Younger philosophers and writers, like Jean Hyppolite and Jean Beaufret (who both began teaching at the ENS after the war), became quite critical of Sartre's effort. The concern of this chapter is Heidegger's "Letter on 'Humanism,'" in particular its radicalization and critique of Sartre's own critique of old humanisms. After first considering Sartre's ambiguously humanist view in "Existentialism Is a Humanism" and the reactions and critiques his thought met with, I will approach the "Letter on 'Humanism'" in its French intellectual context and in its philosophical argument. To understand the "Letter on 'Humanism,'" and particularly its movement *beyond* humanism and *beyond* philosophical anthropology, we should see its force in the late 1940s as rising from the context of the resistance and its breakup.

1. Sartre's effort to identify his thought with humanism, indeed to present it as the only possible and adequate humanism, was at once an accomplishment for antihumanism and a betrayal of the anti-anthropocentric stakes of 1930s thought. It was forceful and ambiguous. No one in recent times had gone to so much trouble to explain why he was a humanist, and no antifoundational realist thinker had avowed his humanism quite that explicitly. "Existentialism Is a Humanism" expressed at once the philosophical and popular success of existentialism, and his willingness to oppose to contemporary humanisms a notion of subjectivity stripped to its bare fact, namely, man's existence. With "Existentialism Is a Humanism" Sartre became emphatic on the need to understand existentialism as not merely dealing with the horror and absurdity of subjective existence in a world that forever exceeds the subject's comprehension and action—a world in which the epistemological insights of antifoundational realism have led to moral anguish. Instead, Sartre sought to demonstrate that it is precisely by arguing that man is unable to control the world that existentialism provides an ethical call to action. But he did not engage in an

all-out acceptance of humanism; indeed, he anticipated the question why he should look to humanism for an ethico-political solution at the very end of his lecture:

People have said to me: "But you have written in your *Nausée* that the humanists are wrong, you have even ridiculed a certain type of humanism, why do you now go back upon that?" In reality, the word humanism has two very different meanings. One may understand by humanism a theory which upholds man as the end-in-itself and as the supreme value. . . . That kind of humanism is absurd . . . an existentialist will never take man as the end, since man is still to be determined. And we have no right to believe that humanity is something to which we could set up a cult, after the manner of Auguste Comte. The cult of humanity ends in Comtian humanism, shut in upon itself, and—this must be said—in Fascism. We do not want a humanism like that. But there is another sense of the word, of which the fundamental meaning is this: Man is all the time outside of himself: it is in projecting and losing himself beyond himself that he causes Man to exist; and, on the other hand, it is by pursuing transcendent aims that he himself is able to exist. Since man is thus self-surpassing and can grasp objects only in relation to his self-surpassing, he is himself the heart and center of his transcendence. There is no other universe except the human universe, the universe of human subjectivity. This relation of transcendence as constitutive of man (not in the sense that God is transcendent, but in the sense of self-surpassing) with subjectivity (in such a sense that man is not shut up in himself but forever present in a human universe)—it is this that we call existential humanism. (EH 90–93 / 309–10)

This passage (echoed in later defenses of Sartre's humanism, notably by Merleau-Ponty) does not quite express the tone of the lecture, but it is suggestive of Sartre's awareness of the step he was taking in declaring existentialism a humanism and a philosophy of man.[2] It is worth emphasizing the track Sartre takes to not be accused of being a humanist in the old or classical sense. Only a couple of years earlier Sartre had himself accused none other than Nietzsche and Bataille of being humanists.[3] Here he emphasizes the disregard for the Comtean, Kantian, and even Communist humanisms: "The cult of humanity ends . . . in Fascism. We do not want a humanism like that."[4] The care he takes provides a distinct (and largely unappreciated) sense that, for Sartre, (a) his own turn toward humanism was no small business, and (b) his overturning of the classical priority of *essentia* over *existentia* seemed radical enough to allow an escape from the limitations of earlier humanisms:

In the philosophic atheism of the eighteenth century, the notion of God is suppressed, but not, for all that, the idea that essence is prior to existence; something of that idea we still find everywhere, in Diderot, in Voltaire, and even in Kant. Man possesses a human nature; that "human nature," which is the conception of human being, is found in every man; which means that each man is a particular example of a universal conception, the conception of Man. In Kant, this universality goes so far that the wild man of the woods, man in the state of nature and the bourgeois are all contained in the same definition and have the same fundamental qualities. Here again, the essence of man precedes that historic existence which we confront in experience. (EH 20–21 / 290)

This second description also highlights a basic tension between humanism as "understood up to then" and Sartre's own version. By contrast to Albert Camus's opposition between the absurd world and the "something in this world which is meaningful—and this is man"—which first assures man's meaning and then compares it to the horror of a lack—Sartre's position rejects concepts of human nature, and of man as the measure of things ethical, philosophical, and political.[5] His minimal humanism and restricted subjectivism ("man cannot transcend human subjectivity" [EH 25/291; trans. modified]) can begin only given this rejection. In other words, this critique of classical humanism grounds the better-known part of Sartre's argument: his emphasis that "man is freedom," his citation from Ponge's poetic contribution to the first issue of *Les Temps modernes* that "Man is the future of man" (EH 38/295), his expectation that in choice, decision, and action, the individual makes or builds the universal (EH 70/304)— and that therefore existentialism is the only political morality "compatible with the dignity of man, it is the only one which does not make man into an object" (EH 65/302). Furthermore, this argument points to a tension between two sorts of influence. On the one hand, as Sartre suggests (EH 9–11/287), his attempt to baptize existentialism a humanism is evidence of the force of the Communist rejection of subjectivism and its pressure on strands of contemporary thought—whose rejection of a subservience of the individual to class politics the Communists regarded as a politics of the will. It also offers a sense of his conviction that a doctrine that emphasizes the morality and priority of engagement should itself be accordingly engaged. On the other hand, if we allow for his express willingness to make existentialism more widely available and to discuss on a "terrain de vulgarisation," if we allow for the demands he saw as placed on him

by his own thought, this humanism becomes the basic link between phenomenology and existentialism, the central step beyond the 1930s attack
on transcendence to which he had contributed.[6] All this involves a redefinition, *in ambiguous terms,* of man: man is devoid of given essence, transcendence, or set goal, and he is premised on the fact of human existence
and the ontological difference of this existence from that of objects and
animals, but man is also the bearer of political action and moral responsibility, the builder of the universal, therefore anew the ideal and unfailing
ground and limit of thought and action. This tension is precisely what, in
1946, allowed Sartre to in one gesture (indeed a gesture that could be easily understood by an intellectual public lacking a philosophical education)
void philosophy of the expectations of a universal human essence and an
aim toward the "pure" human existence that this essence would grant, and
also to bring anthropocentric humanism back from the grave he had lain
it in with *Being and Nothingness.* It is also what gave "Existentialism Is a
Humanism" force and originality in a field crowded by seemingly more
classical humanist ideologies like Communism, a renascent Catholicism,
a persistent resistentialism, and a political commitment to the democratic
values of the Fourth Republic. Indeed, if Sartre's moral philosophy was—
and could be—said to best reflect a situation relevant to occupation and
resistance rather than to peace, intellectual freedom, and reconstruction,
Sartre used "Existentialism Is a Humanism" to deny that after the liberation things had returned to some sort of normality, to deny that the change
of political regime granted any of the humanisms with which his was competing any privileged status or claim to a human essence. In short, rather
than accepting that commitment had basically changed after the liberation, Sartre argued that its stakes had intensified and that his humanism
offered the sole path distanced enough from essentialism and metaphysics.
This ambiguous and minimal humanism thus offered a huge step for antihumanism and its critique of modern metaphysics. On the one hand, it rejected essentialism and offered a surpassing of preexistentialist humanisms;
on the other, it clearly resolved the humanist problem through subjectivism, granting his anthropology (and the praxis that ensues from it) the status of first philosophy and ground for the rest of his thought. Moving away
from his 1930s writing, Sartre brought back the human as a driving force in
thought, leaving aside any attempts to either ground it or to see beyond it.

2. Sartre's effort to assert existentialism's humanism failed to convince committed Marxists at least as badly as it failed to impress Catholics.[7] Indeed, the influence of defenders of Communist humanism in contemporary culture can be easily seen in their attacks on Sartre, whom they accused of providing a subjectivist bourgeois ideology that not only served the petty worries of the bourgeoisie but also resurrected a fascistic voluntarism.[8] But unlike Catholics and Communists, who argued that Sartre's was not a humanism, the thinkers involved in phenomenology and in the 1930s antifoundational and realist reorganization of philosophy *without exception* accused Sartre of being a confused humanist bound to a subjectivism that distorted his phenomenological philosophy. For them, Sartre failed to carry forward the anti-anthropocentric spirit of the 1930s, reverting to Cartesian and Kantian principles (particularly the primacy of the *ego cogito*). Recalling the experience of watching Sartre deliver "Existentialism Is a Humanism" with a group of fellow *khagneux* including Gilles Deleuze, Michel Tournier wrote in his autobiography:

On October 28, 1945, Sartre called us together. It was a mob scene. An enormous crowd pressed against the walls of the tiny hall. The exits were blocked by those who had not managed to gain entry to the sanctuary, and women who fainted had to be piled on a convenient grand piano. The wildly acclaimed lecturer was lifted bodily over the crowd and onto the podium. Such popularity should have alerted us. Already the suspect tag "existentialism" had been attached to the new system. Having tumbled into the darkened nightclubs of Paris, the new star attracted a grotesque fauna of singers, jazz musicians, soldiers of the Resistance, drunkards, and Stalinists. So what was existentialism? We were soon to find out. Sartre's message could be stated in six words: existentialism is a form of humanism. And to illustrate his point he told us a story about peas in a matchbox. We were floored. Our master had gone and fished up that worn-out old duffer Humanism, still stinking with sweat and "inner life," from the trash heap where we had left him, and now he trotted him out along with the absurd idea of existentialism as if he had invented both. And everyone applauded.[9]

But as suggested already, a few nineteen-year-old phenomenology enthusiasts were not the only ones floored. Belgian philosopher Alphonse de Waelhens, who had published the first book-length study of Heidegger's thought in French, and who would soon interpret Heidegger's "Letter on 'Humanism'" as a *humanist* text, wrote a review of the March 1946 publication as a book of Sartre's *Existentialism Is a Humanism* and explicitly criticized it as an unconvincing humanization and bastardization of Sartre's own thought. De Waelhens accused Sartre of misunderstanding categories and priorities of phenomenology and for creating, without solid reasoning or purpose, unphilosophical universalisms that depended on a vague political program of freedom through engagement.[10] To amplify his criticism, De Waelhens actually cited Merleau-Ponty in support of his argument against Sartre's "new" and "utopian" argument on freedom of action: "[The *Phenomenology of Perception*] lets us think that we were not altogether wrong to have attributed to [Sartre] a doctrine of freedom that, under pretext of making freedom the fundamental value, destroys it."[11] In defense of Sartre against Catholic and Communist critics, Merleau-Ponty (whose chapter on freedom in his *Phenomenology of Perception* can also be read as *targeting* Sartre's trust in freedom) emphasized Sartre's caution, writing in *Figaro littéraire* that "if humanism is the religion of man as a natural species or the religion of man as a perfected creature, Sartre is as far from humanism today as he ever was. . . . The savagery of *La Nausée* is still there; it is only that Sartre has come to realize that men were close to his heart, even when he judged them most severely" (SNS 45). Merleau-Ponty was a lone supporter though. Jean Wahl, while clearly receptive to Sartre's thought and excited about existentialism, staked a position ultimately closer to Heidegger's. His talk "A Short History of Existentialism," attended by many thinkers of the early generation of Heidegger's readers (like Koyré, Gandillac, and Levinas), included a critique of Sartre's tendency toward popularization. The publication of Alexandre Kojève's lectures on Hegel also implicitly targeted Sartre, through Kojève's claim on the end of history as a death of man. In a well-known footnote added to the 1947 publication, Kojève suggested that with the end of history, there is nothing left to do: the hopes of a theory of *praxis* or engagement, such as Sartre's, were unfounded.[12] If the end of history *had already come*, as Kojève had suggested in the late 1930s, then human engagement and action had lost its significance.[13] Kojèvian partisans Maurice Blanchot and Georges Bataille also argued against the authenticity attributed to Sartre's engagement, calling it "deceitful" (WF 317). For Blanchot, the literature of action (as presented in "What Is Literature?") erased literature's capacity of addressing its own limit and lacked a genuine relation to death and genuine engagement such as the one he located in the Terror following the French Revolution.[14] In general terms, for Blanchot the humanization of literature's task could only come at the expense of an understanding of its fundamentally nonhuman and inhuman order and its kinship with death. Bataille, whose "mysticism" Sartre had criticized *as a humanism* that was indifferent to fascism, also criticized Sartre's humanism and literature of engagement in terms echoing Blanchot.[15] If anything, Sartre's advocacy of humanism brought forth an explosion of writing on the difficulty and confusion, if not the impossibility of humanism.[16]

3. Seen against this background, Heidegger's postwar incursion into the French philosophical scene came to interest a new and very different readership than the earlier, anti-idealist group of the 1930s. Thinkers of the 1930s had read Heidegger as a slightly older contemporary who provided the crucial philosophical premise that made possible their own innovative thought. But they had no illusions as to his commitment to Nazism. Those who, already influenced by 1930s protoexistentialism and by the import of Hegel and Kierkegaard, came to read Heidegger more closely during the occupation and found in him a major thinker whose politics hardly affected the utility of his thought—a thinker who could be read explicitly *against* the politics he endorsed. Indeed, while collaborationists like Marcel Déat and Robert Brasillach had presented themselves as deeply indebted to German thought, none of the major collaborators and inspirers of collaboration engaged with phenomenology. And only Marxists came to view Heidegger as seriously contaminated.[17] Yet at the same time, Heidegger was read with considerable profit by the resistance.[18] Among later prominent intellectuals, Sartre's is the most obvious case and Jean Beaufret's the most notorious—but Frédéric de Towarnicki, Eric Weil, Gaston Fessard, and Joseph Rovan all touted the value of Heidegger for their thinking and even for their resistentialism, and they consistently contrasted his thought to his personal politics. Sartre, who at the height of his commitment to Husserl in the 1930s had considered Heidegger's thought "barbaric" by comparison, declared himself a "partisan of Heidegger" during the "phony war" period of 1939–40, even teaching him at the camp where he was held with other French soldiers the following year.[19] Beaufret first encountered Heidegger while in the resistance network *Pericles*, when he was given a copy of *Sein und Zeit*

by Joseph Rovan, a Germanist who, under the not insignificant pseudonym Joseph Rosenthal had translated fragments on time from *Being and
Time* in 1943 and who in 1947 would attempt and publish the first, partial
translation of the "Letter on 'Humanism.'"[20] Rovan was an important
résistant, forging identity papers in Lyon; in 1944, he was arrested and
sent to Dachau, but reemerged, having converted to Catholicism, and became a vice-director of Emmanuel Mounier's *Esprit* and a Gaullist advisor
with a career that continued well into the 1980s.[21] For his part Beaufret
was skilled in philosophy, but his German was apparently weak. From a
rightist 1930s nonconformism, he had moved to the resistance and was
sympathetic to the Left, and he (according to Rovan) had concerns over
Heidegger's political and personal failings.[22] Not incidentally, Beaufret
published his own texts on Heidegger and existentialism in *Confluences*,
and the "Letter on 'Humanism'" and his work on Heidegger in *Fontaine*.
Both of these (like *Les Temps modernes*) were journals tied to the resistance.[23] As Ethan Kleinberg has noted, Beaufret later meticulously tied
his resistantialism to his reading of Heidegger (largely to provide political
protection for Heidegger), even claiming that on the day of the Allied
invasion of Normandy on June 6, 1944, he reproached himself for rejoicing
more for realizing some of what Heidegger was all about than about being told about the invasion itself.[24] Meanwhile, Fessard taught Heidegger
throughout the occupation, all the while contributing to the resistance as
the director of *Témoignage Chrétien*, and the author of the major rallying
cry *France, prends garde de perdre ton âme!*, the first and most significant
Catholic intellectual *résistance* document.[25] And as is well known, Sartre,
in *Being and Nothingness*, implicitly contrasted the authenticity of the *résistant* willing to face death against the self-deceiving ill-will of the collaborator who took the easy way out. Jean Wahl's case is more ambiguous:
he expressed vocal opposition to Heidegger's politics, but despite being
arrested and sent to the concentration camp at Drancy (then escaping to
the United States for the remainder of the occupation), he restarted his
teaching at the Sorbonne in 1945 with a Heidegger course.[26] Not only did
these figures relegitimate the study of Heidegger's thought during and
after the occupation, they also helped make Heidegger—particularly his
positions on authenticity and death—a cornerstone of *résistance* morality.
    A very different sensitivity to the political question concerning Hei-

degger became common currency in the group surrounding Alexandre Koyré that had shaped Heidegger's early reception. After 1945, most of them came to share a critical approach to Heidegger, emphasizing both the monumental value of *Being and Time* and their worries over his politics and later thought. Though Wahl relegitimated Heidegger at the Sorbonne in 1945, he was also the first to publicly report, in the American journal *The New Republic*, that during the rectorship Heidegger had barred Husserl from the university library at Freiburg.[27] By the summer of 1946, Wahl had received (and had started to circulate) a copy of Heidegger's "Letter to the University Authorities," his apologia for the rectorship.[28] Later, Wahl would become embroiled in public exchanges with the younger Heideggerians (especially Beaufret), and while teaching Heidegger elaborately and quite carefully, continued to criticize the general aim of his thought and explicitly endorsed the young Jürgen Habermas's 1953 response to the *Introduction to Metaphysics*.[29] Koyré (who, like Wahl, Sartre, Vladimir Jankélevitch, Merleau-Ponty, and others would refuse to attend the 1955 conference at Cerisy because of Heidegger's Nazism), had arrived at a harsh decision on Heidegger's "failure" in his careful and long 1946 study on Heidegger's conception of truth, which opened *Critique*.[30] Levinas's critique of Heidegger gradually became central to his own work, while Kojève came to scorn Heidegger's post-1927 path altogether.[31]

Given these demarcation lines, it is not unfair to mark out the second phase of Heidegger's French reception as beginning not with the postwar emphasis on a "correct" reading of his thought against the original "anthropological" interpretation running from Corbin and Kojève to Sartre, but instead with the resistance-era presentation of Heidegger as a master thinker, the profundity of whose thought on death transcended the problem posed by his political commitment and facilitated a counterreading against this very commitment.[32] The postwar debate in *Les Temps modernes* attests to the significance of this interpretation among non-Communist philosophers. A sign of the growing differences between the Communist and non-Communist resistance, the debate was rooted in the Communist effort to discredit existentialism as a petty bourgeois, individualist, even fascistic ideology. This critique of Sartre found a strong pretext in that Heidegger had been a Nazi; for *Les Temps modernes*, it was imperative to show the incidental character of Heidegger's Nazism—that is, to stake and justify a position that all but contradicted the fundamental belief of existentialists in engagement. As Koyré wrote in 1948, "Only the Marxists are neither infected nor infiltrated [by existentialism], and either explain the existentialists away as easily as everything else, or more simply condemn it as Hitlero-Fascism (because its chief representative, M. Heidegger, has been a Nazi) or Trotskyism."[33] Understandably then, *Les Temps modernes* turned the Heidegger debate into a major issue concerning its own legitimacy. *Les Temps modernes* first published exonerating texts by Sartre, Frédéric de Towarnicki, and Maurice de Gandillac.[34] Karl Löwith's "Les Implications politiques de la philosophie de l'existence chez Heidegger," which appeared in late 1946 and argued the case for the significance of Heidegger's Nazism, came to clearly reflect the perception and frustration of the *older* generation.[35] Löwith's argument that Heidegger's historicity and finitude were fundamentally tied to his Nazi arguments met with hefty criticism in France (and especially in *Les Temps modernes* itself) precisely because of the existentialist link to the resistance, its legacy and memory. Responses to Löwith came from Eric Weil (then director of *Critique*), the Belgian existentialist Alphonse de Waelhens, and Jean Beaufret (in other journals), not to mention the existing engagement of Sartre and others, and the translation and publication of the "Letter on 'Humanism,'" which all evoked the perceived utility of Heidegger in the contemporary political scene.[36]

Heidegger himself was active both in this exonerating effort and in the attempt to relate his recent writings to the postwar state of French philosophy (without accepting what he perceived as reductive interpretations of his thought). In fact, he was even more active than is usually acknowledged, sending texts and writing letters to many French contemporaries—a tendency that increased with his rising status in the early 1950s (for example, the aforementioned typescript of Heidegger's self-defense over the rectorship received by Wahl). Arguing that his political involvement was incidental, Heidegger sought to make an impression on young French officers and philosophers visiting him and wrote favorable letters to Sartre and Beaufret.[37] This last was facilitated by a letter Beaufret had written to Heidegger, one that was preceded by a visit from the French soldier Frédéric de Towarnicki—who by chance was carrying with him Beaufret's publications on existentialism in the resistance journal *Con-*

fluences. These events may have led Heidegger to overestimate Beaufret's importance and occasioned their subsequent exchanges, among them the "Letter on 'Humanism.'"[38] To highlight Heidegger's interest in Paris, it is perhaps fitting to note that Heidegger was aware of the writings of Bataille and Blanchot, and that in 1951 he even sent Wahl an offprint of §26 of "Overcoming Metaphysics"—itself hardly a politically exonerating text.[39]

4. Against the background of the gradual breakup of the resistance into pro- and anti-Communist factions, the returning mistrust in humanist solutions, and the spread of philosophical critiques of Sartre, the "Letter on 'Humanism'" can be read anew with a somewhat different emphasis. This context helps explain both the letter's claims to a superior humanism—which I will call a superhumanism—and its attacks on all existing humanisms and on the supposedly anthropocentric focus of French 1930s thought and Sartre's antiessentialism.[40] The complexity of Heidegger's gesture in the "Letter on 'Humanism'" captures and expresses quite powerfully the dilemmas of ex-*résistants* aware of the fragility of engagement and political impotence of the time they were entering. The text thus offers a consistent and radical *negative anthropology*—a term that needs to be understood in the context of his thinking of the negative and the human. Negative anthropology is useful in explaining, from the perspective of philosophical anthropology, the operation Heidegger carries out in this text—an operation that undermines the claims of philosophical anthropology by systematically showing their limitations and their derivativeness vis-à-vis ontology and language. In what follows, I will attempt first to consider aspects of Heidegger's work that directly address the impetus provided by this context and Heidegger's perception of anthropology and then proceed to show the broader address of philosophy that is involved in the "Letter."

What dominates the first half of the essay is Heidegger's use of terms and motifs central to the languages of Sartrean existentialism and phenomenological anti-anthropocentrism; this forms a core of his philosophical strategy. The "Letter" begins with a crucial and paradigmatic displacement—of Sartre's understanding of *engagement,* which Heidegger references in French and whose facile negotiation of conceptions such as *man* and *action* Heidegger explicitly targets (LH 239). Heidegger's displacement rests on two primary reformulations (LH 254): (i) he responds to Sartre's "précisément nous sommes sur un plan où il y a seulement des hommes" ("we are precisely in a situation where there are only men") with—also in French—"précisément nous sommes sur un plan où il y a principalement l'Être" (we are precisely in a situation where there is principally Being" [LH 254]); and (ii) he redirects the quotidian conception of action as causing an effect to argue that the accomplishment of an action is to bring "into the fullness of its essence" that which already *is* (LH 239). These reformulations ("nous sommes sur un plan où il y a principalement l'Être" and the reconsideration of action) are crucial to Heidegger's argument for a number of reasons. First, they prepare and facilitate further conceptual deployments and reorganizations. For example, Heidegger proceeds to claim that thinking (which is more primordial than all philosophy and is necessarily involved in any engagement) is the "engagement of Being by Being," that it is *Being*'s engagement (LH 239–40).[41] Second, they foreground, as the opening of his position, his emphasis on Being, on language as the "house of Being," and on the human being's turn to thinking as the necessary premise of all access to an understanding of its "ecstatic ek-sistence," its unconcealment in the light of Being *in* and *as* its essence. In order to explain why these statements make sense and allow a different understanding of Being and its history, Heidegger stakes out a long, roundabout path. He first provides a series of historicizations—of humanism and its meaning, but also of *essentia* and *existentia* (the terms through which Sartre defines his own humanism and his opposition to Platonic-Cartesian anthropology)—carefully redefining humanism along the way to demonstrate its dependence on the definition of man (and man's *humanitas*) as *animal rationale* (the Latin is important), and its inability to think the human being beyond this definition and its metaphysical limitations. Heidegger's history of humanism identifies it with

(a)   the Latin translation of Aristotle's *zōon logon ehon* as *animal rationale,* which constructs "a metaphysical interpretation of it," and which for Heidegger abandons "the human being to the essential realm of *animalitas*" (LH 246), allowing humanism to be linked to "life" but also to biologism (LH 247); this identification repeats both Heidegger's organization and critique of philosophical anthropology in *Being and Time* as emerging out of *animal rationale*

and the religious making of man in God's image and resemblance
(BT §10), as well as Heidegger's treatment of the metaphysical
conceptions of man in *An Introduction to Metaphysics*;

(b)   the Roman, Renaissance, and German turns to Greek philosophical
paideia, particularly the Roman "translation" of *paideia* as
humanitas (LH 244);

(c)   the strategic concern "that the human being become free for his
humanity and find his worth in it" (LH 245), a concern that always
depends on conceptions of human nature and freedom and grounds
the humanisms of Marx, Sartre, even Christianity (LH 244–45).[42]

Heidegger makes it clear that these premises and definitions, which retrace
the contours of the metaphysical tradition, not only condition our understanding of man but also do so in such a way that forecloses any possibility
of us interpreting man's existence or dignity as exceeding the metaphysical
tradition—that is, as exceeding these definitions. And it is à propos of this
foreclosure (which largely echoes the "history of the forgetting of being")
that Heidegger writes:

The highest determinations of the essence of the human being in humanism still
do not realize the proper dignity of the human being. To that extent the thinking
in *Being and Time* is against humanism. But this opposition does not mean that
such thinking allies itself against the humane and advocates the inhuman, that it
promotes the inhumane and deprecates the dignity of the human being. Humanism is opposed because it does not set the *humanitas* of the human being high
enough. (LH 251)

For Heidegger, this does not mean humanist determinations are hereby
"declared false and thrust aside." But it does displace, in toto and as derivative and ultimately reductive, the whole tradition from Plato and especially from Rome to the present, that is to say, the entire set of alternatives
to his own thought that might, for his readers, offer a proper humanism.
On one point, however, Heidegger does not yet object: the premise that
"the humanity of the human being . . . lies in its essence" (LH 244). On
the question of essence, Heidegger again offers a history of concepts and,
through them, displaces and reuses Sartre's "existence precedes essence" by
reconceiving its terms. Regarding "existence," Heidegger repeatedly limits
its meaning to "actuality" (LH 249, 250)—in a sense, the facticity of brute

being—then defines Sartre's notion of existence as "the actuality of the *ego cogito*" (LH 261). He leaves aside this—Cartesian, he implies—notion for the sake of the neologism "ek-sistence" that foregrounds the human being's "ecstatic" relation to things and the world in general, in the midst (but *not* the center) of which it exists. This essence derives from the fact that the human being belongs to Being. Now, humanisms, by relating the human being's essence to its actuality, take the essence of the human being to be "obvious" (LH 245) and necessarily identify it with *animal rationale* (whereby they reduce man to a privileged kind of animal). Therein lies their "damage" (LH 241): in complementing and contrasting essentiality with actuality (*existentia*), humanisms rule out the very question whether man can be defined more fundamentally than in terms of this contrast. Heidegger here outdoes Sartre's hostility to notions of human nature, predefined human essence, natural law, and natural right by treating his mode of overcoming such notions as *intricately bound to what it seeks to overcome*, and hence as incapable of doing so. A proper overcoming of such notions would demand the demonstration of this intricate binding and show both its limitations and a way past them. "Sartre expresses the basic tenet of existentialism in this way: existence precedes essence. In this statement he is taking *existentia* and *essentia* according to their metaphysical meaning, which from Plato's time on has said that *essentia* precedes *existentia*. Sartre reverses this statement. But the reversal of a metaphysical statement remains a metaphysical statement. With it he stays with metaphysics in oblivion of the truth of being" (LH 250). In this way, Heidegger re-presents Sartre's thought as providing the latest version of a (Roman) humanism, which he contrasts to his own archae- or superhumanism, his superior care for the dignity of man that does not fall into Latin limitations.

It is worth noting that the attempt to outdo Sartre mirrors—strategically speaking—Sartre's own effort to outdo competing humanisms, only on a grander scale and without any obvious political program.[43] Moreover, though Heidegger objects to Sartre's identification of *Being and Time* with existentialism, and though he unequivocally refuses to be simply termed an atheist (LH 266), he does not mark Sartre's atheist humanism as simply "wrong" or especially damaging. He emphasizes instead that the baggage of engagement and action that existentialism bears and the evocation of *Being and Time* do not suffice by themselves to surpass the troubles and dangers that lie with classical humanism. By accepting humanism, Sartre fails to understand that the insufficiency of his inversion commits him to an engagement that may not be per se violent, but that nevertheless maintains the danger (LH 243, 259, 261), damage (LH 241), and threat (LH 243) that metaphysical humanism has been unable to overcome. Here, Heidegger also strikes a note against the moralism of Sartre's existentialism, particularly against the moral transformation of the critique of anthropocentrism into an existentialism founded on the subject's incapacity.

Next, Heidegger practices in his argument an appraisal of Marxism that echoes *both* his reading of Sartre *and* also Sartre's own give-and-take strategy toward the Communists.[44] Heidegger's attention to Marxism should not be considered as altogether opportunistic: like the Marxists, he was concerned with Sartre's "return" to Descartes' *ego cogito*, which, as was recognized at the time, had "no place in his [Heidegger's] thought."[45] On the one hand, he praises Marx's "essential and significant" recognition that "the estrangement of the human being has its roots in the homelessness of modern human beings" (LH 258) and calls the Communist view of history "superior to that of other historical accounts," a view with which so far "neither phenomenology nor existentialism" has entered into a "productive dialogue" (LH 259). On the other, he counters that Marxism has not been able to sufficiently think "the essence of materialism" (LH 259), and he proceeds to present this failure as constitutive of the present "nihilist" state of Europe.[46]

Whoever takes "communism" only as a "party" or a "Weltanschauung" is thinking too shallowly, just as those who by the term "Americanism" mean, and mean derogatorily, nothing more than a particular lifestyle. The danger into which Europe as it has hitherto existed is ever more clearly forced consists presumably in the fact above all that its thinking—once its glory—is falling behind the essential course of a dawning world destiny that nevertheless in the basic traits of its essential provenance remains European by definition. (LH 259–60)

This argument resonated well in the fragmented French resistance and its perception of both Communism and the return of the Republic as reductive alternatives that tended to "uniformize" or homogenize man and that lacked adequate respect for the experience of resistance—as suggested for example by Maurice Merleau-Ponty and Jean Hyppolite, as well as the translators of the "Letter" into French (some of whom, like Rovan and also Roger Munier, had been members of the resistance) and Jean Beaufret himself, or even by thinkers unrelated to Heidegger, for example, André Malraux. Moreover, by arguing that the dominant metaphysical and political framings of the world were all betrothed to a failure to accord man the dignity he deserved, the "Letter" delegitimates their (occasional or constitutive) forms of violence, especially their formative effects on the individual. At the same time, the "Letter" radicalizes Heidegger's position in *Being and Time*. In the deployment of phenomenological ontology in *Being and Time*, the suspension of "man" was necessary for a correct understanding of the ontological question (the contrast of *Dasein* to the anthropological subject in §10 of *Being and Time*), or was left as a task to be initiated after the completion of the ontological project (BT §7C).[47] But in the "Letter on 'Humanism'" it is not merely important that man accept the primacy and primordiality of *Dasein* over the *human*. Heidegger aims specifically at a general reduction of anthropology and its capacities. Even the uses of the word anthropology are dismissive: for example, nationalism is assaulted for being an "anthropologism" (LH 260), a term that is also explicitly associated with a "moral-existentiell" (LH 253) misreading of Heidegger's work. Heidegger turns the sense of political impotence that he sees as central to the postwar context into a necessity for ontology and for the rejection of anthropologies of action. He opposes "thinking in values" as "the greatest blasphemy imaginable against Being" (LH 265), providing examples of such thinking in treatments of "culture, art, science, human dignity, world, and God" (LH 265). He objects to their idealization ("we everywhere speak against all that humanity deems high and holy" [LH 264]) and to their identification as fundamental to the essence of man.[48] Using such "values" as the foundation of a political anthropology would only lead to a politics of the will, a nihilism presenting itself as an egalitarian redemptive solution, an anthropologism.

Would it be too much to argue that the search of the "Letter on 'Humanism'" for a place or scene untainted by metaphysics and politics reflected the priorities of some in the French ex-resistance in a far more convincing way than Sartre's effort to direct the resistance legacy toward an engagement with the demands of the present?[49] Heidegger suggests the present to be a time for reflection, rather than for engagement, a unique moment in which to escape the entirety of European metaphysics. In doing so, he quietly identifies himself with a wing of the intellectual left that, aware of the impossibility of extending the resistance's "struggle against inhumanity," seeks to reinterpret the present moment in terms of the collapse of Europe and the coming of a Hegelian end of history, an end from which it is necessary and nearly impossible to escape. He is also identifying himself with thinkers unwilling to offer definitive answers to the Communist problem—aware of the utopian hopes of Communism and of the ineluctability of violence in the contemporary world. To put the same example differently, Heidegger implicitly identifies this untainted scene with an *other* Europe. He suggests that this other Europe is the only site that could find its way again (LH 259–60). Only by excising itself from the problematic metaphysics and its own formulation of and dependence on Western destiny could it overcome the danger posed by its present state, bolstered by "Americanism" and Communism, the pincers crushing Europe, as per the geopolitical system he described in the *Introduction to Metaphysics*. Again, this present moment for Europe is not a time for action in the classical sense, but rather a time for profound transformation premised on a rethinking of modernity. Heidegger clearly codes this potential in terms of a task and expectation of philosophical controversy:

Should we keep the name "humanism" for a "humanism" that contradicts all previous humanisms—although it in no way advocates the inhuman? . . . Or should thinking, by means of open resistance to "humanism" risk a shock that could for the first time cause perplexity concerning the *humanitas* of the *homo humanus* and its basis? In this way it could awaken a reflection—if the world-historical moment did not itself already compel such a reflection—that thinks not only about the human being but also about the "nature" of the human being, not only about his nature but even more primordially about the dimension in which the essence of the human being, determined by being itself, is at home. (LH 263)

If all humanisms were mired in a metaphysically constructed present whose violence and damage are inescapable, then the only proper "humanism" was a rejection of humanisms: an antihumanism. Thus, and even though Heidegger's effort could be read as just one more exclusivist humanism that affirms its singular, "more profound" and more universal call to understanding the human while rejecting "competitors" as misguided and ultimately dangerous ideologies, nevertheless its refusal of *all* humanisms, termed as a refusal of *humanism*, its language, spirit, philosophical premises, and hopes, stands apart in offering a place seemingly untarnished by humanism. This place avoids seeking a new "New Man" who would transform Europe radically or inhabit a New Europe and instead attempts to show man in the light and poverty of the openness of Being.

5. How can we interpret Heidegger's claim that showing man in the light of Being restores him to his real, primordial existence, while effecting, to quote Michel Haar, a "mutation" in the essence of the human?[50] How does the refusal of humanism and the effort to explain the essence of the human being translate into the anthropological problem, the question of man? Should we pay heed first to the critical and contextual force of the letter, which would suggest Heidegger's philosophical anthropology to be a denial of philosophical anthropology tout court and an antihumanism, or to Heidegger's offer of a proto- or superhumanism, a thinking prior to and more fundamental than all humanism, which would no longer have use for humanism as a name? How should we interpret the immediate reception of the "Letter," which, like some more recent thinkers, has often turned to see it as a humanist text?

Consider the following two, somewhat divergent passages. First, having already refused the alignment of his thought with humanism, Heidegger writes:

Does not . . . thinking think precisely the *humanitas* of *homo humanus?* Does it not think *humanitas* in a decisive sense, as no metaphysics has thought it or can think it? Is this not "humanism" in the extreme sense? Certainly. It is a humanism that thinks the humanity of the human being from nearness to being. But at the same time it is a humanism in which not the human being but the human being's historical essence is at stake in its provenance from the truth of being. (LH 261)

This passage begins by avowing the "humanism" of Heidegger's thinking: "Is this not 'humanism' in the extreme sense? Certainly." It then identifies the site from which, and in which, the human being can be thought in this "extreme sense" of "humanism": "from nearness to being." Yet once Heidegger has arrived at this point, he immediately undoes the avowal. What is at stake, from the perspective of this site of a nearness to Being is "not the human being" but the provenance of its historical essence—in its ek-sistence—from the truth of Being. At stake in these concluding lines is not the self-mobilization (that is, the humanism) of a definition (that is, the human being), but rather the erasure of this mobilization and self-af-firmation in favor of this being's examination of its provenance from "the truth"—which can only be "the truth of being."

The second passage emphasizes this emergence of the human being while questioning even the utility of the earlier avowal of humanism:

The essence of the human being lies in ek-sistence. That is what is essentially—that is, from being itself—at issue here, insofar as being appropriates the human being as ek-sisting for guardianship over the truth of being into this truth itself. "Humanism" now means, in case we decide to retain the word, that the essence of the human being is essential for the truth of being, specifically in such a way that what matters is not the human being simply as such. So we are thinking a curious kind of "humanism." The word results in a name that is a *lucus a non lucendo* [literally: a grove where no light penetrates].[51]

Besides tying the human being to Being and seeing it as drawn away (ek-) from its actuality, Heidegger addresses here the impossibility of a proper determination of humanism in polemical fashion, at once (i) af-firming his "humanism" as superior, (ii) restoring or redefining the sup-posedly essential meaning of the word "humanism," but (iii) discarding *without* replacing the word "humanism" for its attachment to metaphysical determinations of the past. This gesture of redefining humanism but re-jecting it nevertheless by way of his system of forestry metaphors (clearing, grove, shepherding, light, path, and so on) is crucial. Were he to maintain it, the word "humanism" would just name something without meaning anything: as opposed to the "clearing" or "openness" of Being, humanism, already misdirected, now becomes a dark grove. By linking truth, the *es-sence* of the human being, and Being, Heidegger treats as pleonastic and parasitic the use of "humanism" for the guardianship of the truth of Be-ing—such a humanism, while not a contradiction, would be the dark spot in the forest.[52]

At stake in both passages and their different strategies toward "hu-manism" is the anthropological problem. What Heidegger rejects, *even while redirecting the term humanism through his presentation of the human being qua* Dasein *in its nearness to Being*, is man's tendency of man to affirm himself as himself. Now, precisely because Heidegger (i) denies and denigrates man in the traditional definitions, but then (ii) joins these denigrations with an effort to provide an at once more primordial and more "futural" alternative, and nevertheless (iii) refuses to allow man a self-affirmation, I want to propose here that the treatment of the question of man in the "Letter" can best be described in terms not of a rejection of anthropology tout court but of a negative anthropology.

Up to this stage I have presented negative anthropology in terms of systematic efforts to understand the human being not as the ground of philosophical anthropology, but rather as a construct of different premises and philosophical systems. The negative dimension of Kojève's anthropology rests on the designation of "the human" as a negation of all there is, including itself and its own understanding of its humanity. The human could thus only be defined by way of its negation of itself—to recall Kojève's striking formulation, "*ein nichtiger Mensch, der sich in Nichts gegeben ist, der sich nicht gegeben ist, sich nichtet und vernichtet*" (AT 184).[53] When criticizing classical transcendence, Sartre, Levinas, and Bataille (like Heidegger) practiced a voiding of the human qua positive transcendence, which they compounded by a mistrust of the trap involved in the empirical or realist alternative. What Levinas named *excendence*, the escape he strove for, was precisely the hope that not all was lost to this empiricism. Now, Heidegger's case is perhaps the most significant one in the development of negative anthropology, precisely because the emphatic refusal to accept humanism or to tolerate the thinking of Being as a humanist enterprise leads him to a philosophical reconstruction of the human that explicitly renounces the truth of any foundational status of the human and the human being.[54] Man is "founded" on *Dasein*; he cannot (thus should not) affirm himself as himself; the human being as *Dasein* is defined by way of its lack and its dependence on Being, language, thinking, and a metaphysical construction of "the world-historical moment." At stake here is not merely Heidegger's refusal to let man's self-affirmation occur in the clearing of Being, but rather the establishment of a thinking of the human, of the human being, and of the essence of the human being in terms of its derivativeness from categories and terms of ontology.

Can we name this reorganization of anthropology (which refutes classical anthropology so as to offer a more genuine thinking of the human) a "negative anthropology"?

The reception of the "Letter"—which replicates the ambiguity toward the anthropological question inherent in the "Letter" itself—supports such a naming. On the one hand, Heidegger's undermining of anthropology to the profit of ontology is usually read as an attack on the 1930s "anthropological reading" of his work. Indeed, this reading is central to the rise of the orthodox group of Heideggerians in the 1950s: the "Letter" is contemporary to the derision (by Heidegger and especially by Jean Beaufret) of *réalité humaine* as an insufficient, anthropologistic translation of *Dasein* and the anthropological and Cartesian reading of Heidegger in the 1930s.[55] Together with the critiques of Sartre and Marxism (not to mention other systems of thought and the current condition of Europe), the anti-anthropological frame and force of the essay became foundational to postwar "French Heideggerianism."[56] Yet many of the same readers received the "Letter" as a humanist text—indeed as founding humanity anew, more fundamentally, in a fashion unbound by the limitations of *all* recent competing ideologies and definitions of the human. Alphonse de Waelhens and Maurice Merleau-Ponty explicitly accepted Heidegger's approach *as humanist*, indeed as a new, "deeper" humanism.[57] Jean Hyppolite also saw Heidegger's critique of anthropology as allowing a deeper engagement with the human being and its position in the world and in history. Jean Beaufret concurred; in his 1949 "Sur un nouvel humanisme" he clearly understood the qualified antihumanism of the "Letter" as a deeper humanism than that of the battling humanists of his time. Echoing Heidegger's praise of the Marxist idea of history, Beaufret gave credence to Marxist and Hegelian humanism, arguing that they "restored humanity to its proper history and demanded that this history clarify the present situation." But besides his theoretical Marxist humanism, Beaufret clearly wanted to suggest here that the time of such petty humanisms was over, and the truer, deeper, "new" humanism was about to emerge.[58] Jacques Derrida's famous 1968 essay "The Ends of Man," with its critique of Heidegger's claim to be overcoming humanism, has inspired, and corroborated, several recent readings of Heidegger's essay that refuse reductive identifications of Heidegger's antihumanism with the negative sense in which the term is often evoked today.[59] In other words, the reception of the "Letter" in France broadly suggests that we need to think concurrently the "superhumanism" of the text together with its antihumanist emphasis. Now, is it possible to extend Heidegger's own ambiguous treatment of humanism toward such a "negative" conception of the human?

First, regarding "anthropology": it is worth recalling Heidegger's central objection to anthropology. As Françoise Dastur writes:

[For] Heidegger, the fundamental difficulty in [philosophical anthropology] does not consist in obtaining a systematic unity of the determinations of man, but resides in the concept of "philosophical anthropology itself," which remains fundamentally ambiguous. This is because the term *philosophical anthropology* can signify the search of what specifically constitutes the being of man by contrast to that of other kinds of beings—but which is no more than a regional ontology among others and therefore cannot as such purport to constitute the center of philosophy. Yet philosophical anthropology can also signify a search that is founded on the recognition of man as the definite and absolutely first being, according to the Cartesian definition, which would thus imply the centering of philosophy on human subjectivity.[60]

The specificity of this critique does not simply render impossible a reading of the "Letter on 'Humanism'" that would begin with the trope of the "human." From what I've suggested so far, the "Letter" could be read as an exercise in an alternative anthropology—a *Destruktion*, in Heidegger's term, of anthropology's history and scope, an effort that recognizes (and works with) its regional status. Such a reading would necessarily emphasize the goal of emptying out man's historical and political role, power, and task, for a turn to *Dasein*, and through it Being and logos. It would also note the dependence of "the human" as it exists now on its metaphysical and anthropologistic determinations—determinations that are damaging and reductive but cannot be simply dismissed. In each of these occasions, man is dependent on other categories. Nevertheless, it is *still* man that we are talking about (and that Heidegger talks about), even if his references to a "human being" (the word is maintained) require that it exist only in a different sense (as *Dasein*, not as human) and only in the shadow of Being. In other words, while Heidegger cannot be said to remain within the paradigm of anthropology, he by no means denies "the human": he keeps it suspended and thinkable, if only indirectly. Now insofar as the "Letter" rejects the self-affirmation of man and undermines classical philosophical anthropology, can we speak of its own anthropology in the "negative"?

Here, we are faced with Heidegger's own terminology, and the specificity of his own use of "negation." In "How to Avoid Speaking: Denials," Derrida emphasizes the approach to the negative given by Heidegger in the 1929 lecture "What Is Metaphysics?" Reading this lecture (alongside Heidegger's "On the Essence of Ground" and other works) in relation to onto-theology, and specifically in relation to negative theology, Derrida addresses "What Is Metaphysics?" as "a treatise of negativity" that "establishes the basis for negative discourse and negation," particularly in Heidegger's thinking of anguish as locating "us in a relation to a negating (Nichtung) which is neither annihilation (Vernichtung) nor a negation or a denial (Verneinung)."[61] The treatment of the human offered by Heidegger in the "Letter on 'Humanism'" is negative in exactly this fashion: neither annihilation, nor denial. Heidegger's strategy is one of circumvention and regrounding followed by a reinscription of the question.

Thus the negativity of negative anthropology, indeed the radicalism of Heidegger's position, essentially begins from and involves the inability of anthropology to speak for itself, to offer any determinations that would not necessarily be those already offered by Being (and language). Again and again, Heidegger makes it clear that what takes priority in the relation of man to Being is Being: "that the essence of the human being is essential for the truth of being, specifically in such a way that what matters is not the human being simply as such" (LH 263); "*précisément nous sommes sur un plan où il y a principalement l'Être*" (LH 254). To cite Michel Haar, "Man does not bear his properties and powers of his own accord; he does not give himself Being, nor his relation to Being. He is not the center of entities; he maintains himself 'in the midst of entities' without being their middle."[62] One could add: man does not control his engagements (LH 240), does not fully recognize the *nomos* (assignment and law) under which he acts in relation to Being (LH 274), does not understand his world-historical destiny in relation to being, even finds himself lost before a genuine presentation of the ethos of Being (LH 269–70). In this sense, the "Letter on 'Humanism'" is not a simple deletion but a redeployment of the anthropological questioning, a deployment in the modes of a negativity premised neither on annihilation, nor on denial. In this redeployment, the self-affirmation of the human is neither possible nor desirable. *Affirmation is reserved for Being; affirmation concerning the human being at the clearing of Being is reserved for Being.*

How can we then understand the stakes, characteristics, and radicalism of the human being Heidegger offers? It is worth recalling first of all that Heidegger speaks of his thinking of the human being in terms of a return or a thinking that would be "primordial" (LH 246, 255, 262, 263, 271). This constitutes the novelty, or—to recall Derrida's intonation of Heidegger's understanding of "primordial"—the character of a promise of a new birth.[63] Heidegger himself emphasizes this return as a reopening of the future of man: thinking "the essence of the human being . . . in its origin," means thinking "the essential provenance that is always the essential future for historical mankind" (LH 246). He writes of a hope—in terms of an assumption—that "in the future the human being will be able to think the truth of being" (LH 256), which it can only do from the perspective of *ek-sistence*. The two tropes, the return to the primordial and the opening of a future are tied to each other.[64] They offer and effect a doubling, an opening up, of the present to the *ek-sistence* of the human being; thus, they indicate an interpretation of *ek-sistence* itself—as precisely a self-detachment from existence—and view it anew by way of an attunement to Being. The return to the primordial (that is, the most essential) and the openness toward a future for the human being in the "clearing" of Being offer the ground for a "mutation" of the human being.

This premise of ek-sistence—its location at the very (non-)basis of the human being's self-interpretation and as the opening of its future—is central to this anthropological attention. Compared, for example, to the anti-anthropocentrisms offered in the mid-1930s, one aspect of Heidegger's radicalism rests on the fact that, rather than emphasize the impossibility of transcendence and seek to determine man by virtue of his escape from this trap of immanence, Heidegger's "ek-" maintains its gaze on the human being in its historical ek-sistence, at once from within and from a certain without—a without that involves time (in the recuperative and futural moves) and not just Being. This dual, shifting practice of attention and radicalism in negative anthropology is then marked by two crucial terms: *world* and *language*.

In the "Letter on 'Humanism,'" Heidegger both sidelines and transforms his earlier concept of "world." His "On the Essence of Ground" posited man as casting or projecting "world" over entities and things. "We name world that *toward which Dasein* as such transcends, and shall now determine transcendence as *being-in-the-world*" (EG 109). World in that context serves as the basic structure of coherence and intelligibility that is necessary for *Dasein* to recognize and cope with entities it encounters; it is thus central to the process by which *Dasein* transforms a scattered universe into the scene of one's existence and freedom (EG 126–28). Through the casting of world, *Dasein* finds itself in the midst of a world, wherein beings disclose themselves to it—where it has access not only to their utility but also to their truth.[65] In the "Letter on 'Humanism,'" there is a significant shift of emphasis whenever Heidegger speaks of these questions. First, Heidegger evades the issue of transcendence—except in terms of a reaction to those who think that his work "renounces all 'Transcendence.'"[66] Second, and more importantly, "world" appears not as *Dasein's* unveiling of entities around it, but as a signal of the openness of being.[67] What happens here to the understanding of being-in-the-world is that Heidegger counters the problematics of worldly versus heavenly being, or worldly versus spiritual being (LH 266) (that is, thinking in values) with a presentation of world as a domain of the human being's ontological receptivity and participation in its ontological dimension:

For us, "world" does not at all signify beings or any realm of beings but the openness of being. "World" is the clearing of being into which the human being stands out on the basis of his thrown essence. "Being-in-the-world" designates the essence of ek-sistence with regard to the cleared dimension out of which the "ek-" of ek-sistence essentially unfolds. Thought in terms of ek-sistence, "world" is in a certain sense precisely "the beyond" within ek-sistence and for it. (LH 266)

The novelty does not appear in the remark that world "does not signify . . . any realm of beings"—Heidegger had made that clear as early as *Being and Time*. But here, as an "openness" or "clearing" of being, "world" belongs not to *Dasein*, but to Being. It does not frame *Dasein's* interaction with nature and others. What it frames and organizes is the human being's essentially passive relation to Being—its appearance in the openness of Being, its appurtenance to Being. Prior to any subject-object relation, *world* guarantees the appropriation of *Dasein* by Being: it reveals the human being as ek-sisting ("stands out [among entities] on the basis of his thrown essence [that is, its ek-sistence]"). Man thus cannot be defined through his relation to a world that links and relates the entities man is faced with— once again, however, he is defined through his relation to Being as this is made possible by the latter's "openness." *Dasein's* casting of world is more or less replaced by man's true emergence in the clearing. A concept that used to be central to *Dasein*'s interaction with entities (or at least to its place "in their midst") is given over to Being and frames man (and *Dasein*) as a derivative of Being.

A second major change, strategically similar to the first, concerns the emphasis on language, and in particular on primordial language, logos. Heidegger's conception of language in the "Letter" is dual: language, in its quotidian sense, is formative of the oblivion of being that humanism has participated in, but in its most primordial (read: Heideggerian) sense and usage, it allows an understanding of language, particularly of the Greek *logos*, as "the house of being" (LH 254)—the grounding of man onto language, and the prioritization of language over the speaking agent. "But the human being is not only a living creature who possesses language along with other capacities. Rather, language is the house of being in which the human being ek-sists by dwelling, in that he belongs to the truth of being, guarding it. [§] So the point is that in the determination of the humanity of the human being as ek-sistence what is essential is not the human being but being . . . " (LH 254). In both cases—fallen and primordial language—man is not the origin and basis of speech, but rather its conveyor, the medium in and through which either the oblivion or the truth of Being respectively come into expression. Again, this expression is significant in that language is not in man's control. Rather it constructs the humanity of the man and the coappurtenance of man and being.

Considered separately, the two notions form a signature of the shift in Heidegger's attention during his later writing—in particular a move away from a certain phenomenologically coded address of the problem of operating in and understanding one's world and toward a heightened, more emphatic attention to the question of language. Now, if we interweave the change in the concept of world with the prioritization of language, the move from a *Dasein* that casts world to one that "dwells" in the house of Being that is language acquires yet further significance. What becomes especially striking in the text is Heidegger's use of language that could have made possible a reading of world in an existential or phenomenological analytic, but which Heidegger keeps far from any such approach: terms such as *house, home, clearing, nearness, homelessness,* not to mention *dwelling, shepherding, guarding,* and so on. Precisely what should have occasioned a hermeneutic phenomenology of *world* now serves as a series of technical terms linked to a *literal* "bringing to language" (LH 274) of the problem of being-in-the-world, an effectuation through language of the human being's proximity to Being.[68]

Let us rephrase in terms of negative anthropology and of Heidegger's superhumanism. Because of the dual shift produced by language and world, man now finds himself tied—from different directions—by Being. He is held fast by world, driven into the primordiality of a house of Being. What, then, is man's role? First, as shown, it is principally one of accepting the clearing, as a site in which Dasein can reside and think thanks to and also so as to facilitate its essential provenance. Man does not have properties, abilities, and qualities; nor does he control or even participate in his own definition. Man, here, becomes the "shepherd of Being" (LH 252), but he has lost all central faculties, properties, qualities, and powers that could sustain or occasion a positive determination of his "essence" or "meaning" that could do anything but pull him back to Being. These have all been ceded to Being, to the site of its appearance—the clearing—and its house—language. It is only "the engagement of Being" (ILH 240), man's participation in the "engagement of Being by Being" (ILH 239) that can bring them into full bloom. A second way of reading the role of the human being, keeping in mind its current existence away from Being and in the midst of a metaphysically defined Europe, involves the (ultimately ethical) task of moving toward, and into, this clearing. In this effort to educate the human being so it may go from darkness to the light of the clearing, there remains a certain En-light-enment ideal, but also the warning that in his current metaphysical and dangerous existence, man is still tied to his determinations—albeit to his determinations in a perpetual lie. In the first of these conceptions, the human being is clearly conceived in the negative; in the second form, it strives toward its negation. In both of these ways of conceiving Heidegger's stance toward the human being, there is no doubt that, in its own way, Heidegger's "Letter on 'Humanism'" advocates a humanism opposed to "humanism" in sense, limitation, existing formulations, spirit, and name. Neither of these conceptions allows the self-affirmation of the human being, and no mobilization of the essence of the human is possible. To the extent that it is a humanism, Heidegger's is a humanism without man, a humanism that negates man to get to him—and in this sense, at once a protohumanism and a hyperhumanism.

Man is (or should be) above the idolatry of humanism; Heidegger's effort casts him anew, for a futural return to his primordial belonging. In both cases, the human being is conceived in a negative (which is not to say in an "annihilating" or "denying") fashion. What remains for it is a recognition of its ability to recede before the logos, which can instead bring him to the light of his essential truth.

The radicalism of Heidegger's "Letter" thus lies not with his critique of other humanisms—the visible face of the "Letter"—but in the theorization of an anthropology *in the negative* and the contrast of an authentic existence in this negativity with the bound and inauthentic one of the present life. This assertion of negative anthropology and call to fundamental ontology against the nihilist politics of the will expressed by both East and West, against humanisms incapable of recognizing the priority and engagement of Being, is, for him, the main task of thought.

It is also here that, paradoxically perhaps, the use value of Heidegger's thought in the immediate postwar period becomes clearest. What was important with the end of the war was the destruction of any politics of the will, any political anthropology based on a subjectivist universalism. The place that Heidegger promised in the "Letter," the distance from and superiority over politics is precisely what some *résistants*, having failed in their hopes for a radical transformation of society found themselves denied by the Fourth Republic. Heidegger, whose rehabilitation in France depended almost entirely on former *résistants* and soldiers, offered them an analysis of the human that facilitated a distance from political muddling and sought a new, non- or suprapolitical world. In refusing to term this thinking a humanism while arguing that its light showed the philosophical misery and darkness of humanism, as well as in refusing all possible priority of humanism's anthropological foundation, Heidegger refused the dream of radical social and political change toward a New Man—but also, and no less importantly, the very possibility that such a dream might make sense. Except in one sense: for man to dwell in the luminous court of Being, where self-affirmation is reserved for Being by way of man, and not for some (New) Man.

Atheism and Freedom After
the Death of God: Blanchot,
Catholicism, Literature, and Life

At the outset of this book, I quoted, from Emmanuel Levinas's 1956 interpretation of Maurice Blanchot's literary and philosophical work, a passage that I have used in describing the "new" nonhumanist atheism emerging with the 1930s and the postwar period.

Contemporary thought holds the surprise for us of an atheism that is not human-ist. The gods are dead or withdrawn from the world; concrete, even rational man does not contain the universe. In all those books that go beyond metaphysics we witness the exaltation of an obedience and a faithfulness that are not obedience or faithfulness *to* anyone.[1]

In this claim, Levinas aimed to set the stage for his broader reading of Blan-chot, suggesting that Blanchot at once operated within this contemporary frame, but that he also did not land in the pitfalls of this "surprise," par-ticularly this obedience and faithfulness "that are not obedience or faith-fulness *to* anyone." While such an interpretation of Blanchot's goals and writing is certainly possible, what is more interesting here is that Blanchot not only embraced this nonhumanist atheism but also used it to criticize both traditional atheism and its Catholic critics. In the process, he used this atheism to rethink the question of freedom, a concept that he would place at the foundation of his writing on life and his theory of literature. I repeat the passage here for precisely this reason—but also in order to preface and accentuate Blanchot's radicalization of Kojève's position, indeed the distance traveled by this atheism from the 1930s through (and despite) Sartre's humanist recuperation of atheism, to Blanchot's stance. Here I explore two concise interpretations of texts Blanchot published in the journal *Critique*, which address the importance of this postwar atheism for the stakes of literary philosophy and critique. I begin with Blanchot's critique of Henri de Lubac's *The Drama of Atheist Humanism*, and in particular de Lubac's reading of Nietzsche's understanding of freedom. At stake in that short yet forceful text is Blanchot's effort to move toward an atheism which would explicitly assimilate the Catholic critique of atheist humanism, as a result of which freedom would lose its political and liberatory claims and ethics. From this approach of freedom I turn to its role in Blanchot's theorization of life and revolution, amid a literary and philosophical field profoundly concerned with humanism as a problem. This occurs in a long passage on the 1793 Terror in Blanchot's famous essay "Literature and the Right to Death." In that context, I would like to consider Blanchot's use of, and play on, languages of right, as well as his paradoxes involved in the theory of freedom he uses to target these languages. Before returning to the interplay of the heritage of the resistance and the problem of Communist violence in Maurice Merleau-Ponty's writings, Blanchot's texts can help contribute to a demonstration of the vastly different terrain on which antihumanist questions played after the war. His writing forms at once a counterpoint to Catholic humanism, human rights discourse, and socialist utopianism, a space for literature's theorization of human freedom, history, and life, and a harsh renegotiation of the stakes of action and death in post-1944 French thought.

1. An Atheist Critique of a Catholic Critique of Atheist Humanism

In 1946, Blanchot reviewed Henri de Lubac's recent book *Le Drame de l'humanisme athée* (*The Drama of Atheist Humanism*).[2] Like de Lubac's interwar writings (for example, his 1938 *Catholicisme*) and in line with the general argument of Catholic humanism, *The Drama of Atheist Humanism* targeted atheism as by definition stuck in a tragic situation.[3] De Lubac's claims here are nothing less than exemplary of postwar Christian critiques of humanism, for an emphasis on the failures of atheist humanism remained a major social and intellectual claim among Catholic thinkers. Among writers from Jacques Maritain and Nicolai Berdyaev to Gabriel Marcel, Emmanuel Mounier, François Mauriac, and Jean Lacroix, it became common currency to argue that atheism could not accept that man looks toward the superhuman, the transcendent, and the infinite—that is to say, toward God—in search of definite meaning and spiritual solace. Gabriel Marcel wrote several books on the problem of man and his tendency to undo and destroy himself when distanced from God.[4] Lacroix, who had cofounded the journal *Esprit* with Emmanuel Mounier and who became, in 1945, the principal philosophy reviewer for *Le Monde*, would argue that humanism's construction of man as an absolute amounts to idolatry.[5] Nicolai Berdyaev, who since the early 1930s had been an influential religious thinker conversant in philosophy, spoke of a "self-destruction of humanism," and he explicitly attempted to ground human rights in Christianity.[6] Other writers echoed this approach, arguing also in favor of the adoption and appropriation of human rights discourse by and in the name of theocentric humanism.[7] De Lubac's particular formulation of this problem claimed that atheism's tragedy was its awareness of being unable to provide an alternative to God—an awareness that leads to the suffering of Dostoevsky's characters and the drama of Nietzsche's efforts to posit the Overman. Because of this tragic overreaching, de Lubac announced (again) that in atheism "man has *literally* been dissolved."[8] De Lubac proceeded, in his critique of Feuerbach and Nietzsche, to claim that "Atheist humanism was bound to end in bankruptcy. Man is himself only because his face is illuminated by a divine ray."[9]

Blanchot's assessment (significant for his notions of revolution, literature, and freedom) does not tolerate de Lubac's call for a return to religion; yet, perhaps surprisingly, it accepts without hesitation de Lubac's assault on the conceptual and historical poverty of atheism, a poverty it treats as coextensive with the present state of humanity. Blanchot remarks that though Nietzsche was far from an ordinary atheist (WF 288), de Lubac treats him as exemplifying the modern dramatic situation by seeking—and by performing through his writing—the death, or rather the *murder*, of God. Blanchot praises de Lubac's "excellent study on Nietzsche's atheism," particularly his effort to "clarify the role that [Nietzsche] played in the formation of a world from which God is absent" (WF 289). But that is not enough: "Despite its exactitude, [de Lubac's] attempt lets Nietzsche's presence, and perhaps the meaning of his deed, escape" (WF 289). For de Lubac, Blanchot writes, "Atheism has a positive sense. Nietzsche wants to leave the field clear to affirm man and, even more, to affirm in man this more-than-man that until now was alienated by God" (WF 293). Blanchot's objection to this treatment of atheism paradoxically accepts de Lubac's claim that a turn toward an alternative would be wrong. Like him, Blanchot rejects any effort to find a positive foundation for meaning in Nietzsche's death of God—that is, to grant the status of undisputed affirmation to atheism in general, to see it as a self-sufficient humanism and to find in it a ground for *meaning itself.* "The positive quality of the Death of God is hardly arguable: one can even believe that negation, to be possible, must be not only the negation of God but also the affirmation of something. Still, the meaning of this affirmation remains to be sorted out. It is not actually certain, as Jaspers believes, that the negation of transcendence must be enclosed in a dogmatic affirmation of immanence" (WF 293). This passage sets Blanchot's response in remarkably ambivalent terms: it first turns to what looks like an affirmation of the positivity of the "death of God," only to then wonder whether atheism's affirmation can go further than the negation of God. This doubt is a central motif in Blanchot's review: What might the negation of God and transcendence amount to, and does it translate into an affirmation beyond the obvious turn to immanence? While noting that Nietzsche's affirmation is tied to infinite negation, indeed to the "infinite negation of the infinite" (WF 294), Blanchot doubts the "dogmatic affirmation of immanence"—whether this "infinite negation" of God might still have the character of an affirmation. "'God is dead' cannot live in Nietzsche as knowledge bringing an answer, but as the refusal of an answer, the negation of a salvation, the 'no' he utters to this grandiose permission to rest, to unload oneself onto an eternal truth, which is God for him" (WF 292). The "refusal to answer," the refusal to turn negation into a ground, and the irreducibility of negation are all central to Blanchot's particular approach to meaning, and in particular to the interrelationships between concepts of death, meaning, and freedom. The privileging (and Hegelian inflection) of the term "negation" in the context of Nietzsche turns to both Kojève and Bataille. As is evident from the identification of the atheist with pure negation, Blanchot (like Kojève) claims to solve the problem of the "affirmation" to be found in the negation of God, by declaring this affirmation to be "man's infinite power of negation" (WF 293)—that is to say, by returning to the very negation that announced the problem of affirmation.[10] Kojève explicitly treated God as an element of nature or the given that man (or the atheist) had to negate; Blanchot would be saying the same thing here were he not couching it in Nietzschean (rather than Hegelian) terms. Still, in its restlessness, the "no" that "Nietzsche utters" remains precisely the "no" that can be identified with man in his effort to overcome. It is, nevertheless, a "no" that cannot, as in Kojève's case, be seen as a mark of radical otherness to nature, God, and the world, and a "no" that evades both the dogmatic affirmation of immanence and the "unloading" of "oneself onto an eternal truth" (the identification of truth in transcendence and God). Here, Blanchot implicitly turns to Bataille's 1930s theorization of the dismantling of the self in a world bereft of transcendence, as well as to Bataille's hope, in his books *Inner Experience* and *Guilty*, of reaffirming the need for sovereignty and interiority in a world that cannot tolerate them.[11] On the basis of these arguments, Blanchot denies that a negation of the divine offers an alternative transcendence to be found in the self. Like Bataille, he seems to despair at the possibility of any overcoming that would lead beyond the present—the possibility that negation might have an undoubted affirmative consequence, even in the sense of a sublation.[12]

The force of Kojève and Bataille in the treatment of negation and its attachment to an elusive Nietzsche are clearest in Blanchot's rejection of the Overman. Here, the possible affirmative dimensions of negation become radically ambiguous: "In principle, the Overman replaces God. But, finally, what does Nietzsche say about the Overman? Exactly what he says about the gods: 'Always, we are lured higher, up to the realm of the clouds: there we put our motley empty theories, and now they take on the name of Gods and Supermen. . . . Ah, how tired I am of all that is insufficient'" (WF 293). This reading, with its emphasis on the insufficiencies and failure of the Overman, allows for Blanchot's emphasis on Nietzsche's "elusiveness" (whether as an authorial force behind an argument or as a figure present in Nietzsche's own texts), an elusiveness that is precisely

what de Lubac ignores (WF 298–99). This elusiveness is central to Blanchot's interpretation of Nietzsche against not only de Lubac's but also the
classic reading ("current Nietzscheanism"—WF 293), according to which a
commitment to the Overman offers a privileged scene for the call "beyond
good and evil" and would provide a fictional embodiment for freedom.
By contrast, Blanchot claims that freedom and negation should be seen as
a radical formal openness and a rejection of efforts to define, locate, and
reduce meaning. Insofar as negation cannot simply imply that the refusal
of transcendence is affirmatively figured in the Overman and in becoming, Blanchot maintains the necessity of an "infinite power of negation"
as a largely Kojèvian and Bataillean priority: this "infinite power" is man's

> ability to be always equal to what surpasses him, other than he is, different from
> himself; it is the measureless, limitless dissatisfaction, questioning become pas-
> sion and will to sacrifice; it is, against all the forms of being, revolt, united to
> the search for a form to be capable of putting this revolt in danger and starting it
> again. *Thus the negation of God is indeed linked to something positive, but this posi-*
> *tive is man as negativity without rest, power to deny God without end: freedom.* (WF
> 294; italics mine)

Now, if Kojève had identified man with negation but had also seen man's
overcoming of the human as a loss of what distinguished him from the
natural given, Blanchot instead doubts the positivity of this identification.
Especially interesting here is the coding of freedom in terms of "negativity
without rest, power to deny God without end." The identification of freedom with negation qua denial of God's existence (a denial that is "without
end" and "thus" never reaches its goal) facilitates an elusive and paradoxical
effort that again moderates the reach and implications of atheism's denial
of God. In being infinite, negation is a negation of the infinite; in being
the successful negation of the divine, it demonstrates its own lack of foundation, its existence *as* lack of foundation. Above all, it signifies something
like ontological revolt, the refusal of ground and God, a refusal that, to
quote Blanchot once again, "allows freedom to become aware of the nothing that is its foundation, without making an absolute of this nothing"
(WF 296). But the positivity to which Blanchot points, notably the positivity of this freedom and the benefits it would entail remain in suspension
throughout. If *negativity without rest* is immediately reconfigured here as
"power to deny God without end," this has a specific significance in the

context of Nietzsche: the use of the term "freedom" approaches Nietzsche's own only insofar as it confirms freedom as the denial of both God and (implicitly) the Judeo-Christian tradition imagined as the irreducible ground of Western modernity. The specific sentence reveals a second qualification: it starts with "the negation of God is indeed linked to something positive," but then the reader is struck by the *but* and what follows it: "but this positive is man as negativity without rest, power to deny God without end." That is to say that this positive rejects classical and existential theories of freedom, explicitly denying the conception of freedom in existentialism as extending to every aspect of interpersonal relations. Blanchot's formal critique of freedom turns it from applying to questions and concerns of everyday life and back to an ontological premise for which freedom in human relations is significant precisely as the persistent effort to live as it were in denial of foundations, "in anguish and in risk."[13]

The Death of God is less a negotiation aiming at the infinite than an affirmation of the infinite power to deny and to live to the end of this power. In the Death of God, it is not atheism that counts (whether positive or not) but the experience of man as freedom or, more exactly, the fact that in one and the same experience is disclosed the absence of all recourse to an unconditioned being, along with the structure of human freedom as unconditioned ability to separate oneself from oneself, to escape oneself, to free oneself by means of an infinite questioning. (WF 296)

Is this not to exhaust both freedom and the positivity of "the negation of God" by naming as *freedom* and as "infinite questioning" only the "infinite power to deny and to live to the end of this power?" Isn't this a freedom in the ontological but not in the social or political sense, a freedom that lacks a proper positivity and rejects the supplanting of God by Man or even by the Overman? Can we not say that Blanchot's defense of an explicitly elusive Nietzsche advocates precisely an atheism that no longer offers any transcendence, any sufficient immanence, or even promise of a political or legal equality and freedom? Does his atheism not offer a world of human relations in which freedom would play only a formal role, as ontological ground, and not a social one? Blanchot's argument does this by surprisingly assuming de Lubac's charge that atheism's liberatory ethics cannot offer an alternative anthropotheist transcendence, nor a better humanity. At the same time, it refuses de Lubac's corollaries: first, that Nietzsche (like other atheists) gets out of this quandary by endorsing a life in immanence that posits *overcoming* as transcendence and embodies humanist hope in the Overman; and second, that atheism is thereby bankrupt, and the solution to the problem of transcendence is a turn toward God. Freedom here further sheds its social goals for a formal, ontological meaning largely tied to that of a human being's existence tout court. Atheism appears as a necessary if self-destructive enterprise that man is bound to: thanks to it, Blanchot could later write that classical atheism's attack on God "remains pure pretention," and that instead a proper atheism is thoroughly antisubjectivist, "what excludes every response in the first person."[14]

2. Freedom, the Writing of a New Epoch, and the Last Act

Blanchot's treatment of atheism and freedom, his atheist adoption of the Catholic critique that atheism is not bound to superior and more harmonious human relations, and his resulting claims that the tragic situation surrounding man is inescapable and that the work of freedom is by no means a direct movement toward some sort of universal liberation, resonated strongly with the postwar literary scene.

Indeed, as is well known, the strong political statement of the phenomenological assault on humanism found a significant counterpart and complement in contemporary literature. Writers like Albert Camus, Jean-Paul Sartre, Georges Bataille, not to mention Eugène Ionesco, Raymond Queneau, Marguerite Duras, Jean Genet, or, somewhat later, Alain Robbe-Grillet also addressed major aspects of the critiques of humanism, the questioning of atheism, and the possibilities and philosophical codes surrounding man.[15] Some of them—most successfully Sartre—joined philosophical and literary output, tending carefully to the difference in argument, style, and thought that they could express in each of the two. Without reverting to systematic phenomenology or political philosophy, their literary work presented and expressed problems that it shared with contemporary philosophy.[16] Other philosophers turned to using literary texts as a cultural prop for their treatments of man: Maurice Merleau-Ponty, for example, closed the *Phenomenology of Perception* with a passage from Antoine de Saint-Exupéry that, on its own, stood as a confirmation of his emphasis on intersubjectivity: "Man is but a network of relation-ships, and these alone matter to him" [PhP 456]. Against this philosophi-cal background, the postwar literary reception of Kafka and Artaud, Ni-etzsche and Dostoevsky, clearly contributed to a sentiment—frequently subsumed by the vague qualifier "existential"—that man's relationship to the world was one signed above all by irrationality, violence, entrapment, and perhaps even hopelessness. Perhaps the most remarkable and radical expression in literature and theater of the visibility, resonance, and appeal of antihumanism's principal motifs was Samuel Beckett's dramatic rise to literary prominence during the late 1940s.

Less known at the time yet influential among literary scholars and philosophers in the 1950s was Blanchot's thinking of freedom, death, and literature as this is expressed in his essay "Literature and the Right to Death," first published in two parts in Georges Bataille's journal *Cri-tique*, the first part bearing a different title: "Le Règne animal de l'esprit" ("Spirit's Animal Kingdom").[17] In this famous essay (echoing Jean-Paul Sartre's effort to link freedom and literature in "What Is Literature?" while famously refusing Sartre's solution), Blanchot used his interpreta-tion of atheism and freedom to found a theory of literature, and—more importantly for my purposes here—a theory of human life modeled on literature.[18]

Readings of the essay usually emphasize the treatment of the Revo-lutionary Terror, freedom, and negation as remarks on the premises of literature, on the kind of life that literature thinks, and on the radical transformation that is effected with the act of writing and the production of a text. Still, we could invert these interpretive priorities and approach instead the text as an argument on revolution, as concerned with the turn-ing of life after "the Revolution." The stakes of such a reading are implicit in a reading of Blanchot's essay that Jacques Derrida offered shortly after Blanchot's 2003 death. Derrida wrote, "Isn't ['Literature and the Right to Death'] fundamentally the terrifying document of an epoch of French, very French literature . . . but also of the most equivocal political thought of our literature? Does it not form a counterpoint, in fact in nothing less than the name of literature itself, to the inviolable right to life?"[19] What offers Derrida a chance to distance himself from what he calls a "post-Hegelian and post-Mallarmean discourse of 1948" is precisely the commit-

ment to assigning death (and the death sentence) the status of marker and
defender of freedom, indeed the status of a right.

The dignity of man, his sovereignty, the sign that he accedes to universal right and
raises himself above animality, is that he towers over biological life. He puts his life
in play in right, he risks life, he affirms thus his sovereignty as subject or as consciousness. A right that would give up inscribing, within itself, the death penalty
would not be a right. It would not be a human right, it would not be a right worthy of human dignity. It would not be a right. Not a right of man. The very idea
of right implies that something means more than life. Life must not be sacred as
such, it must be possible to sacrifice it for there to be right. The idea of sacrifice is
common as much to Kant, Hegel, and Heidegger as to Bataille and this Blanchot
here, even when they talk of literature. Right is at once the right of literature and
the right to death, that is, the right to the death penalty.[20]

Derrida proceeds then to deem Blanchot's approach *classical* for not overcoming this sacrificial logic. And he points out both the harshness and ri-
gidity of Blanchot's approach, which sees the right to death—the right to
a human death as opposed to a "merely" animal perishing—as founding
all other rights. Derrida identifies a central tension, between, on the one
hand, the tradition and language of Natural Right and the "rights of man,"
and, on the other, the Blanchotian response, for which the right to death
(and a radicalization of modern anthropology) gives birth to the very freedom that it would annihilate in each individual. This tension, and Blanchot's conscious use of it in his theorization of freedom and human life, is
what I want to consider here: a way for which at stake is not victimization,
nor suffering (these are ineluctable), but the revolution as "writing," without any humanist pretenses, a New World.

I want to address, first, the question of writing and of the relationship of writing to freedom, second, the problem of freedom, death, and
life, and third, the question of life under/after the revolution.

It is well known that early postwar French treatments of "the
Revolution"—a generalization that frequently allowed a mapping of the
French Revolution onto the Russian one—gave the European Left a history of its progress from the "feudal" through the "bourgeois" state and
toward Communism, and also explained away the problem of violence:
"to make an omelet one needs to break some eggs."[21] Blanchot's approach

to the violence does not aim to justify it, nor does it require that violence come in the name of a utopia that is to be realized. Instead, Blanchot holds a much stricter understanding of the revolutionary act according to which the latter does not fully organize a future but only opens the present to it—in other words, one that does little more than deny the given present, the dominance and determination of the present.

At stake in the conception of freedom is not just the Terror as a pre-condition of literature—the ostensible focus of the essay—but also, conversely, the absolute negation that is writing as a model for the negation that is the right to death and that the terrorists "inflict on themselves"—the idea that the operations of the Terror are operations of *writing* a new epoch in the style of writing a text lacking the ambiguities of *life*. This is announced in the explosive passage that opens the treatment of the French Revolution (in fact, of "Revolution," the French being the exemplar):

Revolutionary action explodes with the same force and the same facility as the writer who has only to set down a few words side by side in order to change the world. Revolutionary action also has the same demand for purity, and the certainty that everything it does has absolute value, that it is not just any action performed to bring about some desirable and respectable goal, but that it is itself the ultimate goal, the Last Act. (WF 319)[22]

In being the Last, this Act posits no future; it functions merely as a Ko-jèvian negation of what already is. Revolutionary action—precisely in its "demand for purity"—demands nothing less than absolute value to be placed in its undoing and replacement of the past. This Act is based on the same kind of negation that founds the writer's act, the writer's engagement *through* writing *in* writing. Revolutionary action "is in every respect analogous to action as embodied in literature"; it shares with writing the movement "from nothing to everything" (WF 318).[23]

The metaphor of writing and action is central and frequently repeated: earlier in the essay, Blanchot writes that "the writer only finds himself, only realizes himself, through his work; before his work exists, not only does he not know who he is, but he is nothing." And to explain this argument on the writer, he quotes Hegel on the individual: "'An individual,' says Hegel, 'cannot know what he [really] is until he has made himself a reality through action'" (WF 303).

What is in play in this turn from the writer to the revolutionary actor? First, a sense that negation, which in Kojève was identical with action and hence with freedom, is analogous to the binary range "from nothing to everything" that characterizes the movement of literature. Just as writing brings to a halt the movement of life and history, revolution utilizes violence in the name of a new but absolutely undeterminable epoch, destroying the murkiness and ambiguity of life for a future divided and shared between a nothingness of death and a nothingness of absolute freedom. Each person is universal freedom, and this universal freedom forms the conceptual force uniting nothingness to negation, death to life qua embodied death. Writing of the terrorists, Blanchot says, "The Terror they personify does not come from the death they inflict on others, but from the death they inflict on themselves" (WF 320). Blanchot here extends and formalizes a classic defense of Jacobinism, all the while tying revolutionary action to the fact and act of writing.

Second, because of this absolute movement, Blanchot suggests that in the revolution, death guarantees—indeed *becomes*—the freedom that liberates men. It postulates no future; instead, taking advantage of the all-or-nothing stakes of writing, it formulates the future as set by the finitude that emerges thanks to the unshackling from an old regime that doubles as an unshackling from any ground. Revolution makes men (in a Heideggerian and Kojèvian fashion) both fully responsible for their death and absolutely incapable of thinking life and a life of rights without the priority and foundation that is this death understood as freedom from the old regime (as well as from every regime instituted thus far *by* freedom). What the Revolution allows is for finitude to become a necessary corollary—and by extension a *condition*—of freedom: freedom comes to require death, just as death seems nothing less than something made possible by freedom.

But how is it that such an event can create a worldview based on the experience of such concepts as death and freedom? Because in the Revolution an action becomes "the ultimate goal, the Last Act," Blanchot can highlight that in this Last Act freedom and death come to be interchangeable—though the first is effectively denied by the second. Freedom, as action, is negation; death, as the marker of the absolute value of freedom's action, partakes of the nothing as well, though differently (I will return to this problem soon). As in Kojève, so long as man was anything but pure negation, so long as he failed to be but embodied death and denied his own function and task as that of death, he could not acquire nor hold a right to his own proper death nor by extension to any individual action. This was the Old Regime. But now, with revolutionary action, death itself becomes "the very operation of freedom in free men" (WF 319).

Isn't death the achievement of freedom—that is, the richest moment of meaning? But it is also the empty point in that freedom, a manifestation of the fact that such a freedom is still abstract, ideal (literary), that it is only poverty and platitude. Each person dies, but everyone is alive, and that really also means everyone is dead. But "is dead" is the positive side of freedom which has become the world: here, being is revealed as absolute. "Dying," on the other hand, is pure insignificance, an event without concrete reality, one which has lost all value as a personal and interior drama because there is no longer any interior. (WF 320)

The achievement of freedom: this is what death becomes, rather than freedom's effacement and loss (WF 320). As a result, "freedom or death," which announces the Reign of Terror and which, in it, becomes "the only tolerable slogan," encapsulates the all-or-nothing stakes of action in the construction of a new world. As a philosophy of history, and as a basis of a theory of "universal" freedom, this slogan turns its either/or claim into one about the coextension and radical inversion that links *freedom as negation* and *death as the nothingness on which negation is premised and toward which it tends*.

This coextension depends on the treatment of *negation* and *nothingness*, which Blanchot inherits from Kojève and Sartre but develops in a different sense premised on their status in language (and, by extension, in *writing*).[24] Blanchot carefully orchestrates a contrast of *the nothing* (Fr. *le néant*) to *negation* (Fr. *négation, nier*), a contrast that is especially important because it allows the ambiguity of the question of freedom to become clearer, but also because it imposes this linguistic doubling onto the realm of human relations. Here, terminological similarity and a common etymological origin lead to absolute contrast—Freedom (human negation) as a radical opposite of Death (nothingness)—and back to a coextension and interchangeability—Freedom as all but equal to Death. Life and Death come thus to be premised on a bridge between writing and existence in revolutionary terror, a notion that Blanchot notes as "abstract, ideal (literary)."

This is the point where "death," granted the highest significance in this revolution, refuses precisely the life that preceded it and becomes the essence of freedom in human life. "Freedom or death" comes to mean freedom for finitude; freedom as finitude; better freedom as action leading to death than the old life; better death for others and for oneself than the unworthy prerevolutionary life. Here, History has become void; to use Gerald L. Bruns's term, this "caesura of history" that occurs with the Terror, provides for a posthistorical present in which the absolute transparency of the relation of life to death formalizes every aspect of life. Blanchot utilizes the Law of Suspects of September 17, 1793, to emphasize the figure of transparency as the premise of the Terror's demand for the purity of freedom qua *negation* and its absolute opposition *and* interchangeability with death. "No one has a right to a private life any longer, everything is public, and the most guilty person is the suspect—the person who has a secret, who keeps a thought, an intimacy to himself. And in the end, no one has a right to his life any longer, to his actually separate and physically distinct existence. This is the meaning of the Reign of Terror" (WF 319).[25] Freedom here comes to signify not the possibility of individuality and private life, not freedom as proposed by the contemporary Universal Declaration of Human Rights, but precisely its erasure, the advent of social transparency at its most dramatic and extreme.[26] Naming Saint-Just and Robespierre, Blanchot continues:

The Terrorists are those who desire absolute freedom and are fully conscious that this constitutes a desire for their own death; they are conscious of the freedom they affirm, as they are conscious of their death which they realize, and consequently they behave during their lifetimes not like people living among other living people, but like beings deprived of being, like universal thoughts, pure abstractions beyond history, judging and deciding in the name of all history. (WF 320)

In other words, the Revolution is here the proper moment of Heideggerian and Kojèvian finitude—the moment in which it becomes possible for action to acquire meaning thanks to death. Once again, this meaning is freedom, and it is only possible through the abstraction that is writing. Thus the confined world of the Revolutionary Terror becomes not only the birth of a world of rights *but also its self-limitation*. Finitude also becomes the premise for the closure and emptiness of these very rights, as no life can be based on these rights and this death. Freedom and finitude come to be attached to writing and to the text at the expense of life and living, at the expense of any kind of being that is not equal to a Heideggerian being-to-ward-death. The construction of a world of rights thus depends on the voluntary destructibility of the individual and the human that, in an abstract sense, would be universalized through them.

Now, why insist on this maddening theorization of freedom and death, particularly if Blanchot's readership at the time was somewhat limited?

I have focused on Blanchot's theorization of the future to accentuate a near-eschatological character present in the 1946–47 texts under discussion here and that came to characterize European intellectuals' response to the shadow cast by the war's catastrophe. Such an interpretation of the postwar—*not the war itself but its immediate aftermath*—is present in texts such as Heidegger's "Letter on 'Humanism,'" Camus's *The Plague*, Beckett's *Waiting for Godot*, Koestler's *Darkness at Noon* (published in France in 1945), Malraux's *Walnut Trees of Altenburg*, and even Cocteau's *Orphée*—to cite some of the better-known works most relevant to the present topic. Blanchot's "Literature and the Right to Death" seems to be an apex of this approach.[27] That is to say, once the war was over, intellectuals frequently came to interpret their situation in largely binary terms, frequently asked the value of a life worth living, frequently undermined the future as a category of thought, frequently interpreted the changes that now became possible as able to restore only a semblance of social life but as incapable of instituting any new or improved world, and by and large rejected the very possibility of a theory of history that would or even could rely on progress as a category. Blanchot was by no means alone in forcing a notion of life through a stranglehold of literature to make a point regarding the near-impossibility and violence of change. Many political arguments as well as existentialist and poetic ones from the 1946–48 period tended to effect a retrospective reading of 1945 marked by a profound belief that a major mark in the rise of the West had been crossed; that cultural progress from the nadir of 1944 was only possible under the banner of a revolution (a revolution that neither was forthcoming nor could be trusted to improve things, in Blanchot's language would only write a new world, regardless of that world's content), that France and Old Europe more generally were hostage to a geopolitical pincers made of the new superpowers and capable of crushing on a whim; and that war between the superpowers, with Europe as their casualty, was almost inevitable. To say thus that these postwar intellectuals were *postwar* is to suggest that the horizon of their thought was marked by a recent event whose catastrophic force overshadowed any explicit futurity.

Many of these motifs find a strong (*too* strong, if anything) formulation in Blanchot's discussion of Revolution as a caesura, of the new world as written rather than lived, as tolerating no opacity, as demanding a utopia based on death, negation, and action. His all-or-nothing stakes of freedom already suggest that any life not premised on the "freedom or death" slogan is an unfree life, that any life after the revolution needs to either depend on the freedom for which the right to death founds all rights, on the freedom in which death and action replace life. This is precisely the direction that Blanchot's argument was taking in his review of Henri de Lubac's work.

If disappointment with the failure of the liberation to bring about social change was a major concern for intellectuals of the Left, and disappointment with Vichy and its course was at stake for 1930s right-wing thinkers (and much has been written about the difficulty of interpreting Blanchot's postwar political position), it is not hard to see Blanchot here as talking to both sides.[28] As Blanchot confines his scheme of freedom and finitude to the Revolution—and to literature—it becomes possible to describe his perception of his time as one lost in a life without finitude or clarity, a life bereft of "genuine" death and determination, a life for which even human rights can no longer guarantee freedom and action. Similarly, if the hopes of Communism and of an overcoming of a present situation were also crucial, Blanchot kept himself closer to the opposite stance—that radical change is no longer possible. I am emphasizing this to foreground a problem I will consider in the next chapter, when Merleau-Ponty, in *Humanism and Terror*, designates by Charles Péguy's term *epoch*, "one of those moments where the traditional ground of a nation or society crumbles and . . . man himself must reconstruct human relations" (HT xvii). Blanchot's "Revolution" echoes the former part of Péguy's proposition, though not its second part (the "need for reconstruction"): an actual reconstruction of the *humanity* of these "human relations" has little place in Blanchot's thought—just as his time could not (for him) bring it about. Hope is absent from his argument, and revolution and violence may not be thought of as necessitating a meaningful outcome to history. The fact of the revolution would be the denial of ground and the openness of becoming, of exhausting oneself in becoming—but it would not be the meaningful resolution and surpassing of contradictions and violence. The publication of such a radical binary suggests that for Blanchot, neither an overcoming nor a resolution was possible anymore. Unlike for communists, fellow travelers like Merleau-Ponty, and other intellectuals who had seen the 1945 Purge as bringing about a kind of new social purity (and who still hoped that the Moscow trials of the 1930s had also been carried out in the name of a new world of social harmony and genuine human relations), what justifies terror in "Literature and the Right to Death" is not the move toward such improved and more harmonious human relations. Instead, it is the perpetual operation of freedom in Terror—the operation of the absolute negation that occurs in it and at once justifies and represents humanity as pure freedom. Without the Terror, freedom languishes, which is to say it loses all force.

Having begun an approach of Blanchot's abstract thinking of the Terror in terms of the task of literature moving beyond life, the future of a "right to death," and the death of secular humanism, it is to the reality and possibility of this terror that we now turn.

After the Resistance (2): Merleau-Ponty, Communism, Terror, and the Demise of Philosophical Anthropology

It does not show much love for reason to define it in such a way that it is the privilege of a Western elite released of all responsibility toward the rest of the world and in particular of the duty to understand the variety of historical situations. To seek harmony with ourselves and others, in a word, truth, not only in a priori reflection and solitary thought but through the experience of concrete situations and in a living dialogue with others apart from which internal evidence cannot validate its universal right, is the exact contrary of irrationalism, since it accepts our incoherence and conflict with others as constants but assumes we are able to minimize them. It rules out the inevitability of reason as well as that of chaos. . . . One is not an "existentialist" for no reason at all, and there is as much "existentialism"—in the sense of paradox, division, anxiety, and decision—in the *Report of the Court Proceedings* at Moscow as in the works of Heidegger.

—MAURICE MERLEAU-PONTY, *Humanism and Terror*

If Heidegger responded to the dilemmas of the resistance by advocating a thinker's distance from the political world, particularly in the context of a nihilistic showdown that for him marked the postwar context, and if Maurice Blanchot sought to see a revolutionary life as tying the future with the perishing of life and agency, Maurice Merleau-Ponty, in his contemporary text *Humanisme et terreur* (*Humanism and Terror*), sought to plunge the intellectual back into a debate concerning communism and the possibilities of a New Man. Merleau-Ponty's argument radicalized Sartre's ambiguous humanism and transformed Marxism's theory of history in such a way as to justify the Moscow Trials and the overall Soviet Terror—with the proviso that such violence be in the name of genuine human relations. Merleau-Ponty considered this demand fundamental: what he was asking was whether it could be safely said that the USSR was adequately committing itself to its promise of such a future. If Heidegger was concerned with finding a path more profound and pure than those provided by humanism and metaphysics, a path that would overcome their limitations, Merleau-Ponty responded by inverting the problem and addressing metaphysics differently—at the point where humanism comes to be indistinguishable from violence, indeed from the very violence that one would usually target as undermining humanism.

Merleau-Ponty lived and ended the war as a committed if unorthodox Marxist.[1] Not especially interested in the domestic politics of the PCF, Merleau-Ponty was nevertheless a deep believer in Marxism's support of a humanity freed from the institutionalized violence of capitalism and from its insufficient and misleading offerings—a humanism of culture (SNS 44), a humanism as "the religion of man as a natural species or . . . as a preferred creature" (SNS 45), a humanism of the rights of the citizen, or a humanism as "a philosophy of the inner man which finds no difficulty in principle in his relationships with others, no opacity in the functioning of society, and which replaces political culture with moral exhortation."[2] His argument that the war's principal effect on philosophy was the elimination of prewar liberal philosophies that stood at a distance from "real" political events and that conceived violence as an exception to social life (in "The War Has Taken Place") remained his central political position throughout his years as political director of *Les Temps modernes*, the journal he cofounded with Sartre in 1945. At stake throughout was his appeal for a humanism that would be based on the "concrete improvement" of human relations: this appeal, more than Sartre's "Existentialism Is a Humanism," founded the link between the postwar political anthropology of existentialist phenomenology and a humanism that, while rejecting classical notions of human nature and essence, would remain openly committed to a certain political notion of humanity.

Interestingly, however, this aspect of his thought, expressed above all in his scandalous essay "Le Yogi et le prolétaire," published between October 1946 and January 1947 in *Les Temps modernes* and republished as the crux of *Humanism and Terror* in March 1947, is routinely distinguished from Merleau-Ponty's 1943 *Phenomenology of Perception* and from his late-1950s ontology and critique of anthropology in *The Visible and the Invisible* and in the lectures on *Nature*.[3] On the one hand, this has generally highlighted the shock value and furious politics of *Humanism and Terror* (as well as of similar essays from the period) which does not resonate easily with the formal and unimpassioned analysis of *Phenomenology of Perception*. On the other hand, this distinction has protected Merleau-Ponty's phenomenology from the difficult implications of his treatment of the USSR. It has then led to a misinterpretation of his 1953 break with both Communism and Sartre as a self-distancing from *Humanism and Terror* toward a more "reformist" humanism.[4]

But the emphasis should be placed elsewhere: Merleau-Ponty's approach to communist politics follows from his mistrust of classical conceptions of given meaning, not just in the sense of a political arguments joined to, or translated from a philosophical one, but as the direct, "immediate," necessary component of the anthropological dimension of his phenomenological and psychological ideas. My aim here is twofold: first, to present Merleau-Ponty's philosophy of history and agency in the context of his phenomenological work; and second, to clarify Merleau-Ponty's ambiguous relation to Soviet Communism and the philosophical force of his understanding of violence.[5]

Merleau-Ponty engages head-on with the protoexistentialist narrative of antifoundational realism; indeed, he adopts some of its fundamental positions. First, as per his best-known argument, he conceives meaning as never guaranteed by a ground or ideal but only received from the world through the perceiving subject's interaction with this world. There is nothing to assure us of the truth afforded by the outside world, whose truth lies in our understanding of it. In his discussion of intersubjective interaction in the *Phenomenology of Perception*, Merleau-Ponty treats the subject as "thrown in a nature" (PhP 346). This formulation echoes Heidegger's themes of *Dasein*'s thrownness and being-in-the-world; yet it differs from Heidegger's arguments in that it identifies the subject's world (which for

Heidegger is bound to *Dasein*) with what appears to be a nature in toto, not one partly constituted by the subject (PhP 356), and also in that in this nature and because of its thrownness, the subject needs to find means of ascertaining meaning and truth—means neither given nor "controlled" by the subject. Rather than the drama of a trapped and threatened I, so common from the mid-1930s on, Merleau-Ponty prioritizes the relation between the I and other bodies "inhabited" by consciousness; such inter-subjective interaction utilizes relations of analogy between self and others (PhP 348), conceptual identification, mimesis, and one's understanding of the world around oneself. Merleau-Ponty specifically premises intersub-jectivity on an insufficiency of the self that "causes the other to appear as the completion of the system" (PhP 352). Conversely, the other, this other "pattern of behavior," demonstrates my inability to reduce the world to my perception and subjective construction of it. The other demonstrates my insufficiency. "The cogito of another person strips my own cogito of all value and causes me to lose the assurance which I enjoyed in my solitude of having access to the only being conceivable for me, being, that is, as it is aimed at and constituted by me" (PhP 353). This point extends further. The acknowledgment of subjective insufficiency is at once a constitutive dimension of intersubjectivity and a consequence of it. The interaction between self and other is thoroughly defined by way of a sharing of the world in and through which the two "coexist" (PhP 354), even though this coexistence nevertheless means that the two individuals' "situations cannot be superimposed on each other" (PhP 356). This "superimposing" is central to the emergence and development of conflict because it turns intersubjectivity qua sharing and completion into a coextensiveness and overlap for which the I would deny the other its separate existence and capacity for truth. This offers Merleau-Ponty the occasion to argue at once in favor of a coexistence that should always be shared, that is, "experienced on both sides" (PhP 357) and also against any effort to either reduce the other's I to an object, to take his place, or even to "try to live another's experiences" (PhP 356).

Here Merleau-Ponty comes close to Hegel and Kojève's understand-ing of recognition, which he is clearly addressing. First, he alters the foundation and context of Kojève's interpretation of desire: the conflict of Desires to be found in Kojève is turned into a principally phenomenological effort to understand the boundaries of the I and a recognition of the conflict that occurs when selves are seen to be overlapping. Second, Kojève's concept of *recognition* is inflected into a thinking of intersubjectivity not based on the violence of recognition on reciprocity. Third, though Merleau-Ponty takes from Kojève an identification of human historical action with negation and transformation—and hence, as becomes clear in *Humanism and Terror*, with violence—he limits this identification and does not accept that intersubjective action or interaction can begin from this violence.

Another engagement with a complex quasi-Hegelian problematic appears toward the end of Merleau-Ponty's thinking of intersubjectivity. Returning to the *cogito*, Merleau-Ponty accepts the need for a reason or logos that would be greater than that of individual reason or objective thought (PhP 365 / SNS 63). The meaning of such a claim is elusive because Merleau-Ponty links it immediately to a questioning of phenomenology and time, wherein he largely effaces it. It is nevertheless worth noting here, as the question of this superior logos returns as a significant problem in his hope against hope, in *Humanism and Terror*, that true human relations and a genuine intersubjectivity, "the recognition of man by man" (HT 186) may appear. For our context, the significance of Merleau-Ponty's theorization of the I's self-conception—in the natural and social world it inhabits through the body and perception, in temporal existence, and in the perception of other entities—lies at once in the subject's consequent elaboration of a meaning for man, an ethical theorization of intersubjectivity as requiring the sharing of the world, the evocation of a greater "Reason" that outdoes classical rationalism. Merleau-Ponty's own "humanism" and understanding of his historical situation follows from there.

In writing of "understanding" a historical situation, it is important to not overlook one final early claim of *Phenomenology of Perception*. Merleau-Ponty addresses questions of politics and history right from the beginning of the *Phenomenology*, again with an invocation of Hegel. Following Husserl on what it means to "understand" something, Merleau-Ponty writes that this is "to take in the total intention" of something (PhP xviii), not merely what it is for representation but "the unique mode of existing that is expressed in the properties" of this something—whether this something be a stone or "all the events of a revolution." He then proceeds to identify this "unique mode of existing" that one seeks to take in with a Hegelian Idea: a unique "way of patterning the world which the historian should be capable of seizing upon and making his own." This argument is central to the effort in *Humanism and Terror* to "understand" the Moscow Trials as an expression of Soviet intentions and dreams, and it ties back to his concerns with the individual's efforts to interact with the world.

Now, because of the limitation placed on the individual by his interaction with the world, what might offer something of a human future, for Merleau-Ponty, is the dependence on others, both for the construction of meaning and for a participation in politics or in the conception and conceptualization of truth. Michel Haar notes Merleau-Ponty's anti-anthropocentric turn as taking place in *The Visible and the Invisible*, specifically because of that work's turn toward ontology and away from anthropology.[6] To a certain degree, this turn is already evident in the earlier writings. Insofar as man is not the ground of meaning in the world or the guiding force of history, insofar as the sufficiency of anthropology is already being undermined in the *Phenomenology of Perception*, the anti-anthropocentric turn is already in motion. Even when Merleau-Ponty proclaims himself a humanist, this humanism has been stripped down to a care for man that cannot be reduced to anthropocentrism. And, as Claude Lefort, Michel Haar, Etienne Bimbenet, and other writers have shown, this theme would become associated with and elaborately developed in the questioning of "the crisis of the human sciences" in the turn of the 1950s and in the courses of the late 1950s, notably the course on nature.[7] In *Humanism and Terror*, this problem is addressed not via an existential crisis, but via a philosophy of history coded in terms of an overcoming of violence, in the service of which Merleau-Ponty asks his contemporaries to "look violence in the face."

To look violence in the face: this metaphor recurs often in his writings of the immediate postwar period. First, in "The War Has Taken Place" (October 1945), Merleau-Ponty criticizes the prewar attitude thanks to which "we had secretly resolved to know nothing of violence and unhappiness as elements of history because we were living in a country too happy and too weak to envisage them" (SNS 139): not only was it impossible to "look violence in the face," but also it was impossible to *envisage* it, to give it a face, mark it out, think about it and understand it. As if violence passed beneath and besides this national imaginary that was "too happy and too weak"; or rather as if the pact that this "we" made (a pact that can now be recognized with hindsight) was a pact that could only be made "secretly," only without anyone knowing or admitting they had made it, but one which "we" had nonetheless made. Then, Merleau-Ponty returned to the phrase several times in *Humanism and Terror*: for example, at the very beginning of "The Yogi and the Proletarian" (published in October 1946), where the metaphor denotes the absolute impossibility of its literalization, its experience: à propos of a communist sympathizer Merleau-Ponty evokes so as to suggest himself unsupportive of Soviet terror per se, he writes, "[The sympathizer] has forgotten that violence—anguish, pain, and death—is not beautiful, except as an image, in art and written history . . . the exalted sympathizer refuses to see that no one can look violence in the face" (HT 2; trans. amended). This second use opposes the possibility of seeing violence in positive terms: no one can look at violence as if it, or the politics that employs it were goals in themselves. Written in mid-1946, the phrase also evokes an effort to engage with the "problem of communism" and especially of its terror, *without* limiting the debate to pro- and anti-communist possibilities: here, the "exalted sympathizer" would be a straw man intended to distance Merleau-Ponty's position from the (reasonable) perception that this position offers little else but fellow-traveling support for communism regardless of the latter's violence. Merleau-Ponty returned to this expression once again a few months later, when composing an introduction to "The Yogi and the Proletarian" for its book publication as *Humanism and Terror*. By this stage, he was faced with the critiques that his articles had already roused, and he lamented the general fatigue toward an understanding of the links between humanist promises and violence. This passage is worth citing in its entirety:

The war has so drained everyone, demanded so much patience, so much courage, has so multiplied glorious as well as inglorious horrors that men no longer have the energy even to look violence in the face, to see it at its source. They have so longed to be rid at last of the presence of death and return to peace that they cannot bear to see it elude them; a slightly frank view of history is therefore taken by them as an apology for violence. They cannot bear the thought of still being exposed to violence, of still having to pay with courage to exercise liberty. Although everything in politics *as in the theory of knowledge* shows that the reign of universal reason is problematic, that reason like liberty has to be made in a world not predestined to it, they prefer to forget experience, to drop culture there and solemnly formulate as venerable truths the tired sayings which answer their weariness. An innocent is an innocent, a culprit is a culprit, murder is murder—these are the conclusions of three thousand years of philosophy, meditation, theology, and casuistry. It would be too painful to have to admit that, in a way, the Communists as well as their opponents are right. "Polytheism" is too difficult. And so they choose the god of the East or the god of the West. And—it is always the same—precisely because it is out of weakness that they love peace, there they are, all ready for propaganda and war. In the last analysis, the truth from which they are running is that man has no rights over the world, that, to talk like Sartre, he is not "man by divine right," that he is thrown into an adventure whose happy end is not guaranteed any more than the harmony of mind and will assured in principle. (HT xli–xlii; italics mine)[8]

This time, "to see it at its source" serves to qualify the demand that people (Merleau-Ponty doesn't say *we* here) have the "energy *even* to look violence in the face." This qualification points away from a literal "looking violence in the face," a head-on approach that could lead to facile proclamations ("murder is murder").[9] Instead, looking violence in the face means ignoring its apparently immediate manifestations and its readily identifiable sources, and rather targeting it at its most pervasive, most established foundations (HT xxxvi): seeing it where it is invisible, where it passes as it were *beneath* the gaze. "For, by hiding violence, one grows accustomed to it, one grows accustomed to it and makes an institution" (HT 34). Looking violence in the face means seeing it wherever it manifests itself, wherever people are "exposed" to it, but also recognizing its depth rather than identifying it with whichever of the contemporary gods (of "East" or "West") one rejects. Failing to understand its reach ensures the survival of humanism *as* hypocrisy. To support his approach, Merleau-Ponty turns to three themes from his earlier work, namely, *thrownness into a nature that offers no given or set meaning,* "*an adventure whose happy end is not guaranteed,*" and *a Reason that needs to be constructed.* Merleau-Ponty then offers an extraordinary, and for many an outrageous response to this "hypocrisy": "If one gives violence its name, and if one uses it, as the revolutionaries always did, without pleasure, there remains a chance of driving it out of history" (HT 34).

Humanism and Terror is a lengthy negotiation of the legitimacy of violence and the circumstances in which it affects individuals. Unlike the pre-WWI age of the "shameless" humanism of the Spirit and Reason, where violence was supposed to be merely leftover darkness where the light of reason had not yet reached, contemporary existence now dissociated from "the idea of a humanity fully guaranteed by natural law."[10] In 1946–47, violence could not be reduced to an opposite of Reason and easily eliminated "bit by bit." Claiming that "the value of a society is the value it places upon man" and that "to understand and judge a society, one has to penetrate its basic structure to the human bond upon which it is built" (HT xiv), Merleau-Ponty proceeds to a scathing attack of the Reason of liberalism, which dissimulates and disavows its own violence. This critique (to which we have already pointed) marks a success of French communist thought, and Merleau-Ponty (extending Sartre's existential humanism) agrees here with communist premises (HT xxi).

If the events of the last thirty years lead us to doubt that the world proletariat is about to unite, or that proletarian power in one country establishes reciprocal relations among men, they in no way affect the truth of that other Marxist idea that no matter how real and precious the humanism of capitalist societies may be for those who enjoy it, it does not filter down to the common man and does not eliminate unemployment, war, or colonial exploitation. (HT 175)

Merleau-Ponty continues:

Western humanism is a *humanism of comprehension*—a few mount guard around the treasure of Western culture; the rest are subservient. . . . Western humanism, like the Hegelian State, subordinates empirical humanity to a certain idea of man and its supporting institutions. . . . Western humanism has nothing in common with a *humanism in extension*, which acknowledges in every man a power more precious than his productive capacity . . . as a being capable of self-determination and of situating himself in the world. In its own eyes Western humanism appears as the love of humanity, but for the rest of men it is only the custom and institution of a group of men, their password, and occasionally their battle cry. (HT 176)[11]

In arguments like these, Merleau-Ponty reiterates the same stance: liberalism pretends that its unblemished face irons out the fact and occurrence of violence (a point he repeats over and over [HT xv, 155, 172, 180 et al.]).

It has no way to address, *or even to face*, its violence, and accordingly to seek to gradually overcome it. Merleau-Ponty opens here the following question: Given that liberalism cannot proceed to its own overcoming, in other words cannot eradicate violence and institute proper human relationships, can communism do so instead? More interesting than the attack on liberalism is the ambivalence toward the project of contemporary communism, which Merleau-Ponty implicates with violence at every step, asking of its violence two deeply interrelated questions: Does it work consequentially toward an overcoming of the violence thus far instituted in human relations, and does the communism that utilizes it indeed manage this overcoming?

Two philosophical moves preface the relation of communism to violence: (a) the formation of a philosophy of history, premised on the contingency of the future and the impossibility of knowing it; and (b) the *ethical* demand for a commitment to the fundamental improvement of human relations. Merleau-Ponty here comes close to Blanchot's approach, all the while differing from him absolutely in his prioritization of ethics and the radical claim that violence can be justified only if it results in a world without violence. Merleau-Ponty's trust in a new man, fully egalitarian, within the framework of "Marxist sociology," and tending toward the eradication of violence formulates his organization of "the real question," that is, "Is communism still equal to its humanist intentions?" (HT xviii). Or, as he puts it elsewhere: "The only question which remains . . . whether Bukharin really died for a revolution or a new humanity" (HT xxxiv).

The demand for a philosophy of history is intimately tied to the antifoundational realism of Merleau-Ponty's contemporary phenomenological concerns—especially the claim that vis-à-vis nature, there is no vantage point from which one has superior access to the truth. Merleau-Ponty specifically situates the problems of history and violence in the interrelation of man and world—in the fact that humans are situated beings and not embodied pure consciousnesses. Here he clearly echoes and expands on his position in *Phenomenology of Perception*:

I never encounter face to face another person's consciousness any more than he meets mine. . . . We are both for one another situated beings, characterized by a certain type of relation to men and the world, by a certain activity, a certain way of treating other people and nature. . . . To start with a pure consciousness is beyond my grasp: even if I tortured his body I could not do him any violence. In such a case the problem of violence does not arise. It only arises with respect to a consciousness originally committed in the world, that is to say with violence, and thus can only be solved beyond utopia. We only know of situated consciousnesses which blend themselves with the situation they take and are unable to complain at being identified with it or at the neglect of the incorruptible innocence of conscience. When one says that there is a history one means precisely that each person committing an act does so not only in his own name, engages not only himself, but also others whom he makes use of, so that as soon as we begin to live, we lose the alibi of good intentions; we are what we do to others, we yield the right to be respected as noble souls. . . . *We do not have a choice between purity and violence but between different kinds of violence. Inasmuch as we are incarnate beings, violence is our lot.* (HT 109; italics mine)

A relationship between violence—"our lot"—and concrete intersubjectivity is thus a necessity: "violence is universal" (HT 2). What has appeared so far as an inability to face violence is, in a sense, the unwillingness to recognize the necessary effect of human action and law—its fundamental and irreducible violence (HT xxxvi et al.). This unavoidability is the crucial premise for a philosophy of history, and through its cynicism becomes, for Merleau-Ponty, the headstone in the tomb of liberalism—and, ironically, communism as well:

If I wish freedom for another person it is inevitable that even this wish will be seen by him as an alien law, and so liberalism turns into violence. *One can only blind oneself to this outcome by refusing to reflect upon the relation between self and others.* . . . We are not accusing liberalism of being a system of violence; we reproach it *with not seeing its own face* in violence, with veiling the pact upon which it rests while rejecting as barbarous that other source of freedom—revolutionary freedom—which is the origin of social pacts. *With the assumptions of impersonal Reason and rational Man, and by regarding itself as a natural rather than an historical fact, liberalism assumes universality as a datum, whereas the problem is its realization through the dialectic of concrete intersubjectivity.* (HT 35 n11; italics mine)

In the name of pure human relations, humanism becomes hypocritical: it fails to allow for a philosophy of history that would think of the human world as an unfinished system (HT 188), that would understand the everpresence of violence in this open system or the necessity to seek an overcoming of institutions that facilitate this ever-presence, and finally that would recognize as crucial the goal of reducing violence by attacking it "at its source."

Merleau-Ponty effects here an inversion of Kojève's thematization of the end of history, rejecting determinism in Hegel and the early Marx (particularly in the form granted by Kojève), and criticizing the Hegelian understanding of the State as having control of permanent, institutionalized Terror (HT 150) on the basis of which arises a supraempirical conception of man to which men have to answer (HT 67, 155–56, 176).[12] Somewhat more in line with Blanchot, who sees a revolutionary act as damning the actor to all-or-nothing stakes, to an "achievement" of death, and to a denial of any future to his revolutionary life, Merleau-Ponty argues instead that in their historical course, events come with a precariousness, contingency, or bruteness that defines not their outcome but their retroactive interpretation. To the extent that all actions involve a kind of violence upon others, commitment involves precisely the acceptance (and responsibility) that one's cause could be lost (whereupon one would become a victim) or won (whereupon one's violence would be crowned triumphant).

There is a sort of maleficence in history: it solicits men, tempts them so that they believe they are moving in its direction, and then suddenly it unmasks, events change and prove that there was another possibility. The men whom history abandons in this way and who see themselves simply as accomplices suddenly find themselves the instigators of a crime to which history has inspired them. And *they are unable to look for excuses or to excuse themselves from even a part of the responsibility.* (HT 40)

In this kind of a "possible worlds" argument, history is *not* what offers an ethical confirmation of choices: it is not the case that something is right because its proponents win. Instead, the actual outcome of history is what renders the possible but unachieved courses that "men" take impossible to disavow. Merleau-Ponty's position might perhaps be identified with the classic claim about communist violence—that to make an omelet you need to break some eggs—but it is more far-reaching and ambiguous. In postulating the "maleficence" of history and the ungraspability of the future, Merleau-Ponty rejects the historical necessity of a future confirming and justifying a certain violence. At the same time that he places a premium on intersubjectivity and human recognition, he denies that a politics aiming that high is inescapable or a communist privilege. Putting this claim in somewhat different terms, Merleau-Ponty asks whether the Communist future can be wanted *even though it is philosophically impossible to simply accept its theory of history*. He also explicitly refuses to accord this desired but philosophically problematic future a blanket justification of violence (in radical opposition to Blanchot). He proceeds to argue on the problem of this theory of relations between the present and the future both in general terms and with specific reference to the case of the Moscow Trials.[13]

> *The contingency of the future, which accounts for the violent acts of those in power, by the same token deprives these acts of all legitimacy, or equally legitimates the violence of their opponents. . . . We argue that an action can produce something else than it envisaged, but nevertheless political man assumes its consequences.* (HT xxxvi)

> The Trials remain on a subjective level and never approach what is called "true" justice, objective and timeless, *because they bear upon facts still open toward the future, which consequently are not yet univocal and only acquire a definitively criminal character when they are viewed from the perspective on the future held by the men in power.* (HT 27; see also xxxiii)

Merleau-Ponty does not doubt here that, in the name of a genuine intersubjectivity, it is possible and desirable to "sacrifice those who according to the logic of their situation are a threat . . . [to the] promise of humanity" (HT 110). His ethical and political imperative concerns specifically a belief in humanity rid of the violence so pervasive in institutions, the class system, and the contemporary conception of freedom.[14] For Merleau-Ponty, questions of ownership and the proletariat are fundamentally involved in man's relation to nature and himself (HT 155). If, as cited above, "the problem" is the realization of universality "through the dialectic of concrete intersubjectivity" (HT 35 n11), Merleau-Ponty makes it clear that he considers this realization to be a consequence of the not-unexpected idealist efforts of the past. The present era is (using Charles Péguy's term) an *epoch*, "one of those moments where the traditional ground of a nation or society crumbles and . . . man himself must reconstruct human relations" (HT xvii). As an *epoch* it is especially significant: not only does man exist in a world that is presently crumbling, but he is thereby charged with a grand task; moreover, the epoch confirms, through its exceptional status, the need for a philosophy of history, a thinking that would provide a philosophical and political narrative to history that would explain the latter's movement.

A philosophy of history is thus necessary not only for an understanding of the course and "cruelty" of history (that is, of the fact that violence is a corollary of intersubjectivity). Insofar as the ever-presence of violence turns the fact that humanity is an "open or unfinished system" into precisely an *imperative*, an understanding of commitment premised on the impossibility of knowing the future and the need to persevere toward it (HT 179). A "philosophy of history" is necessary to justify the critique of Communism from a standpoint of a Marxism, or, as noted in the original version of the essay in *Les Temps modernes*, a "proletarian" humanism.[15]

Thus any philosophy of history will postulate something like what is called historical materialism—namely, the idea that morals, concepts of law and reality, modes of production and work are internally related and clarify each other. In a genuine philosophy of history all human activities form a system in which at any moment no problem is separable from the rest, in which economic and other problems are part of a larger problem, where finally the productive forces of the economy are of cultural significance just as, inversely, ideologies are of economic significance. (HT 154)

What Merleau-Ponty attacks (and the part of his argument that is most often overlooked in historians' writings on *Humanism and Terror*) is the Soviet failure to commit to these principles of "proletarian humanism."[16] It is of the utmost significance whether the Moscow Trials in the Soviet Union are applying the institutionalized permanent Terror of the late Hegel, wherein violence is necessary to the uniting of men (HT 150), or a position in which the goal of violence would *necessarily* be the erasure and overcoming of violence itself. Merleau-Ponty accepts that the USSR had to "force the march of history and do violence to it" (HT 136). But, even though he often stands close to accepting this violence, he has no difficulty arguing that, from his perspective, Soviet Communism is *by no means* succeeding in these hopes, that Bukharin died only for a Revolution, that "the USSR is not the proletarian light of history Marx once described" (HT 141), that "Soviet life . . . is the opposite of proletarian humanism" (HT 136), and that it has moved, to quote his chapter title, "from the proletarian to the commissar."[17] For him, the Soviet project has long entered a stage of domestic "regression" or "stagnation" (HT 139–40), and a foreign policy that does not play the democratic game but only seeks a defense of the Soviet state (HT xxv–xxvii). Merleau-Ponty appears at this point like an anti-Stalinist Communist, and his critique, despite its overall support for Communism, is harsh. "If one tries to evaluate the general orientation of the Communist system, it would be difficult to maintain that it is moving toward the recognition of man by man, internationalism, or the withering away of the State and the realization of proletarian power" (HT xx). This present failure is why, though he defends the USSR from the charge of violence à propos of the Moscow trials, Merleau-Ponty declares himself opposed to the USSR, announcing, over and again, that it is as impossible to be for communism as it is to be against it (HT xxi, xxix, xliv). Moreover, this is why, though he defends the USSR from Koestler's charges that the essence of communism is circumscribed by the violence it does to the individual, Merleau-Ponty argues that this is a violence that everyone implicates himself in through an acceptance of the stakes of the de-subjectivizing "grammatical fiction," as Koestler calls the "I," the speaking subject that Marxist politics undermines in favor of the class (HT 3). Yet more significantly, Merleau-Ponty ultimately suggests through this critique that the USSR has undermined the very humanism it is supposed to advance and, with it, the only reason to support communism. In Mark Poster's words, for Merleau-Ponty "men were free *not* to build socialism."[18]

The imperative proposed by Merleau-Ponty can thus be situated at the site of a neither/nor between humanism/terror, liberalism/Sovietism, Communism/anti-Communism. It lies also in the commitment to a Marxist or "proletarian" humanism convinced of the need of overcoming ownership, preserving liberty, and standing its ground against liberalism.[19] But a third way to the two blocs is impossible, and the situation is "inextricable" (HT xxi).[20] Like Heidegger's claim that genuine thought is being crushed by the pincers of contemporary nihilisms of East and West, Merleau-Ponty's position is that France finds itself seeking and incapable of utilizing this third way (HT 184). Commitment is thus needed for a humanism that seeks to overcome violence while remaining acutely aware of Soviet failure.

The stakes of this argument are quite particular. When the essay and the book came out, they angered nearly everyone: anti-communist former *résistants* saw it as a justification of the least acceptable aspect of communism, namely, Soviet terror. Liberals rejected its contemptuous treatment of their humanism as hypocritical. Communists found Merleau-Ponty as accepting only the critical aspect of Marxism and unwilling to understand the significance and goals of *praxis*. Today, the historian who reads the materials on *Humanism and Terror* and who would be tempted to reduce its argument to an early defense of "existential Marxism" and offer a *Rezeptionsgeschichte* of the book would in turn likely call *Humanism and Terror* nothing more than a confused work.[21] For some, the most that Merleau-Ponty can be reasonably said to have provided is a defense of *engagement* from state power—a power that Koestler saw as defending any and all violence, while leaving the individual forced to forever participate in this violence (whether it is directed at others or at himself). Nevertheless, *Humanism and Terror* is a crucial document of its period for four major reasons tied to Merleau-Ponty's refusal to identify humanism with the dominant political camps and his commitment to the ever-presence and indeed value of violence in interpersonal relations.

First, his is a humanism at the limit, a position that can be described as easily as a radical and unforgiving humanism as it can be an antihumanism that under the guise of a hope for the future purity of human existence disregards and even legitimates violence. It is a call for a new humanity that cannot be constructed or reached, for which violence is ever-present but a solution never will be—a new humanity that, in being unreachable, condemns the present to ineluctable violence. This "proletarian" conception of humanism as fundamentally tied to an improvement of concrete human, intersubjective relations during this period involves both a trust of the Marxist impetus whose postrevolutionary universalism promised such an improvement, and a contempt for all politics (including Soviet politics) that fails this task. Indeed, one could even argue that virtually all politics is bound to fail this task—it can neither erase its violence nor bring about a new humanity. The partial disengagement of the utopian hope from existing concrete politics and in favor of an intellectual confrontation with theoretical Marxism came to dominate French thought during this early postwar period, and even more so later.

The critique of Marxism that Merleau-Ponty effects through his peculiar humanism goes further still. Merleau-Ponty counters Marxism's emphasis on a Dialectic of History that moves without the need for individual involvement—and toward whose end individuals cannot avoid working. Merleau-Ponty's ethics by contrast demands *both* engaged agency and the absence of any conviction that such agency might have any effect. The question he poses as fundamental, "whether Bukharin really died for a revolution or a new humanity" thus highlights both the distance between Marxism and Soviet politics and also the dangers of a conviction that any action whatsoever might find assurance in dialectical materialism's theory of history (HT xxxiv).

Second, because of this ambiguous radicalism, *Humanism and Terror* is expressive not just of the pervasiveness and force of Marxist arguments against liberalism but also of a growing disgruntlement with Soviet policies. This discontent would soon become characteristic of former communists renouncing communist *and* anti-communist politics because of their respective kinds of violence and their pretenses to a deeper humanism. It is important not to read *Humanism and Terror* just from a post-1989 perspective, but to see it in the context of a theoretical Marxism involved in doubting Stalinism and hoping for an alternative politics. In *Humanism and Terror,* to work in the direction and for the benefit of human dignity and genuine human relations is to ally oneself with a theoretical Marxism (in its distinct rejection of modern humanism as violent and destructive) and to realize its likely failure to achieve its task. Heidegger, in his 1953 republication of the *Introduction to Metaphysics,* would bring back the trope of a pincers crushing Europe: "This Europe, in its ruinous blindness forever on the point of cutting its own throat, lies today in a great pincers, squeezed between Russia on one side and America on the other. From a metaphysical point of view, Russia and America are the same. . . . "[22] Again like Heidegger, and still within the aftermath of the resistance and the period before the Iron Curtain had become Europe's horizon, Merleau-Ponty marks out France (and Europe) as the terrain of a battle between East and West that can only survive by holding up a *neither/nor* banner to both anti-Communism and Communism (HT 157, 179).

In this context, if Koestler poses a problem for Merleau-Ponty, this is above all because Koestler turns *engagement* into the basis of the Communist state's destruction of the individual—whether this individual is the engaged intellectual or the individual opposed to the State. Koestler sees the engagement of the individual in favor of the State as *always* dependent on the State for its success (state approval) or failure (which leads to an execution). For Koestler, this means being engaged in ruining people in the name of State ideology and pretending one's own shaming and ruin in the name of the State is not to come. Merleau-Ponty's *Humanism and Terror*, by contrast, advocates the need for engagement as a consequence of contingency and of the inability to predict the future—in other words, the ethical command to engage with others in a way that would facilitate a genuine improvement of human relations.

At stake here is also the peculiarly French tradition that posited the intellectual not as trapped into a relation with the State but as operating at a certain distance from the official political realm. Interpreters have noted the lineage between the intellectual resistance and the language of contestation that developed after it in response to its political and social disappointments, and its lack of a defined role in the postwar period. Merleau-Ponty belongs squarely within this tradition, and in this sense his political effort is tied not to a direct relationship to a state that emphasizes an ideological claim that it ultimately abandons for purposes of its own survival but to an ethics that engages with statehood only to the extent that critique, a thinking of history, and an imagination of the future do not belong to it. As the distance between Left Bank intellectuals and the French government appeared increasingly ossified, addressing the USSR was a way of mobilizing an alternative philosophico-political realm for which the immediate political world had little use. Playing with the primacy of the USSR as the utopian and violent state of its time, *Humanism and Terror* is Merleau-Ponty's effort to turn a state into a form of power that has to answer continually, not only *for* but *to* the utopia expressed in its own ideology.

Third, Merleau-Ponty's major achievement in *Humanism and Terror* was his conversion of the earlier phenomenological writings on embodied perception into a philosophy of historical and political ambiguity with a substantial utopian tension. The embodied perceiver, whose thrownness into nature and need of others define a mostly formal experience of the world, turns here into a temporal subject whose existence bends to the fundamental ambiguity of its historicity and of its future. The role of action and engagement as suspended in the uncertainty of history and bound to the impossibility of predicting consequences not only complements the phenomenological argument but also opens it to a reading that would allow for a historical (and, for the late 1940s, thoroughly contemporary) comprehension of the historical and political construction and possibilities of meaning. Through *Sense and Non-Sense* and the politically daring and problematic *Humanism and Terror*, the phenomenological project of the early 1940s became a complex form of negative anthropology: a denial of man's grounding and primary status in his perception of phenomena, his engagement with art and culture, and above all his participation in politics, action, and history. This is a very different negative anthropology than Heidegger's.[23] With Merleau-Ponty (who is often read as Sartre's less political partner in existential phenomenology), this denial of man's grounding becomes a radical call to turn intersubjectivity and recognition into a political project whose violence could only be acceptable so long as it would be in the name of this humanity as intersubjectivity—which, as Merleau-Ponty would later recognize, was virtually impossible, as much as he might here try to redeem communism through an imaginary "proletarian humanism."

Finally, Merleau-Ponty's search for a political support to his "proletarian" humanism that would be neither reduced to strict communist doctrine nor to divergence from communism's original humanist hope is characteristic of the path of *Les Temps modernes* during its first years when its political effort faced both the scandal of its fellow-traveling and communist criticisms based on its distance from the party line.[24] Merleau-Ponty's politico-philosophical approach of humanism in this context is, in retrospect, exemplary of much of the intellectual scene and the dilemmas it would construct for itself: for Communism but not for a Stalinist or anti-Stalinist Communism per se; for a theoretical Marxism but not one linked to extant, practical politics for a "genuine humanism."

Man in Suspension: Jean Hyppolite
on History, Being, and Language

1. *Lucus a Non Lucendo*: Beyond Humanism,
Violence, and Metaphysics

Between Malraux, Sartre, Heidegger, Blanchot, and Merleau-Ponty, thus, the stakes and breadth of antihumanism came to be tied to the problem of the ethics and political anthropology in a post-WWII world, just as they also effectively mapped many of the dilemmas of the *résistant* legacy, the emergence of a new intellectual landscape, and the early postwar perception of Western progress as having come to a barren close. Malraux's Gaullism granted his Nietzschean-Spenglerian thinking of the decline and possible death of Western man a respite only possible through the salvaging of European art. The phenomenologists' intellectual contribution was more substantial to the new antihumanism. Merleau-Ponty and Sartre identified the possibility of engagement with a new thinking of the human (and out of an effort to come to grips with the Communist ownership of the humanist mantle). Heidegger, by contrast, tied the task of the present time to the need for intellectual distance, a turn toward a thinking that would be critical of almost the entire Western tradition and capable of transforming man by ridding itself of all the positive meaning he can be attributed. In this sense, where Merleau-Ponty and Sartre turned the personal and political struggles of the resistance into a new sort of intellectual engagement, an engagement that may well be in vain, but is ethically imperative. Through these arguments, Merleau-Ponty, Sartre, and

Heidegger radically undermined the traditions of natural law and natural right: among philosophers it was not really possible any longer to proclaim that man has natural and inalienable rights, or that such rights belong to a certain essence or given nature of man. (Many who did so, like Cassin, emphasized precisely the fragility of human goodness and the *need* for international legal support for such rights to become inalienable.) Instead, the notion of an essence or nature of man now seemed itself inescapably premodern—thoroughly insufficient as an effort to understand the complexity of modern life. Sartre, Merleau-Ponty, and Heidegger finally agree in their mistrust of humanism, which they tie to political and philosophical anthropologies of the present and past—seeing in the present moment as opening the possibility of thinking the human anew.

In these philosophers we find a radicalization, even a competition over the radicalization of negative anthropology: the critique of Hegelian and Marxist historical anthropology in Merleau-Ponty parallels the critique of faith, foundations, and nineteenth-century humanism in Sartre and the critique of any anthropology not deriving from ontology and language in Heidegger. Sartre's effort to turn "existence precedes essence" into a requirement that man, being freedom, take responsibility for himself, and found on this responsibility the course of all mankind, should not be simply treated as a humanism, but forms a theory of action not premised per se on humanism and its various past political anthropologies. Anthropology here is negated from the status of ground of ontology and philosophy of nature: at stake is the suspension of man from other categories of thought, the erasure of the human from thought and action itself. Where Sartre founds his political and moral theory on the possibility of a renewal, Merleau-Ponty and Heidegger move increasingly away from the possibility of any position on what man is or can be.

This suspension or even near-erasure of the human that emerges with Heidegger and Merleau-Ponty's development of new languages and aims would come to be most clearly codified and established in the maturation of antihumanism that occurs with Jean Hyppolite's postwar writing, particularly the period leading up to and including his 1954 masterpiece *Logic and Existence*. In texts from this period, Hyppolite concludes the process of this emergent "new thinking" that at once attacks faith in political projects and makes possible a thoroughly negative imagination of the New Man, one that, in man's hope against hope for a better world, suggests (even though it does not yet commit to) the impossibility of finding any truth or humanity in political constructions of the future. Writing in decidedly modernist terms, Hyppolite moves from a worry concerning the weak and unstable equilibrium in which man finds himself given the force of history and the complex intermingling of transcendence and immanence, toward a formal (as opposed to historical) theory of man's suspension from being and language. In this argument, Hyppolite's undoing of humanism's hopes comes to be tied to a critique of contemporary Hegelianism as anthropocentric, as well as to the necessity of rethinking modernity and human existence as dependent, in toto, on forces that man emerges from and thinks, but over which he has no control.

2. Dialectical Roadkill and the *en-deçà* ("Humanisme et hégélianisme" *in short*)

In "Humanisme et hégélianisme," a four-page 1949 text included in the posthumous collection *Figures de la pensée philosophique*, Hyppolite defines atheist humanism as a philosophy of immanence (F 148 / U 217) and a philosophical anthropology. He proceeds to contrast humanist immanence to philosophies of transcendence, and humanism's status as an anthropology to both philosophies of nature (for which man leads *only a human*, that is, a *natural* life [F 148]) and religious philosophies (which place man under the banner of a search for the beyond [F 148, 147]). This conceptualization of humanism serves and addresses as much Hyppolite's own intellectual self-positioning as his properly philosophical aims. On the one hand, it explicates and utilizes Hegel's thought for a critique and an overcoming of modern humanism; on the other, it seeks to strategically reorganize the terrain of contemporary thought around Hegel, and therefore to use Hyppolite's own interpretation as a privileged entry point to the study of contemporary philosophical problems. This dual effort is evident in Hyppolite's conclusion: "The interest of the relationship between Hegelianism and humanism is that it allows us to grasp the ambiguity of Hegel's position and to perceive, *in it*, the . . . direction of contemporary problems" (F 149; italics mine). The gesture of privileging the relation between Hegelianism and humanism provides specific direction

and bite for Hyppolite's definition of humanism as a thinking of immanence. Hyppolite emphasizes not only Hegelianism's philosophical importance (which "in the history of European culture could not be exag-
gerated") but especially its divergence from existentialism and Marxism,
treating these movements as reductive if popular appropriations that testify to Hegel's influence, but also to the capacity of his thought to reveal
ambiguities and hidden assumptions of contemporary thought.[1] Thus the
postwar resurgence of humanism, in Marxism and in Sartre's claim that
only existentialism could properly think the dignity of man (F 148), offers
Hyppolite immediate targets through which to consider the philosophical limitations of humanism in general. Having already rejected historical
definitions of humanism that would treat it as a trait of a specific period
(for example, Renaissance or Enlightenment humanism [F 147]), Hyppolite uses the "ambiguity of Hegel's position" to locate the philosophical significance of Renaissance and Enlightenment humanism and even
Christian asceticism. These quick gestures toward a kind of Greco-Chris-
tian conceptual history allow him to then consider the Weberian interpretation of modernity—as emerging from, and furthering, a laicization
and philosophical/social transposition of Christian dogma (F 149). Hyppolite relates this position to a classical expression of the humanist problem after Feuerbach, Marx, and Nietzsche, according to which, "if God
is dead, man must arise to [his place] and actualize in himself the divine"
(F 149). What is interesting here is that Hyppolite does *not* accept this solution. For him, Hegel does not divinize man, he divinizes history—at
once praising in it the emergence of human values and Right and arguing
that History divinized brings about the negation of human personality (F
149). Hyppolite understands this divinization of history not as an immanence (as would be the case in humanism) but as a transformation of vertical transcendence (God) onto horizontal transcendence (History). Hegel
would thus resist the sufficiency of existentialist terms of human dignity
and Marxist terms of social equality because the immanence of their humanism would too quickly impose the divinization of "the human" (itself
not a claim for immanence) on a history that has been reduced to a linear,
self-enclosed movement. Instead, what is at stake for Hyppolite's Hegel is
the unstable equilibrium between the human individual and a divine His-

tory that forms the expression and synthesis of the human spirit but at a cost for the individual.

At the time that he composed "Hegelianisme et humanisme," Jean Hyppolite was on the way to becoming one of France's most important academic philosophers. He was the author of the massive *Genesis and Structure in Hegel's Phenomenology* and the translator of Hegel's *Phenomenology of Spirit*, a considerable undertaking that both Alexandre Kojève and Gaston Fessard—to cite only figures discussed in this present work—had attempted but never completed. After the conclusion of World War II, Hyppolite had started teaching at the Ecole Normale Supérieure; after composing his very influential *Logic and Existence* in the early 1950s, he would become its director, before being elected to the Collège de France.[2] In other words, his power in Parisian intellectual circles was considerable. Second, his influence as a Hegelian thinker was substantial, as attested by pupils and colleagues as different as Jacques Derrida, Georges Canguilhem, Gilles Deleuze, Guy Debord, Michel Foucault, and Alain Badiou. Hyppolite's reading of Hegel served as an antisubjectivist counterweight and corrective to the one by Kojève, which was broadly considered too Marxisant, too subjectivist, too wild, too often incorrect. As will become evident, Hyppolite, who engages here at least implicitly with a number of contemporaries (Kojève, Merleau-Ponty, Tran Duc Thao, and Heidegger), offers a particularly useful case for seeing how the overall problems of antihumanism (negative anthropology, an atheism that is not humanist, critiques of humanism) interplay and affect postwar philosophical thought; this, moreover, despite Hyppolite's distance from express political claims and problems (for example, violence). Amidst his debates with contemporaries, the stakes, ambiguity, and radicalism of Hyppolite's concept of an *unstable equilibrium* becomes much clearer if we interplay the short aforementioned text with a second, longer, and lesser-known version delivered as a lecture at a 1949 international conference titled "Umanesimo e Machiavellismo" in Bolzano, Italy, where Hyppolite objected strongly to any solution that would take up either of these sides, arguing that each engages with an unacceptable humanism, and instead supporting this equilibrium in all its instability.

3. Man in Suspension I ("Humanisme et hégélianisme," the Lecture Text)

The second version of "Humanisme et hégélianisme" differs from the short one in that it is at least three times longer, and in that through the different ordering of some of its passages, it reuses the apparent conclusions of the shorter text as entry points to more elaborate problems. It provides a much more complex definition of humanism, and a far clearer balancing of its stakes. Hyppolite again begins by treating humanism as an *immanence* opposed to transcendence—whether horizontal or vertical. Using a second contrast that also appears in the short essay, namely between Christian asceticism and Greek rationalism, he suggests that an oscillation between these two positions leads to the rise of humanism in modernity, a thinking for which man and historical humanity becomes the "measure of all things," or, "*better*, the meaning of all things" (U 217). He then proceeds to read this rise of humanism a third time, now through a specifically Hegelian lens—a quick account of 'Self-Consciousness' through 'Reason,' particularly the movement from the Master-Slave through the Unhappy Consciousness. Hyppolite sees the result of this movement as a specific marker of the dependence of human dignity on a transcendental ground. "If humanism is an affirmation of human dignity and grandeur, this dignity and this grandeur manifest themselves as beyond the individual man, and it is the idea of God that enunciates this transcendence" (U 220). This "idea of God" allows for a new interpretation of the contrast between Christianity and post-Christian humanism, and *this* contrast—which emphasizes the continued need of a "beyond"— is what forms the centerpiece of the lecture. Hyppolite begins by supporting the thesis that the essence of Christianity can be found in a recognition of the identity of human and divine nature (U 223), that is to say, the incarnation and its evolution in the Christian *ekklēsia*. If the religious community orients itself toward the God-Man's actions, toward continuous reform or reformation through them (U 223), this is because of a need to understand the Incarnation, qua foundation of Christianity, as a foundation of humanity as such. But precisely this repeated reformation of the *ekklēsia* through its continued turn and return to an understanding of the incarnation, death, and resurrection of the God-Man leads to a loss of the

Christo-centrism of the Bible: which is to say, toward a reformulation of the Absolute in anthropocentric terms. Hyppolite thus contrasts, in the *Phenomenology*, the hope of the *ekklēsia* for salvation in the Second Coming, with the effect of this hope, the "total revelation" of God, which is the total revelation of the human spirit in History (U 224). Echoing and de-Christianizing the Jesuit theologian Gaston Fessard's reading of Hegel (U 224)—for which history is a theodicy—Hyppolite emphasizes that the revelation of the (human) Spirit in History leaves History as nothing less than a self-revelation of the transcendent, and the embodiment in it of the Absolute.[3] This is *not* to say that Hyppolite sees this revelation as taking place "in" or "by way of" man: "If nonetheless Hegel does not push his analysis of man's relation to God that far, this is because he perceives that this reduction of man to himself alone, the reduction of all that is divine into the human, culminates in the loss [*perte*] of man" (U 221). Hyppolite elides, through this new contrast, not only Christian and Old Hegelian readings of Hegel, which often appeal to a religious imperative, but also atheist readings with Young Hegelian or Kojèvian overtones; he also specifically opposes the idea that the *Enlightenment* constitutes a liberation of man, instead marking it as man's *dégénérescence* (degeneration) (U 221).[4] Hyppolite's Hegel is very clear on this: to the extent that belief in God involves man's self-idealization coded as a "vertical" Transcendence, the evacuation of the place of God also strikes at man's capacity and hope to accede to God's place—as humanism would require. If in the shorter essay the "unstable equilibrium" between *history* and *the human that has to fill the void left by God's death* does not fully explain the impossibility of this accession, here the interpretation of modernity explicitly rejects man's capacity to claim this empty site. Hyppolite determines the transformation of Hegel that takes place with Feuerbach, Marx, and Nietzsche, as insufficient and politically motivated (U 220, 222), insofar as their call for an overcoming of man is premised on the humanism of the *Aufklärung* (U 220,221). Hegel's conceptual schema, by contrast, doesn't tolerate the humanizing interpretation except by basing it on horizontal transcendence—which largely annuls it. Thus man's inability to fill the void left by God's death leads to his loss, his negation (U 220).

With the divinization of History appear a number of further issues. On the one hand, history allows us to turn from the fallen Absolute toward the rights of community and the "rights of Right" (U 224). Differently put, this historicism also appears to facilitate the emergence of certain human(ist) values—especially private right and the State (U 221). But, on the other hand, right and the State only engage with man insofar as he is and remains a member of the herd (U 221). Because history has no humanist sense or core, because it operates expressly against the particulars that stand in its way, a community or a state founded on right do *not* safeguard for the individual the meaning of the Absolute. "Man, unable to grasp himself in this absolute certainty of self, ends by placing his absolute in finite things, in *private right*, in *contracts*, in the *money* that condenses to itself the universal of the modern world—and given that finite things necessarily escape man—man becomes the prey of a dialectic that he does not dominate" (U 221). Between post-Christian community and the immanence of humanism, man finds himself deprived of innate meaning and transformed into a victim—and, importantly, a victim *not only of history but of its modern creatures as well*—the private right, contracts, and money that are supposed to codify human resistance to History's overarching force.

This model for the emergence of modernity allows Hyppolite to offer a systematic alternative to competing accounts. First, it steps aside and undermines the "Enlightenment" interpretation I have already pointed out, and its conception of Man as rising to a sort-of-Kantian subjectivity and cosmopolitan outlook to the world. Rejecting these is also a first way of setting up an objection to Sartrean and Marxist humanisms, their liberation ethics and their accounts of the modern subject's political engagement, and social role. We can also see how Hyppolite's argument demolishes the (for him) classical account of a rise of humanism *within* Hegelianism—that is to say, the influence of the Young Hegelians and of Kojève's, Sartre's and Merleau-Ponty's readings, and through it the claim that the "tribunal of History" suffices as a humanism (U 224). Hyppolite suggests, no fewer than five times, that the power of History forces the individual to turn to things that render him a *prey* to the dialectic.

Thus, the problem that Hyppolite is faced with is man's acceptance and framing of his own devaluation: that Hyppolite rejects the Hegelians' humanization of History is not to say that he finds himself obliged to criticize Hegel's nonhuman History for destructively walking over the particular. While disdaining humanism as insufficient, Hyppolite does not place himself on the side of the subject against this divinized History, on the side of a protection of man against a transcendence that leads him to subhuman status.

When Hegel studies the historical phenomenon of the struggle of the Aufklärung against faith, he is very close to justifying this struggle against a beyond in which man would tend to find refuge against the *en deça* [—] but he discovers at the same time the consequences of this victory of the *Auflkärung*, the risk that humanity courts when reduced to itself, which is to get itself stuck in a world that would be no more than an animal world, a society comparable to an animal society. (U 221; italics mine)

Hence the role of the "unstable equilibrium": as a balancing act between horizontal transcendence (History) and immanence (humanism of the subject), between Greek humanism and Christianity, *between* an engagement with right and a fear of right's dual destruction of modern individuality and Christian community (U 224). That Hyppolite arrived at doubts over Hegelian humanism is no news; Deleuze himself based his review of Hyppolite's *Logique et existence* precisely on this theme.[5] But more important than the mistrust of a Hegelian humanism or any announcement of antihumanism is the philosophical anthropology that is negatively represented through this equilibrium. In it, man finds himself *suspended* from (a) a dialectical, divinized History that crushes all particularity, and (b) the finitudes of money, private right, and so on, which replace humanism and deface the Absolute. Hence the description of man in terms of animality and prey. While the strong tone of "prey" would ostensibly allow for a defense of the individual—by *foregrounding* the violence that can be expected of a history that is moving toward what is by no means a humanist utopia—this suspension denies man any capacity to act in his own defense. In this Absolute, Man is neither a subject that acts or speaks as a free historical individual, nor a kind of particle of History. Deprived of the theological self-idealization and self-definition that provided him with a claim to transcendence, self-knowledge, and salvation; deprived of meaningful action or participation in History; deprived of a direct relation to the Absolute except for deceitful reductions like money, contracts or right, Man is finally an index for the loss of meaning that follows the loss of God.

4. From Contentless Antithesis to Unbalanced Category (Hyppolite and Kojève)

The novelty of this conception of man in suspension is easy to miss—some of its themes recall Adorno; others were systematized and radicalized in the 1960s. More recently, the work of Jean-Luc Nancy has also echoed and furthered similar insights.[6] Hyppolite himself further complicates his conception in *Logique et existence*. But in order to explain, within the corpus of French Hegelianism, the specificity and significance of Hyppolite's negative anthropology, I want to change terrain a little and contrast it to that of certain contemporaries, starting with Alexandre Kojève. Hyppolite explicitly worked against Kojève's interpretation of Hegel, and in many ways helped shape Kojève's legacy and status as a "Marxist thinker." As he would make clear later, it is Kojève that he saw, in "Humanisme et hégélianisme," as the main advocate of humanist Hegelianism. It is important, in this context, to mark out the differences between (a) Kojève's ontology, (b) the picture Hyppolite has/constructs of it in the period of "Hegelianisme et humanisme," and (c) Hyppolite's own Hegel.

(a) Kojève's Ontology and Negative Anthropology

Let us quickly recall elements of Kojève's thought. Kojève's anti-anthropocentric ontology is based on his idea that the contrast of the observing and observed systems in Heisenberg's uncertainty principle parallels Heidegger's distinction of *Dasein* from *Vorhandensein*—of the being of man from the worldhood of the world. Kojève directly transposes these onto a dualist ontology that distinguishes between man and world and treats the world as given, and man as its negation. This basic schema Kojève maintains throughout his reading of Hegel in the seminar, slanting sublation into negation and equating negation with man, while treating Hegel's notions of *thesis* and Being as equal to the given world. Having worked out his own ontology, Hegel can only provide him with an anthropology intimately connected to history, in which Kojève sees man rising to divinity, a divinity already exemplified in Christ's dual, divine/human nature, which Man in turn achieves at the end of history through a sort of imitation without imitation of Christ. Thus, throughout history, Man lacks himself—whether as grounded or as an absolute end: he is nothing other than a negation of every world, he has no basic *essence* but only a status as continuous destruction of the given. But by finally becoming God, man breaks this dualism and becomes equal with nature, with the given, that is also to say, undoes the achievement that is his divinization and becomes no longer human but undifferentiated from Being, nature, the world. The ambiguous conclusion of History—a divinization that is also a dehumanization of the human subject in that it erases even the ungrounded character of Man's existence as negation—further troubles any positive identification of his status and condition in this History.

(b) Hyppolite's Reconstruction of Kojève's Negative Anthropology as a Positive One

If Kojève's 1930s attack on French idealism was premised on a need to turn against the Neo-Kantian conception of man as his own highest being and ideal and resulted in a Christomimetic conception of Man as *free, finite historical individual*, such a conception hardly suffices for Hyppolite. Hyppolite writes explicitly on Kojève in a 1957 essay ("La 'Phénoménologie' de Hegel et la pensée française contemporaine"), and he identifies Kojève's thought with a claim that Hegel's *Phenomenology* is an anthropology, imposing on him the critique of Feuerbach and Marx. He echoes Kojève's suspicion of the Enlightenment and Kantianism (especially on the *in itself*), and he agrees with Kojève that man should be seen as creative negativity, not static essence (F 239). But here the similarities end. Hyppolite explicitly objects to Kojève's dualist ontology, identifying it (somewhat too quickly) with Sartre's *Being and Nothingness* (F 240), and specifically distinguishing sublation from man. While concurring with Kojève that Jesus is the paradigm for humanity's realization of its divine nature, Hyppolite rejects Kojève's treatment of Jesus as an exemplar for the lived experience of a *free, finite historical individual*—which for him culminates in Kojève's treatment of Napoleon as bringing humanity to a direct identification with the Absolute. A further implication of this criticism is that Kojève's attempt to construct an anthropology, by seeing Man as negation and leading him to a dramatic, anthropotheist end of history where Man basks in purveying his own historical ascent, leads to a self-assured and ludicrous conception that we, after WWII, can claim the end of history as our historical success.

Kojève's conception is thus far too humanist now both because it conceives of Man as always directing history, and because it sees the reconciliatory outcome of History as a tribunal for its course (F 238). For Hyppolite, this ignores the tragedy of a History that moves without caring not to squash the particular and also the ambiguous role of incarnations of the Absolute. More importantly, Kojève humanizes precisely what is least humanist about Hegel—therefore destroying Hegel's "discoveries" of the speculative and of the absolute revelation (F 241), the very themes that confound any reduction to anthropology or theology and undermine the historicist account. In a fashion that clearly recalls Adorno, Hyppolite seeks instead to see the notion of the subject as always under threat, while at the same time denying the subject any defense through humanism: the goal is to undo any possibility of interpreting man as an agent of History. If, in relentlessly targeting all ground, Kojève's human becomes the free historical individual that serves as historical agent, Hyppolite's human is but a noncategory, a force in suspension, a contradiction born of unacceptable options.

(c) Hyppolite, Tran Duc Thao, Merleau-Ponty

Hyppolite's attack on "humanizing interpretations of Hegel" has two additional targets. The first is his personal friend and copresenter at the conference "Umanesimo e Machiavellismo," Maurice Merleau-Ponty. Hyppolite specifically targets Merleau-Ponty's convictions in *Humanism and Terror* concerning the contingency of history and the necessity of agency as the central ethical and political question concerning fellow traveling; Hyppolite criticizes in particular the claim that one *must* take part in history, that a utopia or even hope that history might end in a life in equality (for example, Communist equality) suffices as a defense of violence perpetrated in its name.[7] *Humanism and Terror* is significant for Hyppolite's point of view insofar as it advocates something that even Kojève's thought lacks, namely, utopia (even at the level of a hope against hope) as *ethical command*, a belief that everyday life in true Communism might provide the humanism that bourgeois politics destroys and cannot

imagine, and that such everyday life deserves a genuine commitment un-
less Soviet violence were done solely with the goal of preserving the revolution and not for the rise of a new, genuine humanity.[8]

The second, implicit target is the Vietnamese Marxist phenomenologist Tran Duc Thao. Thao's 1951 *Phenomenologie et materialisme
dialectique* formalized an argument he had pursued from his position as
chief writer of *Les Temps modernes* on decolonization, where he became
a major influence on writers such as Frantz Fanon.[9] Echoing somewhat
Lukács's critique of existentialism (but from a much closer place to existentialism), Thao argued that phenomenology had inescapable limitations
when it came to real matters—limitations he wished to overcome through
an effort to use dialectical materialism to "ground" Husserl and subvert
Hegel. If the Hegel who was perceived as most radical, and who remained
useful for intellectual efforts linked to decolonization (Thao's, Fanon's,
and the later Sartre's included), Hyppolite's negative anthropology based
on a thinking of history was instead much more formal and ambivalently
political. His critique of Western humanism and his notion of the violence
of History may have facilitated an assault against the West from the outside and for a construction of alternative humanisms, but they also found
themselves critiqued by those invested in intellectual struggles against
material oppression.

Now, when Hyppolite speaks of the violence of a progressive and
teleological, even transcendental History, he affirms an other radicalism,
a formal antihumanism, for which man as a grounding category of ethics and politics must be overcome. Without falling back on a humanism
defending the subject against history (the humanism that Merleau-Ponty
targeted as an expression of Western imperialism), Hyppolite insists,
against Thao and Merleau-Ponty, on the priority of an antihumanism
that rejects all claims to a harnessing of the horizontal transcendence has
broken (1) man's relation to his self-idealization and self-representation in
God, as well as (2) the individual's relation to the community.

5. Marionette: Man in Suspension II

Hyppolite's solution to the problems of contemporary Hegelianism
is eventually to claim that the historical and anthropological position is

founded on, and eclipsed by, an ontology of the human subject. This he elaborates on in his work *Logic and Existence* (*Logique et existence*), which centers on the relations between the *Logic* and the *Phenomenology of Spirit*. *Logic and existence* proceeds explicitly from concerns suggested in "Humanisme et hégélianisme" by both highlighting the political status of these concerns and reducing their ontological priority; instead, his Hegel turns here to a more complicated suspension of the human that now (a) depends on a specifically ontological questioning, and (b) leads to a theory of a production of meaning that is guaranteed neither by history nor by man. The conclusion to *Logic and existence* appears crafted as a radicalization of questions considered thus far—an attempt to reorganize them. As has been noted before, Hyppolite's reading of Heidegger's "Letter on 'Humanism'" and *What Is Called Thinking?* is crucial in this respect— once again, not because Hyppolite picks up Heidegger's announcement of an opposition to humanism, but rather because he echoes and even follows Heidegger's reprioritization of the relationship between man and *Dasein* (as well as of *Dasein* and Being), by reorganizing the relations between subject and Being, subject and logos, subject and Universal.[10] "The leading difficulty of Hegelianism is the relation of the Phenomenology and the Logic. Today we would speak of anthropology and ontology. The one studies the properly human reflection, the other the absolute reflection that passes through man" (L 189). Through this *rapprochement* with Heidegger, whom (like Kojève twenty years earlier) he mixes with Hegel without explicitly indicating the influence, Hyppolite reinscribes the human subject in the *Logic* in such a way as to radically emphasize the priority of the *logos* and *Being*. Both the terms of this reinscription and of the priority of *the logic of thought* over *the subject that thinks* follow from the critique of anthropocentrist Hegelianism and the rejection of humanist immanence considered thus far. Here Hyppolite continues, "Humanity as such is not the supreme end for Hegel. When man is reduced to himself, he is lost: this is how he is in Greek comedy and the *Aufklärung*. He makes use of his freedom in order to retreat into abstract self-certainty, but this certainty is contentless and gives itself an empirical, a finite project. Man is an intersection; he is not a natural *Dasein* that would have a primordial positivity" (L 186). It is thus that Hyppolite arrives at a formula that echoes Heidegger as much as it angles his claim that "language is the House of Being": "Man does not possess the freedom that allows him to wander from one determination to another or to be dissolved in abstract nothingness; rather, freedom possesses man. Through this freedom [. . .] man does not conquer himself as man, but becomes the house (*la demeure*) of the Universal, of the Logos of Being, and becomes capable of Truth" (L 187).[11] This ontological priority of Being and language over the subject, the confident overcoming of humanisms based on History and individuality respectively, and the construction of truth thus become the constitutive bases for a theory of meaning, history, and the very possibility of human freedom. Moreover, this conception of the human is both less dystopian (in the sense that the subject's dissolution in language renders it far less vulnerable to a logic of divinized History) and, at the same time, far more restrictive of the human subject's positivity and subjectivity—in the sense that it leaves the individual as a kind of vehicle for the experience of notions, selfhood, existence, and universals it cannot comprehend or participate in.

Nevertheless, *Logic and Existence* neither resolves nor effaces the equilibrium between History and the human introduced in "Humanisme et hégélianisme." What it does do is destroy its ontological priority, emphasizing instead a different suspension of "the human" between, on the one hand, *this historico-anthropological site of balancing*, and on the other, *an ontological (and, from the earlier perspective much more formal) construction of Being, the Universal, and Logos.* Man's submission to divinized History is joined by man's suspension from Being and his condition as vehicle of logos. In a sense, man is assaulted both from within and without—that is to say, man is reconstructed both as the prey of history's interplay with a self-effacing individuality and as the space for the play of the Absolute. What this means is that, reading *Logic and Existence* with the stakes of philosophy today in mind, Gilles Deleuze would correctly note that "if Hyppolite's thesis 'philosophy is ontology' means one thing above all, it is that philosophy is not anthropology," but reading the same text with the question of man in mind, we are left less with a delegitimation of the anthropological question than with its submission to ontological and historical priorities.[12] Human dignity and hope for social equality are no longer the crucial issues because their status as fundamental categories is now undone and they have become side-effects for both a reaction to History and an ontology in which subjectivity holds no priority and no capacity for independent action, choice, and so forth, even less for a positive politics. If human subjectivity can be granted any positive or determinate role or value, this is specifically derivative of, and consequent to, the organization of *logos* and *being* that traverse its facticity, existence, and relation to others as all this occurs against a historical backdrop. Were one to start pointing out the differences between logos, the Universal, and Being (differences that Hyppolite does not iron out), then man, expressing or balancing from these bases of absolute knowledge, balancing even from their differences, becomes a veritable marionette for the Absolute.

6. On Ambiguity

I began my analysis of Hyppolite by arguing that his definition of humanism can be read in both properly philosophical and intellectually strategic terms: "The interest of the relationship between Hegelianism and humanism is that it allows us to grasp the ambiguity of Hegel's position and to perceive, *in it*, the . . . direction of contemporary problems."[13] At stake here is not really whether Hegelianism formed the philosophical horizon of the postwar period. Rather it is the way in which this "ambiguity of Hegel's position" allows Hyppolite to avoid what he perceives as a Scylla of historicism (with the possible traps of a subjectivist messianism or an endorsement of violence on ideological premises) and a Charybdis of a direct phenomenological, existentialist, or ontological displacement of man for an alternative (whether that would be the fact of existence or the ambiguous relation between man and Being). Hyppolite keeps both of these in play: putting man in suspension is his way of at once arguing for the reach of these inversions of man and outdoing them. This human marionette at once denies the sufficiency of each of these two interpretive systems and transforms Hegel's *Logic* into the basis for combining them and radicalizing them, all the while completing and stepping beyond a grand history of the Greek, Christian, and humanist modernity. Because of this movement, Hyppolite's ambiguity plays with and seeks far more than he openly claims. It plays with virtually the entire twentieth-century philosophical tradition considered thus far in this work—not only the thought of Kojève, Heidegger, and Merleau-Ponty as suggested already but also the series of philosophical moments—from the scientist/

man described by Koyré, Kojève, and Bachelard, who must now recognize there is no purity of knowledge and no translation of mind to world, to Levinas's, Bataille's, and Sartre's subject trapped in immanence, and to the later Heidegger's reorganization of the relationship of man to Being and logos. Hyppolite's endorsement of ambiguity seeks the establishment of premises for a new system of thought, whose announcement of the derivativeness of man and humanism would not mean raising a political banner in philosophy. It would instead facilitate the *address* and interplay of questions of history, violence, and empirical knowledge in *almost* the same breath as the more fundamental questions of language, being, and Absolute knowledge, and it would leave man to hang from these terms, problems, and issues—a being with neither historical resolution nor philosophical self-organization and ground. In this way, Hyppolite's ambiguity reconfigures and rethinks many of the problems posed by Heidegger and Merleau-Ponty. Both in his critique of historicism and in rejection of anthropological foundationalism in ontology, Hyppolite sets the problem as a thoroughly contemporary one: his ontological effort ultimately refuses Heidegger's turn to the pre-Socratics for a new thinking of the world, just as it ignores (if not undermines) the ethical demands toward the subject and political actor that Merleau-Ponty posits as necessary despite the cunning of history. Hyppolite's ambiguity is thus by no means a mere expression of doubt in humanism or a reflection of the lack of definitive responses to the humanist problem.

What is striking in this ambiguity is its indifference toward humanism. Hyppolite's negative anthropology renders humanism—whether based on human rights or on Marxist premises—quite insignificant, as both the historical and the formal arguments that would be involved in its theorization, delimitation, and political deployment cannot alter the basic fact that man is neither grounded in himself nor able to aim for an ideal that would be decidedly (and undoubtedly) humanity's own. If man's submission to History is joined by his suspension from Being and logos, then ambiguity only signifies the impossibility and indifference of choosing and relying on a particular "humanist" claim. In this sense, Hyppolite completes the early postwar movement of antihumanism's radicalization and codification: against humanisms we find not a rejection, but instead a modern atheist anthropology indifferent to their competition and dismissive of their aims.

Conclusion

Throughout the present work, I have sought to offer a history of the emergence of a new atheism unbound by humanism, by interplaying a general tripartite (theological, philosophical, critical) structure with a series of philosophically significant moments in its elaboration. Central among these have been (a) the emergence of antifoundational realism, its dismantling of subjectivity, and its participation in a profound transformation of philosophy of science and philosophy of nature; (b) the political and philosophical undoing of idealism and classical humanism, primed in particular by the competition between the different and ostensibly exclusive humanisms of Communists, nonconformists, and Catholics; (c) the construction of new terms and radical limitations for anthropotheism, which articulate an erasure of man in a universe bereft of God; (d) the undoing of classical transcendence and the existentialist (and antihumanist) sense of entrapment; and (e) the postwar emergence of new, minimal humanisms, and their rejection by phenomenologists and some literary authors as insufficient, still violent, and incapable of even understanding the terms of their hope and promise. I have tried to intersperse with these themes a number of further problems: the offering and fares of Catholic anti-anthropocentrism beyond the Christian confine; the undoing of utopia and the elaboration of philosophical and political antimessianisms; new genealogies of modern thought; the transforming interplay of violence and sovereignty; the abandoning of ideals of a harmonious secular society; the critical rethinking of transparency as a scientific and social goal; the reception of Martin Heidegger and G. W. F. Hegel's thought; and the transformation of models of the philosophy of history and the understanding of French modernity.

From the emergence of antifoundational realism in the 1930s through the effort to move from anthropology to ontology in the late 1940s and early 1950s, the transformation and impact of the new philosophical claims on man was at once slow and monumental. Importantly, what matters in this philosophical system is not that the new atheism and philosophical anthropology "overcame" humanism—by and large, they did not. Merleau-Ponty's stance toward the human and its future is so explicitly and broadly ambiguous regarding violence as to deal only with difficulty against humanist accusations of advocating it.[1] Heidegger's self-distancing from humanism, as Jacques Derrida later noted, gave the illusion of having reached "a new shore" without really doing so.[2] No less significantly, if the "conflict of humanisms" persisted well into the 1960s and the literary appropriation of antihumanist tropes came to express and echo in broader terms what philosophical, scientific, and critical thought claimed, at the same time the need for *some* minimal humanism became necessary throughout the period and came to characterize not only philosophy but also a public opinion removed from many of the stakes expressed here but still concerned with problems of social policy, Catholicism, communist violence, colonialism, and so on.

The change was nevertheless monumental because it transformed a host of political, religious, philosophical, scientific, and intellectual premises. Politically, it led from a world where "progressive" meant imagining a harmonious anthropocentric universe purged of violence to a generally left-leaning rejection of political projects treating Man as a banner and utopian dream; it thus contributed to the secular rejection of teleological narratives of progress. Philosophically, it led to a depreciation of man from a fundamental category (if not *the* foundation and ground) of thought, existence, and ethics to a limited concept and aporia. It all but annihilated, in French thought and beyond, notions of a stable human nature or essence, of natural law, of right or rights as guaranteeing equality and identity. Theologically, it came to radically transform the conceptual premises of atheism and paralleled a significant conceptual change in the social philosophy of Catholicism. In a perhaps more profound fashion, negative anthropology's kenosis of human subjectivity facilitated a profound rethinking of the very metaphysical and religious tradition it sought to supercede: it offered a critical distance from secular hopes as well as from narratives of religious salvation, complicating the ambiguity of man's relation to the world and to God and hence linking atheism not just to a rejection of God but also to a radical negative theology premised on the complete inaccessibility of the divine. It is this ambiguity and inaccessibility that perhaps explains Emmanuel Levinas's aforementioned criticism that this new atheism "that is not humanist" tends toward the "exaltation of an obedience and a faithfulness that are not obedience or faithfulness *to anyone*"—not an other, not "the" Other, nor God as *autrui*—and partially directs his own effort to offer a radical new humanism.[3] By undermining the ability of man to understand and control the world, emphasizing the violence that is inescapable in man's relations to other men and to nature, and denying the subject sovereignty over language and action, the thinkers examined here offered the metaphysical and religious tradition a way ahead—not exactly by exalting "an obedience and a faithfulness," but rather by aiming to settle beneath man and God so as to lay the foundations for new forms of thought and politics. It is not altogether unfair to claim that existentialism was one result of this aim and structuralism would be another. In a more general intellectual sense, these thinkers contributed to a cynicism toward political promises and helped produce a new language of politics and culture. This new language sought not only to sideline contemporary ideologies as sites of philosophical truth but also to deal with (if not do away with) political religion and ideology by according the problem of the future a sense of indeterminacy and irredeemable movement. The political result was a rejection of messianism and liberationism, and a turn to a perpetual and irreducible critique of the forms and guises of ideology and of presupposition—a turn to taking apart the photographic negative of everyday life.

The story that I have told in this book does not end in the early 1950s. It is essential to open with a few words to the question of structuralism, as this movement became the single most influential inheritor of early antihumanism, the tradition that reconfigured and systematized many of the problems and arguments discussed here. As is well known, structuralism in the 1950s and 1960s became, in terms of both method and intellectual polemics, a sort of standard-bearer of antihumanism; it did so in large part by finding a theory of language in Saussurean linguistics that allowed for this systematization and by attempting fundamental reinterpretation of anthropological, psychological, and social-scientific problems. But it also did so by expanding on movements described or addressed in the present work. What Saussurean linguistics afforded structuralism's anthropological and philosophical dimensions was precisely a profoundly antisubjectivist and anti-anthropocentric approach to human phenomena, the understanding of this approach as scientific (by most significantly Emile Benveniste and Claude Levi-Strauss).[4] In this sense, the call of the major figures of the later 1940s to establish a sufficient antihumanism and a forceful negative anthropology was answered—albeit in somewhat different philosophical language—by Claude Levi-Strauss, Jacques Lacan, and (though at a distance from structuralism) Michel Foucault and Jacques Derrida. Thinkers discussed in this book also played an important role: Merleau-Ponty and Hyppolite facilitated the 1950s legitimation of structural linguistics within philosophical inquiry, while others of the then-old generation, like Merleau-Ponty and Bataille (as well as *Les Temps modernes* in its early years), supported Levi-Strauss's postwar rise. Bataille in particular wrote at great length on Levi-Strauss, in his *Eroticism* and in the second, posthumously published volume of *The Accursed Share*.[5] Merleau-Ponty's turn back from politics to phenomenology and ontology brought him to rethink consciousness from the perspective of language.[6] Some of structuralism's stars had also been present in the 1930s emergence of antihumanism: Levi-Strauss had been a participant at Bataille's late-1930s Collège de Sociologie, while Lacan had been a student of Kojève at the Ecole Pratique des Hautes Etudes and remained a reader of Heidegger in the 1950s. The attention Foucault and Derrida paid to Heidegger is tied in part to their subsumptions of different aspects of both his early writing in *Being and Time* and also of the ontological critique of anthropology of the "Letter on 'Humanism'" in their respective *The Order of Things* and "The Ends of Man."

Two elements of the antihumanism I have been tracing took off with structuralism. The first might be described as *No Antihumanism Except Mine!* The stakes of structuralism were closely intertwined with a rejection of the limitations of the generation of antihumanists discussed here, as well as the effort to establish a philosophically impregnable negative anthropology. The series of critiques and countercritiques between Foucault, Derrida, Levi-Strauss, Lacan, and others can in some part be understood precisely as an effort to effect the *proper* anthropology. If, as argued thus far, the maturation of antihumanism toward the end of the first half of the twentieth century resides in the turn to ontology, philosophy of history, and language, this later struggle of antihumanisms reflected at once a quarrel among the conceptual premises of different disciplines and philosophical priorities, and foregrounded the instability and ambiguity built into the very enunciation of claims that can be seen as belonging to philosophical anthropology. Thus the history that is offered in the present volume will not be readable merely as an archaeology or genealogy of structuralism; rather, structuralism could perhaps be seen as a radicalization of the overcoming of humanism that became instrumental after World War II, on the basis of a linguistic theory that at once served the movement toward being and language and offered it a new ground. This history could also help distance structuralism—especially the later figures related to it, Foucault and Derrida—from the persistent suspicions that their thought assaulted a prevalent democratic and socialist humanism, by showing that, in many respects, their effort to rethink man at once relied on a 1930s and 1940s effort to undermine the unreliable dominant humanisms, yet also stood apart from the radicalism of both the late 1940s thinkers and the early structuralists like Levi-Strauss and Lacan.

A second element that is crucial to structuralism's adoption of "antihumanism" is the codification of negative anthropology and antihumanism in the study of "the human sciences" and thus both in and beyond philosophy itself. In his infamous lambasting of Sartre's anthropology in *La Pensée sauvage* (*The Savage Mind*), Levi-Strauss set the task and goal of the human sciences as "not to constitute but to dissolve man"—a problem raised anew and addressed by Foucault (albeit in very different terms) in *Les Mots et les choses* (1966; *The Order of Things*).[7] In that very essay, Levi-Strauss writes of anthropology as "the principle of all research," and he emphasizes that "we can hope to find in [Sartrian phenomenology] only a point of departure, not one of arrival." In this process, anthropology becomes a study of the human that aims for a new, scientific, and nonhumanist understanding of men, ostensibly without humanistic preconceptions: "The idea of some general humanity to which ethnographic reduction leads will bear no relation to any one may have formed in advance."[8] Similarly Michel Foucault's *The Order of Things* and *Discipline and Punish* would offer a stunning reinterpretation of many philosophical categories crucial to a humanist worldview, so as to demonstrate precisely how this worldview depended not on the philosophical systems criticized by the thinkers approached here, but rather on the human sciences that made modern philosophy (including these thinkers) possible, as well as on the power structures that in turn made such human sciences as well as theorizations of freedom and action possible and granted them so much hope. Ever attentive to possible systematizations of human thought and experience, such approaches moved the tripartite basis of antihumanism well beyond what their predecessors thought possible.

Yet what is at stake after 1950 is not just Levi-Strauss's use of structural linguistics in an endeavor to turn social anthropology into a science, the debate on humanism among Marxists (and especially Althusser's contribution to it), Foucault's explicit and broadly discussed assault on the traditional anthropocentrism of discourse, or Jacques Derrida's dismantling of the rhetoric of "The Ends of Man."[9] Though it is tempting to offer an outline of those developments—an outline that would remain far too tentative—a different temptation is harder to resist: to show, if only in a couple of pages, that post-1950 developments in the tripartite history of antihumanism went *far* beyond the structuralist and Heideggerian matrix with which they are usually identified. This is particularly important insofar as a claim is frequently made that structuralist antihumanism resounded while public opinion turned away from its postwar mistrust of humanism.

A telling example of antihumanism's broader influence comes from French historians of science—and practicing scientists—especially of biology. Philosophers and practicing scientists from Georges Canguilhem and René Leriche, through Jacques Monod and François Jacob and beyond, have made significant efforts to establish anti-anthropocentrism not only in the philosophical understanding of their science but also in their approach to a scientific philosophy of nature and in the relationship between science and politics.[10] In 1949, Jacques Duclaux, who had long been a professor of general biology at the Collège de France and a member of the French Academy of the Sciences, wrote, "The entirety of scientific knowledge leads to two results. The first is the enunciation of natural laws. The second, which is much more important, is the creation of a new nature, which is superimposed on the first and for which a different name should be found given that it is not natural and would have never existed without man."[11] Duclaux does not cite quantum physics in this passage, but the implication is clear— after physics, biology too had reached a non- and indeed antipositivist methodology. Canguilhem, who cites this very passage, clearly suggests a continuity between wave mechanics—which he references as a paradigm for the understanding of diverse models in science—and Duclaux's claim on nature—which he quotes precisely to suggest that "modern science is primarily the study of para-nature or a super-nature rather than of nature itself."[12] The hope thus emerges for him as well that (to use Wahl's expression), science's cognizance of "its limits" allows for the possibility of overcoming these by a dismantling of its humanist pretenses. Canguilhem would explicitly praise Hyppolite after his death as a major harbinger of antisubjectivism, but he also joined philosophy of nature with an anti-anthropocentric critique of the overreaching of man throughout his own career, writing (for example) on the subject of disease that "the concept of man covers with a false appearance of specific identity individual organisms whose existence is thus deprived of different powers of resistance to aggression."[13] It is essential to note that Canguilhem's writings on "the normal and the pathological" explicitly criticized the link of such normative terms to the philosophies of progress used by supposedly humanist theories of biology and applied medicine. Motifs of this sort became influential also for biologists like François Jacob and Jacques Monod, and sociologists of technology like Georges Friedmann and André Leroi-Gourhan, who made considerable use of "antihumanist" elements, without explicitly engaging with antihumanism itself. To take one example, the critique of anthropocentrism in science was no less significant for Jacques Monod (1965 Nobel Laureate in medicine, director of research in cellular biochemistry at the Institut Pasteur, and professor at the Collège de France), who in his best-selling 1970 book *Chance and Necessity* (*Le Hasard et la nécessité*) wrote of anthropocentrism as an "illusion," a "myth," and a "mirage" that the theory of evolution finally managed to escape in "the second half of the 20th century."[14] And Henri

Atlan (professor of philosophy and biology at the Ecole des Hautes Etudes en Sciences Sociales, director of the Human Biology Research Center at Hadassah Hospital in Jerusalem, and a pioneer of theories of biological self-organization) has written critically of renewed anthropocentric illusions ever since his earliest work. In his 2002 *La Science est-elle inhumaine?* ("Is Science Inhuman?"), he declares himself a partisan of an *antihumanist* perspective on freedom in a world of biological causation.[15] Despite their differences and despite their disagreement with some of the apparently more radical antihumanisms from the late 1950s, these thinkers (whose posts I recall here to emphasize their status in French education and science) help demonstrate the spread and influence of the anti-anthropocentrism that first emerged in the 1930s. Such biological problems extended easily to further aspects of philosophy of nature (conceptions of life; the relationship of nature to technology and human involvement in it; the relations of the human to other species and to evolution in general), as well as to philosophy of science and technology (for example, genetics and eugenics; artificial intelligence; theories of work and its impact), not to mention political anthropology.

Now if we can glimpse such an explicit and consequential anti-anthropocentrism in the history and philosophy of biology—a science notoriously averse to philosophy—should we then be surprised to find similar (and at times more radical) approaches emerging in interwar and postwar sociology, history, cultural anthropology, or the theorization of technology—in other words, in *sciences humaines* that, to justify the specificity of their object of study, became increasingly averse to premature determinations and generalizations of "the human"? Perhaps it is more surprising to suggest that these approaches did not have a simple political purpose, be it left-wing or right-wing, but rather responded to and aided a much more metapolitical and antipolitical exigency. It is worth noting, for example, that the antipolitical and antiliberationist tendencies of the trajectories of the Annales School, of early linguistic structuralism, and of the philosophers of science did not produce elaborate political problems for their projects. Similarly, the rise of negative anthropology and the turn to ontology in philosophy lost, during the 1950s, the attachment to troubling contemporary politics that Heidegger and Merleau-Ponty's arguments could not in the late 1940s escape.

Three closing points. (1) As we have seen, a definitive aspect of the emergence of antihumanism was the critique of competing definitions of the human and of the humanisms that such definitions were seen to entail. This is true not only at the political level—the conflict of exclusivist humanisms in the 1930s, among Christian, liberal, Communist, and fascisant thinkers, and the postwar struggle between Marxists, Christian thinkers, existentialists, Gaullists, and so forth—but also absolutely prevalent in a philosophical framework. The present work has described a number of further such philosophical criticisms, and they bear repeating here: André Malraux's Spenglerian critique of his contemporaries, André Masson's praise of Bataille's *The Blue of Noon* as opposed to the unwitting and half-hearted antihumanism he diagnosed as a component of 1930s culture, the widespread 1930s critique of Brunschvicg, Sartre's critique of Bataille, Heidegger's critique of Sartre and of the "anthropologization" of his thought in 1930s France, Merleau-Ponty's critique of Koestler, Blanchot's critique of both Sartre and Merleau-Ponty, Hyppolite's critique of Kojève, Merleau-Ponty, and Sartre, and so on. The centrality of these histories of criticism to antihumanism cannot be overestimated because they produced a self-radicalizing demand that anti-anthropocentrism and the critique of anthropology become consistent and systematic. From the perspective of this self-radicalizing demand we can also see, left behind, not only humanisms but also a number of positions that only with great difficulty could pass as humanist: Sartre, Bataille, and the nonconformists offer three such examples. But this was precisely the impulse of negative anthropology's radicalizing reformulation and retheorization of the human, which persisted well into the 1960s and 1970s.

(2) Equally important in the emergence of antihumanism was its contribution to the construction—avowed or not, systematic or not—of new "humanisms," new mobilizations of "the human"—even if these were mobilizations that became progressively more limited and indeed unpolitical and minimal. Atheism's transformation reached a point where the claims and differences between possible minimal humanisms (based on a shared equality in weakness and loss) no longer really made a difference. Not only because these new, more particular, and indeed more constrained humanisms competed with each other, but also because they disqualified more classical and moderate positions, not to mention anthropologies

they considered too affirmative or politically facile. As Jacques Derrida would suggest in his "The Ends of Man" apropos of Heidegger's "Letter on 'Humanism'" each new radicalization, each new antihumanism failed to fully overcome the human as it proclaimed and brought with it a new humanism.[16]

From this perspective, and given in particular the gradual development of more radical humanisms, the force and significance of even the early 1930s alternative and exclusivist humanisms becomes clear. The effort to produce a specific and politically useful restriction or reorganization of "the human" already denied the vague universalism that one often associates with "humanism" to an extent that could be used both to refine (and radicalize) these new humanisms and to deny them. Nevertheless, despite humanism's delegitimation, it was the development of negative anthropology that, by systematically treating man as a construct of thought, history, existence, language, and so on, pointed beyond this duet of humanism and antihumanism and toward a new series of possibilities in philosophy and the legacy of this period. The influence of negative anthropology, which grew in both scope and radicalism in the 1950–75 period, remains paramount in both European philosophy and strains of cultural, anthropological, and literary analysis. It is also crucial to our understanding of contemporary man: with the return of religion in contemporary culture and philosophy, with the ambivalent politicization of human rights, and with the advent of cultural and political anxieties concerning the question of what comes "after" the human in an age marked by virtual reality, artificial intelligence, and DNA mapping, the phenomenon of a philosophy seeking to overcome dominant philosophical and theo-political paradigms of God and Man so as to construct a metapolitical approach and language for dealing with man and his ontological importance *by way of the negative* remains of exceptional relevance and critical potential.

Thus (3), this book ends at a moment of profound ambiguity in French thought, a moment that anticipates the different antihumanisms and new humanisms of the 1960s and 1970s: from structuralist antihumanism to the celebratory humanisms of late Marxism and May '68, from the anticolonial thinkers of the 1950s like Frantz Fanon to the new theorists of democracy of the 1970s like Claude Lefort, Pierre Rosanvallon, and Cornelius Castoriadis, and to the many postmodern obsessions and critiques of the 1970s and 1980s. All of these movements owed a great deal (to paraphrase Pascal's famous term) to the reproportioning of man that occurred in the second quarter of the twentieth century, even if they frequently doubted or refused this debt. At the same time, this postwar moment was one that could see the atheist humanism that emerged with the Enlightenment and the nineteenth century as in need of being over-come and perhaps indeed coming to a close. This is the goal established and pursued with the new nonhumanist atheism and the turn toward a negative anthropology. Insofar as the early postwar period is the moment when European thought became conscious of its own finitude, we can say, without doubt or velleity, that antihumanism is precisely the signature of this self-consciousness: the promise of a world without promises, the violence of a world hoping to ending violence, the humanity of men no longer able or willing to trust any humanity at all.

Notes

INTRODUCTION

1. Feuerbach, *Essence of Christianity,* inter alem 17, 336–37.
2. Feuerbach, *Principles,* §1, 5.
3. Comte, *Catéchisme positiviste.* See also Wernick, *Auguste Comte.*
4. Janicaud, *L'Homme va-t-il dépasser l'humain?* 15. Janicaud is probably refer-ring to Proudhon's *Philosophie de la misère,* particularly because of Proudhon's crit-icism of "humanism's" lack of social implications and its construction of what he sees as a surrogate religion and his effort to redirect it. Michael Allen Gillespie, in *The Theological Origins of Modernity,* suggests that the application of "humanism" to the Renaissance derives in large part from nineteenth-century scholars. See Gil-lespie, *Theological Origins of Modernity,* 71.
5. Koyré, "Present Trends," 534. For this expectation, see, for example, Brunschvicg, *Écrits philosophiques I,* esp. 9, 304.
6. Levinas, *Sur Maurice Blanchot,* 10; translated in Levinas, *Proper Names,* 127.
7. For Germany, see Rabinbach, *In the Shadow of Catastrophe;* for France, see Hughes, *Obstructed Path.* For cultural implications of World War I, see, among others, Eksteins, *Rites of Spring.*
8. Bataille, "La 'Vieille taupe' et le préfixe sur dans les mots surhomme et sur-réaliste" (OC II, 102); translated in Bataille, *Visions of Excess,* 38.
9. See, for example, Merleau-Ponty, "La Guerre a eu lieu," in *Les Temps mod-ernes* I (October 1945); translated as Merleau-Ponty, "The War Has Taken Place," in *Sense and Non-Sense,* 141–42, 144; and Koyré, "Present Trends," 533–35.
10. Aron, "Future of Secular Religions," in *Dawn of Universal History,* 177–201.
11. Kojève, *L'Athéisme;* Kojève, *Introduction à la lecture de Hegel,* 435.
12. See the young Sartre's critique of Kant and the Neo-Kantians in "Transcen-dence of the Ego" (TE 17–19 / 35–36).
13. Wahl, *Vers le concret.* Bataille, *L'Expérience intérieure.*
14. See Heidegger, *Qu'est-ce que la métaphysique.*
15. It is important to understand that the scope of this approach is so far-reach-ing that, from the perspective of the 1930s, it altered the perception of the history of European thought all the way back to Descartes and Galileo, as I will show in

Chapter 2. If, during the Copernican Revolution and the Reformation, Man became at once convinced of his capacity to sort out and systematize the world and gradually transformed a theocentric universe into an anthropocentric one, then during the 1930s it was broadly argued that knowledge and science had overestimated man's stability as a foundation of knowledge and misjudged his ability to control the world. Accordingly, we can expand Marc Richir's argument that phenomenology reverses Copernican cosmology and accord this massive reversal to this atheism that is not humanist, the antihumanist climate that formed its background, and the negative redefinition of anthropology that it helped elaborate. Richir, *Au-delà du renversement copernicien,* 82.

16. The idea that humanism is directly based on definitions of humanity can also be found in Lacoue-Labarthe, *La Fiction du politique,* 138. Lacoue-Labarthe proceeds to consider Nazism as a humanism precisely on this ground.

17. Sartre, *L'Existentialisme est un humanisme.*

18. Pascal, *Pensées,* 33.

19. De Maistre, *Considerations on France.*

20. Classic among the origins of this modern Catholic position is Augustine's juxtaposition of St. Paul (who points the way to God, thus allowing salvation from this "body of death") to the Neoplatonists (who don't), in his *Confessions* VII. xxi.27, 131. During the 1930s, the most significant (and among the most liberal) arguments in favor of a Catholic rejection of atheist humanism were by Jacques Maritain, Henri de Lubac, Gabriel Marcel, and Gaston Fessard.

21. For a far-reaching definition of the Counter-Enlightenment that is useful here, see Lilla, "What Is Counter-Enlightenment?"

22. Arguments for reading a kind of mysticism and/or negative theology in midcentury literary and philosophical texts has been made by several writers in recent years, among them Connor, *Georges Bataille;* Hart, *Dark Gaze,* and elsewhere; Hollywood, *Sensible Ecstasy;* Nancy, *La Déclosion;* Szafraniec, *Beckett, Derrida, and the Event of Literature.* Note also the growing literature around negative theology and the writings of Jacques Derrida, including works by Hent de Vries, John D. Caputo, Rodolphe Gasché, and Mark Taylor.

23. For this reason, and while Alexander Nehamas is right to treat "humanism, at its most extreme" as "a position that attributes to human beings absolute importance in the universe, absolute freedom from any outside forces in the world, absolute knowledge and control of themselves," I am not fully in agreement with his definition of "antihumanism at its own extreme" as claiming that "individual human beings are of no consequence in the universe, that they are totally controlled, even constituted, by outside forces (economic, social, sexual) that are the real subjects of history, that they are essentially incapable of seeing themselves for what they are." But see his overall argument in the foreword to Renaut, *Era of the Individual,* vii–xviii. The quotes are from xiv.

24. The frequent demonization of critiques of humanism is particularly troubling for both historians and philosophers seeking an understanding of the evolution of notions of the human in modernity. Typical such reductions are, for example, the remarkably reductive treatment of Adorno and Horkheimer's *Dialectic of Enlightenment* typical today in accounts of the French Enlightenment (for example, Hunt, "Paradoxical Origins," 4, and esp. 15 n2), and the assault on late twentieth-century efforts (often placed under the unhelpful and frequently misunderstood rubric of postmodernism) to move beyond and resituate the Enlightenment (for example, in D. Gordon, *Postmodernism*). An effort to maintain an Enlightenment spirit in contemporary thought should not lead historians to ignore the tremendous historical transformations of the nineteenth and twentieth centuries or to endorse a return to the eighteenth century on the basis of philosophers' imperfect or reductive historical imaginations.

25. Significantly, it was not just a few philosophers who probed the relationship among man, world, and the death of God. Various contemporary theoretical movements participated in this reorientation: critiques of classical psychological theories of consciousness, the rise of psychoanalysis, Durkheimian developments in anthropology (notably the efforts of the Collège de Sociologie to explain the survival and dispersion of forms of the sacred in a profane world), and the statistical/sociological emphasis of the Annales School of history. See Hollier, *Le Collège de sociologie*. See, on the philosophical problematization of mysticism, some of the essays in *Recherches philosophiques,* vols. 1 and 2. On the "antihumanism" of Durkheim's sociology, see Hirst's *Durkheim, Bernard,* 137. Hirst's Althusserian background facilitates this reading; the elaboration of theory of social anthropology from Durkheim through Mauss and Levy-Bruhl and then Levi-Strauss and others would require an analysis that I have not been able to offer here, notably with a parallel reading of the Annales School and its competitors in history. Cited also in Jay, *Marxism and Totality,* 280.

26. Blanchot, for example, could write that the atheists attack on God "reste de pure prétention," announcing that pure atheism is "Ce qui revient peut-être à exclure toute réponse en première personne," thus at once linking atheism with the contemporary critiques of subjectivism, with what I will call negative anthropology, and with the lack of any possibility of "humanist horizon." Blanchot, *L'Entretien infini,* 377 / 252.

27. See Deguy, *Sans Retour,* 113–15. Deguy's more poetic approach to the term is of similar inspiration to my own. By contrast, I take a certain distance from Ulrich Sonnemann's *Negative Anthropologie,* insofar as I understand his intellectual targets as participants in the intellectual transformation he also points to. Theodor Adorno notes his affinities to Sonnemann's work in a (strangely untranslated) moment of his introduction to *Negative Dialektik.* Adorno's treatment of dehumanization, his critique of the "jargon of authenticity," and his reading of Beck-

ett can also be said to sketch a negative anthropology, though I will not consider his work here. Also, James Bernauer has noted preferring "negative anthropology" over "negative theology" in the case of reading Foucault, but (though I agree on this point) Bernauer's definition and approach also differ significantly from mine; nevertheless, see Bernauer, *Michel Foucault's Force of Flight*, 178.

28. This tradition of grounding conceptions of man and understanding and defining the human by its faculties or qualities (a tradition by no means unitary and in fact marked precisely by the broad clashes it can from the present perspective be said to involve) spans from Descartes's *Meditations* and David Hume's *Treatise on Human Nature* through Condillac's writings and the conclusions of Comte's *Cours de philosophie positive*. It is far too broad to consider here in appropriate detail—and my aim is to precisely suggest that negative anthropology responds to it in terms of a broad bloc to be surmounted. For a nuanced approach to this claim, considering the limitations of the dominance of man over nature, see the classic study by Lovejoy, *Great Chain of Being*, esp. 186–207.

29. These references should not suggest that Diderot was never skeptical about humanism, individuality, and freedom. In other texts, such as *Jacques le fataliste*, *Le Neveu de Rameau*, and *Le Rêve de D'Alembert*, he makes his doubts very clear. Still, the anthropocentric drive is forceful and crucial to his thought. On a second matter worth noting here, Odo Marquard correctly notes that Enlightenment definitions like the one cited above mask broader currents and transformations, and he confirms nevertheless that the "boom in philosophical anthropology" in the second half of the eighteenth century "puts forward man as someone whom, even in the most recent form of the old metaphysics—in dualistic Cartesianism—man was not allowed to be: as the psychosomatic 'whole person'—that is not simply *res cogitans* (a thinking being), but *homo naturalis et individualis* (natural and individual man)." Marquard, *Farewell to Matters of Principle*, 40.

30. Kant, *Logic*, 29.

31. The first three questions are first brought up in the *Critique of Pure Reason*, 635.

32. Kant, *Anthropology from a Pragmatic Point of View*, 3. After playing a crucial role in Martin Heidegger's reading of Kant in *Kant and the Problem of Metaphysics*, this reference became a regular starting point in philosophical writings on the interstices between anthropology and phenomenology or anthropology and other philosophical questions. See, for example, Ricoeur, "L'Humanité de l'homme," 309; and Michel Foucault's course "Problèmes de l'anthropologie" at the Ecole Normale Supérieure in 1954–55 (IMEC, Fonds Foucault, C.2.1/FCL 2. A03–08, transcription by J. Lagrange); Haar, *Heidegger and the Essence of Man*, xxiii; and Bimbenet, *Nature et humanité*, 9.

33. Again, this is not to suggest that philosophical anthropology had up to the 1930s been simply and unambiguously affirmative, foundationalist, or universal-

ist, but that philosophers contributing to this "negative anthropology" tended to picture it in that way. In the French context, the case of Pascal is particularly significant (for example, the *Pensées*, §199, "The Disproportion of Man") in influencing nonanthropocentric evocations of and references to man in the nineteenth and twentieth centuries. Marx's case is also significant, notably in the shift from his early to his later work, where the humanist Hegelianism recedes (see Seigel, *Marx's Fate*, chaps. 7–9). Nevertheless, from the perspective of philosophers of the 1930s it was retroactively conceived as *having been just that*, precisely because of the readiness of thinkers in the dominant wave in philosophy in the 1920s— Kantian neocriticism—to identify it as such. In fact philosophical anthropology was very equivocal as an enterprise, and a certain understanding of "man" as a mystery or aporia is characteristic of both the Christian theological tradition and in much of modern philosophy. For Christian philosophers, man, created by God in His image and resemblance, is—in the very least—to be conceived in terms of a lack or insufficiency by comparison to God's attributes and Christ's promise; he is fallen and depends on a mixture of grace, conversion, and works in his search for salvation. In modern philosophy, moreover, the meaning of man is often left ambiguous or presented as unsolvable. Descartes, while famously defining the (human) subject as *cogito ego sum*, also treated it in mechanistic terms—hence, for many, leaving unanswered the question of where the humanity of the human lies. Kant, while emphasizing the significance of the question "what is man?" also noted that this last cannot be answered either phenomenologically or through man's self-examination (an idea that became dear to French neocriticism).

34. Althusser, *Humanist Controversy*; Foucault, *Order of Things*; Derrida, "Ends of Man," in *Margins of Philosophy*.

35. Merleau-Ponty, "Man and Adversity" (1951), in *Signs*, 226.

36. "Man and Adversity" is contemporary to Merleau-Ponty's self-distancing from Communism and exactly contemporary to his writings against "human engineering." In that vein, see his "Introduction" to Michel Crozier's article "Human Engineering," in *Les Temps modernes* 69 (July 1951): 44–48; republished in *Parcours I: 1935–1951*, 230–34. Along a different line, concerned in particular with the problem of machinism—and the question of what is being molded and what can instead survive and liberate itself against the power of machinism—runs through Georges Friedmann's work *Machine et humanisme*.

37. The philosophical and political story of Martin Heidegger and his French readers—the core of the French phenomenological reception—is well known. I subsume here the excellent accounts by Ethan Kleinberg and Dominique Janicaud, and I also offer certain alternatives to their interpretations, especially of the problem of *réalité humaine*. See Janicaud, *Heidegger en France*, vol. 1. Kleinberg, *Generation Existential*.

38. Heidegger, *Pathmarks*, 254.

39. See Haar, *Heidegger and the Essence of Man*; Derrida, *De l'esprit*, V–VII.

40. Clearly, my approach offers a definition of "antihumanism" at the same time that it traces its history. Several reasons necessitate and guide this redefinition. First, it facilitates an understanding of the complexity of antihumanism, by offering a parallel explanation of its theological and philosophical force—its most radical and systematic but largely quiet dimension—*as well as* its ambiguous political and anti-ideological argument—its most visible and critical face. I am particularly interested in the complex and very different series of philosophical projects and concerns involved in antihumanism, including the attempted dissolution of the subject and the self, the critique of Western Reason, the anti-Kantian and anti-Cartesian reconceptualization of man, and other motifs that so dramatically defined the course of French thought. Second, this tripartite definition explains the philosophical emergence of antihumanism in the 1930s and emphasizes the maturation of its worldview in the early postwar years. In particular, it shows both links to, and major differences from, earlier critiques of liberalism, while emphasizing the singularity and significance of the intellectual and political contexts of the 1930s and 1940s, and offering an alternative account for the scope of the philosophical reorganization that occurs in the period and the shared positions underlying very different movements. Third, historians and philosophers have, in recent years, used the same term to describe other moments in, or aspects of modern thought and intellectual history (see, for example, Gouhier, *L'Antihumanisme au XVIIe Siècle*; and Zimmerman, *Anthropology and Antihumanism in Imperial Germany*); the present definition helps emphasize the distance between the movement I am describing and such and other "antihumanisms." Finally, a definition such as the one I'm staging here is necessary precisely because of the insufficiency of the classical, somewhat quotidian understanding of "antihumanism." Fuzzy, overdetermined, and often pejorative, the term "antihumanism" was often used from the mid-1970s on by antagonists of its purported philosophical partisans to present the latter as disrespectful toward the humanist tradition, an attitude that does not adequately address the complex emergence we are discussing here. See, for example, Dufrenne, *Pour l'homme*, as well as Ferry and Renaut, *La pensée '68*, translated as *French Philosophy of the Sixties*. Dufrenne explicitly takes the term from Althusser, but notes that its idea exists "everywhere" in the texts he is discussing (9). See notably his opposition to antihumanism in philosophy (122). It is important to note that even Althusser (whose argument on Marx's "theoretical antihumanism" was perhaps the most explicit endorsement of the term by someone describing his own argument) uses "antihumanism" in principally strategic—rather than philosophical—terms, preferring "a-humanism." See Althusser, *Humanist Controversy*, 232. By the time that antihumanism came to be seen through the lens of a series of intellectual debates such as Althusser's "Humanism debate" in Marxism in 1963–65, or the 1960 debate between Levi-Strauss and Sartre, most of the an-

thropological and theological transformations had long taken place. That traditional use of the term is especially misleading in that it suggests a generally identifiable movement that organized itself around an opposition to humanism, and that did so in the years around 1968. (See Ferry and Renaut, *French Philosophy of the Sixties*, xviii–xix). Not only was this far from the case, but humanism was not in itself the heart of its critique. Moreover, the lack of a core movement is significant precisely because "antihumanism" did not always exist in explicit form (nor in even remotely the same form) in the thinkers discussed here—in other words, because it was a theoretical and political constellation rather than a strict ideological position. Even thinkers who refuse this critique tend to accept this particular 1960s constellation as definitive of antihumanism (see, for example, Alain Badiou's definition (in *Ethics*, 5–6), which also uses the same constellation, though his identification of antihumanism's sense is similar to the one I offer here). By considering antihumanism as a system of thought guided in general by the three aspects of the definition offered here, we can allow both the radicalism and the internal complexity of this "movement" to appear.

41. This is also to say that in modern France, the role of Renaissance forms of humanism was not of the highest significance. Herein lies one of the major differences between French and German forms of humanism (in the late nineteenth and the early twentieth centuries), and even more, of the meaning of "antihumanism" in Germany since the late nineteenth century. For Germany, see Marchand, "Nazism, Orientalism and Humanism," 267–305, esp. 268–74; and Zimmerman, *Anthropology and Antihumanism in Imperial Germany.*

42. See Worms, "Introduction," in *Droits de l'homme et philosophie*, 7–8. In his analysis, Worms correctly points out that the relationship between philosophy and the "rights of man" is fundamentally ambiguous, inasmuch as (i) the declarations and discourses of the rights of man, while proclaiming an affinity with the Enlightenment, often sought out the political realm and distanced themselves from philosophy, while (ii) philosophers involved in human rights debates often argued against one right or another, sometimes seeking less to found rights on philosophy than to refute their philosophical injunction or connection. See also Gauchet, "Rights of Man," 818–28.

43. In Kant's *Anthropology*, the transformative goal concerned man as "citizen of the world." Utopian socialism, particularly among the Saint-Simonians, is also crucial in this regard. Comte, who attempted to connect anthropocentric scientific knowledge with his "Religion of Humanity" (thus linking the heavily anthropocentric scientific positivism he is most famous for with a political and ultimately utopian project) was for a time Saint-Simon's secretary. Comte's balancing of a relativism regarding different societies with the general progress of humanity as a whole played a significant role in his "religion of humanity." See his use of Lamarck in defending the progressive organic improvement of man, especially

"that of [Man's] intellectual development" in Comte, *Positive Philosophy of Auguste Comte*, 2:88–89. The influence of the Young Hegelians in Germany, particularly Feuerbach, Wagner, and Marx, also famously emphasized an anthropocentric and anthropotheist agenda in atheism.

44. Marx, "Introduction," in *Marx-Engels Reader*, 65; the passage as a whole reads: "The criticism of religion ends with the teaching that man is the highest being for man—hence, with the categorical imperative to overthrow all relations in which man is a debased, enslaved, abandoned, despicable being." See also p. 60: "The emancipation of Germany is only possible *in practice* if one adopts the point of view of that theory according to which man is the highest being for man."

45. This is not to imply that anthropology as the science of man in the sixteenth to nineteenth centuries marched together with a political or progressivist humanism. See Blanckaert, "L'Anthropologie en France: le mot et l'histoire (16ᵉ-19ᵉ siècle)," 20.

46. Heidegger, "Letter on 'Humanism,'" in *Pathmarks*, 241. See, for similarly general definitions of humanism, Ricoeur "Que signifie 'humanisme'?" 84–92. Jean Wahl's definitions of humanism also tended to be vague: see his notes for the lectures "Dépassement des humanismes" and "Les Composantes anti-humanistes de l'humanisme," in IMEC, Fonds Wahl, II:11, Dossier Humanisme.

47. Nancy, *L'Oubli de la philosophie*, 26.

48. Ibid., 35.

49. Worms points out that the "rights of man" were under attack from two sides already in the late eighteenth century: at times for not caring enough about the individual, and for not emphasizing the priority of society over the individual. See Worms, *Droits de l'homme et philosophie*, 28.

50. De Lubac, *Drama of Atheist Humanism*. See also Jacques Maritain's *Integral Humanism* and many others among his works; and Lacroix, *Le Sens de l'athéisme moderne*.

51. Catholic humanism in the Third Republic was largely associated with a conservative, often nationalist and anti-Semitic politics, a politics that until the Papal Decree of 1926 that banned the Action Française was largely tied to it. Eugen Weber, *Action Française*. Only after 1926 did a different theorization of humanism really emerge: *this* is what I will call Catholic humanism here. This was by no means the most aggressive, public face of Catholic politics in the first three decades of the century.

52. Sternhell, *Neither Right nor Left*, 33. As Sternhell has shown, these factions were often united in their opposition to the Republic and often shared certain presuppositions or arguments. Sternhell, *La Droite revolutionnaire 1885–1914*, 325–28, and, Sternhell, *Neither Right nor Left*, esp. intro., chap. 1.

53. Lindenberg, *Les Années souterraines*, 86–93, and also chap. 1.

54. For example, Pierre Drieu La Rochelle welcomed the demonstrations of protofascist *ligues* in February 1934, praising the Action Française and especially the Croix de Feu, but he also appreciated the reactions of the Left as a second attack on capitalism. He saw the combination of the two as sounding liberalism's death knell and only chose fascism over Communism in 1935–36, as a consequence of its nationalism—though given the fundamental antifascism of Communists, the profascist groups Drieu already frequented, and his adhesion to a nationalist and antiproletarian position, this wasn't much of a surprise. Drieu is by no means the exception in this climate: most nonconformists rejected the republican middle much more easily than they did the opposite extreme. Winock, *Le Siècle des intellectuels*, 234–35, 238.

55. Nizan, *Watchdogs*, 12.

56. See Judt, *Past Imperfect*, chap. 12. Khilnani, *Arguing Revolution*, 121.

57. Malraux, *L'Homme et la culture artistique*. The atom bomb and the unprecedented mechanization of warfare compounded the fear that technology had escaped its utilitarian role and had come to acquire power over individual men, their actions and goals. Fundamental to this reaction was the argument that these disasters were not murders perpetrated against humanity by mad beliefs propagated by seductive demonic leaders who turned already questionable characters into killers, but as a confirmation of humanity's arrogant self-confidence in its own judgment, righteousness, and power. Worse, Western humanism failed completely to defend against such abuses—which, the Communists argued, democracies had long practiced on their colonies.

58. See the classic critique of human rights in Arendt, "Decline of the Nation-State," in *Origins of Totalitarianism*, 267–304.

59. See René Cassin's advocacy of human rights against "Leviathan states" in Winter, *Dreams of Peace and Freedom*, 115. Winter also discusses the Soviet response on page 118. See the readings of Arendt by Hamacher, "Right to Have Rights," 343–56; and Rancière, "Who Is the Subject of the Rights of Man?" 297–310.

60. Human rights, seen under this rubric, often seemed to have "served to legitimate the creation of new forms of sovereign political power (forms which, by appropriating [the] critical language [of human rights], deprived those who sought to protect themselves against the excess of this new power of a crucial weapon." Khilnani, *Arguing Revolution*, 180. Khilnani refers to the post-1789 era, but his formulation expresses the sentiments of many of the figures to be discussed here.

61. This position is most commonly identified with Alexandre Kojève, and I will consider it in Chapter 3. See also the discussion and critique of this position in Merleau-Ponty, *Les Aventures de la dialectique*, 12. See also Axelos, *Marx, penseur de la technique*. The situationists also agreed on a modified version of this approach.

62. For a Catholic approach criticizing secular essentialisms, see Fessard, *De l'actualité historique*, 201–2. See also Sartre's critique of a Comtean humanism, and Merleau-Ponty's critique of his elders' humanisms, quoted above.

63. "Heideggerian antihumanism provided a framework of thinking for people who had abandoned the possibility of a politics that we can make meaningful." Roth, *Knowing and History*, 79.

64. See the discussion of humanisms "without illusions," in Lévi-Valensi and Guérin, "Peut-on être humaniste dans la France des années cinquante?" 159ff.

65. Here, I am in agreement with what Hent de Vries says of Levinas's *philosophical antisubjectivism*, in *Minimal Theologies*, 535–37.

66. Merleau-Ponty, *Signs*, 226. Merleau-Ponty also refused to simply repudiate humanism in "The War has Taken Place" (SNS 152).

PART I: INTRODUCTION

1. Malraux, *La Condition humaine*.

2. Malraux, *Les Noyers de l'Altenbourg*.

3. "Le problème qui se pose pour nous, aujourd'hui, c'est de savoir si, sur cette vieille terre d'Europe, oui ou non, l'homme est mort." Malraux, *L'Homme et la culture artistique*, 14. Malraux repeated more or less the same lecture at the *Rencontres internationales de Genève* conference "Défense de la culture Européenne" on December 23, 1947. See also the reviews of the lecture: "Is Europe Dead?" *The New Leader* (January 18, 1947)—with an English translation of an excerpt; *Combat* (November 15, 1946); and *Carrefour* (November 7, 1946), with a publication of only that part of the lecture that dealt with his worries over the survival of European culture.

4. Todd, *Malraux*, 61–62.

5. Still, this difference should not be overestimated. Strictly speaking, because the two characters differ only in part and in style, Ling is the first to announce a death of Man. A. D. avoids discussing Ling's point until the end of the book, when he announces it himself, as if for the first time. His reasons for arguing it are quite different from Ling's, particularly as A. D. does not fully accept Ling's diagnosis of the West as simply based on an absurd core—on the basis of which Ling provides his criticism of Western man as considering himself as eternal and, by extension, as mired in anxiety and absurdity. Though the two characters espouse more or less the same ideas, and though the argument on absurdity is and remains central to Malraux's overall position on contemporary culture and thought, it is important that A. D. sees the death of Man as coming specifically with the advent of Western secular humanism and the death of God. Regarding absurdity in Malraux, see Loubet del Bayle, *L'Illusion politique*, 300–304.

6. Todd, *Malraux*, 65. Lyotard writes that Malraux discovered Spengler through his wife Clara, during a 1925 trip to Berlin. See Lyotard, *Signed Malraux*, 77. Regarding Nietzsche, see Le Rider, *Nietzsche en France*, 191. I am not fully convinced by the claim of Le Rider that "'L'homme précaire' selon Malraux est une des modalités de la 'surhumanité' nietzschéenne" insofar as this claim undermines both the extent to which "precarious man" is as much a modality of the *last man* in Nietzsche as of the Overman, but also the extent to which for Malraux this collapse is not really cause for excitement. See also Caute, *Fellow-Travellers*, 190.

7. See, for example, Paul Nizan's December 1933 article "L'avenir de la culture" (ALP 283–85), where Nizan explicitly argues that the demise of capitalism is obvious even to fascists, and notes Spengler's *Decline of the West* is an insider's perspective of this bourgeois demise.

8. Daniel Lindenberg identifies Spengler with the turn to myth in the 1930s. Lindenberg, *Les Années souterraines*, 73. See also p. 96 for the conservative constellation involving Spengler in the period.

9. As does, for example, Richard Wolin, in his critique of French 1930s thinkers. See Wolin, *Seduction of Unreason*, chaps. 4–5, passim.

10. For the elaboration—and limits—of human rights around the turn of the century, see Worms, *Droits de l'homme et philosophie*, pt. 3.

11. Hyppolite, *Figures*, 1:230–31. On the politics of students at the Parisian *khagnes* and the École Normale Supérieure, see Sirinelli, *Génération intellectuelle*, chaps. 9–13.

12. Besides the figures to be discussed below, other major figures of this aging generation were the philosophers of science Emile Meyerson and Pierre Duhem, the sociologists Celestin Bouglé and Emile Durkheim, and the anthropologist Lucien Lévy-Bruhl.

13. I do not have the space to present all these figures here—nor can I write sufficiently of the philosophical differences between, for example, spiritualism, intellectualism, and neocriticism. There are relatively few studies of French philosophers of the late nineteenth–early twentieth century, and they are by and large aimed at explaining the thinkers that came later. Among these, see Schrift, *Twentieth-Century French Philosophy*, 5–8, 10–18ff; Beaufret, *Notes sur la philosophie*; Brooks, *Eclectic Legacy*, chaps. 1, 4. For a different perspective that prioritizes spiritualism and philosophies of life, see Lefranc, *La Philosophie en France*. Moreover, see Fabiani, *Les Philosophes de la république*, 94. According to Jean Hyppolite, Lachelier, Boutroux, and Brunschvicg "continually referred" to Kant. See Hyppolite, *Figures*, 1:231. For a short treatment of Renouvier, see Schrift, *Twentieth-Century French Philosophy*, 6. For the significance of a reading of Kant for the thought of Lachelier and Boutroux, see Beaufret, *Notes sur la philosophie en France*, chaps. 2, 3.

14. Michel Winock argues that "republican manuals" in both the 1840s and 1870s were dominated by Kantian morality and were closely connected to Kantian philosophers of significance in the 1870s (notably Boutroux, Renouvier, Lachelier, Lévy-Bruhl, and others). Michel Winock, *Le Siècle des intellectuels*, 104. See also Brooks, *Eclectic Legacy*, chap. 5. For the role of anthropology in late nineteenth-century thought, see Hecht, *End of the Soul*, chap. 7. Alexandre Koyré, who taught at the section for religious studies of the Ecole Pratique des Hautes Etudes, once discussed its founding in the early years of the Third Republic as the construction of the first nondenominational (and by implication, for him, first scientific) school for religious studies in France (Koyré, *De la mystique à la science*, 8, 12–13).

15. Kant, *Anthropology from a Pragmatic Point of View*, 3.

16. Kant, *Anthropology from a Pragmatic Point of View*, 3–4, 186–87, 196–98.

17. Kant, *Logic*, 29.

18. As they were for the neocriticists, these were also goals for Benda in *The Treason of the Intellectuals*.

19. Brunschvicg, "L'Humanisme de l'occident," *Écrits philosophiques*, 1:8–9.

20. Brunschvicg's divergences from Kant are treated in Merleau-Ponty, *La Nature*, 47–58. Alan Schrift remarks that Brunschvicg's *Geistesgeschicthe* owed much to Hegel (Schrift, *Twentieth-Century French Philosophy*, 11). Given Brunschvicg's known dislike for Hegel (see, for example, his "Le Rationalisme métaphysique de Hegel," in Deschoux, *Brunschvicg*, 124–25), this Hegelianism should not be over-emphasized: one could instead point to the peculiar role played by Victor Cousin in the 1820s in at once importing certain Hegelian elements (like historicism) while distancing French thought from Hegel's altogether, as well as the Comtean kind of historicism that paralleled Hegel's in the French context. One should also point to the more general prevalence of a Hegel-like historicism in Neo-Kantianism in general, that is, even Cassirer's, as suggested by Friedman in *Parting of the Ways*, 105–10, 155–56.

21. Brunschvicg, *L'Esprit européen*, lectures 9 and 10. As we will see in the next chapter, this emphasis is precisely what Heidegger and younger French thinkers would resist in Brunschvicg from the turn of the 1930s onward.

22. Brunschvicg, *L'Expérience humaine*, 457–65. For an ethical critique of realism and naturalism, see also Brunschvicg, *Le Progrès de la conscience*, 718. Theau, *La Philosophie française*, 53.

23. Brunschvicg, *Le Progrès de la conscience*, 704–7. Brunschvicg does *not* reduce the progress of mathematics to Kant's conception of it (705), but specifically argues that Kant's forms and categories set the critical project on the correct path that allows not only for an understanding of "the positivity of science" but also for that of its progress. As a result: "La réflexion sur le devenir de la science aboutit ainsi à redresser perpétuellement la perspective historique de l'humanité, comme la science elle-même, d'approximation en approximation, rend la struc-

ture de l'univers toujours plus cohérente et plus vraie. Le progrès de la perspective humaine et de la structure cosmique sont au fond un seul et même progrès: le progrès de cette conscience intellectuelle, dont Kant avait laissé sans doute échapper certains traits fondamentaux, mais à laquelle il avait su du moins lier le sort de l'idéalisme critique" (706).

24. Brunschvicg, *Le Progrès de la conscience,* 726. The passages from pp. 710–26 argue for the moral and political consequences of this progress of "western consciousness."

25. Brunschvicg, "Appendice II: Le Rôle de l'homme occidental," *Écrits philosophiques,* 1:304.

26. A more substantial and far more sympathetic treatment of Brunschvicg's humanism can be found in Deschoux, *La Philosophie de Léon Brunschvicg,* esp. 134–62. Because his concern is to explicate Brunschvicg's thought, rather Deschoux does not deal adequately with the problems suggested here.

27. This is not the place to consider this range of possibilities. I nevertheless want to provide a couple of suggestions. The clearest engagement of these questions can be found in the implicit debate (and shared premises) between the qualified realism of Meyerson's *Identité et réalité,* and the mixture of mathematics and Kantianism in Brunschvicg's *Les Étapes de la philosophie mathématique, L'Expérience humaine et la causalité physique,* and *Le Progrès de la conscience.*

28. Benda, *Treason of the Intellectuals,* 201. See also Schalk, *Spectrum of Political Engagement,* chap. 2. Schalk usefully presents Benda's concern against intellectual passions as following from a belief, held since the Dreyfus Affair among many French thinkers, that intellectuals supporting their opposing positions inevitably betrayed their functions as intellectuals (26).

29. The most sustained criticism of Brunschvicg's radical idealism can be found in Merleau-Ponty, *La Nature,* 47, 54–55. Merleau-Ponty openly accuses Brunschvicg's humanist radicalization of Kant of reducing the relationship between man and his world to a subject-object relation in which the object is *fully* dependent on man and his thought.

30. *Bulletin de la Société Française de Philosophie* (1921): 50–51; cited in Descombes, *Modern French Philosophy,* 21. Cresson and Brunschvicg had been friends since their time at the Ecole Normale Supérieure (*promotion* 1888).

31. Again, see Theau, *La Philosophie française,* 55–56. Though Theau sees this as Brunschvicg's "central idea," it is of course dependent on Kant's "Remark" in the *Anthropology* as regards whether man can know his inner self on the basis of an examination of his outer self, and his objection that anthropology cannot provide an adequate response to this problem. Kant, *Anthropology from a Pragmatic Point of View,* 15n.

32. Proust, *Swann's Way,* 109.

33. Sartre attacked philosophical solipsism in *Being and Nothingness*, 301–15. Merleau-Ponty's criticism of Lachelier in *Phenomenology of Perception* also targets idealism as a solipsism: see *Phenomenology of Perception*, 349–50. See also Paul Ricoeur's criticism: "Mais cet intellectualisme est-il capable, non pas bien sûr de maîtriser les démons—car personne finalement ne le peut—mais simplement de rendre raison des démons qui habitaient l'homme européen et qui terrassèrent à la fin de ce premier tiers du vingtième siècle ? N'avait-on pas sousestimé les forces constructrices et destructrices de la vie ? N'avait-on pas été aveugle au nihilisme qui, montant du 19ᵉᵐᵉ siècle, avait depuis longtemps tranché les racines spirituelles—platoniciennes et chrétiennes—du rationalisme tempéré?" in "L'Humanité de l'homme: contribution de la philosophie française contemporaine," in *Studium Generale* 15 (1962), 312. It would be interesting to read Emmanuel Levinas's thought on "the other" as targeting Brunschvicg's idealism: their wildly different reactions to Davos debate and Brunschvicg's rejection of Levinas's teaching aspirations through a comment that his accent in French precluded any university career in France would provide a useful background as to why Levinas's objections to Hegel and Heidegger did not direct him toward Kantianism. Levinas also criticizes Brunschvicg in his *Humanisme de l'autre homme*, 37.

34. See Etienne Gilson's wide-ranging criticisms of Brunschvicg after the latter's talk "La Querelle de l'athéisme," in *Bulletin de la Société Française de Philosophie* (1928): 56–61, 66–69. See, finally, Brunschvicg's long-standing quarrel with Gabriel Marcel, noted in Deschoux, *Brunschvicg*, 12–14; and in Levinas, *Difficult Freedom*, 44. See also the lectures by Kuki Shuzo in the next chapter (notably Kuki, "General Characteristics of French Philosophy," in Light, *Shuzo Kuki and Jean-Paul Sartre*). The timeliness of the Sfp's interests was often criticized by younger philosophers and writers in this period. See, for example, WD 41, where Nizan accuses the Sfp of irrelevance, ideological proselytizing, and complete failure to understand the problems of the world surrounding it.

35. These include Henri Delacroix, Elie Halévy, and Louis Weber.

36. Bayer, *Travaux du 9eme congrès international de philosophie.*

37. As Alexandre Koyré put it in 1946, in the later interwar period, both Bergson and Brunschvicg, with their idealism and optimism, seemed rather inadequate, *inactuels*. The world as it is did not seem to fit into their categories; they seemed not to be able to give an answer to the most burning questions of the day." Koyré, "Present Trends in French Philosophical Thought."

38. See the *Revue de Metaphysique et de Morale*, the *Revue philosophique*, and the *Recherches philosophiques* during the 1930s.

39. See specifically the wide-ranging critique of rationalism reported in Loubet del Bayle, *Les Non-conformistes des années trente*, 253, 262.

CHAPTER 1

1. In a 1969 interview with *L'Express* (which he disavowed in a subsequent letter to *Der Spiegel* (November 15, 1969) perhaps because of a promise of exclusivity for the "Only a God Can Save Us" interview), Heidegger (or his anonymous yet extraordinarily informed impersonator) remarked, "It was a Japanese prince who studied with me in 1929 and who brought my work to Sartre," fifteen years before Heidegger got his own chance to read Sartre. See *L'Express* 954 (October 20–26, 1969): 171. See also Heidegger's references to Kuki in Heidegger, *On the Way to Language*, 1–6. See Light, *Shuzo Kuki and Jean-Paul Sartre*.

2. De Beauvoir, *La Force de l'age*, 141; trans. as *Prime of Life*, 112. Levinas, *Théorie de l'intuition*.

3. Kuki, "General Characteristics of French Philosophy," in Light, *Shuzo Kuki and Jean-Paul Sartre*, 92–95.

4. Heidegger, *On the Way to Language*, 1. For Kuki's relation to Heidegger, see also Buchner, *Japan und Heidegger*, 127–39, 268–69, passim.

5. For the Davos debate, see Cassirer and Heidegger, *Débat sur le kantisme et la philosophie*; P. Gordon, *Rosenzweig and Heidegger*, chap. 6; Friedman, *Parting of the Ways*. Part of the Davos debate has been republished in Heidegger, *Kant and the Problem of Metaphysics*. For the French context, see Maurice de Gandillac's testimony, which contrasts Brunschvicg and Levinas; see de Gandillac, *Le Siècle traversé*, 95, 132–35; Janicaud, *Heidegger en France*, 1:30–31; Bourdieu, *Political Ontology of Martin Heidegger*, 58–60. Cassirer visited Paris for a talk at the Sfp on Rousseau. See the *Bulletin de la société française de philosophie* (February 27, 1932).

6. Heidegger's *Kantbuch* was eventually translated into French by de Waelhens and Biemel as *Kant et le problème de metaphysique*. This was the first translation of a complete book by Heidegger into French.

7. During the debate, both Heidegger and Cassirer attempted to distance themselves from anthropologism and anthropocentrism. See also Heidegger, *Kant and the Problem of Metaphysics*, 183.

8. See the references in de Vries, *Minimal Theologies*, 361. Friedman, *Parting of the Ways*, 3. See also my review of Friedman's book in *MLN* 117, no. 5 (December 2002): 1127–31; and Lilla, "Ménage à Trois," 13.

9. P. Gordon, *Rosenzweig and Heidegger*, 279; Taubes, *Political Theology of Paul*, 104; de Gandillac, *Le Siècle traversé*, 134. Levinas's difficulty in the Parisian academic context, and Brunschvicg's dismissal of Levinas, is noted in Kleinberg, *Generation Existential*, 42. In later years, Levinas was ambivalent toward Brunschvicg and his legacy—warmer than most of his contemporaries, but still very critical philosophically.

10. See Brunschvicg, "Préface," in Gurvitch, *Les Tendances actuelles*, 8.

11. De Gandillac, *Le Siècle traversé*, 134.

12. See Descombes, *Le Même et l'autre*. Waldenfels, *Phänomenologie in Frankreich*. Roth, *Knowing and History*.

13. For Heidegger's approval of the translation, see Corbin, "Post-Scriptum biographique à un entretien philosophique," in *Cahier de l'Herne*, 43: "Il me faisait entièrement confiance, approuvait tous mes néologismes français, et me laissait une responsabilité un peu lourde." Also cited in Ethan Kleinberg, *Generation Existential*, 70.

14. Extending a long tradition of critiques of this term (in one of his classic polysemous gestures, Derrida termed it "monstrous"), Janicaud calls Corbin's term "execrable" in *Heidegger en France*, 1:46.

15. On Soviet exiles and Paris as the capital of Russians in exile, see Chamberlain, *Philosophy Steamer*, 230. Chamberlain mentions in passing both Koyré and Kojève (231, 234).

16. A useful study of this generation is Louis Pinto, "'(Re)traductions: Phénoménologie et 'philosophie allemande' dans les années 1930," in *Actes de la recherche en sciences sociales* 145 (December 2002): 21–33.

17. Jay, *Marxism and Totality*, 277. For Gide see his *L'Immoraliste*; for Malraux, see his *La Condition Humaine*. See also the work (especially the translations and erotic writings) of Pierre Klossowski.

18. Koyré, *From the Closed World*.

19. Heidegger, "Qu'est-ce que la métaphysique?" trans. H. Corbin, in *Bifur* 8, with Alexandre Koyré's introduction, 1–8. Heidegger, "De la nature de la cause," trans. A. Bessey, *Recherches philosophiques* I (1931–32): 83–124. Koyré, review of N. Hartmann *Das Problem des geistigen Seins*, 407–10; reviews of G. Van der Leeuw, *Phänomenologie der Religion*, and N. Hartmann, *Zur Grundlegung der Ontologie*, 420–24.

20. This much was suggested already in the mid-1930s by Raymond Aron of *Recherches philosophiques* and Bachelard's work in a review for the *Zeitschrift für Sozialforschung* (*Zeitschrift für Sozialforschung* 6 [1937]: 417–20), cited in the "Translator's Introduction" to *New Scientific Spirit*, xxiii.

21. "Avertissement," vii.

22. "Tendances actuelles de la métaphysique," 2–124. The rest of the review published material from a symposium on mysticism, a section on philosophical strategy, and essays on philosophical research abroad—besides an extensive section reviewing recent materials in epistemology, philosophy of religion, and other fields.

23. Among the authors published or reviewed, we find Reichenbach, Whitehead, Eddington, Bohr, Weyl, and elaborate studies of the "contemporary situation" of particular sciences in other European countries. For further information on the publishing scene, particularly the significance of publishers Gallimard and Aubier-Montaigne, see Pinto, "(Re)traductions: Phénoménologie et "philosophie

allemande" dans les années 1930," 23. See also Cornick, Nouvelle Revue Française *under Jean Paulhan.*

24. Canguilhem, *La Connaissance de la vie,* 47/58.

25. The Heidegger translation was, moreover, among the most careful over the next decade, more respectful to Heidegger's thought per se than Corbin's were to be: the translator, A. Bessey, uses *existant* and *être* and refers to paragraphs 38, 59 of *Sein und Zeit* (*Recherches philosophiques* I [1931–32]: 83) to mark out the significance of the ontological difference. For Bessey, and in a position that perhaps reflects that of Wahl, Being itself must be found in "des analyses de l'être antérieures et d'un niveau inaccessible." It should be noted that Heidegger's own conception of Sein postulates it as less "inaccessible" than his early French readers insist. Kojève's first contributions are in *Recherches Philosophiques* II (1932–33): 470–75. Levinas had already reviewed a book concerning Heidegger and interpersonal relations in *Recherches Philosophiques* I (1931–32): 385–88. Regarding the role of *Recherches philosophiques* in the development of existentialism, Jean Wahl wrote after the war that: "C'est . . . en tenant compte de l'activité de la revue *Recherches philosophiques,* fondée par Koyré et où parut le premier travail de Sartre, en même temps que Gabriel Marcel y étudiait Jaspers et qu'on y traduisait Heidegger, que l'on peut comprendre le développement de l'existentialisme français." Jean Wahl, "Situation présente de la philosophie française," II:39–40.

26. Koyré, *De la mystique,* 8, 12–13.

27. Koyré, *De la mystique,* 28. Auffret, *Alexandre Kojève,* 363.

28. Corbin, "Post-Scriptum philosophique," 43.

29. See his interview in *La Quinzaine littéraire,* June 1–15, 1968, 18–20.

30. Kojève's analysis of the Master/Slave relation first appeared in *Mésures.* See Bernard Groethuysen to Alexandre Kojève, letters of January 1, 1938, and December 7, 1938, in BNF Mss. Occ., Fonds Kojève, boite 20, "Groethuysen."

31. Sirinelli, *Génération intellectuelle.* The difference of EPHE and the *Recherches philosophiques* from the ENS as intellectual hubs is evident both in their philosophical directions and long-term (postwar) influence.

32. Husserl, *Méditations cartésiennes,* 14. It is worth noting that Maurice Merleau-Ponty insisted on the relation between science and phenomenology until the end of his life. See his discussions of psychology in *Phenomenology of Perception* and especially his discussion of physics in *La Nature.* This interest in linking phenomenology and science continues: see, for example, writings by Sean Dorrance Kelly and Hubert Dreyfus in the United States, and Catherine Malabou in France, which have continued the emphasis on a philosophical link between phenomenology and philosophy of science.

33. This list is not necessarily complete—it concerns only those figures whose lectures Alexandre Kojève attended and from which his notes survive. See BNF Mss. Occ., Fonds Kojève, boite 4.

34. The question of *indeterminisme* (uncertainty) may here be seen specifically against the background of a resistance to scientific determinism elaborated in
French sociology since the late nineteenth century, and perhaps yet more importantly, the legacy of spiritualism and the influence of Henri Bergson's objections
to science. A useful guide to the critique of scientific determinism can be found in
Hecht, *End of the Soul*, chap. 7.

35. Kojève, *L'Idée du déterminisme*. Meyerson, *Réel et déterminisme*. Bachelard,
Le Nouvel esprit scientifique.

36. NES 132–33 / 133–34 and 175–77 / 172–74. See also Kojève, review of "Archives d'Histoire des Sciences et Techniques [Archiv istorii nauki i tekhniki], Académie des Sciences de l'URSS. Travaux de l'Institut d'Histoire des Sciences et des
Techniques," Ière série, vols. V and VI (1935), in *Thalès*, X (1935), 237–53, including
a long review of an article by S. F. Vassilev on Meyerson, which Kojève uses to criticize both Meyerson and Vassilev. Kojève also noted that "Heisenberg contradicts
Meyerson," when reading the latter's *Identité et réalité* in 1928–29. See BNF Mss.
Occ., Fonds Kojève, "Carnets sur la science," II:41.

37. The following pages should not be read as if I were staking a claim on a
certain interpretation of quantum mechanics; what is presented here is specifically
seen through the eyes of the philosophers considered here, and it is by no means a
settled or established view of quantum physics or of nature at the quantum level.

38. See ID 143–44; Heisenberg's discussions in *Principes physiques de la théorie
des quanta*, cited in NES 84/86; and Heisenberg's less technical and more readable
Physique et philosophie, 19–27. See also a remarkable book that considers many of
the problems of complementarity in relation to the writing of Bataille and Derrida, Plotnitsky's *In the Shadow of Hegel*. In his more recent work, Plotnitsky has
situated Bohr between Hegel and Kant, ultimately reading him closer to Kant. See
his books *The Knowable and the Unknowable* and *Reading Bohr*.

39. Henri Atlan, citing J.-M. Lévy-Leblond, explains that part of the force of
quantum physics, also for the major physicists working on questions they posed,
was precisely that "when quantum concepts were first elaborated their fathers
could understand them only by reference to classical concepts, even those they
were meant to replace." Kojève, Bachelard, and Wahl echo and expand philosophically from this point as well. See Atlan, *Enlightenment to Enlightenment*, 250. For
an evocation of precisely this capacity to destabilize classical systems, see Lyotard,
Postmodern Condition, 55. This prioritization of quantum physics persists and is
one of its main popular claims. See, for example, Gray, *Straw Dogs*, 23–24.

40. This argument is most clearly made in NES 16 / 16–17. Bachelard's *La Valeur inductive de la relativité* received a glorifying review by Albert Spaier in the
same first volume of *Recherches philosophiques*: "Il y a là de quoi troubler tout
homme habitué à penser qu'une solution de continuité existe toujours entre les
vérités *a priori* et les faits" (*Recherches philosophiques* I [1931–32]: 368). Kojève also

suggests a filiation between non-Euclidian geometry and "modern" (quantum) physics; see ID 302.

41. NES 161–62, 166 / 161, 164–65. For Koyré, see his essays "Galilée et Platon" (1943) and "Galilée et la revolution scientifique" (1955), in *Etudes d'histoire de la pensée scientifique,* 170, 193, 199. It is important to note that Bachelard does not object to a mathematization of nature, but to an antiempiricist, idealist such operation.

42. Bachelard made the same argument on the need for a new conception of the noumenon in his article "Noumène et métaphysique" for (the opening section of) *Recherches philosophiques* I (1931–32): 55–65; reprinted in *Etudes.*

43. For Kojève's studies of quantum physics, see BNF Mss. Occ., Fonds Kojève, boite 4, "Carnet Paris 1928–29" and "Carnet 'Boulogne 1929,'" where Kojève first notes that unlike relativity, quantum physics did involve an overturning of classical physics ("Carnet 'Boulogne 1929,'" 47, 62).

44. Kojève submitted *L'Idée du déterminisme* to the Sorbonne, where it was accepted in 1932. See Kleinberg, *Generation Existential,* 65.

45. Kojève also criticizes the Kantian thing-in-itself in his posthumously published 1953 text, *Kant,* 104–10.

46. A related parallel to Kojève's conception of quantum physics, which I will not discuss here, is his contemporary interpretation of Kandinsky, with whom Kojève had an extensive correspondence and on whom he wrote twice. The connection is made in somewhat biographical terms in Auffret, *Alexandre Kojève,* 272–92.

47. Like Meyerson and Bachelard, Kojève distinguishes the two. The relationship between physics and mathematics (particularly the significance of geometry) is typical of the French Neo-Kantian tradition and a considerable theme in Brunschvicg's aforementioned *L'Expérience humaine,* not to mention Husserl's *Crisis of the European Sciences.* As I will suggest later, this played a paramount role in Koyré's theorization of the beginnings of modern science. For the role of physics in Kojève's later concept of "energology," see Kojève, *Essai d'une histoire raisonnée,* 1:304.

48. Kojève, "Zum Problem einer diskreten Welt" typescript, 74 n26 (BNF Mss. Occ., Fonds Kojève, boite 9). See the review of *L'Orientation actuelle des sciences* cited earlier, a review written by Kojève *and* published under Koyré's name in *Revue philosophique* (1932: 9–10): 315–18. Why Kojève would ghostwrite for Koyré is not clear; to offer just one answer, unlike Kojève who had no established position, Koyré, as a student and protégé of Gilson could easily find cover over such an attack on Brunschvicg (Gilson was very critical of Brunschvicg), while Kojève's drafts for the review include far harsher treatments of Brunschvicg and Langevin (see BNF Mss. Occ., Fonds Kojève, boite 8–9; see also his notes in Mss. Occ., Fonds Kojève, boite 4, "Carnet 'Boulogne 1929'").

49. Wahl, *Philosopher's Way,* 206; henceforth abbreviated to PW.

50. See his note in "On the Essence of Ground" where Heidegger writes that *Sein und Zeit* was poorly received in Germany as based on an "anthropocentric perspective." Heidegger, *Pathmarks*, 371 n66. This expressly concerns his debate with Cassirer, who (somewhat like Brunschvicg, who saw man as his own ideal) emphasized the priority of anthropology, as well as the recurrent comparisons to Max Scheler. See also some of the more recent interpretations of his work, for example Françoise Dastur's *Heidegger et la question anthropologique*, whose second chapter presents the Heideggerian reading of Kant (central to his early post-1927 years) as specifically seeking a philosophical anthropology and the relation of such anthropology to the problem of finitude.

51. See Wahl's *Existence humaine et transcendance*, 134–35.

52. Heidegger, "Letter on 'Humanism,'" in *Pathmarks*, 250–51. In Chapter 5 we will return to the way in which Heidegger's position at once reduced the novelty of Sartre's articulation of anti-anthropocentrism in the "Existence precedes essence," and also indeed radicalized it and attached it, against Sartre, to the postwar attempts at antihumanism.

53. "My belated thanks for the Kafka letters and Kojève's Hegel book. Both were important to me. . . . Kojève has a rare passion for thinking. French thought of the past few decades is an echo of these lectures. Even the abandonment of these talks is itself an idea. But Kojève only reads *Being and Time* as an anthropology." Martin Heidegger to Hannah Arendt, letter of September 29, 1967, in Arendt and Heidegger, *Letters 1925–1975*, 133.

54. Rockmore, *Heidegger and French Philosophy*, 38. Janicaud, *Heidegger en France*, vol. 1, chaps. 4–5 (contrast to chap. 2). Ethan Kleinberg, *Generation Existential*, also contrasts the "first," anthropological reading of the 1930s to the second and third, postwar and nonanthropological readings. Anson Rabinbach also implies this in his *In the Shadow of Catastrophe*, 120–21.

55. Corbin's term, while indeed a poor substitute for *Being-there*, is not necessarily a bad translation of *Dasein* in the essay "What Is Metaphysics?" and reflects the specifically *metaphysical* argument Heidegger presents, not to mention provides a *realist* (as I argue here) interpretation of the definition of the human. As Corbin noted Heidegger approved the term during a discussion in 1937, and it is possible that this evasion of questions of existence and the ambiguity of "human reality" are precisely what factored in its favor. Whether *réalité humaine* involves an anthropologization of Heidegger, it inversely serves in the French context as an emptying out of anthropological categories—rejecting that human reality is anything other than the there-ness of *Dasein*. Heidegger's *Dasein* and Kojève's repeated use of *réalité humaine* in his lectures on Hegel in different ways postulate a being that elides and undermines anthropological determination; in Kojève's case, the identification of *réalité humaine* with nothingness is explicit and fundamental. Critiques, like Janicaud's and Derrida's, do apply more closely to Sartre's overuse

of *réalité humaine* in *Being and Nothingness*; Corbin's use of *réalité humaine* in his translation of passages from *Being and Time* is also more suspect than his use for "Qu'est-ce que la métaphysique?" where its utility is much clearer.

56. Levinas, *La Théorie de l'intuition*. See also Levinas, *En découvrant l'éxistence*. That Husserl and Bergson function as (radically different) philosophical carriers of modernity is a position shared by thinkers as diverse as Heidegger and Adorno. See Adorno, *Negative Dialectics*, 8–9.

57. For a (short-lived, but nonetheless significant) late 1920s and early 1930s appreciation of Scheler, see Gurvitch, *Les Tendances Actuelles de la Philosophie Allemande*. Groethuysen, *Introduction à la philosophie allemande depuis Nietzsche*. Bachelard, *La Psychanalyse du feu*, 169–72ff. See also Kojève's reviews in *Recherches philosophiques* 1932–33 and 1934–35 (signed Kojevnikoff).

58. On the contentious issue of reality in Heidegger, see Greisch, *Ontologie et temporalité*, 243–47; P. Gordon, "Realism, Science, and the Deworlding of the World," in *Companion to Phenomenology and Existentialism*, 425–44; Taylor, "Engaged Agency and Background," in *Cambridge Companion to Heidegger*, chap. 7. I would like to note that I do not use "realism" and "reality" here outside of this specific Heideggerian context.

59. In Heidegger's terminology, *existential* points to an analytical understanding of existence, by contrast to *existentiell*, which refers to one's understanding of existence on the basis of one's lived experience.

60. Kojève, "Zum Problem einer Diskreten Welt," typescript, 74 n26.

61. Kojève, "Note sur Hegel et Heidegger," 38.

62. Kojève, *Introduction à la lecture de Hegel*, 485–87n; 430–32, 435, 440–43 (English trans., 212 n115–215; 150–55, 166–68).

63. "Comme souvent chez Hegel, le Fürsichsein signifie l'entier des objets isolés du Verstand: c'est le Vorhandensein de Heidegger: l'homme [. . .] est [*Dasein*]. La *Totalität* als ein *Einzelheit*—c'est le *Jemeinigkeit* du *Dasein* de Heidegger. Mögliches et Tod [référent à] Möogliches et Tod dans Heidegger aussi. Et vous voyez que Heidegger et Hegel disent également la même chose; l'homme est non pas Vorhandene (nicht fürsichtsein) mais *Dasein*, sein eigen Möglichkeit (an ihn selbst ein [Ihn] möglich); le *Dasein* est je-meines (als eine [Einzelheit]) seulement dans la mesure où c'est un *Sein zum Tode* (immer zum Tode [bereit])." BNF Mss. Occ., Fonds Kojève, boite 11, "Note sur le panthéisme hégélien: Projet inachevé d'une conférence qui devait avoir lieu après la XVIe conference du 2e cours, commencée le 30/3/35," 6. Kojève, *L'Athéisme*, 94. Kojève wrote *L'Athéisme* in August–October 1931.

64. Kojève, *L'Athéisme*, 95.

65. By *Befindlichkeit* I mean—and I take Kojève to mean—existential disposition: the subject's existence as always already an engagement with things around it.

66. The survival of Kojève's interpretation of Heisenberg in his course and his legacy is also suggested (in somewhat joking terms) in Queneau, *Journeaux 1914–1965*, 669.

67. Wahl, *Poésie, pensée, perception*, 12.

68. Sartre, *Search for a Method*, 19.

69. Koyré, "Present Trends in French Philosophical Thought," 534. Schrift, *Twentieth-Century French Philosophy*, 17–18. Schrift specifically notes the aim of *Vers le concret* as being the overcoming of French spiritualism and idealism.

70. Gary Gutting also argues that the effort to search of the concrete was definitive of the interest in Husserl and Heidegger, and he uses Wahl's book title as a chapter heading in his *French Philosophy in the Twentieth Century*, 107.

71. Alan Schrift agrees on the priority of Wahl's reading of Heidegger over his analysis of Marcel, Whitehead, and James. See Schrift, *Twentieth-Century French Philosophy*, 18 n23.

72. The problem of pragmatism is central to Wahl's early writings. Wahl, *Les Philosophies pluralistes*.

73. To the extent that this treatment of subjectivity led to Wahl's later reading of Heidegger with Kierkegaard, it is well known that Heidegger, already criticized as an anthropocentric metaphysician in Germany, rejected Wahl's synthesis. See Heidegger's letter to Wahl, in which Heidegger (probably in Wahl's own translation) notes, "I must [. . .] insist that, even though *Being and Time* engages with 'Existenz' and 'Kierkegaard,' my philosophical tendencies cannot be classified as *Existenzphilosophie*.[§] I am absolutely in agreement with your claim that the 'philosophy of existence' is exposed to the double danger of falling either into theology or into abstraction. But the question that preoccupies me is not that of man's existence; it is that of Being in its totality and as such. Nor is Nietzsche a philosopher of existence—but in his doctrine of the will to power and the eternal return he poses the ancient and unique question of Being. Yet the question posed in *Being and Time* is by no means treated by either Kierkegaard or Nietzsche, and Jaspers passes it by altogether" (Wahl, *Existence Humaine et Transcendance*, 135).

74. By the time *The Philosopher's Way* appeared, moreover, the epistemological impact of the uncertainty principle had moved far beyond the limits of quantum physics and echoed the resolution of a number of problems. For example, referring to problems of experimentation in biology and physiology, Georges Canguilhem (who was much indebted to Gaston Bachelard on a number of methodological and philosophical problems) would write, "How is it possible to avoid, here as elsewhere, the fact that observation—which is an action because it is always to some degree prepared—troubles the observed phenomenon?" and, while considering cell theory, would explicitly cite wave mechanics as a paradigm for synthesizing irresolvable differences of approach. See Canguilhem, *La Connaissance de la vie*, 34/42 and 45/55, respectively. In the same work, Canguilhem also referenc-

es and quotes Jacques Duclaux to argue that, even in biology, "modern science is primarily the study of a paranature or a supernature rather than of nature itself" (Canguilhem, *La Connaissance de la vie*, 28n/35n). The quoted text is from Duclaux, *L'Homme devant l'univers*, 273.

75. This is by no means to say that Bohr, Heisenberg, or especially de Broglie would agree to Wahl's descriptions and positive argument.

76. Wahl shows also his accord with this analysis in a short objection to the interpretation of physics by Raymond Ruyer. See Wahl's response to Raymond Ruyer after the latter's presentation "'Le Psychologique' et 'le vital'" at the *Sfp*, November 26, 1938; published in the *Bulletin de la Société Française de Philosophie* (1938): 183.

77. This problem of inaccessibility is to a degree a result of Wahl's elision of Heidegger's distinction of *existentiell* from *existential*. I take Wahl's resolution (that man is somehow aware but incapable of experiencing or thinking the concrete in any analytic fashion) to recall Niels Bohr's famous and oft-repeated statement that "the new situation in physics has so forcibly reminded us of the old truth that we are both onlookers and actors in the great drama of existence" (see *Philosophical Writings of Niels Bohr*, 1:119). I would like to thank Arkady Plotnitsky for citing this passage to me.

78. Bataille, "Le Labyrinthe," 364–72; trans. as "The Labyrinth," 171–78, esp. 173. See the analysis in Merleau-Ponty, *La Nature*, 125–38, which plays a pivotal role for the development of his argument. Kojève argues that in the quantic universe, "l'anthropomorphisme naturel a peu de prise" (ID 245); Bachelard seems to agree (NES 128/128).

79. Wahl's later role in the reception (in the philosophical community) of Heidegger and his Nazism is ambiguous and worthy of note. Besides the 1938 and 1945 lectures based on a typescript of Heidegger's winter 1928–29 course *Einleitung in die Philosophie* (*Gesamtausgabe* 27) that Koyré had brought to Paris (the first of which courses criticized Heidegger's politics, the latter ignored the political issue), his later praise of Habermas's critique of Heidegger, and his rivalry with Jean Beaufret, two documents are worth noting. The first, in Father Gaston Fessard's archive, are two copies "sur l'originel, le 10.VIII.1946, prêté par J.W." of Heidegger's November 4, 1945, letter to the university authorities, which suggests that Wahl procured the letter through official channels or acquired it directly from Heidegger (see Archives Jésuites [Vanves], Fonds Fessard, 33/1/1, 33/1/7). The second is a section of Heidegger's "The Overcoming of Metaphysics," in Wahl's own archive, sent to him by Heidegger's printer and student Egon Vietta ("Martin Heidegger, 'Ausschrift 1939/40,'" in IMEC, Fonds Wahl, Dossier Heidegger, Chemise "Egon Vietta / texte sur M. Heidegger"), offprint from Fritz, *Ernst Barlach*.

80. But see the positive review of *Vers le concret* by Spaier, 468–69.

81. See the essays grouped in "Symposium sur les transcendances," in *RP* II: 1–187. Also Wahl, "Le Problème du choix," 404–44; and his *Existence humaine et transcendance* in general.

82. Roudinesco, *Jacques Lacan*, 89. Koyré, *L'Idée de Dieu*. See Centre Alexandre Koyré (Pavillon Chevreul), Fonds Koyré, Boite "Conférences et textes divers." A very useful bibliography of Koyré's published work (and of work on Koyré) is Stoffel, *Bibliographie d'Alexandre Koyré*. For Koyré's influence on his students in these matters, see, for example, Georges Bataille's contribution to his shared article with Queneau, "Critique of the Foundations of the Hegelian Dialectic" (Bataille, *Visions of Excess*, 109), where Bataille explicitly treats some of the above figures as originators of Hegel's thought. Koyré's main publications in *Recherches philosophiques*, in addition to a few reviews, were sizable bibliographical overviews, mostly on medieval and modern philosophy. See *RP* I (1931–32), 466–501; II (1932–33), 563–98; IV (1934–35), 476–522; and V (1935–36), 507–40.

83. See the *Annuaire de l'Ecole Pratique des Hautes Etudes, V^e section*, from 1921 through 1939; Koyré's course descriptions are reprinted in *De la mystique à la science*, 21–54.

84. Corbin, "Post-Scriptum biographique à un entretien philosophique," 44.

85. See his introduction of Martin Heidegger, "Qu'est-ce que la métaphysique?" trans. H. Corbin, in *Bifur* 8 (June 1932): 1–8. It is also rumoured that Koyré brought a typescript of Heidegger's 1929 *Einleitung in die Philosophie* course (Janicaud, *Heidegger en France*, 1:96). Wahl used this manuscript twice (in 1938 and 1946) to construct his course almost literally out of Heidegger's. I did not find the manuscript either in Koyré's archive or in Wahl's. But see also de Towarnicki, *À la rencontre de Heidegger*, 251; Wahl, *Introduction à la pensée de Heidegger*, 9 n2. For Wahl's 1938 course, which uses this one of Heidegger's courses as an introduction to philosophy, see IMEC, Fonds Wahl Dossier Heidegger (Chemise "Heidegger" 10pp+ 3*32pp).

86. Koyré's early critique of Bergson also followed in part from his studies under Husserl at Göttingen. Koyré criticized Bergson in "Bemerkungen zu den Zenonischen Paradoxen," 610–13. Husserl, "Briefwechsel," 355–62. See also de Gandt, *Husserl et Galilée*, 97–104. De Gandt suggests, somewhat unconvincingly, that Husserl was principally influenced by the German Neo-Kantians in his treatment of Galileo and largely passed this position to, or found it confirmed in Koyré's work. That strikes me as too straightforward. As regards Husserl's Galileo, see also the first text published on the *Crisis of the European Sciences* in France, namely, Levinas's "L'oeuvre d'Edmund Husserl," in *En découvrant l'existence*, 44. The figure of Husserl's *Krisis* in French thought works well with that of Koyré's presentation of modern science as relying on a suppression of its metaphysical origins. As the role of the Krisis in the reception of phenomenology has been widely discussed, I will avoid addressing it at length here; for a quick description relevant to

the present concerns, see Stiegler, *Technics and Time 1*, 3. See also Aron Gurwitsch's remark on Koyré's opinion of Husserl's Galileo study in Gurwitsch, *Phenomenology and the Theory of Science*, 39.

87. A. Koyré, review of Werner Heisenberg, 457–58. Alexandre Kojève, review of J. Perrin et al., 315–18. Alexandre Koyré, reviews of A. N. Whitehead, *Nature and Life*; L.-S. Stebbing, *Logical Positivism and Analysis*; L. Silberstein, *Causality, a Law of Nature or a Maxim of the Naturalist?* P. Langevin, *La Notion de corpuscules et d'atomes*; Centre International de Synthèse, *Science et loi*; and the general overview "Histoire des sciences" (with G. Bachelard) in *Recherches philosophiques* IV (1934–35): 398, 434–40, 517–22, respectively. See also the review of A. Eddington, *New Pathways to Science*, 455–57.

88. Koyré, "L'Evolution philosophique de Martin Heidegger," 161–83, esp. 180.

89. Koyré, "Etudes sur Calvin" (course), *De la mystique*, 44–45.

90. See the course description for "Galilée et la formation de la science moderne," in Koyré, *De la mystique*, 44. See also Koyré, *Etudes galiléennes*. It is through his argument for a sort of prescientific background that Koyré provided the possibilities for someone like Thomas Kuhn.

91. Regarding Duhem, see the critical appraisals in Koyré, *De la mystique*, 29, 36, 40, 43, and the critique in "Galilée et Platon," *Etudes d'histoire de la pensée scientifique*, 171–72. For a discussion of Koyré's critique of Duhem, see Cohen in *Scientific Revolution*, 106ff. *Etudes galiléennes* was dedicated to Meyerson, whom Koyré makes use of in order to criticize on the one hand Boutroux and Poincaré (see EHESS, Centre Alexandre Koyré, Fonds Koyré, Boite "Conferences et texts divers," dossier *Conférences à verifier: Physique Epistémologie Meyerson* [texte incomplet]), and on the other Brunschvicg (see "Sur la pensée de Brunschvicg," 3–4, in EHESS, Centre Alexandre Koyré, Fonds Koyré, Boite "Conferences et texts divers"). Yet Meyerson himself comes under critique in Koyré's work: see Koyré, "Die Philosophie Emile Meyersons," 197–217; and Koyré's review of Meyerson's *Du cheminement de la pensée*, 5–6, 647–55. Even beyond these reviews, Koyré's treatment of rationalism involves an entirely different viewpoint than Meyerson's.

92. Mieli, "Il tricentenario dei *Discorsi* di Galileo Galilei," 281; cited in Koyré, *De la mystique à la science*, 35.

93. Koyré, *De la mystique*, 36–37. Redondi does not note that, while curtly dismissive of Koyré, at least one of these reviewers, Aldo Mieli, was positive toward Duhem's work; see Mieli, "Souvenirs sur Duhem et une lettre inédite de lui," 139–42. H. Floris Cohen agrees that Koyré felt "little but scorn" for positivism's influence in scientific research and its influence in the historiography of science (see Cohen, *Scientific Revolution*, 85).

94. Contemporary echoes of this conception of the mathematization of nature and world in the early modern period can be found in Badiou, *Being and Event*, 143ff.

95. Recent critiques have shown varying limitations in Koyré's antiempiricism and have criticized his claims on a variety of levels—but at stake here is less the accuracy of his argument than its role in the 1930s treatment of science, reality, and the status of phenomenology. Nevertheless, see the critiques of Koyré in *Cambridge Companion to Galileo*, as noted above. See also Beltrán, "Wine, Water and Epistemological Sobriety," 82–89. Even though he appears to have been faulty on experimental data, Koyré was arguing against the practice of experiment—and a comprehension of Heidegger's notion of unconcealment explains the argument that experiment proves the preconceived ideas and existential conceptions one bears—Heidegger makes the exact same claim on truth as logical correctness (vis-à-vis the more "primordial" conception of truth as unconcealment).

96. See Segre, "Never-Ending Galileo Story," in *Cambridge Companion to Galileo*, 403–5. See also, in the same volume, Hooper, "Inertial Problems in Galileo's Preinertial Framework," esp. 159–60. Koyré, "Galilée et l'expérience de Pise," in *Etudes d'histoire*, 217, 223.

97. See Barthel, *Beiträge zur transzendentalen Logik*. Koyré reviewed Barthel's *Beiträge* in *Revue philosophique* 116 (1933): 288–90; and quotes in the review from Barthel's argument that the falling bodies experiment could neither have been properly deduced nor experimentally carried out. Koyré, "Galilée et l'expérience de Pise," 216–19.

98. That Koyré's critique of the primacy of experiment was shared by important contemporary historians of modern science (for example, Eduard Jan Dijksterhuis) is noted by Cohen in *Scientific Revolution, 185*.

99. Koyré, "Galilée et la révolution scientifique du 17ᵉ siècle," *Etudes d'histoire*, 210–11.

100. Koyré, "Orientation et projets de recherches," *Etudes d'histoire de la pensée scientifique*, 11.

101. Koyré, "Galilée et la formation de la science moderne" (course), *De la mystique*, 44; italics mine.

102. Koyré, "Galilée et Descartes," in Bayer, *Travaux du 9e congrès international de philosophie*, II:42.

103. Koyré, "Galilée et la formation de la science moderne" (course), *De la mystique*, 43, 44; Koyré, "Etudes sur Galilée" (course), *De la mystique*, 48. Koyré elaborated on this argument in his "Galilée et Platon," *Etudes d'histoire de la pensée scientifique*, 170; see also his analysis of the law of inertia, which involves an extensive contrast of the modern geometrization of real space as opposed to the Aristotelian physical conception of reality, in "Galilée et la révolution scientifique du 17ᵉ siècle," 199–205.

104. See, among other texts, "Galilée et Platon," *Etudes d'histoire de la pensée scientifique*, 168.

105. The debate on the (non)existence of an external, independent nature continues after the war and can be found in the structuralist debates concerning culture, in Derrida's treatment of the *trace*, Debord's theorization of the all-encompassing spectacle, etc. The elision of nature in scientific study is foregrounded in both the Heideggerian antiscientific argument and various (more scientifically reliable) works on the philosophy of science. Besides Heidegger's discussion of world and reality, see his postwar emphasis on the *Gestell* and the irreversible denaturing of reality. For the French reception of the discussions on the *Gestell,* see Axelos, *Marx;* Beaufret, *Dialogue avec Heidegger vol. III;* and the discussion in Janicaud, *Heidegger en France*, vol. 1, chap. 11. See also Canguilhem's discussion of the distinction of the experimental from the normal (*La Connaissance de la vie*, 34/42) and the primacy of anthropology over anthropomorphism (35/43).

106. Koyré, "Galilée et la révolution scientifique du 17ᵉ siècle," *Etudes d'histoire de la pensée scientifique*, 197. Koyré, "Les Etapes de la cosmologie scientifique" (1948), in *Etudes d'histoire de la pensée scientifique*, 87; Koyré, "Sens et portée de la synthèse newtonienne," in *Etudes newtoniennes*, 42–43; trans. as "Significance of the Newtonian Synthesis," 20–24.

107. Koyré, quoted in Cohen, *Scientific Revolution*, 87. Also cited, in reference to Lacan's conception of modernity, in Elisabeth Weber, "Elijah's Futures," 208.

108. Koyré, "Théologie et Science," lecture at the Collège philosophique; Koyré, *De la mystique*, 180.

109. Koyré's history undermines the rationalism of Brunschvicg (who thought science originated in a rational scientific spirit and would not find it originating in non- (or pre- or anti-) rational religious and metaphysical approaches. Theau, *La philosophie française*, 55n.

110. See, for example, Roger Caillois, *Man and the Sacred*. Less directly, see also Levi-Strauss, *Le Cru et le cuit.*

111. Bataille alludes to Bachelard's rhetoric of a "psychoanalysis of objective knowledge" and specifically writes that "science represses intention" in "Critique of Heidegger," *October* 117 (summer 2006): 27.

112. See, by way of an example, the entire "project" of Georges Bataille in the mid-1930s, and, more "collectively" the Collège de Sociologie.

113. Corbin, "Post-Scriptum biographique à un entretien philosophique," 44.

114. The adjustment is noted by Janicaud, in *Heidegger en France*, 1:577; and by Hollier, in *Le Collège de sociologie 1937–1939*, 323n.

115. Heidegger, *Kant and the Problem of Metaphysics*, §36–37, 145–46. See Dastur, *Heidegger et la question anthropologique*, 41. The centrality of Heidegger's *Kant-buch* in France is borne out first of all by the fact that it was the first of Heidegger's book-length works published in translation by Alphonse de Waelhens and Walter Biemel at Gallimard in 1953. There are also numerous French studies of Heidegger on Kant. Both Foucault and Derrida engaged the question while at

the ENS: Derrida wrote a paper on "Kant, Hegel, Heidegger" in 1954–55 (University of California at Irvine, Special Collections and Archives, Jacques Derrida Papers (MS-C01), Series 1.2, box 1 folder 47 [www.hydra.umn.edu/derrida/uci.html, last accessed January 16, 2006]). As noted in the Introduction, Foucault taught a 1954–55 course on "Problems of Anthropology," which does not address but clearly subsumes Heidegger's argument on a number of points, particularly his reading of Kant and the organization of the Kantian perception of anthropology (IMEC, Fonds Foucault, C.2.1 / FCL 2. A03–08: Problèmes de l'anthropologie [notes prises par Jacques Lagrange]).

116. Heidegger further discusses Kant's *Anthropology*, its construction of "world," and (more implicitly) its consideration of political problems in EG 119.

117. See Dastur, *Heidegger et la question anthropologique*, 35–36.

118. The problem of the polis, of Plato's *agathon*, and Kant's world is one that I cannot treat in the present context, but it is extraordinarily important in terms of the political stakes involved in Heidegger's early thought and in particular of his understanding of *Dasein* as existing "for the sake of itself."

119. Angelika Pillen reads Heidegger alongside Koyré on different topics, especially the questions of *time* and *Spirit* in Hegel. That analysis does not contradict the present one. See Pillen, *Hegel in Frankreich*, 92–95.

120. See Hollier, *New History of French Literature*, 895.

121. Georges Gurvitch's setting of Husserl against German Neo-Kantianism can easily be seen as a critique of Brunschvicg; see his *Les Tendances actuelles de la philosophie allemande*, 11–13, a book that Brunschvicg prefaced. See also Merleau-Ponty, *Parcours II*, 251.

122. Kojève, review of J. Perrin et al., *L'Orientation actuelle des sciences* (signed by Koyré). See also Koyré's talk "Sur la pensée de Brunschvicg" where Koyré presents Brunschvicg and Meyerson, from the new post-Kantian perspective that he himself holds, as two sides of the same coin. EHESS, Centre A. Koyré, Fonds Koyré, Boite "Conférences et extes divers," "Sur la pensée de Brunschvicg," 3–4.

123. Merleau-Ponty, *Phenomenology of Perception*, 54–56, 349–50; citation on 56. Merleau-Ponty also criticizes Brunschvicg, 394.

124. "L'homme occidental, l'homme suivant Socrate et suivant Descartes . . . est celui qui enveloppe l'humanité dans son idéal de réflexion intellectuelle et d'unité morale." In Brunschvicg, "Appendice II," 304.

125. For the commonplace "3-H," see Descombes, *Modern French Philosophy*, 9; Descombes is referring to Sartre's "Hegel, Husserl, Heidegger," in *Being and Nothingness*, 315–39.

CHAPTER 2

1. Eksteins, *Rites of Spring*, chaps. 3–5.

2. On humanitarianism and its failures in WWI, see Becker, *Oubliés de la grande guerre*, 229–317. On the memory of the war, see Sherman, *Construction of Memory;* and Becker, *Oubliés de la grande guerre*, 359–70.

3. Eksteins, *Rites of Spring*, 223.

4. On the image of the wounded in and after WWI, with occasional considerations on the impact of these men on the contemporary human condition, see the remarkable work by Delaporte, *Gueules cassées*. On the reconstruction of gender roles and masculinity, see Roberts, *Civilization Without Sexes*.

5. Audoin-Rouzeau and Becker, *14–18*, 170.

6. For example, the spectacle of the February 6, 1934, riots, with right-wing leagues besieging the Chamber of Deputies after the Stavisky and Chiappe affairs (not to mention the Daladier government's lack of power and eventual fall), gave the impression that "France is at the gates of civil war." Winock, *Le Siècle des intellectuels*, 244. See also Paxton, *Vichy France*, 243–49.

7. Arbousse-Bastide, *Pour un humanisme nouveau*.

8. Arbousse-Bastide, *Pour un humanisme nouveau*, 18.

9. Maritain, *Le Docteur angélique*, 85–86. I would like to thank Samuel Moyn for pointing out this reference to me. Maritain in Arbousse-Bastide, *Pour un humanisme nouveau*, 224.

10. Furet, *Passing of an Illusion*, 212–13, and chap. 7 in general.

11. Rabinbach, "Legacies of Antifascism," 4–5, 8–9.

12. On the roots of twentieth-century French socialism in Marxism, see Judt, *Marxism and the French Left*, chap. 1, 25, 144ff. Michel Winock argues that the Proudhonian and anarchist tendencies in French socialism were appropriated by the nonconformist personalists at *Esprit*. See Winock, *Histoire politique de la revue 'Esprit' 1930–1950*, 98–101. For revolutionary syndicalism and nonconformism, see Sternhell, *Neither Right nor Left*, 16.

13. It is not by accident that the PCF's daily newspaper was called *L'Humanité*.

14. Zhdanov et al., *Problems of Soviet Literature*. Boterbloem, *Life and Times of Andrei Zhdanov*, 115–16. Rubenstein, *Tangled Loyalties*, 130–33.

15. Marx "On the Jewish Question," in *Marx-Engels Reader*, 26–52.

16. See, again, Furet, *Passing of an Illusion*, 210–13; and Caute, *Fellow-Travellers*, 146. Jackson, *Popular Front in France*, 259. See also Judt, *Marxism and the French Left*, 138–46. Caute, *Fellow-Travellers*, 223.

17. Jackson, *Popular Front in France*, 66–67. Useful discussions of *la main tendue*, its context, and Catholic responses to it, can be found in Murphy, *Communists and Catholics in France, 1936–1939*; Hellman, "French 'Left-Catholics' and Communism in the 1930s," 507–23.

18. Success on this front was limited; see Jackson, *Popular Front in France*, 241–48.

19. Jay, *Marxism and Totality*, 277. Rabinbach, "Legacies of Antifascism," 4ff.

20. On Gide and Rolland, see Caute, *Fellow-Travellers*, 101–6, 134–45. On Rolland's significance in French Communism, see Ory, *La Belle Illusion*, 188. For Gide, also see his *Retour de l'URSS*.

21. The deaths of Kyo and Katov make the reference more explicit. See Pascal, *Pensées*, 165: "Imagine a number of men in chains, all under sentence of death, some of whom are each day butchered in the sight of the others; those remaining see their own condition in that of their fellows, and looking at each other with grief and despair, await their turn. This is an image of the human condition." Todd, *Malraux*, 170–74. Chanussot and Travi, *Dits et écrits d'André Malraux*, 118–20. As Chanussot and Travi show, Meyerhold and Eisenstein are by no means the only directors to have eventually abandoned attempts to turn the book into a script. In an ironic aside, success in adapting *La Condition humaine* into a theatrical production came in 1955 to none other than Thierry Maulnier, who (as we shall see) during the 1930s was an anti-Semitic, radical fascist critic of fascism and who wrote for *Action Française* and small fascist journals even during the occupation. Maulnier explicitly recalled his past in the program for the play, all but apologizing to his audience for this production of an ostensibly left-wing play. The production received bad reviews. Malraux supported it, which should not be too surprising politically—following his wartime shift to Gaullism, he wrote in 1946 that *écrivains maudits* (writers who had participated in the politics of the Right and were accused of intellectual collaboration) should not be marginalized. See also Maulnier, "*La Condition Humaine* au théâtre." For Maulnier in the late 1930s and early 1940s, see Carroll, *French Literary Fascism,* chap. 9. See also Sternhell, *Neither Right nor Left,* chap. 7, passim.

22. On the interplay between hope and the end of man in Malraux, see Blanchot, *Work of Fire*, 210.

23. Malraux, "L'œuvre d'art n'est pas une pierre," in *André Malraux*, 286. Cited in Hollier, *Absent Without Leave*, 148.

24. My citation here retains only the passages of Gisors's thoughts on Kyo and his relationship to others.

25. For example, in Maritain, and also in Nizan (ALP 306). See also Merleau-Ponty, "Man, the Hero," in *Sense and Non-Sense*, 184.

26. Note, for example, the failure of the party leadership to understand the significance of the revolt in Shanghai in "Part III" of the novel, as well as König's scoff at Kyo's defense of human dignity, his identification of Communist humanism as something that would not, and did not, include him (König). Caute has a lot of trouble considering Malraux a fellow traveler; his account from the perspective furnished by the question of the fellow travelers is informative (Caute, *Fellow-Travellers*, 189–92), echoes many of my suggestions here.

27. *Literaturnaya Gazeta/Le journal littéraire* (June 12, 1934); (ALP 305). Also cited in Lyotard, *Signed, Malraux*, 164. Nizan also argues for a parallel between the two works in his "Les enfants de la lumière," 107–8 (ALP 263). Regarding his respect for Heidegger's thought: Nizan had been the editor of *Bifur*, where Henri Corbin's translation of "What Is Metaphysics?" appeared. Merleau-Ponty notes Nizan's admiration for Heidegger's philosophy in *Signs*, 26. See also Hollier, "1931, June: Plenty of Nothing," in *New History of French Literature*, 895. Mark Poster notes that Nizan's critique of bourgeois humanism could also be seen as following from surrealist or existentialist positions. While Martin Jay correctly argues that this aspect should not be overestimated, it is true that Nizan's attack on humanism does parallel his interest in Heidegger, and that the critical dimension of *The Watchdogs* is run through and through with protoexistentialist themes. See Jay, *Marxism and Totality*, 278 n7.

28. Nizan's evocation of *homo faber/artifex/noumenon/phenomenon* may well be a reference to Brunschvicg, whose *Le Progrès de la conscience dans la philosophie occidentale* makes occasional use of these terms throughout (for example, xiii–xvii, 728ff). Nizan also attacks Brunschvicg in WD 92.

29. WD 9–10. Nizan's manifesto at times appears to fall into the trap of contenting itself with ad hominem accusations against contemporary philosophers (of which there are plenty in the book, above all against Brunschvicg, Bergson, and Boutroux, against the popularizer of a detached ethos Julien Benda, but also against younger figures like Gabriel Marcel or Jean Wahl [WD 40–42]). For Nizan's intellectual duel with Benda, see Schalk, *Spectrum of Political Engagement*, 49–51. Nizan also attacked Alain, in more or less the same terms, in his review of the latter's *Propos pour l'education* in *L'Humanité* (December 30, 1932), 4 (ALP 164–66).

30. Gary Gutting notes the echo of this exact rejection by Catholics, notably Gabriel Marcel. See Gutting, *French Philosophy*, 104.

31. See Teroni and Klein, *Pour la défense de la culture.*

32. Ory, *La Belle illusion*, 189–90. For the organization of the Congress, see Rubenstein, *Tangled Loyalties*, 141–46.

33. Nord, "Catholic Culture in Interwar France," 4, 9. Hughes, *Obstructed Path*, 67.

34. Sternhell, *Les Anti-lumières*, chaps. 2, 5. Regarding the warming of the Catholic Church during the late nineteenth century (under Leo XIII) to philosophical education for the purposes of attracting young philosophers to Catholicism, and on its implications for the French context, see Fabiani, *Les Philosophes de la république*, 150–51.

35. Paxton, "France," in *Catholics, the State*, 68–69.

36. Nord, "Catholic Culture in Interwar France," 3. See, for example, de Lubac, *Catholicisme*, 305–51.

37. In the riots of February 1934, the Action Française reached at once the last high peak of its influence and the loss of its capacity to embody the French version of the "fascist temptation" (which it had in some ways spawned), a loss that rendered its monarchism obsolete—its Catholicism having already been undermined by the Papal interdiction. On the Action Française, see Prévotat, *Les Catholiques et l'Action française*; and Eugen Weber, *Action Française*.

38. Quoted without citation by Blanchot in "On Nietzsche's Side," in *Work of Fire*, 289.

39. Nord, "Catholic Culture in Interwar France," 9. See, for example, Masure, *L'Humanisme Chrétien*.

40. De Lubac, *Catholicisme*, 353. Among de Lubac's works, see especially his *Corpus Mysticum*. Regarding de Lubac's influence on Ernst Kantorowicz, see Pranger, "Politics and Finitude," in *Political Theologies*, 115.

41. It should be noted that the position that Western humanism, even at its most anthropocentric, depends heavily on elements it plucked out of, or inherited from, Christian thought is a widespread argument among thinkers of Catholicism's political theology—from Carl Schmitt to Jean-Luc Nancy. For an account of early Christian humanism (during the Renaissance) and its relationship to civic humanism, see Gillespie, *Theological Origins of Modernity*, 73-77.

42. This attention on Maritain's behalf should be read in conjunction with Max Weber's influential reading of Calvinism's distancing of God from Man—influential not least because the claim was repeated in France until *at least* Maurice Merleau-Ponty's 1955 *Adventures of the Dialectic* (Merleau-Ponty, *Les Aventures de la dialectique*, 24).

43. On the effects of Jansenism with regard to God's influence and role in the City of Man, see Gauchet, *Disenchantment of the World*, 51–57; Bell, *Cult of the Nation in France*, 17, 28.

44. See, in this regard, the attempt to "remake the Renaissance" as announced by *Esprit* in its opening issue. Cited in Loubet del Bayle, *Les Non-conformistes des années trente*, 266. The theme of returning to the Middle Ages in order to proceed anew and in a better fashion was typical of many writers, including Berdyaev. See Henri de Lubac's discussion of Nicolai Berdyaev's call for a "new" Middle Ages in *Drama of Atheist Humanism*, 72.

45. In 1945, Alexandre Koyré would treat "the revival of Catholic philosophy" as central to the transformation of "even the 'climate' of philosophy," and he would mention Fessard first among such figures as Henri De Lubac, Maurice Blondel, and Gabriel Marcel with regard to this revival. Koyré, "Present Trends in French Philosophical Thought," 530–31.

46. See the short intellectual biography of Fessard by Sales, "Gaston Fessard," in *Hegel, le Christianisme et l'histoire*, 17–21.

47. Fessard presented his interpretation of Hegel in Kojève's concluding seminar; see Fessard, *Hegel, le christianisme et l'histoire*, 261–68.

48. For an explicitly personalist approach, sympathetic to certain theoretical aspects of Marx (and even more to arguments of Proudhon, see Berdyaev, "Personne Humaine et Marxisme," in *Le Communisme et les chrétiens*, 178–202. Berdyaev repeats the central charge: Marxism may perhaps be interpreted "in a humanist fashion," but it is fatalistic and erases the human spirit [193]).

49. Fessard, *France, prends garde de perdre ton âme!* (also known as *Témoignage Chrétien* 1 [November 1941]). Noting its significance, Robert Paxton writes also, "The major point is that no Catholic authority in France or in Rome gave public support to *Témoignage Chrétien's* protest against Vichy's own anti-Semitic measures." Paxton, "France," 84. After the liberation, Fessard's tract was seen as founding Catholicism's participation in the *résistance*. Nevertheless, that Fessard was respected does not mean he remained uncontroversial; his later writings are often filled with strong if polite objections against Catholic thinkers critical of his Paulinianism, his conception of Hegel as providing a powerful philosophical basis for Catholic thought, or his attempt to provide an adequate Catholic response to Marxism (without this making him a supporter liberation theology). See his *De l'actualité historique* (2 vols.); for his defense of a "dialectic of pagan and Jew," see 1:53–55, 1:215–29. See his copies of Schmitt's *Nationalsozialismus und Völkerrecht; Das Begriff des Politischen;* and *Staat, Bewegung, Volk,* in Archives Jésuites de Vanves, Fonds Gaston Fessard, 77.

50. Galatians 3:27–29, Revised Standard Edition.

51. See the reading of Fessard by Hellman in "French 'Left-Catholics' and Communism in the 1930s," 523.

52. Nizan, *Pour une nouvelle culture*, 259.

53. June 1937 reviews of Gaston Fessard, *Pax nostra* (1936) and *La Main tendue?* (1937), in BNF, Fonds Kojève 8, Comptes Rendus III; published in Hesbois, Le Livre et la Mort, 152–60, and, in modified form, in DKH 131–36. Kojève wrote to Fessard about reviewing his books on June 21, 1937. Fessard responded to Kojève (at once humorously and seriously) that this review in turn left him (Fessard) open to his Catholic critics: "Je vous avais dit de ne point craindre de m'opposer très carrément votre position négatrice. . . . Vous l'avez fait; je vous en suis très reconnaissant. Même vos petites pointes sur mon «orthodoxie»—puisque mes livres sont publiées avec l'imprimatur—ou le conservatisme de tout ce qui s'intitule «chrétien» tel le régime autrichien, m'ont bien amusé! Je prévois le jour où mes adversaires «Catholiques» reprendront vôtres phrases sur l'imprudence qu'il y a à se servir pour la réparation d'une chose d'un outil qui a été forgé pour la détruire! C'est de bonne guerre." Fessard to Kojève, August 11, 1937, included in BNF Mss. Occ., Fonds Kojève, boite 20.

54. The antiparliamentary position greatly accentuates their proximity to fascism, insofar as from the viewpoint of committed antifascists and liberals, such a proximity, with its frequent connections to fascist organizations and its later collaborationist consequences, could not be underplayed or mistaken.

55. See Winock, *Histoire politique de la revue 'Esprit,'* 81. For the Nietzsche with Marx motif, see Lindenberg, *Les Années souterraines,* 86–94.

56. Brasillach is cited as seeking to "retrouver l'homme" in LCr 246. On a reading of Marcel Déat with Alexis Carrel, see Lindenberg, *Les Années souterraines 1937–1947,* 166–94. On Drieu La Rochelle's conception of Europe, see Carroll, *French Literary Fascism,* chap. 5, esp. 136–42.

57. On Mounier's consideration of bourgeois man as dead, see Winock, *Histoire politique de la revue 'Esprit,'* 13–23.

58. Loubet del Bayle, *Les Non-conformistes des années trente,* part II:1, chap. 5, esp. 248–53. Loubet del Bayle, *Les non-conformistes des années trente,* 292.

59. It is important to emphasize that though nonconformism ultimately fed into a far-right ideology, its difference with respect to the Action Française conception of man and the threats man faced was substantial; their frames of reference to the past and to past conceptions of man also differ. See, by comparison, Maurras, "L'Homme," in *Oeuvres capitales II,* 159–70.

60. Merleau-Ponty, *Sense and Non-Sense,* 106.

61. I borrow the term from Sternhell's *Neither Right nor Left* and from Carroll's *French Literary Fascism.*

62. See Sternhell, *Neither Right nor Left,* esp. 141, and 187–96. See the positive Catholic reactions to Communism, as described for example by Hellman in "French 'Left-Catholics' and Communism in the 1930s," 510.

63. Loubet del Bayle, *Les non-conformistes des années trente,* 338–39. Mounier continued to preach a kind of left-wing Catholic personalism after the war, though its political implications changed from the pre-WWII ones. See Judt, *Past Imperfect,* passim.

64. Winock, *Histoire politique de la revue 'Esprit,'* 84–85, 103.

65. Sternhell, *Neither Right nor Left,* 215–21, 288–91, 376–80. It is very important to note here that personalism as a movement and a philosophy cannot be tied to the politics of Mounier or the fascisant tendencies of some of its proponents, and this discussion should not be taken to endorse that approach. As noted already, its principal anthropological innovation in Catholic thought, that is, the emphasis on the "person," influenced many contemporaries, including de Lubac, Maritain, and Fessard—but also Marcel, Blondel, Berdyaev, and others.

66. See Hellman, *Emmanuel Mounier,* 24–50ff.; Winock, *Histoire politique de la revue 'Esprit,'* 37–39, 43–52; and Amato, *Mounier and Maritain.*

67. Major articles on humanism by Mounier are "Notre humanisme"; and "Fin de l'homme bourgeois."

68. Winock, *Histoire politique de la revue 'Esprit,'* 101.

69. Italics mine. Winock writes of Mounier's lack of a political compass in Winock, *Histoire politique de la revue 'Esprit,'* 84. Sternhell's reading of Mounier is far more critical, suggesting a complicity (intentional or not) with fascism. Sternhell, *Neither Right nor Left*, 290–91.

70. The book was published simultaneously in French and English. Regarding the acclaim that *Man the Unknown* received, see Jean Paulhan's cautious response to Roger Caillois's review which denounced the book as a "shocking mediocrity" and a "vapid display of elementary knowledge" that was popular only due to "incompetence or self-interest" of readers. Caillois's review and a description of Paulhan's comments can be found in Caillois, *Edge of Surrealism*, 107–9. In the United States, where Carrel was a frequent subject of newspapers and periodicals such as *Time* or *The New York Times*, criticisms were largely restricted to the academic realm; see Carlson's review of *Man the Unknown, 677–78.* See also Reggiani, *God's Eugenicist.*

71. Carrel was heavily influenced by contemporary eugenic theories, which were quite widespread. As is well known, by 1936 several European countries, and many U.S. states, had adopted far-reaching eugenicist laws (see, for example, Michaud, *Cult of Art in Nazi Germany*, 125–26). It was the heavily nationalist and especially the racial emphasis of the Nazi eugenics that delegitimized programs in other countries (which were directed principally toward criminals and the mentally ill). Pichot's reference to Carrl as 'un grande humaniste' is in his *La Société pure de Darwin à Hitler*, 29.

72. André Pichot argues against granting too much significance to Carrel in French eugenicism (and suggests that most of his ideas were in the mainstream of contemporary thought in his *La Société pure*, 8–11).

73. Pichot, *La Société pure de Darwin à Hitler*, 10.

74. Remarkably enough, until recently Carrel went largely unnoticed in most histories of France in the mid-1930s. Pascal Ory in *La Belle illusion* and Julian Jackson in *The Popular Front in France* do not even mention him. Ory presents science in the 1930s largely in traditional terms of progress and lack thereof.

75. Nancy, *L'Oubli de la philosophie*, 26, 35.

76. "During the 1930s, if you were a young person with literary ambitions, . . . you read both *L'Humanité* . . . and the *Action Française*, for the book reviews. . . . Even Walter Benjamin read the *Action Française*." Kaplan, *Collaborator*, 11.

77. See, for example, a well-known article by Mauriac, "Un écrivain devant les soviets," 1; see also Noth, "Struggle for Gide's Soul," 12–20.

78. Sternhell and others have emphasized the applicability of the "les extrêmes se touchent" link between the radical Left and the radical Right; for Sternhell, the turn of a large number of left-wing nonconformists toward an antimaterialist, au-

thoritarian revolutionary nationalism formed the basis for a radical theoretical fascism that would ideologically sustain and radicalize the "National Revolution." Sternhell, *Neither Right nor Left*, 15–19ff.

79. Sunil Khilnani calls this a "negative consensus." See Khilnani, *Arguing Revolution*, 21.

CHAPTER 3

1. Compare the passage on Neoplatonism and Christianity (ILH 257) with the critique of Paul (ILH 262–23).

2. See the text in *Critique*, on "Hegel, Marx et le christianisme," 339–66, which, coming in the very opening issues of Bataille's new journal, established Kojève's fame as a "Marxist" reader of Hegel. See also Kojève's 1937 review of Fessard's books *Pax nostra. Examen de conscience international* (1936) and *La Main tendue? Le dialogue catholique-communiste est-il possible?* (1937), in BNF, Fonds Kojève 8, Comptes Rendus III (1937–39); published in modified form, in DKH 131–36.

3. See Nietzsche, "Anti-Christ," in *Twilight of the Idols*, 166–69, 173–75. The proximity of Kojève's reading of Jesus to Nietzsche's own reading is noteworthy. See also the fragment cited by Taubes in *Political Theology of Paul*, 80–81.

4. See Solovyov, *Lectures on Godmanhood*; *Lectures on Divine Humanity*. For the influence of German thought in midcentury Russia, see Berlin, *Russian Thinkers*.

5. The standard biography of Kojève is by Auffret, *Alexandre Kojève*. See also the intellectual biography by Filoni, *Kojève prima di Kojève*, and the useful biographical synthesis in Kleinberg, *Generation Existential*, chap. 2.

6. It is often noted that Jean-Paul Sartre may well have been in attendance. The list of attendees, published by Roth in *Knowing and History*, 225–27, is decidedly incomplete. One should add also the participants in the College of Sociology where Kojève lectured on "Hegelian Concepts" (participants to this talk included Claude Levi-Strauss, Michel Leiris, Roger Caillois, and other regulars of the Collège, and, interestingly, Walter Benjamin).

7. Kojève attacks Hegel's "dialectical metaphysics and philosophy of nature" as "visibly unacceptable" in lectures from 1934–35 (ILH 486n). In the very same note, he rejects Hegel's ontology as a consequence of this unscientific philosophy of nature. Elsewhere, he writes that Division I of *Being and Time* moved Hegel's anthropology in the *Phenomenology of Spirit* toward an ontology, while Division II (which never appeared) could be expected to replace the "faulty [fausse] ontology" of Hegel's *Logic* (*RP* V [1935–36], 416). Even more importantly, Kojève calls Hegel's ontology a "grandiose and complete failure" in his "Note sur Hegel et Heidegger" (1935), *Rue Descartes* 7 (1993), 38. In both of these texts, Kojève explicitly espouses Heidegger's "dualist ontology" as opposed to Hegel's. That this point was influential is testified to by Hyppolite, *Figures de la pensée philosophique*,

1:240; and by Descombes, *Le Même et l'autre*, citing from Scott-Fox and Harding's translation as *Modern French Philosophy*, 34–35. See also Wahl, "A propos de l'introduction," 77–100, and esp. 86–87, 97–99.

8. Heidegger, *Hegel's Phenomenology of Spirit*.

9. Also, Kojève makes no distinction between the Terror in the French Revolution and radical transformative violence in general, indeed seeing the first as exemplary of the latter.

10. Stoekl, "Round Dusk: Kojève at 'The End.'" Stoekl goes on to cite a remarkable passage from the *Introduction à la lecture de Hegel*: "The negativity that made the arrival of the end possible will, in retrospect, be judged moral, no matter how it seemed at the time. And since Man himself is defined as temporality and negation (IRH 160), even the bloodiest violence or the grossest injustice, if necessary for the eventual completion, will be (or will have been) good. The true moral judgments are those borne by the State (moral=legal); States themselves are judged by universal history. But for these judgments to have a meaning, History must be completed. And Napoleon and Hegel end history. That is why Hegel can judge States and individuals. The 'good' is everything that has made possible Hegel, in other words the formation of the universal Napoleonic Empire (it is 1807!) which is 'understood' by Hegel (in and through the *Phenomenology*). What is good is what exists, the extent that it exists. All action, since it negates existing givens, is thus bad: a sin. But sin can be pardoned. How? Through its success. Success absolves crime, because success—is a new reality that *exists*. But how to judge success? For that, History has to be completed. Then one can see what is maintained in existence: definitive reality" (ILH, 95).

11. Judt, *Past Imperfect*, 77.

12. See Merleau-Ponty, *Humanism and Terror*.

13. Glucksmann, *Les Maîtres penseurs*. See Aron's famous discussion of how "Kojève fascinated an audience of superintellectuals inclined toward doubt or criticism" (Aron, *Memoirs*, 65–66). Vincent Descombes describes Kojève as a master thinker, indeed as *the* master thinker of twentieth-century French thought in his *Modern French Philosophy*, 9–55. Descombes's essay is among the most consistent and useful interpretations of Kojève, though as it will be clear from my account, I think he tends to read Kojève through the lens of Sartre, interprets ontological dualism a bit too quickly as a "humanization of nothingness," and finally provides a reading of the origins of negation that could use some updating, given, for example, the publication of Kojève's *L'Athéisme*. There are exceptional convergences between Kojève and Sartre's thought, especially between Kojève's utilization of man as pure negation, and Sartre's recognition of nothingness in the human and his crafting of the for-itself. But the humanization of nothingness *could* be said to occur in Sartre, whereas in Kojève the gesture is different—toward a "nothingization" or erasure of the human.

14. Comparisons can be made to notes taken by Georges Bataille during years two and five, and by Denyse Harari in year four. These are kept in BNF, Fonds Bataille, 8B and 13D; they can also be compared to Kojève's scripted lectures, to be found in Fonds Kojève 10–11. Many thanks to Marco Filoni for identifying for me Harary as the author of the anonymous notes in Bataille's archive. See Kojève's letters to Strauss and his "Tyranny and Wisdom" in Strauss, *On Tyranny*. Raymond Aron would later often say that Kojève *always* lectured without notes—which is unlikely given the gigantic volume of his notes. Cf. Kleinberg, *Generation Existential*, 68. With the exception of the final year of his course, 1938–39, where his lectures numbered to twelve, Kojève always gave more than twenty lectures (twenty-one the first year, twenty-two the second, twenty-four the third, twenty-six the fourth, and twenty-five the fifth). Kojève numbered the pages of his lecture notes, including in this count the translations he worked off. Though notes from the first four years are relatively scarce, the translation survives in full, and the final page numbers in each of these years indicate a total of more than 2,682 pages of notes 11. Ethan Kleinberg exemplifies the victims of this myth when he writes that he will assume Kojève's Marxism and "not discuss it except when made explicit by Kojève." Kleinberg, *Generation Existential*, 71–72.

15. Jarczyk and Labarrière, *De Kojève à Hegel.*

16. Allan Bloom's "Preface" to the English translation of (parts of) the *Introduction à la lecture de Hegel* is the classic elegiac text on Kojève. Fukuyama's references in *The End of History and the Last Man* are also uncritical (Fukuyama, *End of History and the Last Man*, for example, 66–67). Laurent Bibard's editing, translation, and introduction to *L'Athéisme* in French which not only interprets this 1930 text on the basis of Kojève's 1950s attempt to "update" Hegel's System, but betrays the author's ignorance of Heidegger (for example, in his note to p. 123) whose centrality in that text is endlessly underscored and would probably be even more marked in a proper translation. Finally the prominence of the Auffret biography, which is quite informative but often appears unsubstantiated and is not very adept to philosophical questions, can also be explained on these premises.

17. See the back cover to Jarczyk and Labarrière, *De Kojève à Hegel.* This situation is changing a bit, but a serious discussion of Kojève's role in modern thought, as well as of persistent philosophical tropes in Kojève's own thought, is still to come. See the useful intellectual biography by Filoni, *Kojève prima di Kojève.* See also the first serious attempt to treat Kojève's philosophical anthropology, by Pirotte, *Alexandre Kojève, un système anthropologique.* Richard Rorty dismisses Kojève altogether: "Derrida asks: 'Who can deny that the neo-Marxist and para-Heideggerian reading of the *Phenomenology of Spirit* by Kojève is interesting?' I can. Kojève's book on Hegel is, as Derrida charmingly admits, written 'in that profoundly offhand, nutty and pataphysician manner which is, to be sure, his genius, but which is also his entire responsibility[. . . .] Kojève's offhand nuttiness gets

tiresome pretty quickly" (Rorty, *Philosophy and Social Hope*, 218; citations from Derrida, *Specters of Marx*, 71–72). Robert Pippin also laments the value usually attributed to Kojève: "It is commonplace among those who admire Kojève to grumble about the 'Hegel scholars' who just don't get it when they criticize Kojève's eccentric reading, don't see that Kojève was no mere 'professor' and was after world historical goals not limited by textual fidelity. But Kojève was a child of his own time, too. . . . Kojève's embodiment of such a finite *Geist* clearly limits and diminishes his work, particularly because it so limits what he can see in Hegel. . . . That strain of Hegelianism that produced both 'scientific' revolutionaries and existentialist heroes has now, it is safe to say, played itself out. Its limitations are clear and its limited and painful historical results also clear. And the great dangers (particularly political dangers) of that strain in Hegel that produced both a reactionary attack on politics itself and a kind of radical historical fatalism are also manifest." Pippin, *Idealism as Modernism*, 260. See also Derrida's discussion of Kojève (far more ambiguous than Rorty allows) in *Specters of Marx*, 14–15, 61–62, 70–74.

18. It is important to note here that Kojève's emphasis on the given is very far from Jean-Luc Marion's concept of givenness. Marion does not appear to have been informed by it (and in any case could not have known of Kojève's *L'Athéisme* because the latter was only published in 1998. See Marion, *Being Given;* and Marion, *Reduction and Givenness*.

19. Ontological dualism, Kojève indicates repeatedly in *L'Athéisme* and other texts from the 1930s (like the "Note on Hegel and Heidegger" of 1936), is not the same as what had long been approached as "metaphysical dualism" Heidegger had recently disparaged in *Being and Time*—notably in the Platonic opposition of Forms to matter, or the Cartesian distinction of extension from thought. Indeed, Kojève's writing is largely unopposed to Hegel's metaphysical monism or to Heidegger's critiques of Descartes and Neo-Kantianism, all the while rejecting Hegel's *ontological* monism as a disaster. I will return later to Kojève's consideration of metaphysical problems (such as homogeneity).

20. If we are to believe Kojève's own later statement, he had not understood "a word of" the *Phenomenology of Spirit* until he started preparing for the course (and therefore *L'Athéisme* would not be seriously influenced by Hegel). *La Quinzaine littéraire* (July 1–15, 1968), 19. However, Kojève was notoriously unreliable as a narrator of his own life; how literally this statement should be taken is unclear. The connection of Negation to Hegel's own concept of determinate negation is largely accepted in the French context, notably by Hyppolite in *Figures de la pensée philosophique*, 1:239.

21. It is not clear whether this rendition is the responsibility of Kojève or his translator. But it is also unclear that the translator of *L'Athéisme* knows Heidegger. For example, he completely misses the Heideggerian undertones in page 123. Thus, the rendition of *Dasein* as "Homme" and Being-in-the-World as "Homme-

dans-le-Monde"—or, differently put, the approach to these renditions—is potentially misleading. This could be taken also as a critique of Heidegger's distinction of presentness-at-hand [*Vorhandenheit*] and readiness-to-hand [*Zuhandenheit*]. On the one hand, it emphasizes the readiness-to-hand of everything in the world (even one's own body); on the other, it questions whether something can ever really be ready at hand, in the sense of being recognized as an object independent of its utility or relation to man's usage of it.

22. This is a central problem of Kojève's interaction with Strauss, and a major complaint from Strauss regarding Kojève's approach to his work. Kojève writes to Strauss that were Strauss correct on his interpretation of nature, then Strauss would be correct in general. But of course, the implication is, his (Strauss's) dependence on Plato for a theory of nature is both antiquated and misdirected. Kojève refuses any notion of human nature to Strauss. See Strauss et al., *On Tyranny*, 261–62.

23. See Kojève, "Note sur Hegel et Heidegger," 37–39. Here, see also, "[Le] donné est une espèce de l'interaction: or celle-ci exprime, réalise, et suppose comme sa condition, l'homogénéité des modes d'être des membres qui interagissent" (AT 118).

24. Kojève, "L'Idée de la mort dans la philosophie de Hegel," ILH 532; IDPH 30–31. See also Wahl's reading of Kojève: "Il n'y a pas une essence immuable de l'homme; l'homme n'est pas le représentant d'une espèce qui serait déterminée dans son essence," in Wahl, "A propos de l'introduction à la phénoménologie de Hegel par Alexandre Kojève," 99.

25. Judith Butler also describes this by noting that Kojève's "extension" of "Hegel's doctrine of negation" relies on his "rejecting the premise of ontological harmony." See Butler, *Subjects of Desire*, 63.

26. On this point, see also Dastur, *Heidegger et la question anthropologique*, 35–36.

27. On this point, I am in agreement with Judith Butler's statement that "Kojève's subject is an essentially intentional structure." See Butler, *Subjects of Desire*, 67.

28. Apropos of Heidegger's problematization of philosophical anthropology, Françoise Dastur writes: "(Pour) Heidegger, la difficulté fondamentale en (anthropologie philosophique) ne consiste pas dans l'obtention d'une unité systématique des déterminations de l'homme, mais réside dans le concept même d'«anthropologie philosophique», qui demeure foncièrement ambigu. Car ce terme d'anthropologie philosophique peut signifier la recherche de ce qui constitue de matière spécifique l'être de l'homme par contraste avec celui des autres types d'étants, mais elle n'est alors qu'une ontologie régionale parmi d'autres et ne peut donc à ce titre prétendre constituer le centre de la philosophie. Il peut aussi signifier une recherche qui se fonde sur la reconnaissance de l'homme com-

me étant absolument premier et certain, selon la définition cartésienne, ce qui implique alors la centration de la philosophie sur la subjectivité humaine" (Dastur, *Heidegger et la question anthropologique*, 42). This discussion, to which I will return to in Chapter 5, is helpful here: as I have argued, the latter definition is not applicable to Kojève because of his emphasis on ontological dualism as the core problem of contemporary philosophy. Kojève appears to be closer to the former definition ("la recherche de ce qui constitue de matière spécifique l'être de l'homme par contraste avec celui des autres types d'étants"), but implicitly rejects Heidegger's critique that this philosophical anthropology concerns a regional ontology by rejecting the possibility of (and even the significance of Heidegger's argument as lying in) ontological monism—and by implication, rejects Heidegger's second point, the idea that this philosophical anthropology claims to be the center of philosophy.

29. This theme is not just characteristic of Kojève's work, nor is it just a Hegelianism "without reserve." The addition of Non-Being to Being is characteristic of, for example, Levinas's *De l'evasion*, where he asserts, "against Parmenides, that Non-Being is." Levinas, *On Escape*, 71. Sartre's "néant" also relates closely to Kojève's own thought. See also Butler, *Subjects of Desire*, 66–67.

30. To accentuate Kojève's difference from other readers of Hegel, suffice it to note that Jean Hyppolite repeatedly objected to identifying *man* (or the self) with *negation* and instead argued that man (or the self) is produced in the clash between negation and Being, in their proximity and distance. Hyppolite, *Figures de la pensée philosophique*, 1:236; see also his essay "Situation de l'homme dans la phenomenologie de l'Esprit" in the same volume.

31. Kojève later said in an interview that until Koyré gave his lectures on Hegel in 1932 and he himself started working on the Hegel course in 1933, he did not understand the *Phenomenology of Spirit* at all. As I have suggested already, Kojève's statements of this order need to be taken with a grain of salt. Nonetheless, in *L'Athéisme* Hegel appears in very ambivalent terms (AT 212 n7), as does Feuerbach (AT 182); in a course on Russian philosophy of religion (and Solovyov) that Kojève drafted for the EPHE before giving his course on Hegel, there are no notes on Hegel—which is significant, insofar as Solovyov is sometimes read as an interpreter and adapter of Hegel and Nietzsche, and also given that in these lectures Kojève discusses wisdom elaborately (see Fonds Kojève 10, Dossier "Philosophie Religieuse en Russie"). The same must be said of the writings on science from the 1920s. In all the essays and works prior to 1933, Hegel appears no more than do the remnants of Neo-Kantianism Kojève carried with him from his early studies.

32. "Et ce devenir révélateur signifie que la Totalité implique la réalité *humaine* qui n'est pas un *donné* éternellement identique à elle-même, mais un acte d'autocréation progressive temporelle" (IDPH 30; trans. modified).

33. "L'Homme de Hegel . . . est le Néant (Nichts) qui anéantit l'Être-donné existant en tant que Monde, et qui néantit lui-même (en tant que temps histo-rique réel ou Histoire) dans et par cet anéantissement du donné" (trans. modified, from IDPH 70).

34. Kojève, "Note sur Hegel et Heidegger," 38. Kojève also announces his de-sire to update Hegel and show his "real" aims and significance in a letter to Tran Duc Thao of 1946, published in DKH 64.

35. Like the basic claim to ontological dualism, this betrays Kojève's attempt to join contemporary mathematics and science (here his interest in set theory) with Heideggerian ontology. See his *Zum Problem einer Diskreten "Welt,"* in Fonds Ko-jève 9.

36. BNF, Fonds Bataille, 13–D, 49 (Bataille's notes).

37. ILH 110, 146, 148–49. This is the crux of Fukuyama's interpretation of Ko-jève; see *End of History and the Last Man*, 206–7, 288–89.

38. In part IV of *The Claim of Reason*, Stanley Cavell gives a somewhat dif-ferent reading of universal satisfaction (explicitly à propos of Hegel) at the end of history, by pointing out that were such a civilization of the end to come, then "(its members) would not be dissatisfied. They would have lost the concept of sat-isfaction." The advent of such a civilization might also mean, Cavell notes, the "vanishing of the human" (Cavell, *Claim of Reason*, 468). I think Kojève's argu-ment about universal satisfaction at the end of history could and perhaps should be presented this way, instead of in terms provided by Kojève's exchange with Leo Strauss and the latter's unwillingness to acknowledge the possibility of universal satisfaction.

39. Here, the parallel to the Frankfurt School (in whose *Zeitschrift* Kojève pub-lished repeatedly). On the one hand, Theodor Adorno also read Hegel with Hus-serl, though he did so mostly to find the Hegel in Husserl and largely as a critique of Husserl's "idealism," rather than in order to read Hegel through Husserl. See Adorno, *Hegel*, for example, 139. On the other hand, Walter Benjamin wrote to Max Horkheimer, praising Kojève's clarity and reading of the *Phenomenology of Spirit* (he heard him speak at the Collège de Sociologie), but he also rejected Ko-jève's interpretation of dialectics as too idealist. See Benjamin, *Gesammelte Briefe*, 5:621.

40. "Pour Hegel pas de diff. essentielle à l'intérieur de l'être, / donc pierre _ chien _ homme: homogénéité " BNF Mss. Occ., Fonds Bataille, 13–D, 79.

41. For Kojève's attention to the struggle for recognition, see the following: "The Idea of Death in Hegel's Phenomenology" (the last two lectures of I:1933–34, ILH 529–74; IDPH); "Note sur le panthéisme hégélien" (planned as lecture XVII of II:1934–35, reworked for a publication of "The Idea of Death in Hegel's Phenomenology" and perhaps given as a lecture in the later part of the third lec-ture series (1935–36), see Fonds Kojève 11, dossier "Note sur le panthéisme hégé-

lien"; lectures of May 28 and June 4, 1934 (perhaps a somewhat different version of "Note sur le panthéisme hégélien," given in its place; see BNF, Fonds Bataille, 13–D, 85–94). See also the text published in early 1939 in *Mésures* and reused as "En guise d'introduction" (ILH 9–34); and several lectures from year two, specifically concerned with the Master/Slave state of consciousness, including the lectures on phenomenology and the dialectic of the real in ILH 445–527.

42. BNF Mss. Occ., Fonds Kojève, boite 4, "Carnets sur la science." De Man, *L'Idée socialiste.*

43. June 1937 reviews of Gaston Fessard, *Pax nostra. Examen de conscience international* (1936) and *La Main tendue? Le dialogue catholique-communiste est-il possible?* (1937), in BNF, Fonds Kojève 8, Comptes Rendus III (1937–39); published in Hesbois, Le Livre et la Mort, 152–60, and, in modified form, in Jarczyk and Labarrière, *De Kojève à Hegel*, 131–36. See the bulletin announcing a lecture by Kojève in BNF, Fonds Kojève 13, "Colonialisme dans une perspective européenne." The lecture, given at the invitation of Carl Schmitt, is published in *Commentaire* 87 (1999), 557–65, and as "Kolonialismus in europäischer Sicht," in *Schmittiana*, 126–40.

44. Of course, "rationalism" is a very different issue to Hegel's approach of Reason. Kojève's critique of rationalism concerns specifically Brunschvicg's neo-criticism, as I discussed it in the opening section of Part One—the conception of rational determination as capable of mapping and correctly understanding the world. As he criticized Brunschvicg's perception of science (Alexandre Kojève, review of J. Perrin et al., *L'Orientation actuelle des sciences*, in BNF Mss. Occ., Fonds Kojève, boite 9, published under Alexandre Koyré's name in *Revue philosophique* (1932: 9–10), 315–18; again, the drafts in Kojève's archive are harsher than the final product), Kojève was clearly interested in objecting to this human capacity to control this Reason, and thus could emphasize the Hegelian interpretation and approach without accepting that the culmination of Spirit involves the triumph of Reason.

45. BNF, Fonds Bataille, 13–D, "Hegel notes de cours," 19 (notes by Denyse Harary, February 19, 1937).

46. See his conclusion regarding Bayle's *Dictionnaire*: "La Raison, qui domine la vie de l'intellectuel, tend—en principe—vers une *vérité* universellement valable, c'est-à-dire communicable et démontrable, se rapportant aux choses de ce monde. Mais, en fait, la Raison détruit toutes les vérités proposées, en mettant en évidence les contradictions qu'elles impliquent. Aussi, le citoyen de la « République des lettres » doit-il se contenter d'une participation au progrès indéfini d'un mouvement intellectuel collectif, allant vers un but commun, mais inconnu et jamais atteint. Le croyant, par contre, se trouve en possession d'une Foi qui lui donne la certitude absolue d'avoir atteint—*hic et nunc*—la vérité définitive se rapportant à

la seule chose qui l'intéresse véritablement—à son *salut* strictement personnel."
Kojevnikoff, "La critique de la religion au 17e siècle," 70.

47. Kojève had read Franz Rosenzweig's *Hegel und der Staat* in preparation for
the first course on Hegel (his preparatory reading list, dated August 15, 1933, is in
BNF, Fonds Kojève 10, chemise *Premièrs cours sur Hegel*). Also, Kojève may have
met (and, more likely, read) Benjamin and Adorno, the first during Benjamin's
long stay in Paris (where Benjamin attended Kojève's lecture at the College of Sociology), and because of their common friendship with Bataille, the latter through
Kojève's reviews in the *Zeitschrift für Sozialforschung*. Biographers have not linked
Kojève with either of Adorno or Benjamin. If for Rosenzweig and other contemporary Hegelians (Benedetto Croce, for example), the History of Spirit is the coming to maturity of Reason, the arrival of Reason to such a point as to unveil and reveal the truth of humanity, its knowledge etc., as Reason, this is not the case with
AK, in whose thinking there is little to be said about Reason either in the end of
History or in the general path from anthropogenesis with the struggle for recognition through Napoleon and the end of history. Kojève's use of "totalitarian" is
significant, insofar as the term, which was used in Italy, had no currency in France
and really became broadly used only after WWII, notably with Arendt's *Origins of
Totalitarianism*. On the origins of the term "totalitarianism," see Rabinbach, "Totalitarianism Revisited," 77–84, esp. 78.

48. To locate these works in Fessard's oeuvre, see the short intellectual biography of Fessard by Sales, "Gaston Fessard," in *Hegel, le Christianisme et l'histoire*,
17–21.

49. "L'homme de la raison cesse de diviniser les terribles dans la nature. La réalité extérieure cesse d'être divine, *cesse d'être autonome*." BNF, Fonds Bataille, 13–
D, 59 (from the lectures of 1937–38).

50. In this regard, Fukuyama's concluding note on Kojève, namely that History would "vindicate its own rationality" is not quite right. There is nothing rational about the end of history. Fukuyama, *End of History and the Last Man*, 339.

51. BNF, Fonds Bataille, 13–D, 111 (dated January 6, 1939).

52. Aron is well analysed in Kleinberg, *Generation Existential*, 87–94. It seems
to me that Kleinberg still underestimates Kojève's influence on Aron when he sees
the latter as deviating from the former, and particularly when he describes a "two-
tiered" model of history in Aron, on the one hand "natural," hence adhering to
scientific laws, on the other "human," hence based on action and choice. I would
argue that this follows Kojève's ontological dualism almost to the letter—though
neither Aron nor Kojève saw a genuine history playing itself out in the natural
realm.

53. For example, Butler presents work as historical action and later considers the philosophical thinker as the paradigmatic abstract creator in Kojève's
thought. These examples fall within the range suggested here, but do not indicate

its breadth and hence are not by themselves sufficient elaborations of what constitutes *action* in Kojève's thought. See Butler, *Subjects of Desire*, 68, 70.

54. Most commentators on Kojève's work interpret his idea of action as committed to Marx's 11th thesis on Feuerbach and therefore identify his concept of "Action" with revolutionary action. I have shown here and in the previous chapter that for Kojève it suffices to introduce a *Befindlichkeit* (existential disposition) into an imaginary "pure nature" in order for negation to take place, in order to allow for an observation of this "pure nature" to take place, and hence (according to the reading of Heisenberg and the opposition of negation to *givenness* in *L'Athéisme*) for interpretation and (material) action. Kojève extends this position in some of the texts usually interpreted as favoring violence, particularly in the "Idea of Death in Hegel's Philosophy" (ILH 542), where he emphasizes that the radical assumption of finitude involves revolutionary action—and indicates a certain support for or even a justification of the Russian revolution. See Hollier, *Le Collège de Sociologie*, 61–70. Kojève gradually came to emphasize the more active and aggressive of these aspects. Nevertheless, revolutionary action does not by itself satisfy the ontological definition of action. Even when he criticizes the contemplative dimension of existence, Kojève suggests over and over that Discourse is *the descriptive side* of negativity qua action. Moreover, Kojève repeatedly translates "action" as "realization" or "self-realization" (ILH 91), as a way of actualizing oneself and one's thought and Discourse. In ontological terms, Kojève resolutely identifies action and negation in the sense fully that follows from his exposition in *L'Athéisme*. The discussion of man in ILH 504–26 is also extremely important, at once because it clearly defines man as negating action, distinguishing him from nature and the animal, and also because it completely sidesteps the reduction of action to "material," "real," or revolutionary action.

55. See Hegel, *Three Essays 1793–95*. Regarding a different problem: the influence of Nietzsche on Kojève should not be underestimated, as it invariably has been. Kojève refers to Nietzsche in his description of Jesus' instauration of Christianity, in particular his human life of works and death as a God and death as death of God. "Vous voyez, c'est un texte tout à fair nietzschéen. Dieu est *mort*, et c'est le *Christ* qui assure à l'homme cette (*verité*)." BNF, Fonds Kojève 10, "Cours sur Hegel" 1937–38, lecture XX, 13 [E 399].) The conception of Jesus as a Overman overturning pagan morals in favor of humanity's radical self-conception *as superhuman*, and the rejection of Paul as a philosopher remoralizing the forceful example of Jesus marks the most emphatic evocation of and reference to Nietzsche. Kojève's Nietzsche has many things in common with Marc Crépon's image of Nietzsche (though Crépon does not cite or evoke Kojève) in "La Communauté en souffrance," in *Le Malin genie des langues*, 51–70.

56. Zouboff, "Introduction," to Solovyev, *Lectures on Godmanhood*, 7, 51, 53.

57. Solovyev, *Lectures on Godmanhood*, 205ff. Solovyov was himself much influenced by German idealism and Hegel, whom he occasionally references. In his

discussion of Solovyov, Kojève repeatedly brings up points in common between the two.

58. On Solovyov and the Russian avant-garde of the early 1920s, see Groys, *Total Art of Stalinism*, 18–19, 27. Kojève does not explicitly retrieve such a call in his exaimination of Solovyov's writings and reads him specifically as a religious philosopher. Koschewnikoff, "Die religiöse Philosophie Wladimir Solowjews"; "Die Geschichtsphilosophie Wladimir Solowjeffs"; and "La Métaphysique réligeuse de Vladimir Solovyov."

59. ILH 256; see also BNF Mss. Occ., Fonds Bataille 13–D, 62.

60. "Hegel prend à la lettre le mythe chrétien du Dieu—unique—qui en devenant homme, *meurt* en tant que Dieu."

61. "La dure parole" is clearly an ironic reference to the Jesuit reference to "la parole heureuse," the promise of Salvation brought by Christ. Kojève had Jesuit students—most prominent among them Gaston Fessard.

62. By discussing theology in these terms, Kojève opens up a confrontation with Feuerbach, designed as much to follow the latter's suggestion regarding the relationship between theology and anthropology as to condemn and reject the project it fits in and the philosophical ground it emerged from. It is important here to note Kojève's hostility to reading Hegel through Feuerbach, surpassed perhaps only by his hostility to reading Hegel through Marx. As is well known, Feuerbach's central contribution to Young Hegelianism was his inversion of theology into anthropology, his claim that theology was but displaced and idealized anthropology (expressed, notably, in the famous opening exhortation in the *Principles of the Philosophy of the Future*: "The task of the modern era was the realization and humanization of God—the transformation and dissolution of theology into anthropology." Feuerbach, *Principles of the Philosophy of the Future*, 5). Kojève, for his part, repeatedly hinted that Feuerbach was wrong to emphasize sensualist materialism as the anthropological consequence of this inversion. He also historicized the inversion and specifically disengaged it from the progressivist claim that some sort of utopia could be expected to follow from it. Third, without leaving any traces of having reread Feuerbach during his course (the list of secondary readings he compiled in 1933 includes a number of old Hegelians, Rosenzweig, and Marcuse, but neither Marx nor Feuerbach), Kojève apparently claimed to reach a highly similar argument, presumably independently. For Feuerbach, see the excellent treatment in Löwith, *From Hegel to Nietzsche*, 71–83, 310–13, 335–42.

63. In his first surviving letter to Kojève, Carl Schmitt noted that this position would transform "die ganze bisherige Philosophie" in the same breath that he announced his opposition to atheist readings of Hegel. See Tomissen, "Der Briefwechsel Kojève-Schmitt," 101.

64. It is remarkable that Kojève finds Hegel's atheism in precisely the same passage that others (including the later Hegel himself) see evidence of Hegel's

identification of Spirit and Christian Spirit, and which they therefore utilize to advance the argument that Hegel was a Christian philosopher.

65. "L'homme à compris que la *résurrection* du Dieu sous forme divine, dont parle la *théologie* chrétienne, n'est qu'un (reste) du Paganisme" (HRP XX.3 [E.389]).

66. Nancy, *La Déclosion*, 57, 206, 213ff.

67. "Nous (savons) en effet . . . que pour Hegel le Christianisme n'est pas une Religion entre autres, mais *la* Religion (étroite/droite), en ce sens qu'il s'agit là d'une Religion évanouissante, en voie de disparaître. . . . (Le) Christianisme est l'évanouissement des Religions, de toutes les Religions, de *la* Religion en tant que *telle,* du thème de la foi en un Dieu . . . en général." Words in brackets are approximations of terms that are difficult to read.

68. Kojève also adopts this attitude of standing above both camps, Catholic and Communist, and shoving the two sides as different versions of each other in a 1946 review of Gaston Fessard's *France, prends garde de perdre ta liberté*, 195.

69. A good example of reductive approaches can be found in Giorgio Agamben's references to Kojève. In *The Open*, 5–12, Agamben uses Kojève specifically to contrast men to animals, which makes perfectly good sense in the context of his own project of tracing the contours of the difference between human and animal, but most of his readings are little effect in the context of Kojève's own argument.

70. Indeed, Kojève in 1933–34 suggests that men at the end of history are human only because of the universal homogeneous State (ILH 506). Judith Butler's description of Kojève's end of history clearly centers on this early part of the argument insofar as it emphasizes the end of history as an anthropogenetic instance, a ground for an anthropocentric posthistorical existence (Butler, *Subjects of Desire*, 64–65, 68ff.). Kojève's later arguments share none of the "optimism" indicated and argued for here.

71. Adorno, "Jargon of Authenticity," in *Can One Live After Auschwitz?*, 181.

72. Kojève wrote a first version of the *Système du Savoir* (System of knowledge) in 1940. See BNF, Fonds Kojève, 14; published in Hesbois, *Le Concept, le temps et le discours*. After this first version, Kojève wrote an as-yet-unpublished 900-page manuscript in Russian, titled "Sofia Philo-Sofia i Fenomeno-logia" ("Wisdom, Philosophy and Phenomenology"-BNF, Fonds Kojève 12). Postwar drafts of the (never-completed) *Système du Savoir* are also included in *Le Concept, le temps et le discours*.

73. Au moment où l'idéal est *réalisé*, le dualisme disparaît et avec lui la Réligion et le Théisme. Or l'idéal se réalise dans et par l'Action négatrice révolutionnaire (ILH 213).

74. See ILH 215, where Kojève explains, in these terms, the negation of representations of man in transcendental space.

75. This is a central premise of Maurice Blanchot's treatment of freedom in "Literature and the Right to Death," (in *Work of Fire*, 302, 318–20); noted also in Allan Stoekl's introduction to Blanchot's *Most High*, xiv–xvii.

76. "Hegel . . . identifie l'Espace et le *Sein*, l'Être-statique-donné, ce qui est banal et très cartésien. Par contre, l'identification du Temps et du Selbst (Moi-personnel), c'est-à-dire de l'Homme est nouvelle."

77. The affinity of Kojève's argument on the end of Time with Heidegger's conception of the *Ereignis* (appropriation, advent) is usefully explored in Agamben, *Homo Sacer*, 59–61.

78. See the extension of this argument, which clearly evokes the terms of Kojève's discussions of quanta and Heidegger that I have already presented in Chapter 2, in ILH 433.

79. Fonds Kojève 11, dossier "Note sur le panthéisme hégélien," 2.

80. See also Judith Butler's analysis of Kojève on Time in Butler, *Subjects of Desire*, 72.

81. Wahl, *Etudes kierkegaardiennes*. See the treatment of the threat of a giant totality extinguishing individuality, a theme central to existentialism and, in many ways, even to postexistentialist French thought, in the following secondary sources: Hyppolite, *Figures de la pensée philosophique*, 1:233; Roth, *Knowing and History*, chap. 4, also 2–3, 189; Baugh, *French Hegel*—throughout, given his emphasis on the Unhappy Consciousness; Jay, *Marxism and Totality*, chap. 9.

82. This letter originally appeared as an addendum to Bataille's *Guilty*. It is reprinted in *The Bataille Reader*, 296.

83. Jean Hyppolite interprets Kojève's effort to systematize the phenomenology as the attempt to solve an enigma that has been forced on him (see Hyppolite, *Figures de la pensée philosophique*, 1:237). Hyppolite's figure of an enigma, together with the existential implications of the "struggle for recognition," as well as with Georges Bataille's heavily Kojève-influenced *Summa Atheologica* (the triad of his wartime books *Inner Experience, Guilty*, and *On Nietzsche*), which form some of the most significant modern efforts following in the tradition of spiritual exercises, seems to support my suggestion that Kojève's systematic reading of Hegel's *Phenomenology of Spirit* was itself heavily invested in operating as such a spiritual exercise for its readers.

84. According to Raymond Queneau, Lacan consciously imitated Kojève's seminar on Hegel in setting up his own famous seminars on Freud. See Queneau, *Journaux 1914–1965*, 852.

85. Descombes, *Modern French Philosophy*, 11.

86. Judith Butler also suggests that while "Kojève's reading of Hegel is clearly influenced by the early Marx's recapitulation of Hegelian views of action and work," Kojève diverges from Marx in several crucial ways. To these ways I would add the lack of any support for Marx's understanding of alienation, which she still sees as part of his argument (Butler, *Subjects of Desire*, 64). Butler eventually suggests that Kojève's political philosophy amounts to a "brand of democratic Marxism" (Butler, *Subjects of Desire*, 68).

87. See also Fonds Kojève 12, Dossier "Bayle et Fontenelle," 6.

88. "Autonomie et dépendance de la conscience de soi," in *Mesures* (January 14, 1939), republished as "En guise d'introduction," in ILH 3–30.

89. Kojève, *Outline*, 135n17.

90. See his review of "Archives d'Histoire des Sciences et Techniques [Archiv istorii nauki i techniki], Académie des Sciences de l'URSS. Travaux de l'Institut d'Histoire des Sciences et des Techniques," 1ère série, vols. V and VI, in *Thalès* X (1935), 237–53. In another review, of Bernhard Bavink's *Ergebnisse und Probleme der Naturwissenschaften*, where he criticizes Bavink's claim to belong "body and soul" to National Socialism, Kojève appears to argue in favor of the independence of science from political motivation. See Kojevnikoff, "La Philosophie des sciences de M. B. Bavink," 234–35.

91. BNF, Fonds Kojève 13, Dossier "Colonialisme dans une perspective européenne," 4; translated as Kojève, "Colonialism from a European Perspective," 117–18 (trans. amended). Kojève's 1957 critique of Khrushchev can be found in Queneau, *Journaux 1914–1965*, 965.

92. Merleau-Ponty's distance from Kojève would be often significant. See his letter of March 19, 1950, written to Bataille or Eric Weil and included in Kojève's correspondence files (Fonds Kojève 20, "Merleau-Ponty"), in which Merleau-Ponty rejected Kojève's "Tyranny and Wisdom" as submitted to *Les Temps modernes*. In Chapter 5, I will try to show that Merleau-Ponty's theory of history differed considerably from Kojève's, and Merleau-Ponty even made fun of the "end of history." Also see for this Bien, "Intellectual and Action" 139.

93. It is interesting to see the force of the interpretation of Heisenberg persist not only in Kojève's discussion with others, but even in anecdotes relating to Kojève and told by former students. In a curious 1949 note in his journal, Raymond Queneau writes that during a lunch with Jean Piel (executive editor of *Critique* and an economist) Piel brought up his interest in Kojève's thought and ideas. Queneau writes: "Emporté, j'invente la suivante: dans les sciences sociales joue le principe d'Heisenberg. Si Marx n'avait pas fait *savoir* sa théorie, si Lénine n'avait pas tenté de l'appliquer, tout se serait passé comme prévu. Mais la connaissance active de Marx impliquait 'réaction', conscience, etc. et c'est là toute la dialectique du marxisme. Ce qui rend inexact, ou plutôt réduit au rang polémique, le livre de Collinet. Piel a l'air frappé." It is not surprising, but indeed symptomatic that Queneau would choose Heisenberg to play this strange joke on Piel. Queneau, *Journaux 1914–1965*, 669.

94. The labor of linking an anthropological reading with a Marxist one is carried out in Hyppolite, "Conclusion: Logic and Existence," in *Logic and Existence*. Hyppolite explicitly refers to Kojève's interpretation as anthropological and tries to explain this identification in his 1957 "La 'Phénoménologie' de Hegel et la pen-

sée française contemporaine," in *Figures de la pensée philosophique*, 1:241, and also 1:238–40. Derrida, "The Ends of Man," in *Margins of Philosophy*, 117. Descombes, *Modern French Philosophy*, 27. Kleinberg, *Generation Existential*, 83. DKH 29.

CHAPTER 4

1. Hollier sees the sheer desire or aim of escape as a foundation of the College of Sociology: "The College of Sociology cast its lot against life that would be exclusively quotidian. It was imperative to escape." Hollier, *Absent Without Leave*, 122.

2. Levinas specifically targets Marxism, in Levinas, "Reflections on the Philosophy of Hitlerism," 66–67.

3. This position was sheared by Bataille; see my "An Anthropology of Exit," 3–24.

4. See the review of *L'Imagination*, 398–99.

5. Sartre makes a few comments regarding Heidegger's discussion of *the world* (TE 58/75), but it is difficult to judge what these comments indicate regarding his understanding of Heidegger in the mid-1930s. Sartre's later comments suggest that his fluency came in the later 1930s, even during his time as a prisoner of war. See Cohen-Solal, *Sartre*, 141.

6. Levinas, *Difficult Freedom*, 44.

7. Jean-Paul Sartre, "Une idée fondamentale de la phenomenologie de Husserl: l'intentionnalité," 31–32. Names included in the parenthesis also include those mentioned by Sylvie Le Bon in her footnote to Sartre, *La Transcendance de l'ego*, 14 n2. Sartre, *La Transcendance de l'Ego*, 14–16, but see also 84–86 where the solipsist charge is made clearer.

8. Hollier, "When Existentialism Was not yet a Humanism," in *Absent Without Leave*, 149.

9. Hollier, "When Existentialism Was not yet a Humanism," 155.

10. André Masson, letter of July 8, 1935, in *Les Années surrealists* (Paris: Manufacture, 1990), 270; cited in PL 1037.

11. A distinction that, by the way, antedates considerably the 1950s texts on sovereignty that Jean-Luc Nancy discusses by a long period and does not fully completely parallel his definitions and approach in "The Inoperative Community." See Nancy, *Inoperative Community*, 21–23, especially for evocations of late passages of *Inner Experience* and 1950s texts from *Sovereignty* (in English in *The Accursed Share*, vols. 2–3). Nancy more or less agrees on the difference between the pre- and postwar texts in his *La Communauté affrontée*, 32.

12. The project of the Collège and of Bataille's involvement in it are very important in terms of the late 1930s rethinking of the relation between the human and the religious; for reasons of space—and also because I would have to read it in

relation to contemporary social anthropology and broader contemporary efforts in the human sciences and history—I cannot discuss them here, but see Hollier, *Le Collège de sociologie, 1937–1939*.

13. The boys' choir contrasts radically to Bataille's description of a broadcasting of a boys' choir singing mass in 1933: that is "maddeningly beautiful," showing a "superhuman force" emerging from these children's attempts to grasp Christian transcendence. See J.-F. Louette, "Notice," in PL.

14. I elaborate on Bataille's parallel of Nazism to Heidegger's thought, and to the context of his philosophical writing, in "An Anthropology of Exit."

15. Letter to Michel Leiris (April 1935), in Bataille, *Choix de lettres 1917–65*, 105.

16. The standard readings of *The Blue of Noon* and its politics are: Stoekl, *Politics, Writing, Mutilation*, chap. 1; Hollier, "Bataille's Tomb," in *Absent Without Leave*, 53–60; and the important introduction to *The Blue of Noon* in the Pleiade edition, which suggests that the clarity of the "blue of noon" is what the handsome Nazi officer Troppmann sees in the street exhibits. The present section may also be read as a corrective to recent depictions of Bataille's relation to fascism, for example, in Wolin, *The Seduction of Unreason;* or Frost, *Sex Drives*; and also Giorgio Agamben's interpretation of Bataille with regard to themes like animality, sovereignty, and bare life, in his *Homo Sacer*, 61–62, 112–13; and *The Open*, 5–8.

17. It is also worth noting that, according to Jean-François Louette, in his "Notice" for the recent Pleiade edition of Bataille's novels, the "Introduction" comes from Bataille's very first novel, *W.C.*, which does not survive—and thus occupies a different place here than do the two parts of *The Blue of Noon*. See PL 1041.

18. See the analysis in Hollier, "Bataille's Tomb," in *Absent Without Leave*, 53–60. For Hollier, the Don Juan theme is central to the novel.

19. See the opening section of Bataille, "The Pineal Eye," in *Visions of Excess*, esp. 82. Bataille, "Le Labyrinthe," 366; translated as "The Labyrinth," in *Visions of Excess*, 173. For Bataille on Meyerson, see "Lorsque M. Meyerson," in *OC* II:167–69.

20. See PL 222; and, in altered form, IE 79.

21. See PL 221 and IE 78.

22. Dirty, Xenie, and Lazare are identified with the Commander in BN 44, 68, 75, respectively.

23. For the link between Levinas and Blanchot's "second night," see Levinas, "The Poet's Vision," in *Proper Names*, 133.

24. The suggestion that the S.A. officer's untroubled eyes may represent "the blue of noon" is made by J.-F. Louette in PL 1060.

25. Bataille, "Le Labyrinthe," 365; "The Labyrinth," in *Visions of Excess*, 172. The same passage is repeated in *Inner Experience*, 81–82.

26. Heidegger, "On the Essence of Ground," in *Pathmarks*, 120.

27. See my "Anthropology of Exit," esp. 17.

28. This approach closely recalls Heidegger's use of the *mine* in certain sections of Division II of *Being and Time*.

29. Jean-Luc Nancy and Giorgio Agamben both consider Bataille's treatment of sovereignty, but their arguments concern his later work, notably the discussion of the instant etc. in *Sovereignty: Accursed Share 3*. See Nancy, "Inoperative Community"; and Agamben, *Homo Sacer*, 61–62.

30. Philippians II:7, where Paul says Christ "ekenōse eauton," "emptied (voided, evacuated) himself." The *Oxford English Dictionary* points to W. H. Mill in 1844 as introducing the term to dogmatics in English.

31. See Bataille, *On Nietzsche*; and "Letter to Blank, Instructor of a Class on Hegel," in *Guilty*, 123–25.

32. See BNF Mss. Occ., Fonds Bataille 13–D, 88. The interest in Schmitt was widespread among Kojève's students and certainly predates Kojève's implicit engagement with him in the famous *Mesures* article on Hegel's Master/Slave relation and his postwar correspondence with him. Gaston Fessard, to name just one of them, owned 1930s copies of Schmitt's *Concept of the Political* and *Nationalsozialismus und Völkerrecht* and studied them extensively. For Rousseau and Schmitt, see Guénoun, "Théorie de l'assemblée pure," in *L'Enlèvement de la politique*, esp. the opening of the book. Regarding Agamben's treatment of Bataille in the context of bare life, my treatment here suggests a conception of interiority that resists the terms of "bare life" and an opposition to the legalistic reduction or reinterpretation of ontology. Where Troppmann could have been a nice case for an argument on bare life, he is, unmistakably, its disavowal.

33. Mill, "On Liberty," in *Utilitarianism*, 135 and elsewhere.

34. The application of Jeffrey Herf's term is inexact but nonetheless useful. See Herf, *Reactionary Modernism*.

35. Levinas, "Reflections on the Philosophy of Hitlerism," 64–71.

36. Levinas, "Reflections on the Philosophy of Hitlerism," 63.

37. Levinas, "Reflections on the Philosophy of Hitlerism," 71, 67. Also cited by Jacques Rolland in E 29–30.

38. The expression "the harmonizing ideal of *being-human*" is from de Vries, *Minimal Theologies*, 380.

39. See, for example, his discussion of the remnants of idealism in Husserl, where Levinas echoes Sartre: "But above all, [in Husserl] the subject is maintained with a special dignity. *In no way is the subject involved with the reality it constitutes. It doesn't identify with its legacy or its work*" (Levinas, *Discovering Existence with Husserl*, 106).

40. Here Levinas could be said to expand from Heidegger's understanding of fundamental moods in BT §29, especially his comment that in particular moods, Being becomes manifest as a "burden" (173).

41. Thus Levinas considers and puts aside a number of possible kinds or movements of escape: (i) the philosophy (E 51) and mysticism (E 54) of Being (Heidegger); (ii) literary criticism (E 52); (iii) romantic aversion to "lowly realities" (E 53); (iv) escapism from the servitude imposed by the thereness of the body (E 53); (v) Bergson (E 54, 70); (vi) transcendental/religious solutions (E 51) and claims to the infinity of Being (E 69). Moreover, he rejects the possibility that escape would mean just (vii) a movement-toward, a gesture with a destination (E 53–54); (viii) nostalgia for death (E 54); (ix) a search for pleasure (E 62), with the peculiar relation to time that it enforces (E, part IV); (x) a dive into intimacy (E 65); (xi) creative activity and the imitation of "the Creator" (E 72); and finally, (xii) a freeing-oneself from time (E 71) or (xiv) a thinking of nothingness (E 70). Despite their character as formal indications of escape, these "applications" or "instances" are no more than indices of the existent's need to exit (its) being (E 53).

42. Bataille, *Guilty*, 89.

PART II: INTRODUCTION

1. Malraux, *L'Homme et la culture artistique*, in Bibliothèque Nationale (Site François Mittérand) Réserve des livres rares, RES P-R-845. In page 1, Malraux notes "Lecture improvised at the Sorbonne on November 4 1946, at the request of UNESCO."

2. Malraux, *L'Homme et la culture artistique*, 13–14.

3. See its publication in *Carrefour* (November 7, 1946). See also Malraux's interview with Albert Ollivier à propos of the talk in *Combat* (November 15, 1946); and "Is Europe Dead ?" in *The New Leader*, January 18, 1947, which includes a partial English translation of the talk.

4. Malraux, *L'Homme et la culture artistique*, 44.

5. Malraux, *L'Homme et la culture artistique*, 45–46.

6. Interpretations of the *Walnut Trees of Altenburg* differ on the hopefulness of that novel. Maurice Blanchot, reviewing Gaëtan Picon's book *André Malraux* writes: "Picon emphasizes that Malraux' last book, *The Walnut Trees of Altenburg*, makes one hear a hymn to life and marks a stubborn assertion in favor of the victorious role of man." Blanchot adds, "It is true. We can even find a striking symbol of it." Yet he then proceeds to a remarkably ambiguous parallelization of Berger, the protagonist of the *Walnut Trees* to Chen, the famous terrorist of *Man's Fate*, finally writing that Berger's secret is "the impossibility of living" and illustrating this secret through the following quote from Malraux: "Bloodshed is strong enough to decompose the state of distraction that allows us to live." If this is a "hymn to life" or a "stubborn assertion in favor of the victorious role of man," then it is far from the one Malraux politically advocated ("Malraux has always chosen hope,

but he has also always chosen to go all the way to the end of hope"). See Blanchot, *Work of Fire*, 217.

7. To a degree, Malraux was also anticipating Louis Aragon's Communist critique that would follow his talk. Aragon's critique was so harsh and anti-German as to decry Karl Jaspers's participation in the *Rencontres internationales de Genève* and even insinuate that Jaspers was no different than a Nazi. André Pichot points out that in the early 1940s, Huxley saw eugenicism as an "integral part of the religion of the future." See Pichot, *La Société pure de Darwin à Hitler*, 9.

8. Malraux, *L'Homme et la culture artistique*, 14ff. See the report on and critique of Huxley's philosophy of UNESCO in Louis Aragon's talk that followed Huxley's and Malraux's in the same conference.

9. Michel, *Les Courants de la pensée de la résistance*, 618–19.

10. France Combattante, "Déclaration des droits de l'homme et du citoyen (étude du 14 Octobre 1943)," and André Philip, "Une nouvelle déclaration des droits de l'homme: extraits d'une conférence prononcée à New York, le 7 Novembre 1942," in Michel and Mirkine-Guetzévitsch, *Les Idées politiques et sociales de la résistance*, 283–86 and 278–79, respectively. Also *Ligue française des droits de l'homme*, Bulletin #1 (1944–45). For "literary evocations," see Albert Camus's claim that what has meaning is man—a crucial claim amidst his engagement with the absurd in *Lettres à un ami allemand*, 78–79.

11. Furet, *Passing of an Illusion*, 364.

12. The quote is from Hughes, *Obstructed Path*, 158. Historians frequently emphasize what Mark Poster calls a "longing for basic renewal, social, political, and intellectual." See Poster, *Existential Marxism in Postwar France*, 4. The best discussion of revolutionary hopes, in the maquis and beyond is in Jackson, *France: The Dark Years*, 541–43. See also Buton, *Les lendemains qui déchantent*, 56.

13. On the combination of *socialism*, European integration, and a *new democratic humanism emerging from the resistance,* see Lipgens, *Documents on the History of European Integration*, 1:333, 1:339–40, 1:347, 1:351–52ff. On De Gaulle's support for a new appreciation of "democracy," see Mazower, *Dark Continent*, 184.

14. See Gildea, *Marianne in Chains*, 364; Judt, *Past Imperfect*, chaps. 2–3; and Lévi-Valensi and Guérin, "Peut-on être humaniste dans la France des années cinquante?" particularly the discussion of Malraux.

15. Bataille, "Nietzsche est-il fasciste?" Bataille's goal in this text and statement is by no means to rehabilitate fascism, but to indicate its irreducibility. The ambiguities and struggles around the postwar purge of fascist writers, and the rather fast cooling-down of tempers, are notorious, and address to some degree intellectual perceptions of Bataille's point. See, for a very good discussion of this problem, Kaplan, *Collaborator*, 192–93, 195–97, 215–18.

16. Francis Ponge, republished in *Le Parti pris des choses*, 218.

17. Hughes, *Obstructed Path*, 154–55.

18. Bataille, unpublished review of Maurice Merleau-Ponty's *Humanism and Terror*, BNF Mss. Occ., Fonds Bataille 14N, 89–90). Merleau-Ponty himself shared this interpretation of the difference between the postwar present and the turn of the century; see, for example, his, "Man and Adversity," in *Signs*, 226.

19. Supporters of human rights often note this character. In a recent review of Jay M. Winter's *Dreams of Peace and Freedom*, Anthony Dworkin agrees with Winter in considering human rights as a "minor utopia": "The idea of human rights is an anti-utopian idea. It is a universal ideal which at the same time sets limits on what can be done in the name of universal ideals" (Dworkin, "Case for Minor Utopias," 45). Winter explicitly places human rights among his "minor utopias" and notes especially the emergence of human rights as a success of the French republican tradition at its darkest hour. Winter, *Dreams of Peace and Freedom*, 99–120. See also Mazower, *Dark Continent*, 197–99, 210.

20. For one classic critique, see Arendt, "The Decline of the Nation-State and the End of the Rights of Man," in *Origins of Totalitarianism*, 267–302.

21. The case for the significance of that declaration among the efforts of the Constituent Assembly is made by Gordon Wright in *Reshaping of French Democracy*, 134–42.

22. See notably the 1949 meeting with contributions by (among others) Karl Barth, Henri Lefebvre, J. B. S. Haldane, and Karl Jaspers, published as *Pour un nouvel humanisme*.

23. Some of the better known ones include "L'Humanisme aujourd'hui: Enquête de l'UNESCO" (proceedings published in *Comprendre* #15 [March 1956] and #16 [September 1956]); as well as the publications *Le Droit d'être un homme*, ed. Jeanne Hersch (Paris: UNESCO, 1968); and *L'Avenir de l'homme*. Institut International d'études Européennes "Antonio Rosmini."

24. Lévi-Valensi and Guérin, "Peut-on être humaniste dans la France des années cinquante?" 152–53.

25. The ambiguities of the intellectual engagement with Communism have been extensively discussed in Tony Judt's *Past Imperfect*, and elsewhere, and I will not address them in detail.

26. Rabinbach, "Communist Crimes and French Intellectuals," 64.

27. Koestler, *Darkness at Noon*. Kravchenko, *I Chose Freedom*. Rousset, *L'Univers concentrationnaire*; and Rousset, *Les Jours de notre mort*. On Rousset, see Judt, *Past Imperfect*, 113–15, 173.

28. Regarding the languages of political criticism, see Khilnani, *Arguing Revolution*, 18–19ff.

29. Furet, *Passing of an Illusion*, 361–96.

30. Merleau-Ponty, "Autour du marxisme," translated as "Concerning Marxism," in SNS 102–3.

31. For the rising critiques of alternative humanisms, see the texts by Kanapa, *L'Existentialisme n'est pas un humanisme*, Garaudy, *Une littérature de fossoyeurs*. Cited in Lévi-Valensi and Guérin, "Peut-on être humaniste dans la France des années cinquante?" 162.

32. Judt, *Past Imperfect*, 75–76, 95–98.

33. On Sartre during World War II, see Judaken, *Jean-Paul Sartre and the Jewish Question*, chaps. 2–3.

34. Aronson, *Camus and Sartre*, 78.

35. The lecture appeared in book form in March 1946. On the political and intellectual stakes and argument of "Qu'est-ce que la littérature?" see Sunil Khilnani, *Arguing Revolution*, chap. 3. On its stakes and reception, see Hollier, "Must Literature Be Possible?" in *Absent Without Leave*.

36. For the longer engagement of existentialism and Marxism, see Poster, *Existential Marxism*, chap. 1, 4–7.

CHAPTER 5

1. See, for example, Michel Tournier's account cited later in this chapter, and Michel Foucault's later comment that the humanism expressed by *Les Temps modernes* is all he was trying to escape from. Cited in Eribon, *Michel Foucault*, 280.

2. For Merleau-Ponty's reference to *Nausea* as involving a new humanism, see Merleau-Ponty, *Parcours II*, 239. See also *Parcours deux*, 258, for his avowal of influence Sartre's quasi-phenomenological antihumanism on him.

3. Jean-Paul Sartre, "Un nouveau mystique," in *Situations I*, 165.

4. See the critique of solipsism in *Being and Nothingness*, 306–15.

5. "Quelque chose en (ce monde) a du sens et c'est l'homme." Camus, *Lettres à un ami allemand*, 78–79. On early philosophical differences between Camus and Sartre, see Ronald Aronson, *Camus and Sartre,* 12.

6. See the French edition: Jean-Paul Sartre, *L'Existentialisme est un humanisme*, 101, 103.

7. To address Communist and Catholic critiques was the explicit goal of "Existentialism Is a Humanism" (EH 287–28). See also Cohen-Solal, *Sartre*, 221.

8. See the presentation of Sartre as a last vestige of bourgeois ideology and a fascism in *Pravda*, January 23, 1947, cited with other Marxist attacks on him in Aron, "Sartre and the Marxist-Leninists," in *Marxism and the Existentialists*, 19. Cuvillier, *Les Infiltrations germaniques*. Henri Lefebvre wrote in 1946 that "the analyst does not find, in Heidegger's thought, Hitleric politics or racism; more profoundly and seriously, he finds Hitler's style, the style of the S.S." He disdainful-

ly responded to Heidegger's *Being-towards-Death*—the thought that man propels himself toward death and must live resolutely in anticipation of that "moment"— that man is the being that fights against death and its accomplices. See Lefebvre, *L'Existentialisme*, 217 and 255–56, respectively. See also p. 13 of that work. Kanapa, *L'Existentialisme n'est pas un humanisme*; see also Merleau-Ponty, as described by Hubert and Patricia Allen Dreyfus in *Sense and Non-Sense* (xix–xxii). And, perhaps most surprisingly, see Julien Benda in *Les Lettres françaises* (December 23, 1944) (cited in Janicaud, *Heidegger en France*, 1:110 n105). It is not insignificant that the Communist attack on Malraux (in fact by the same Garaudy and Kanapa) follows more or less the same terms and considerations—with the exception that it seeks to discredit Malraux as a Spenglerian (and Sartre as a Heideggerian). The Marxist critiques of Sartre are nicely described in Poster, *Existential Marxism*, 109–61.

9. Tournier, *Wind Spirit*, 132. My thanks to Giuseppe Bianco for this reference.

10. De Waelhens, "L'Existentialisme de Sartre est-il un humanisme?" 291–300. His claims that Sartre cheapens *Being and Nothingness* are harshest in 299.

11. De Waelhens, "L'Existentialisme de Sartre est-il un humanisme?" 299.

12. This is from the footnote to the first edition in 1946, modified by Kojève in the 1960s.

13. In 1962, Kojève wrote in his note for the second edition (which would only appear in 1968) that, as of 1946, he was not convinced the end of history *had* come and only became convinced of this later. Yet there is ample evidence that, even if he was ambivalent, he had long been quite open in arguing this end had come. See Bataille's 1938 "Letter to X (Lecturer on Hegel)," in *Bataille Reader*, 296.

14. For Blanchot's "Literature and the Right to Death," see chap. 6; see also Hollier, *Absent Without Leave*, 7.

15. The difference here between Bataille and Blanchot, on the one hand, and Roger Caillois on the other, is significant; Caillois's resuscitation of concepts concerning human nature and its "grandeur" stands far apart from the movement I am describing here. See Caillois, *Babel*.

16. To give but a couple more examples of the confusion regarding the status of humanism at the time, see the review of a publication of lectures of Jean Wahl's Collège philosophique in the journal *Critique*, where the (anonymous) author writes that the essential dimension of this publication "nous paraît tourner autour de la question de l'humanisme, du sens et de la possibilité meme de cet humanisme" (*Critique* 40 [1949]: 765).

17. Déat, *Pensée allemande et pensée*. For Brasillach, see Kaplan, *Collaborator*. See also Khilnani, *Arguing Revolution*, 38.

18. Ethan Kleinberg provides a lot of useful information on the network of soldiers and résistants—and on the ways contacts among Heidegger, Sartre, and Beaufret were established. See Kleinberg, *Generation Existential*, chap. 5.

19. Sartre, *Carnets de la drôle de guerre*, 226. Cohen-Solal, *Sartre*, 141. Sartre repeats the remark "barbaric" apropos of Heidegger in *Being and Nothingness*, 330. See also the discussion by Janicaud in *Heidegger en France*, 1:56–59.

20. Rovan, "Mon témoignage sur Heidegger," 2. Rovan's translations appeared as "Fragments sur le temps," trans. J. Rosenthal (pseudonym), *L'Arbalète* (summer–fall 1941): 33–48. Rovan would publish "La remontée au fondement de la métaphysique," *Fontaine* 63 (November 1947): 786–804, and the first translation of the "Letter on 'Humanism,'" *Fontaine* 58 (March 1947): 888–98, next to Beaufret's essay on Heidegger's notion of truth.

21. On Heidegger and Beaufret, see Rovan's *Mémoires d'un Français*, 183, 287.

22. In the 1930s Beaufret belonged to the Catholic if not the fascisant Right. He was a close friend of Marcel Jouhandeau, himself a radical nonconformist described by Zeev Sternhell as a "super-collaborationist" (Sternhell, *Neither Right nor Left*, xxv–xxvi). On Beaufret's 1943 concerns vis-à-vis Heidegger's Nazism, see Rovan, "Mon témoignage sur Heidegger," 2.

23. Beaufret worked for *Confluences* during its brief, postwar run.

24. Beaufret, *De l'existentialisme à Heidegger*, 10. Beaufret, *Entretiens*, 4. See Kleinberg, *Generation Existential*, 161.

25. On the existential and not just political influence of *Temoignage Chrétien*, see Rovan, *Mémoires*, 171. See Fessard's 1943 course on Hegel, Heidegger, and time. Archives Jésuites (Vanves), Fonds Fessard, 29G.

26. The 1945 course is published in Wahl, *Introduction à la pensée de Heidegger*.

27. Jean Wahl had already reprised Heidegger's 1929 course Einleitung in die Philosophie in 1938. At that point, Wahl opened with an explicit expression of his displeasure with Heidegger's public function in Nazi Germany (the 1933–34 rectorate), a function that politically tainted his philosophical call for "*inner Führerschaft*" through Being-toward-death. Working on Heidegger's 1928–29 course, Wahl told his students, would dispense with this more recent problem. IMEC, Fonds Wahl, Dossier Heidegger, Chemise "Heidegger," 6. See Heidegger's *Gesamtausgabe 27*; Wahl's 1945 reprisal is interesting especially for its distortions: Wahl, *Introduction à la pensée de Heidegger*, and see Janicaud, *Heidegger en France*, 1:96–98. Wahl wrote in late 1945 in *The New Republic* that Heidegger "in the early days of Nazism, prevented [Husserl] from entering the university buildings of Freiburg, because Husserl was a Jew." Wahl, "Existentialism: A Preface," 443.

28 Gaston Fessard, to whom "J. W." (Jean Wahl) lent a copy of the letter in August 1946), made several copies and perhaps distributed more of them. It is significant that Wahl had a copy of the letter, though it is unclear whether he received it from Heidegger, what he got from reading it (if he was convinced or more worried by it), and who, besides Fessard, he lent it to. See Archives Jésuites (Vanves), Fonds Fessard 33/1/1 (copies in 33/1/7). Heidegger's "Letter to the Rec-

tor of Freiburg University, November 4, 1945" is available in English translation in Wolin, *Heidegger Controversy*, 61–66.

29. See Wahl, *Vers la fin de l'ontologie;* where Wahl goes so far as to ask whether Heidegger's prized question of Being is not after all a *question mal posée.*

30. See Koyré's letter to Anne Heurgon-Desjardins, August 30, 1955: "Permettez moi de me prévaloir d'une amitié déjà fort ancienne et de mes liens, encore plus anciens, avec Pontigny, pour vous dire combien j'ai été peiné d'apprendre qu'un Nazi—je parle de M. Heidegger—a été invité et reçu à Cerisy." (Institut mémoires de l'édition contemporaine, Fonds Centre Culturel International de Cerisy, CRS 4.2.) Koyré, "L'Évolution philosophique de Martin Heidegger," *Critique* I (June 1946) : 73–83; *Critique* 2 (July 1946): 161–83. As Dominique Janicaud argues, a short earlier review, by Koyré, of Heidegger's *Vom Wesen der Wahrheit* in *Fontaine* (the review that published the "Letter on 'Humanism'") was yet more aggressive. This is *not* to say that Koyré's postwar relation to Heidegger was one of complete rejection: his 1948 review of the translation of this same text by Walter Biemel and Alphonse de Waelhens was generally positive, critical of certain terminological choices, and certainly engaged with the essay's argument (see *Critique* 23 [1948]: 377–78). Jean Beaufret's first notable essay on Heidegger's thought "Martin Heidegger et le problème de la vérité" (*Fontaine* 62–63 [November 1947]—published next to Rovan's translation of the "Letter on 'Humanism'") should be read as a response to Koyré's "L'Évolution philosophique de Martin Heidegger," particularly of Koyré's rejection of Heidegger's notion of truth.

31. See Kojève's March 1968 interview (posthumously published in *Quinzaine Litteraire* 18–20), where Kojève, asked why he no longer sought out philosophers, replied "Philosophers? who? . . . Heidegger? You know that Heidegger, as a philosopher, turned out really bad."

32. The classic generational division is a staple of interpretations of Heidegger's legacy in France. See Rockmore, *Heidegger and French Philosophy;* Ferry and Renaut, *Heidegger et les modernes;* and Ethan Kleinberg, *Generation Existential,* v, 17–18.

33. Koyré, "Present Trends of French Philosophical Thought," 533–34.

34. Gandillac and Towarnicki, "Deux documents sur Heidegger," 713–24. As Anson Rabinbach has noted, Sartre wrote the preface to the materials by Gandillac and Towarnicki in *Les Temps modernes* 4 (January 1946): 713; see Rabinbach, *In the Shadow of Catastrophe*, 119.

35. Löwith, "Les Implications politiques de la philosophie de l'existence chez Heidegger," 343–60. Translated as "The Political Implications of Heidegger's Existentialism," in Wolin, *Heidegger Controversy*, 167–85. It is important to note a point that goes somewhat against the overall thrust of my argument on the different generations of readers (without nevertheless supporting the classic interpreta-

tion of these generations), namely, that the translator of Löwith's text was none other than Joseph Rovan.

36. See the responses to Löwith: Weil, "Le Cas Heidegger," and Waelhens, "La Philosophie de Heidegger et le Nazisme"; and Löwith's own response: "Réponse à M. de Waelhens," 370–73, followed by Waelhens's own response (374–77). Beaufret's articles are reprinted in *De l'existentialisme à Heidegger*.

37. The list of known visitors is long: Fréderic de Towarnicki, the filmmaker Alain Resnais, Edgar Morin, Roger Munier, Maurice de Gandillac, in September 1946 Jean Beaufret himself, while Sartre and Beauvoir were also set to meet Heidegger in 1946 (though the meeting never came off). See Safranski, *Martin Heidegger*, 350. Beaufret, *Entretiens avec Fréderic de Towarnicki*, 7. See also Munier, *Stele Pour Heidegger*; Towarnicki, *À la rencontre de Heidegger*; Towarnicki, *Martin Heidegger*. Cf. Safranski, *Martin Heidegger*, 348–49. The letter to Sartre, written *after* Heidegger and Sartre missed an opportunity to meet at Baden-Baden, is curiously dated October 28, 1945 (the very date of Sartre's delivery of "Existentialism Is a Humanism"), and precedes by a few weeks the (far less enthusiastic) first letter to Beaufret. In it, Heidegger praises Sartre's thought and largely concurs with the latter's transformation of his terms.

38. Heidegger's first letter to Beaufret (November 23, 1945) can be found in Heidegger, *Lettre sur l'humanisme*, 180–85.

39. In the early 1950s, Heidegger apparently called Bataille "France's best thinking head" ("la meilleure tête pensante française"). But according to a 1962 letter by Bataille to Jerôme Lindon, Heidegger was mistaking him for Blanchot who was the actual target of the compliment. See Bataille, *Choix de letters 1917-1962*, 582-83. IMEC, Fonds Wahl, Dossier Heidegger, Chemise "Egon Vietta / texte M. Heidegger." Published in Fritz, *Ernst Barlach*.

40. A contrary reading is offered, for example, by Ferry and Renaut, *French Philosophy of the Sixties*, xxiv, xxvii. Dufrenne, *Pour l'homme*, 17–27.

41. This interpretation of thinking as "the engagement of Being" is crucial for Heidegger's peculiar reinterpretation, during the 1968 seminar at René Char's house at Le Thor, of Marx's famous eleventh of the Theses on Feuerbach. Heidegger, in that discussion, attempts to bridge theory (*Interpretation*) and *praxis* and to show that Marx's call to philosophers "to change the world" meant nothing if not to interpret the world more primordially, more authentically, as the participants in the seminar were doing. Heidegger, *Gesamtausgabe 15*, 352–53; recently translated as *Four Seminars*.

42. Regarding *An Introduction to Metaphysics*, see Derrida's *De l'esprit*, section VI, 75–76ff.; translated as *Of Spirit*, 47–48. Derrida emphasizes the continuity of the treatment of "animal rationale" in the *Introduction to Metaphysics* with that in the "Letter on 'Humanism'" (*De l'esprit*, 169 / *Of Spirit*, 103, 139 n6). Françoise Dastur correctly points out that, in the "Letter on 'Humanism,'" Heidegger's pre-

sentation of the "first humanism" shifts from Plato to Rome. See Dastur, *Heidegger et la question anthropologique,* 68.

43. Sartre's own responses to Heidegger were no less ambiguous. In his reports to acolytes like Jean Cau, Sartre expressed contempt for Heidegger, who "vomited commitment" (Towarnicki, *Martin Heidegger,* 94). By contrast, in a 1960 talk at the Ecole Normale Supérieure, Sartre expressed respect for Heidegger and for the criticisms in "Letter on 'Humanism'" (Janicaud, *Heidegger en France* 1, 183–84). For a philosophical analysis of Sartre's response to Heidegger, see Haar, *La Philosophie française entre phénoménologie et métaphysique,* 35–66.

44. Heidegger also wrote favorably of Communism vis-à-vis democracy elsewhere. See Heidegger, *Gesamtausgabe 69,* 188n and 208n (cited in Thomä, "Difficulty of Democracy," in *Nazi Germany and the Humanities,* 92).

45. See Wahl, in *Fontaine* (May 1946): 840. Cited in Janicaud, *Heidegger en France,* 1:115. The accusation of opportunism is in itself not that useful: if Heidegger was being opportunistic, he could have certainly done a better job of it— here, he all but bites the Sartrean hand that feeds him.

46. In his rereading of materialism as "concealed in the essence of technology" (LH 259), Heidegger opens a path that would be followed by Kostas Axelos, notably in his *Marx, penseur de la technique; Einführung in ein künftiges Denken;* and *Vers la pensée planétaire,* 1964.

47. Heidegger, *Being and Time,* 38.

48. This could be contrasted to Malraux's contemporary lecture discussed above (though it is very unlikely that Heidegger had any intimation of when he wrote the "Letter").

49. To quote Michael S. Roth, "Heideggerian antihumanism provided a framework of thinking for people who had abandoned the possibility of a politics that we can make meaningful." Roth, *Knowing and History,* 79.

50. Haar, *Heidegger and the Essence of Man,* 57 n1.

51. LH 263; the clarification is by the editor and translator of *Pathmarks.*

52. At that time, Jean Wahl also joked on this theme, writing that "Leibniz had said that monads have no windows. But for Heidegger, individuals have no windows because they are always essentially outdoors." Wahl, "Existentialism: A Preface," 442. Derrida's famous "mushroom" metaphor for Nazism plays precisely on (and against) Heidegger's own metaphor of the forest. See Derrida, *De l'esprit,* 179 / *Of Spirit,* 109.

53. "A negating Man, who is given to himself in the Nothing, who is not given to himself, who negates and annihilates himself."

54. Heidegger's rejection of questions of social and cultural anthropology, which is not at stake in the present study, is the subject of Edith Wyschogrod's essay, "Fear of Primitives, Primitive Fears: Anthropology in the Philosophies of Heidegger and Levinas," in *Crossover Queries,* 488–503.

55. In an early 1945 article in *Confluences*, Beaufret wrote of Levinas's 1932 essay "Martin Heidegger et l'Ontologie" and de Waelhens's book as the only competent (though still insufficient) works on Heidegger, but still saw them as too Cartesian. Beaufret, *De L'Existentialisme à Heidegger*, 18. The post-1945 critiques of anthropologism rest in large part on Corbin's translation of *Dasein* as *réalité humaine*.

56. On the other hand, first-generation Heideggerians could see in Heidegger's "Letter" nothing less than a repudiation of the very relation between the individual and the world that Heidegger had made possible in *Being and Time*. In one stroke of the pen, Heidegger had turned the entire 1930s effort to destroy anthropocentric idealism into an anthropology and had turned to a mystical understanding of Being (the accusation is made especially by Koyré and Kojève) and of man's relation to it. What was at stake here was not merely these philosophers' "anthropological" reading of his ontology, as is often noted, but the fact that for Heidegger the phenomenological ontology of *Being and Time* was now being put in brackets, that it was itself derided as insufficient. Together with a revulsion against Heidegger's whitewashing of his Nazism, this explains the aforecited criticisms of Heidegger lodged by the first generation—by Koyré, Wahl, and Kojève.

57. Merleau-Ponty, *La Nature*, 183. Waelhens, "Heidegger, Platon, et l'humanisme," 490–96.

58. Beaufret, "Sur un nouvel humanisme," 120–23.

59. Haar, *Heidegger and the Essence of Man*, esp. part II. Françoise Dastur, in her *Heidegger et la question anthropologique* (77, 79), is categorical in seeing Heidegger as a radical humanist and rejecting "le soi-disant 'anti-humanisme,'" le "supposé 'antihumanisme.'" See also de Vries, *Philosophy and the Turn to Religion*, chap. 3.

60. Dastur, *Heidegger et la question anthropologique*, 42.

61. Derrida, "How to Avoid Speaking: Denials," 122.

62. Haar, *Heidegger and the Essence of Man*, 58.

63. Derrida, *De l'esprit*, 176–77; trans. in Derrida, *Of Spirit*, 107.

64. See also the note on "remembrance" and the future (LH 258).

65. As suggested already in Chapter 2, this position is crucial for the hermeneutic phenomenology of *Being and Time* because it involves not only the structures through which *Dasein* comes to understand entities around it, but also the limitations forced on it in the world (Heidegger would rather say the liberation from metaphysical misconceptions involved in thinking about the world).

66. The ambiguity that resides in the treatment of transcendence is furthered with the warning that "world" can be metaphysically (and poorly) understood as a *value* (LH 264). Value, for Heidegger, cannot direct thinking about being, but only forecloses it.

67. "World" also appears the problem of the "world-historical" (where it seems used in a largely quotidian sense; this problem folds back onto the problem of the history of Being and metaphysics).

68. Perhaps this is Heidegger's "acosmisme" (to use Marc Richir's term) at its most radical—one yet more far-reaching than the rejection of a single, finite world in *Being and Time*. Richir, *Au-delà du renversement copernicien*, 82–83.

CHAPTER 6

1. Levinas, "La Vision du poète," citation on 10; "The Poet's Vision," in *Proper Names*, citation on 127.

2. De Lubac, *Le Drame de l'humanisme athée*.

3. De Lubac, *Catholicisme*.

4. See, notably, Marcel's *Homo Viator*; *Les Hommes contre l'humain*; and *L'Homme problématique*.

5. See Lacroix's *Le Sens de l'athéisme moderne*, esp. 65; and his "Danger de l'humanisme," in "L'Humanisme aujourd'hui: Enquête de l'UNESCO," 166–67.

6. Quoted in De Lubac, *Drama of Atheist Humanism*, 65–66. Regarding Berdyaev, see moreover the claim: "le principal mensonge sur lequel repose l'humanisme consiste dans l'idée présomptueuse que l'homme professe sur lui-même, dans la suffisance avec laquelle il s'érige lui-même en Dieu, autrement dit dans la négation du théo-andrisme. L'ascension de l'homme, son élévation à la hauteur suppose l'existence de quelque chose qui lui est supérieur. Et lorsque l'homme reste en tête-à-tête avec lui-même, s'enferme dans l'humain, il se crée des idoles, sans lesquelles il lui est impossible de s'élever. C'est ce qui forme la base de la vraie critique de l'humanisme." N. Berdyaev, *Dialectique existentielle du divin et de l'humain*, 139–69, quote on 145. Berdyaev, *Fate of Man in the Modern World*, 41–42, but see chap. 2 in general.

7. See, moreover, any number of less well known and influential figures. A systematic critique of atheist humanism in the same vein is offered by Etcheverry, *Le Conflit actuel des humanismes*. An interestingly more complex attitude is offered by Maurice de Gandillac's attitude toward the Catholicism he espoused; see "L'homme d'aujourd'hui devant le christianisme," in *Civitas*, 67–90. The case of Maurice Blondel is also significant, though I don't have the space to discuss it here; for his critiques of philosophy, including his postwar critique of Spinozist atheism, see Blondel, *Dialogue avec les philosophes*. Among the many conferences on humanism, politics, and Christianity, see *L'Humanisme et la grâce*. Finally, see the analysis by Hughes, "Catholics and the Human Condition," in *Obstructed Path*; and by Lévi-Valensi and Guérin, "Peut-on être humaniste dans la France des années cinquante?" 156–57; and the books and articles they cite (among them by Mauriac and Pierre-Henri Simon) in 163 nn34–37.

8. De Lubac, *Drama of Atheist Humanism,* 31.

9. De Lubac, *Drama of Atheist Humanism,* 67.

10. The link between Blanchot and Kojève has been repeatedly established, and I will not examine it further here. Some of the most remarkable parallels are noted by Hart in *Dark Gaze,* 116. But see also Simon Critchley's contrast of Blanchot to Kojève in Crichley, *Very Little . . . Almost Nothing,* 32, 81.

11. Bataille's expression, "the wound that is my life," expressing the status of the self in a posthistorical Hegelian world in the famous "Letter to X," comes to mind here. Bataille's 1938 "Letter to X (Lecturer on Hegel)," in *Bataille Reader,* 296.

12. Blanchot relies on Bataille throughout—to start with, in the very *possibility* of addressing Nietzsche, but also in the critique of any easy turn to the Overman for sociopolitical solutions. Bataille's critique of the Overman and his emphasis on reading Nietzsche against Nazi anti-Semitism, which dated to *Acéphale* and are indirectly cited by Blanchot (WF 295), had helped provide enough distance for French readers—including de Lubac—so as to save Nietzsche from an intellectual dustbin of history. See Bataille's critique of the Overman and of the belief that the death of God "la bourgeoisie ayant tué Dieu, il en résulterait tout d'abord un désarroi catastrophique, le vide et même un appauvrissement sinistre." (Bataille, "La 'Vieille taupe' et le préfixe sur dans les mots surhomme et surréaliste," in *Œuvres Complètes II,* 102). De Lubac also points to Bataille in his separation of Nietzsche from the Nazis: he writes that "the prophet in *Zarathustra* would be the first to find abundant reasons for cursing a great many of those who invoke his name" and is clearly referring to Bataille when he writes of the "other interpreters" who would disagree with Alfred Rosenberg, Bäumler, and others who claim "Nietzsche as an inspirer of National Socialism." De Lubac, *Drama of Atheist Humanism,* 31 n1.

13. Here, Blanchot's discussion of freedom comes close to Jean-Luc Nancy's, in *Experience of Freedom.* For this specific point, see p. 2: "freedoms do not grasp the stakes of freedom." On freedom, foundation, Hegel, and Heidegger, compare the present discussion with Nancy, 82–83.

14. Maurice Blanchot, *L'Entretien infini,* 377/252 (trans. modified).

15. "Peut-on être humaniste dans la France des années cinquante?" by Lévi-Valensi and Guérin (in *Cahiers de Fontenay,* 39–40) links several of these authors with the cultural history of the time and the problem of humanism.

16. See Adorno's essay on Beckett regarding the latter's distance from existentialism and his proximity to a series of problems of importance here, in *Can One Live After Auschwitz?* On Beckett and concerning problems we are interested in here—see also Cavell's "Ending the Waiting Game," in *Must We Mean What We Say?* 115–63; Tresize's *Into the Breach;* and Szafraniek, *Beckett, Derrida and the Event of Literature.*

17. Blanchot, "Le Règne animal de l'esprit," 387–405; "La Littérature et le droit à la mort," 30–47.

18. For the critique of Sartre and the theorization of freedom, see WF 307–8.

19. Derrida, "Maurice Blanchot est mort," 272.

20. Derrida, "Maurice Blanchot est mort," 277–78.

21. Judt, *Past Imperfect*, 41.

22. As is well known, the case of Sade is also particularly significant here. On Sade and the relationship of literature to revolution in this text, see, among many others, Derrida, "Maurice Blanchot est mort," 273–74.

23. As has been repeatedly noted, Blanchot in this argument engages with Jean Paulhan's *Les Fleures de Tarbes*. For a useful discussion, see Syrotinsky, "How Is Literature Possible?" in *New History of French Literature*, 953–58.

24. To some degree Blanchot utilizes Kojève's understanding of negation to critically radicalize the theory of freedom that follows from Sartre's theorization of the *fact* of negation (and of the *for-itself*). Regarding Sartre and freedom, most relevant here is the famous passage in *Being and Nothingness*, 709–12, where Sartre defines freedom as involving responsibility for an entire world.

25. Here, Blanchot is echoing Saint-Just's "A patriot is one who supports the republic as a whole; whoever resists in detail is a traitor," a frequent trope in Communism which Merleau-Ponty also discusses in *Humanism and Terror* (34).

26. Samuel Moyn offers an genealogy of François Furet's consideration of transparency in relation to the Terror (in *Interpreting the French Revolution*) by way of Claude Lefort, Marc Richir, and (further back) Starobinski and Baczko in his "On the Intellectual Origins of Furet's Masterpiece," in *Tocqueville Review/La Revue Tocqueville*, 11, 18–19 n18. Starobinski, of course, had been a careful reader of Blanchot, also serving with him on the editorial board of *Critique*.

27. I have not delved into Blanchot's literary writing after 1945 here; Blanchot's rethinking of literature and its goals has traditionally offered a way of reading it; his last novel, *Le Très-haut* (1948), was much invested in the problem of life after a revolution not dissimilar to the idealized version of the French Revolution he describes in "Literature and the Right to Death." In that novel's posthistorical world, the only agent left is disease: the revolutionary State has rendered the possibility of a future and of a humanist world lost once and for all. Humanity is lost to a diseased and moribund posthistorical state, which holds it captive to the Terror of a complete eradication of individuality and an advent of impersonality. The right to death leads further to the universe of Blanchot's later *récits*, in which there is no right any longer, in which the right to death is effaced and leaves nothing behind. Literature thus becomes not only the only place in which any consideration of the absolute is possible—having left "life" behind—but in which this absolute is itself gone.

28. See Stoekl, "Introduction: Death at the End of History," in *Most High*; Ungar, *Scandal and Aftereffect*.

CHAPTER 7

1. Sartre writes in his *Les Temps modernes* obituary for Merleau-Ponty, "It was Merleau-Ponty who converted me. . . . " Cited in Dreyfus and Allen Dreyfus, "Translators' Introduction," in *Sense and Non-Sense*, xx.

2. Merleau-Ponty, "Note on Machiavelli," in *Signs*, 223 (trans. amended).

3. Exemplary of the tendency to "protect" Merleau-Ponty's phenomenology is Étienne Bimbenet's otherwise interesting *Nature et humanité*, which surprisingly excises from the anthropological questioning *any* consideration of historical or political problems from *Humanism and Terror*, *Sense and Non-Sense*, and even *Signs*, and as these inform the ontological questioning of *The Visible and the Invisible* and the lecture series *Nature* and *Philosophy and Non-Philosophy*. Bimbenet in this regard follows an impetus offered by Renaud Barbaras, whose exciting readings of Merleau-Ponty revived the study of his work in the 1990s. On the other hand, some readers, like Barry Cooper in his *Merleau-Ponty and Marxism,* tend to consider Merleau-Ponty's political writings with little more than a passing glance to his nonpolitical texts. In recent years, the major exception to this interpretive tendency is the work of Claude Lefort, whose essays on Merleau-Ponty span the breadth of the latter's oeuvre and refuse to simply reduce the different problems to each other. For an effort, set in terms of intellectual biography, to think together Merleau-Ponty's phenomenology with his politics, which acknowledges but is not intimidated by the "scandal" of the political texts, see Imbert, *Maurice Merleau-Ponty*, 40–44. See, finally, Dreyfus and Allen Dreyfus, "Translators' Introduction," in *Sense and Non-Sense*, which explicitly seeks to link the phenomenological with the historical and political projects.

4. In later years, Merleau-Ponty continued to explicitly reject liberal humanism; see *Parcours II*, 307.

5. Claude Lefort warns that it is less the mirroring of philosophical positions than the analogy or symmetry of the questions posed that marks the connection of the different texts, that provides "the sentiment of wandering in the same universe": "Si nous allons d'un écrit à l'autre, par exemple de la *Phénoménologie de la perception* aux *Aventures de la dialectique*, avec le sentiment d'errer dans un même univers, c'est que de l'un à l'autre la même interrogation se refait. Les termes du problème du corps ne sont pas ceux du problème de la société, ni ceux de la perception ceux de l'action, et je ne puis, passant d'un domaine à l'autre, prendre l'un pour référence et penser l'autre par analogie. La vérité est seulement qu'il y a une manière d'interroger qui s'apprend partout à la fois, qui s'atteste dans le penser, où l'œuvre s'éprouve en chacun de ses moments comme œuvre de l'Être." Lefort, *Sur une colonne absente*, 40.

6. Haar, *La Philosophie française entre phénoménologie et métaphysique*, 16. Marc Richir offers a different anti-anthropocentrism: whereas in the Copernican *renversement* the idea of the infinite is still held to the subject, as something the subject does not see (but can come to do so), does not recognize (but can), in Merleau-Ponty this is no longer the case. Instead of the infinite, the invisible is there in its absence and may only be touched on qua said absence. Merleau-Ponty's "phenomenalization of man" thus involves a movement into the beyond of this Copernican world. See Richir, *Au-delà du renversement copernicien*, chap. 3, esp. 57–58.

7. See Etienne Bimbenet's analysis of Merleau-Ponty's argument on the conditioning of positive content of man by the human sciences in the nineteenth century. Bimbenet, *Nature et humanité*, 17; the argument on the conditioning by the human sciences of a positive knowledge of man in the nineteenth century.

8. Minor amendments to the translation.

9. Merleau-Ponty repeats "an innocent is an innocent, a murderer is a murderer" in *Humanism and Terror*, for example, xxxvii.

10. Merleau-Ponty, "Man and Adversity," in *Signs*, 226.

11. See also the critique of the humanism of the previous centuries and of Julien Benda in Merleau-Ponty, *Causeries*, 52 and 68, respectively.

12. See Merleau-Ponty's *Les Aventures de la dialectique*, 12.

13. Merleau-Ponty goes so far as to suggest that the "glory" of the resistance also presupposes this contingency (HT 41–42, also 37–39)—a claim certainly profiting from hindsight but nevertheless significant as per the ambiguity he is presenting. That this position was criticized is attested to in HT xxxv.

14. Regarding ethics and political Machiavellianism (Koestler cites Machiavelli at the outset of *Darkness at Noon*), Merleau-Ponty emphatically argues with Marxism against the opposition of the two (HT 129; also 120, 154). As he notes in the introduction "the purity of principles not only tolerates but even requires violence" (HT xiii). See also "Note on Machiavelli," in *Signs*, 222–23.

15. "Théorie et déclin de l'humanisme prolétarien" is the title of the third section of the original publication of "Le Yogi et le prolétaire" in *Les Temps modernes*, and corresponds to pp. 103–48 of *Humanism and Terror*, that is, roughly the chapter titled "From the Proletarian to the Commissar."

16. Cf. Judt, *Past Imperfect*, 120–21. Roth, *Knowing and History*, 51.

17. See, for example, the review of *Humanism and Terror*, by Roland P. Caillois, "Destin de l'humanisme marxiste." This would become the standard critique of the book. As Merleau-Ponty makes clear, he declares as much not in the service of a Trotskyist project, and not of any redemptive liberalism of the future. Merleau-Ponty rejects Trotskyism throughout part I, chap. 3 and in p. xxii. See also Cooper, *Merleau-Ponty and Marxism*, 75.

18. Poster, *Existential Marxism*, 159.

19. Pierre Macherey, "Les Philosophes français de l'après-guerre face à la politique: *Humanisme et terreur* de Merleau-Ponty et *Tyrannie et Sagesse* de Kojève" in *Materia Actuosa: Antiquité, Âge Classique, Lumières*, 720. Similarly: "l'alternative du titre [est] laissée en suspens," in Imbert, *Maurice Merleau-Ponty*, 41.

20. The particularity of Merleau-Ponty's argument and his neither/nor attitude is highlighted by Martine Poulain in her account of the French reception of Koestler's *Darkness at Noon*, "A Cold War Best-Seller: The Reaction to Arthur Koestler's *Darkness at Noon* in France from 1945 to 1950," in *Libraries & Culture* 36, no. 1 (winter 2001): 172–84.

21. See Poster's discussion of the reception in *Existential Marxism*, 157. Poster cites Roger Garaudy's criticism as well as the liberal and non-Communist left-wing response. See also Judt, *Past Imperfect*, 121–22; Martin Jay has addressed Merleau-Ponty's *Humanism and Terror* as an effort to fuse holism and Marxism in *Marxism and Totality*.

22. Heidegger, *Introduction to Metaphysics*, 37.

23. This, even though in his later thought (esp. in *La Nature* and the *Notes de cours*) Merleau-Ponty came often to positions close to Heidegger's. See also Michel Haar, "Proximité et distance vis-à-vis de Heidegger chez le dernier Merleau-Ponty," in *La Philosophie française entre phénoménologie et métaphysique*, 9–34.

24. Dreyfus and Allen Dreyfus, "Translators' Introduction," in *Sense and Non-Sense*, xx, xxii–xxiii.

CHAPTER 8

1. Hyppolite explicitly makes fun of the Hegel engendered Feuerbach engendered Marx argument (F 146).

2. A quick philosophical sketch of Hyppolite's influence and significance, and of his role in postwar Paris and the Ecole Normale, is offered by Alain Badiou in his lecture "Jean Hyppolite, un style philosophique," at *Jean Hyppolite entre structure et existence* conference (May 27, 2006). Recording available on http://www. savoirs.ens.fr/diffusion/audio/2006_05_27_badiou_podcast.mp3 (last accessed on September 20, 2007).

3. Fessard, *Hegel, le christianisme et l'histoire*, 139.

4. Here, as much as he may be differentiating himself from Kojève, Hyppolite also distances himself from a second contemporary Hegelian he was personally and to some extent intellectually close to, namely, Gaston Fessard (sj). Hyppolite occasionally invited Fessard to lecture in his courses.

5. Deleuze, "Logique et existence de Jean Hyppolite," 457–60; translated as "Jean Hyppolite's *Logic and Existence*," in Deleuze, *Desert Islands and Other Texts*, 15–18. Similarly, in his intellectual history of French Hegelianism, Michael S. Roth argues that Hyppolite abandoned Hegelian humanism for Heideggerian Being.

(*Knowing and History*, 66, 74–75, 77.) But this answer is, as I have suggested so far and will continue to address, far too clean.

6. That Hyppolite's position remains central to contemporary concerns in political theology and the question of what comes after the subject is perhaps best clarified by way of Jean-Luc Nancy's work—his engagement with the self-deconstruction of Christianity, his questioning of community, his address of the relation between meaning and "the we" (Nancy, *Being Singular Plural*; see also Nancy's *Hegel: The Restlessness of the Negative*); his treatment of humanism as an ideology (Nancy, *L'Oubli de la philosophie*, 26; translated in *The Gravity of Thought*), and his attention to the singular/plural problem of ontology. All these themes, though not premised on Hyppolite directly—and though often in explicit critique of some of Hyppolite's emphases—offer a clear sense of how the ontologization, depoliticization, and formalization of "the human" provides a way of asking anew a series of most basic questions of the human.

7. As is well known, Merleau-Ponty had been Kojève's student in the concluding years of the latter's Hegel seminar; moreover, Merleau-Ponty wrote the long preface and the conclusion to *Humanisme et terreur*, the two sections that emphasize the book's philosophy of history and the call for taking sides in it, only *after* the publication of Kojève's *Introduction à la lecture de Hegel*.

8. Merleau-Ponty's support for this sort of Communist humanism (coupled with his maxim that in today's political situation it is impossible to be a Communist just as much as it is impossible to be an anti-Communist) expresses and indeed plays out what Kojève himself argued in his private politics was the consequence of his reading of Hegel, but also what Kojève never infused into his reading of Hegel, namely, a belief in liberation and human dignity after the end of history.

9. Thao, *Phenomenology and Dialectical Materialism*. Thao also was a major influence on the American journal *Telos* in its early years.

10. Roth, *Knowing and History*.

11. "Language still denies us its essence: that it is the house of Being." Martin Heidegger, "Letter on 'Humanism,'" in *Pathmarks*, 243.

12. Deleuze, "Jean Hyppolite's *Logic and Existence*," 15.

13. F 149; my emphasis.

CONCLUSION

1. Judt, *Past Imperfect*, 121, 124ff.

2. Derrida, *Margins of Philosophy*, 119.

3. Levinas, *Sur Maurice Blanchot*, 10; translated in *Proper Names*, 127.

4. See Benveniste, "De la subjéctivité dans le langage"; Levi-Strauss, "Language and the Analysis of Social Laws."

5. Bataille, *Sovereignty.*

6. See Merleau-Ponty, *Consciousness and the Acquisition of Language,* chap. 3.

7. Levi-Strauss, *Savage Mind,* 247.

8. Levi-Strauss, *Savage Mind,* 247.

9. Althusser, *Humanist Controversy.*

10. Among very recent works, see also Guillaume Le Blanc's strongly Canguilhemian critique of notions of the "normal man" in *Les Maladies de l'homme normal.*

11. Duclaux, *L'Homme devant l'univers,* 273.

12. Canguilhem, *La Connaissance de la vie,* 20, translated in *Knowledge of Life,* 158 n31.

13. Canguilhem, after Hyppolite's death, would write that it is "sous son influence [. . .] que la philosophie française [avait] commencé à perdre conscience de ce qu'était pour elle, auparavant, la Conscience." Canguilhem, "Hommage à Jean Hyppolite," 130. I would like to thank Giuseppe Bianco for this reference. Canguilhem would also pay homage to Hyppolite with "De la science à la contre-science," in *Hommage à Jean Hyppolite,* 173–80. Canguilhem, "Diseases," 105.

14. Monod, *Le Hasard et la nécessité,* 53; translated as *Chance and Necessity,* 42.

15. Atlan, *La Science est-elle inhumaine?* 31–32. Atlan, *Les Étincelles de hasard.*

16. Derrida, "The Ends of Man," in *Margins of Philosophy,* 133–34.

Bibliography

I. ARCHIVAL RESEARCH

Archives Jésuites (Vanves)
Fonds du Père Gaston Fessard
Fonds du Cardinal Henri de Lubac
Bibliothèque Littéraire Jacques Doucet
Fonds André Breton
Fonds Marcel Jouhandeau
Fonds André Malraux
Bibliothèque Nationale de France, Département des Manuscrits Occidentaux
Fonds Georges Bataille
Correspondence Files, Georges Bataille
Fonds Alexandre Kojève
Fonds André Malraux
Fonds Maurice Merleau-Ponty
Bibliothèque Nationale de France, Site Mitterrand, Département des Livres Rares
Jean Wahl, Private Library
Lectures of Jean Wahl at the Sorbonne (1945–65)
École des Hautes Etudes en Sciences Sociales, Centre Alexandre Koyré
Fonds Alexandre Koyré
Institut Mémoires de l'Edition Contemporaine
Fonds du Centre International de Cerisy/Pontigny
Fonds du Collège Philosophique (1945–69)
Fonds Michel Foucault
Fonds Jean Wahl

II. BOOKS AND ARTICLES

Adorno, Theodor W. *Can One Live After Auschwitz? A Philosophical Reader.* Stanford: Stanford University Press, 2003.

———. *Hegel: Three Studies.* Trans. Sherry Weber Nicholsen. Cambridge, MA: MIT Press, 1993.

———. *Metaphysics.* Stanford: Stanford University Press, 2001.

———. *Negative Dialectics.* New York: Continuum, 1970.

Agamben, Giorgio. *Homo Sacer: Sovereign Power and Bare Life.* Stanford: Stanford University Press, 1998.

———. *The Open: Man and Animal.* Stanford: Stanford University Press, 2004.

Althusser, Louis. *The Humanist Controversy and Other Writings.* Trans. G. M. Goshgarian. London: Verso, 2003.

———. *Lénine et la Philosophie.* Paris: Maspero, 1969.

Amato, Joseph. *Mounier and Maritain: A French Catholic Understanding of the Modern World.* Ypsilanti, MI: Sapientia, 2002.

Arbousse-Bastide, Paul, ed. *Pour un humanisme nouveau.* Paris: Foi et vie, 1930.

Arendt, Hannah. *The Origins of Totalitarianism.* New York: Harcourt & Brace, 1966.

Arendt, Hannah, and Martin Heidegger. *Letters 1925–1975.* Ed. Ursula Ludz; trans. Andrew Shields. Orlando, FL: Harcourt, 2003.

Aron, Raymond. "Future of Secular Religions." In *Dawn of Universal History*, 177–201. New York: Basic Books, 2002.

———. *Marxism and the Existentialists.* New York: Harper & Row, 1969.

———. *Memoirs.* London: Holmes and Meyer, 1990.

Aronson, Ronald. *Camus and Sartre.* Chicago: University of Chicago Press, 2004.

Atlan, Henri. *Enlightenment to Enlightenment: Intercritique of Science and Myth.* Trans. Lenn J. Schramm. Albany: State University of New York Press, 1993.

———. *La Science est-elle inhumaine?* Paris: Bayard, 2002.

———. *Les Étincelles de hasard*, vol. 1: *Connaissance spermatique.* Paris: Seuil, 1999.

Audoin-Rouzeau, Stéphane, and Annette Becker. *14–18: Understanding the Great War.* Trans. C. Temerson. New York: Hill & Wang, 2002.

Auffret, Dominique. *Alexandre Kojève: la philosophie, l'État, la fin de l'Histoire.* Paris: Grasset, 1990.

Augustine. *Confessions.* Oxford: Oxford University Press, 1998.

Axelos, Kostas. *Arguments d'une Recherche.* Paris: Minuit (Arguments), 1969.

———. *Einführung in ein künftiges Denken: Über Marx und Heidegger.* Tübingen, Germany: Niemeyer, 1966.

———. *Marx, penseur de la technique.* Paris: Minuit, 1961. Translated by Ronald Bruzina as *Alienation, Praxis, and Techne in the Thought of Karl Marx.* Austin: University of Texas Press, 1976.

———. *Vers la pensée planétaire.* Paris: Minuit (Arguments), 1964.

Bachelard, Gaston. *Etudes.* Ed. Georges Canguilhem. 1970. Reprint, Paris: Vrin, 2000.

————. *La Formation de l'esprit scientifique.* Paris: Vrin, 1938.

————. *La Psychanalyse du feu.* Paris: Gallimard, 1938.

————. *La Valeur inductive de la relativité.* Paris: Vrin, 1929.

————. *Le Nouvel esprit scientifique.* Paris: PUF, 1958. Translated by Arthur Gold-hammer as *The New Scientific Spirit.* Boston: Beacon Press, 1987.

Badiou, Alain. *Being and Event.* London and New York: Continuum, 2006.

————. *Ethics: An Essay on the Understanding of Evil.* London: Verso, 2001.

Barthel, Ernst. *Beiträge zur transzendentalen Logik auf polaristischer Grundlage.* Leipzig, Germany: R. Noske, 1932.

Bataille, Georges. *The Bataille Reader.* Ed. Fred Botting and Scott Wilson. Oxford: Blackwell, 1997.

————. *The Blue of Noon.* New York: Consortium, 2002.

————. *Choix de letters 1917-1962.* Paris: Gallimard, 1997.

————. *Guilty.* Venice, CA: Lapis Press, 1988.

————. *L'expérience intérieure.* Paris: Gallimard, 1943. Translated by Leslie Anne Boldt as *Inner Experience.* Albany: State University of New York Press, 1988.

————. "Le Labyrinthe." *Recherches philosophiques* V (1936): 364–72. Translated by Allan Stoekl as "The Labyrinth," in Bataille, *Visions of Excess.* Minneapolis: University of Minnessota Press, 1985.

————. "Nietzsche est-il fasciste?" *Combat* 113 (October 20, 1944); republished in *OC* XI, 9.

————. *Oeuvres complètes,* vols. I, II, and XI. Paris: Gallimard, 1969–80.

————. *On Nietzsche.* St. Paul, MN: Paragon House, 1994.

————. *Romans et récits.* Paris: Gallimard (Pleiade), 2004.

————. *Sovereignty* in *The Accursed Share.* Vols. 2–3. New York: Zone Books, 1993.

————. *Visions of Excess: Selected Writings 1927–1939.* Trans. A. Stoekl. Minneapolis: University of Minnesota Press, 1985.

Baugh, Bruce. *French Hegel: From Surrealism to Postmodernism.* New York: Routledge, 2001.

Bayer, Raymond, ed. *Travaux du 9ème congrès international de philosophie. Congrès Descartes.* 2 vols. Paris: Hermann, 1937.

Beaufret, Jean. *De l'existentialisme à Heidegger: Introduction aux philosophies de l'existence.* 2nd ed. Paris: Vrin, 2000.

————. *Dialogue avec Heidegger.* Vol. 1. Paris: Minuit (Arguments), 1973.

————. *Dialogue avec Heidegger.* Vol. 2. Paris: Minuit (Arguments), 1973.

————. *Dialogue avec Heidegger.* Vol. 3. Paris: Minuit (Arguments), 1974.

————. *Dialogue avec Heidegger.* Vol. 4. Paris: Minuit (Arguments), 1985.

————. *Entretiens avec Fréderic de Towarnicki.* Paris: Presses Universitaires de France (Epiméthee), 1984.

————. "Martin Heidegger et Le Problème de la Vérité." *Fontaine* 62–63 (November 1947).

————. *Notes sur la philosophie en France au XIXe siècle.* Paris: Vrin, 1984.

————. "Questions du Communisme." *Confluences* 18–20 (1947).

————. "Sur un nouvel humanisme." *La Nef* 60 (December 1949–January 1950).

Beauvoir, Simone de. *La Force de l'age.* Paris: Gallimard, 1960. Translated as *The Prime of Life.* New York: Paragon, 1992.

Becker, Annette. *Oubliés de la grande guerre.* Paris: Noesis, 1998.

Bell, David A. *The Cult of the Nation in France.* Cambridge, MA: Harvard University Press, 2002.

Beltrán, Antonio. "Wine, Water and Epistemological Sobriety: A Note on the Koyré-MacLachlan Debate." *Isis* 89 (1998): 82–89.

Benda, Julien. *La trahison des clercs.* Paris: Grasset, 1927. Translated as *The Treason of the Intellectuals.* New Brunswick, NJ: Transaction Publishers, 2007.

Benjamin, Walter. *Gesammelte Briefe.* Vol. 5 (1935–37). Ed. Chr. Gödde and H. Lonitz. Frankfurt: Suhrkamp, 1999.

Benveniste, Emile. "De la subjéctivité dans le langage." 1958. In *Problèmes de linguistique générale.* Paris: Gallimard, 1966.

Berdyaev, Nicolai. *Dialectique existentielle du divin et de l'humain.* Paris: Janin, 1947.

————. *The Fate of Man in the Modern World.* London: Student Christian Movement Press, 1935.

————. "Personne Humaine et Marxisme." In *Le Communisme et les chrétiens,* ed. François Mauriac. Paris: Plon, 1937.

Berlin, Isaiah. *Russian Thinkers.* New York: Viking, 1978.

Bernauer, James. *Michel Foucault's Force of Flight.* Atlantic Highlands, NJ: Humanities Press, 1990.

Bianco, Giuseppe. "La réaction au bergsonisme. Transformations de la philosophie française de Politzer à Deleuze." Ph.D. thesis, Université de Lille-III, 2010.

Bident, Christophe. *Maurice Blanchot: Partenaire invisible.* Paris: Champ Vallon, 1998.

Bien, Joseph. "The Intellectual and Action." In *Merleau-Ponty's Later Works and Their Practical Implications: The Dehiscence of Responsibility,* ed. Duane H. Davis. Amherst, NY: Humanity Books, 2001.

Bimbenet, Étienne. *Nature et humanité: le problème anthropologique dans l'œuvre de Merleau-Ponty.* Paris: Vrin, 2004.

Blanchot, Maurice. *L'entretien infini.* Paris: Gallimard, 1969. Translated by Susan Hanson as *The Infinite Conversation.* Minneapolis: University of Minnesota Press, 1993.

———. "La littérature et le droit à la mort." *Critique* 20 (1948): 30–47.

———. "Le règne animal de l'esprit." *Critique* 18 (1947): 387–405.

———. *Le Très-Haut.* Translated by Allan Stoekl as *The Most High.* Lincoln: University of Nebraska Press, 1996.

———. *The Work of Fire.* Trans. Charlotte Mandell. Stanford: Stanford University Press, 1995.

———. *The Writing of Disaster.* Trans. Ann Smock. Lincoln and London: University of Nebraska Press, 1995 edition.

Blanckaert, Claude. "L'Anthropologie en France: Le Mot et l'histoire (16e–19e siècle)." *Bulletins et Mémoires de la Société d'Anthropologie de Paris,* nouvelle série I, nos. 3–4 (1989): 20.

Blondel, Maurice. *Dialogue avec les philosophes.* Paris: Éditions Montaigne, 1966.

Bohr, Niels. *The Philosophical Writings of Niels Bohr,* vol. 1, *Atomic Theory and Human Nature.* Woodbridge, CT: Ox Bow Press, 1987.

Boterbloem, Kees. *The Life and Times of Andrei Zhdanov, 1896–1948.* Montreal: McGill-Queen's University Press, 2004.

Bourdieu, Pierre. *The Political Ontology of Martin Heidegger.* Stanford: Stanford University Press, 1991.

Brooks, John I. *The Eclectic Legacy: Academic Philosophy and the Human Sciences in Nineteenth-Century France.* Newark, NJ: University of Delaware Press, 1998.

Bruns, Gerald L. *Maurice Blanchot: The Refusal of Philosophy.* Baltimore, MD: Johns Hopkins University Press, 1997.

Brunschvicg, Léon. *Écrits philosophiques,* vol. 1: *L'Humanisme de l'Occident. Descartes, Spinoza, Kant.* Paris: PUF, 1951.

———. *L'Esprit européen: Leçons professées en Sorbonne, Décembre 1939–Mars 1940.* Neuchâtel, France: la Baconnière, 1947.

———. *L'Expérience humaine et la causalité physique.* Paris: Alcan, 1922.

———. *Le progrès de la conscience dans la philosophie occidentale.* Paris: Alcan, 1927.

———. *Les étapes de la philosophie mathématique.* Paris: Alcan, 1912.

Buchner, Hartmut, ed. *Japan und Heidegger: Gedenkschrift der Stadt Messkirsch zum hundertsten Geburtstag Martin Heideggers.* Messkirsch, Germany: Jan Thorbecke Vlg, 1989.

Bulletin de la Société Française de Philosophie, 1918–1940.

Butler, Judith. *Subjects of Desire: Hegelian Reflections in Twentieth-Century France.* New York: Columbia University Press, 1987.

Buton, Philippe. *Les lendemains qui déchantent: Le parti communiste français à la libération.* Paris: Presses de la Fondation nationale des sciences politiques, 1993.

Caillois, Roger. *Babel.* Paris: Folio (essais), 1946/1996.

————. *The Edge of Surrealism: A Roger Caillois Reader*. Durham, NC: Duke University Press, 2003.

————. *Man and the Sacred*. Glencoe, IL: Free Press of Glencoe, 1959.

Caillois, Roland P. "Destin de l'humanisme marxiste." *Critique* 22 (March 1948).

Camus, André. *Lettres à un ami allemand*. Paris: Gallimard, 1948.

Canguilhem, Georges. "De la science à la contre-science." In *Hommage à Jean Hyppolite*. Paris: PUF, 1971.

————. "Diseases." Trans. S. Geroulanos and T. Meyers, in *Anthropologies*, ed. Meyers and R. Baxstrom. Baltimore, MD: Creative Capitalism Press, 2007.

————. "Hommage à Jean Hyppolite." *Revue de métaphysique et de morale* (1969): 2.

————. *La Connaissance de la vie*. Paris: Vrin, 1965. Translated by Stefanos Geroulanos and Daniela Ginsburg as *Knowledge of Life*, ed. Paola Marrati and Todd Meyers. New York: Fordham University Press, 2009.

Carlson, A. J. Review of Alexis Carrel, *Man the Unknown*. *The American Journal of Sociology* 41, no. 5 (March 1936): 677–78.

Carrel, Alexis. *Man the Unknown*. London/New York: Harper and Brothers, 1935.

Carroll, David. *French Literary Fascism: Nationalism, Anti-Semitism, and the Ideology of Culture*. Princeton, NJ: Princeton University Press, 1995.

Cassirer, Ernst, and Martin Heidegger. *Débat sur le kantisme et la philosophie*. Trans. P. Aubenque. Paris: Beauchesne, 1972.

Castelli, Enrico, ed. *Umanesimo e scienza politica*. Milan, Italy: C. Marzorati, 1951.

Caute, David. *Les Compagnons de route*. Paris: Laffont, 1979. Translated as *The Fellow-Travellers: Intellectual Friends of Communism*. New Haven, CT: Yale University Press, 1988.

Cavell, Stanley. *The Claim of Reason: Wittgenstein, Skepticism, Morality and Tragedy*. 2d ed. Oxford: Oxford University Press, 1999.

————. "Ending the Waiting Game: A Reading of Beckett's *Endgame*." In *Must We Mean What We Say?* Cambridge: Cambridge University Press, 1976.

Chamberlain, Lesley. *The Philosophy Steamer: Lenin and the Exile of the Intelligentsia*. London: Atlantic Books, 2006.

Chanussot, Jacques, and Claude Travi. *Dits et écrits d'André Malraux*. Dijon, France: Editions Universitaires de Dijon, 2003.

Cohen, H. Floris. *The Scientific Revolution: A Historiographical Inquiry*. Chicago: University of Chicago Press, 1994.

Cohen-Solal, Annie. *Sartre: A Life*. New York: Pantheon, 1987.

Comte, Auguste. *Catéchisme positiviste; ou, Sommaire exposition de la religion universelle en treize entretiens systématiques entre une femme et un prêtre de l'humanité*. Rio de Janeiro: Temple de l'Humanité, 1957.

————. *The Positive Philosophy of Auguste Comte.* Ed. Harriet Martineau. New York: Appleton and Co., 1853.

Connor, Peter T. *Georges Bataille and the Mysticism of Sin.* Baltimore, MD: Johns Hopkins University Press, 2003.

Cooper, Barry. *Merleau-Ponty and Marxism: From Terror to Reform.* Toronto: University of Toronto Press, 1979.

Corbin, Henri. "Post-Scriptum biographique à un entretien philosophique." In *Cahier de l'Herne: Henri Corbin.* Paris: Herne, 1981.

Cornick, Martin. *The* Nouvelle Revue Française *Under Jean Paulhan, 1925–40.* Amsterdam: Rodopi, 1995.

Crépon, Marc. *Le Malin génie des langues.* Paris: Vrin, 2000.

Crichley, Simon. *Very Little . . . Almost Nothing: Death, Philosophy, Literature.* London: Routledge, 1997.

Cuvillier, Armand. *Les Infiltrations germaniques dans la pensée française.* Paris: Universelles, 1945.

Dastur, Françoise. *Heidegger et la question anthropologique.* Louvain: Editions de l'Institut Supérieur de Philosophie / Editions Peeters, 2003.

Davis, Duane H. ed. *Merleau-Ponty's Later Works and their Practical Implications: The Dehiscence of Responsibility.* Amherst, NY: Humanity Books, 2001.

Déat, Marcel. *Pensée allemande et pensée française.* Paris: Aux Armes de France, 1944.

Deguy, Michel. *Sans Retour.* Paris: Galilée, 2004.

Delaporte, Sophie. *Gueules cassées: Les Blessés de la face de la Grande Guerre.* Paris: A. Viénot, 2001.

Deleuze, Gilles. "Logique et existence de Jean Hyppolite." *Revue philosophique,* 144, nos. 7–9 (July–September 1954): 457–60. Translated as "Jean Hyppolite's *Logic and Existence,*" in Deleuze, *Desert Islands and Other Texts 1953–1974.* New York: Semiotext(e), 2004.

Derrida, Jacques. *Aporias.* Stanford: Stanford University Press (Meridian), 1993.

————. *De l'esprit: Heidegger et la question.* Paris: Galilée, 1987. Translated as *Of Spirit: Heidegger and the Question.* Chicago: University of Chicago Press, 1990.

————. *Heidegger et la Question.* Paris: Flammarion, 1990.

————. "How to Avoid Speaking: Denials." Trans. Ken Frieden. In *Derrida and Negative Theology,* ed. Harold Coward and Toby Foshay. Albany: State University of New York Press, 1982.

————. *Margins of Philosophy.* Trans. Alan Bass. Chicago: University of Chicago Press, 1982.

————. "*Of an Apocalyptic Tone Recently Adopted in Philosophy.*" In *Raising the*

Tone of Philosophy, ed. Peter Fenves. Baltimore, MD: Johns Hopkins University Press, 1993.

———. *Parages*. Paris: Galilée, 2003.

———. *Points . . .* Stanford: Stanford University Press (Meridian), 1995.

———. *Specters of Marx: The State of the Debt, the Work of Mourning, and the New International.* Trans. Peggy Kamuf. London: Routledge, 1994.

Deschoux, Marcel. *Brunschvicg: l'idéalisme à l'hauteur de l'homme.* Paris: Seghers, 1969.

———. *La philosophie de Léon Brunschvicg.* Paris: PUF, 1949.

Descombes, Vincent. *Le même et l'autre, Quarante-cinq ans de philosophie française (1933–1978).* Paris: Minuit, 1978. Translated by L. Scott-Fox and J. M. Harding as *Modern French Philosophy.* Cambridge: Cambridge University Press, 1982.

Dosse, François. *History of Structuralism.* 2 vols. Minneapolis: University of Minnesota Press, 1997.

Duclaux, Jacques. *L'Homme devant l'univers.* Paris: Flammarion, 1949.

Dufrenne, Mikkel. "Heidegger et Kant." *Revue de métaphysique et de morale* (January 1949).

———. *Pour l'homme.* Paris: Seuil, 1968.

Dworkin, Anthony. "The Case for Minor Utopias." *Prospect* (July 2007): 45.

Eksteins, Modris. *Rites of Spring: The Great War and the Birth of the Modern Age.* Boston: Houghton Mifflin, 1989.

Eribon, Didier. *Michel Foucault.* Trans. Betsy Wing. Cambridge, MA: Harvard University Press, 1991.

Etcheverry, Auguste. *Le Conflit actuel des humanismes.* Paris: PUF, 1955.

Fabiani, Jean-Louis. *Les philosophes de la république.* Paris: Minuit, 1988.

Ferry, Luc, and Alain Renaut. *Heidegger et les modernes.* Paris: Grasset (Figures), 1988. Translated as *Heidegger and Modernity.* Chicago: Chicago University Press, 1990.

———. *La Pensée 68: Essai Sur L'Anti-Humanisme Contemporain.* Paris: Gallimard (Le Monde Actuel), 1985. Translated as *French Philosophy of the Sixties.* Amherst: University of Massachusetts Press, 1990.

Fessard, Gaston. *De l'actualité historique.* 2 vols. Brussels, Desclée de Brouwer, 1960.

———. *France, prends garde de perdre ton âme! Témoignage Chrétien* 1 (November 1941).

———. "Christianisme et communisme," *Critique* 3–4 (1946): 311–12. Translated as "Christianity and Communism," *Interpretation* 19, no. 2 (winter 1991–92): 195.

———. *Hegel, le christianisme et l'histoire.* Ed. Michel Sales. Paris: PUF, 1990.

———. *La main tendue? Le dialogue catholique-communiste est-il possible?* Paris: Grasset, 1937.

Feuerbach, Ludwig. *The Essence of Christianity.* Amherst, NY: Prometheus, 1989.

———. *Principles of the Philosophy of the Future.* Trans. Manfred H. Vogel. Indianapolis, IL: Hackett, 1986.

Filoni, Marco. *Kojève prima di Kojève: Fenomenologia dell'uomo moderno.* D. Phil, Università degli Studi di Macerata, 2005.

Foucault, Michel. *Aesthetics, Method, Epistemology: The Essential Works of Foucault 2.* New York: New Press, 1999.

———. *L'Archéologie du Savoir.* Paris: Gallimard, 1969.

———. *The Order of Things.* New York: Vintage, 1994.

Friedman, Michael. *A Parting of the Ways: Carnap, Cassirer and Heidegger.* Chicago: Open Court, 2000.

Friedmann, Georges. *Machine et humanisme.* 2 vols.: vol.1, *La Crise du progrès*; vol. 2, *Problèmes du machinisme industriel.* Paris: Gallimard 1935/1946.

Fritz, Egon, ed. *Ernst Barlach: Dramatiker, Bildhauer, Zeichner.* Darmstadt, Germany: Eduard Stichnote, 1951.

Frost, Laura. *Sex Drives: Fantasies of Fascism in Literary Modernism.* Ithaca, NY: Cornell University Press, 2002.

Fukuyama, Francis. *The End of History and the Last Man.* New York: Avon, 1993.

Furet, François. *The Passing of an Illusion.* Chicago: University of Chicago Press, 2000.

Furet, François, and Mona Ozouf, eds. *A Critical Dictionary of the French Revolution.* Cambridge, MA: Harvard University Press, 1989.

Gandillac, Maurice de. "Entretien avec Martin Heidegger." *Les Temps modernes* 4 (January 1946).

———. "L'homme d'aujourd'hui devant le christianisme." *Civitas* (Zurich) (November 1946): 67–90.

———. *Le Siècle traversé: Souvenirs de neuf décennies.* Paris: Albin Michel, 1998.

Gandt, François de. *Husserl et Galilée: sur la crise des sciences européennes.* Paris: Vrin, 2004.

Garaudy, Roger. *Une littérature de fossoyeurs.* Paris: Éditions sociales, 1947.

Gauchet, Marcel. *The Disenchantment of the World.* Princeton, NJ: Princeton University Press, 1997.

———. "Rights of Man." In *A Critical Dictionary of the French Revolution,* ed. François Furet and Mona Ozouf. Cambridge, MA: Harvard University Press, 1989.

Geroulanos, Stefanos. "An Anthropology of Exit: Bataille's Interpretation of Heidegger." *October* 117 (summer 2006): 3–24.

———. "Transparency Thinking Freedom: Maurice Blanchot's *The Most High*." *MLN* 122, no. 5 (December 2007): 1050–78.

Gide, André. *L'Immoraliste*. Paris: Mercure de France, 1902.

———. *Retour de l'URSS*. Paris: Gallimard, 1937.

Gildea, Robert. *Marianne in Chains: Daily Life in the Heart of France During the German Occupation*. New York: Picador, 2002.

Gillespie, Michael Allen. *The Theological Origins of Modernity*. Chicago: University of Chicago Press, 2009.

Glucksmann, André. *Les maîtres penseurs*. Paris: Grasset, 1977.

Gordon, Daniel. *Postmodernism and the Enlightenment*. London: Routledge, 2000.

Gordon, Peter Eli. "Realism, Science, and the Deworlding of the World." In *A Companion to Phenomenology and Existentialism*, ed. Mark Wrathall and Hubert Dreyfus, 425–44. London: Blackwell, 2005.

———. *Rosenzweig and Heidegger: Judaism and German Philosophy*. Berkeley: University of California Press, 2003.

Gouhier, Henri. *L'Antihumanisme au XVIIe Siècle*. Paris: Vrin, 1987.

Gray, John. *Straw Dogs: Thoughts on Humans and Other Animals*. London: Granta Books, 2002.

Gregg, John. *Maurice Blanchot and the Literature of Transgression*. Princeton, NJ: Princeton University Press, 1994.

Greisch, Jean. *Ontologie et temporalité*. Paris: PUF, 2002.

Groethuysen, Bernhard. *Introduction à la philosophie allemande depuis Nietzsche*. Paris: Stock, 1926.

Groys, Boris. *The Total Art of Stalinism: Avant-Garde, Aesthetic Dictatorship, and Beyond*. Trans. Charles Rougle. Princeton, NJ: Princeton University Press, 1992.

Guénoun, Denis. *L'Enlèvement de la politique: une hypothèse sur le rapport de Kant à Rousseau*. Paris: Circe, 2002.

Gurvitch, Georges. *Les Tendances actuelles de la philosophie allemande: E. Husserl, M. Scheler, E. Lask, M. Heidegger*. Paris: Vrin, 1930.

Gurwitsch, Aron. *Phenomenology and the Theory of Science*. Evanston, IL: Northwestern University Press, 1974.

Gutting, Gary. *French Philosophy in the Twentieth Century*. London: Cambridge University Press, 2001.

Haar, Michel. *Heidegger and the Essence of Man*. Trans. William McNeill. Albany: State University of New York Press, 1993.

———. *La philosophie française entre phénoménologie et métaphysique*. Paris: PUF, 1999.

Hamacher, Werner. "The Right to Have Rights: Four-and-a-Half Remarks." *The South Atlantic Quarterly* 103, nos. 2–3 (spring–summer 2004): 343–56.

Hart, Kevin. *The Dark Gaze: Maurice Blanchot and the Sacred.* Chicago: University of Chicago Press, 2004.

Hecht, Jennifer Michael. *The End of the Soul: Scientific Modernity, Atheism, and Anthropology in France.* New York: Columbia University Press, 2003.

Hegel, G. W. F. *Critique of Pure Reason.* Trans. Norman Kemp Smith. New York: St. Martin's Press, 1965.

——. *Phenomenology of Spirit.* Trans. A. V. Miller. Oxford: Oxford University Press, 1977.

——. *Three Essays 1793–95.* Ed. and trans. by P. Fuss and J. Dobbins. Notre Dame, IL: University of Notre Dame Press, 1984.

Heidegger, Martin. *Being and Time.* Trans. Macquarrie and Robinson. New York: Harper and Row, 1962.

——. "De la nature de la cause." *Recherches philosophiques* I (1931–32): 83–124.

——. "Fragments sur le temps." Trans. J. Rosenthal (pseudonym of J. Rovan). *L'Arbalète* (summer–fall 1941): 33–48.

——. *Gesamtausgabe 15.* Frankfurt am Mein: Vittorio Klostermann, 1986. Translated as *Four Seminars: Le Thor 1966, 1968, 1969, Zahringen 1973.* Bloomington: Indiana University Press, 2003.

——. *Gesamtausgabe 27: Einleitung in die Philosophie.* Frankfurt: Klostermann, 1996.

——. *Gesamtausgabe 69: Die Geschichte des Seyns.* Frankfurt: Klostermann, 1998.

——. *Hegel's Phenomenology of Spirit.* Trans. P. Emad and K. Maly. Bloomington: Indiana University Press, 1988.

——. Interview with *L'Express.* *L'Express* 954 (October 20–26, 1969).

——. *An Introduction to Metaphysics.* Trans. Ralph Manheim. New Haven, CT, and London: Yale University Press, 1959.

——. *Kant and the Problem of Metaphysics.* Trans. Richard Taft. Bloomington: Indiana University Press, 1997.

——. *Kant et le problème de la metaphysique.* Trans. A. de Waelhens and W. Biemel. Paris: Gallimard, 1953.

——. *Lettre sur l'humanisme.* Trans. Roger Munier. Paris: Aubier, 1964.

——. *On the Way to Language.* Trans. P. D. Hertz. San Francisco: Harper, 1982.

——. *Pathmarks.* Cambridge: Cambridge University Press, 1998.

——. "Qu'est-ce que la métaphysique?" Trans. H. Corbin. *Bifur* 8 (1931).

——. *Qu'est-ce que la métaphysique?* Trans. Henri Corbin. Paris: Gallimard, 1938.

Heisenberg, Werner. *Physique et philosophie.* Paris: Albin Michel, 1961.

——. *Principes physiques de la théorie des quanta.* Paris: Gauthier-Villars, 1932.

Hellman, John. *Emmanuel Mounier and the New Catholic Left 1930–1950.* Toronto: University of Toronto Press, 1981.

———. "French 'Left-Catholics' and Communism in the 1930s." *Church History* 45, no. 4 (December 1976): 507–23.

Herf, Jeffrey. *Reactionary Modernism: Technology, Culture and Politics in Weimar and the Third Reich.* Cambridge: Cambridge University Press, 1984.

Hersch, Jeanne, ed. *Le Droit d'être un homme.* Paris: UNESCO, 1968.

Hesbois, Bernard. "Le Livre et la Mort. Essai sur Kojève." PhD diss., Université Catholique de Louvain, 1985.

Hill, Leslie. *Maurice Blanchot: Extreme Contemporary.* London: Routledge, 1997.

Hirst, Paul. *Durkheim, Bernard, and Epistemology.* London and Boston: Routledge and K. Paul, 1975.

Hollier, Denis. *Absent Without Leave: French Literature Under the Threat of War.* Trans. Catherine Porter. Cambridge, MA: Harvard University Press, 1997.

———, ed. *Le Collège de sociologie 1937–1939.* Paris: Gallimard (nouvelle edition), 1995.

———, ed. *A New History of French Literature.* Cambridge, MA: Harvard University Press, 1994.

Hollywood, Amy. *Sensible Ecstasy: Mysticism, Difference, and the Demands of History.* Chicago: University of Chicago Press, 2002.

Hughes, H. Stuart. *The Obstructed Path: French Social Thought in the Years of Desperation.* New York and London: Harper Torchbooks, 1966.

Hunt, Lynn. "The Paradoxical Origins of Human Rights." In *Human Rights and Revolutions,* ed. Lynn Hunt, Jeffrey N. Wasserstrom, and Marilyn B. Young. Boulder, CO: Rowman and Littlefield, 2000.

Husserl, Edmund. "Briefwechsel." In *Husserliana,* vol. 3: *Briefwechsel,* Teil III: "Die Göttinger Schule," ed. Karl Schuhmann. Dordrecht, Germany, Boston, and London: Kluwer Academic Publishers, 1994.

———. *Crisis of the European Sciences and Transcendental Phenomenology.* Chicago: Northwestern University Press, 1970.

———. *Méditations cartésiennes.* Translated into French by G. Peiffer et E. Levinas. Paris: Vrin (new edition), 1992.

Hyppolite, Jean. *Figures de la pensée philosophique.* 2 vols. Paris: PUF, 1971.

———. *Logique et existence: Essai sur la logique de Hegel.* Paris: PUF (Epiméthée), 1952. Translated by Leonard Lawlor and Amit Sen as *Logic and Existence.* Albany: State University of New York Press, 1997.

Imbert, Claude. *Maurice Merleau-Ponty.* Paris: ADPF, 2005.

Institut International d'études Européennes "Antonio Rosmini," Bolzano. *L'Éducation de l'homme européen—fondements et limites: Actes de la 7ème rencontre internationale* (August 29–September 1, 1962). Bolzano: Tipografia Athesia, 1964.

Jackson, Julian. *France: The Dark Years 1940–44*. Oxford: Oxford University Press, 2001.

———. *The Popular Front in France: Defending Democracy 1934–1938*. Cambridge: Cambridge University Press, 1988.

Janicaud, Dominique. *Heidegger en France*. 2 vols. Paris: Albin Michel, 2001.

———. *L'Homme va-t-il dépasser l'humain?* Paris: Bayard, 2002.

Jarczyk, Gwendoline, and Pierre-Jean Labarrière, *De Kojève à Hegel: Cent cinquante ans de pensée hégélienne en France*. Paris: Albin Michel, 1996.

Jay, Martin. *Marxism and Totality: The Adventures of a Concept from Lukacs to Habermas*. Berkeley: University of California Press, 1980.

Judaken, Jonathan. *Jean-Paul Sartre and the Jewish Question*. Lincoln: University of Nebraska Press, 2006.

Judt, Tony. *Marxism and the French Left: Studies in Labour and Politics in France, 1830–1981*. New York: Oxford University Press, 1986.

———. *Past Imperfect: French Intellectuals, 1944–1956*. Berkeley: University of California Press, 1992.

Kanapa, Jean. *L'existentialisme n'est pas un humanisme*. Paris: Editions sociales, 1947.

Kant, Immanuel. *Anthropology from a Pragmatic Point of View*. Trans. Mary J. Gregor. The Hague: Martinus Nijhoff, 1974.

———. *Logic*. Trans. R. S. Hartman and W. Schwarz. New York: Dover Publications, 1988.

Kaplan, Alice. *The Collaborator: The Trial and Execution of Robert Brasillach*. Chicago: University of Chicago Press, 2000.

Kaufmann, Walter, ed. *Existentialism from Dostoyevsky to Sartre*. New York: Meridian Publishing Company, 1989.

Keenan, D. K., ed. *Hegel and Contemporary Continental Philosophy*. Albany: State University of New York Press, 2004.

Khilnani, Sunil. *Arguing Revolution: The Intellectual Left in Postwar France*. New Haven, CT, and London: Yale University Press, 1993.

Kleinberg, Ethan. *Generation Existential: Heidegger's Philosophy in France, 1927–1961*. Ithaca, NY: Cornell University Press, 2005.

Klossowski, Pierre. "Sur Maurice Blanchot." *Les Temps modernes* 40 (1949): 298–314. Altered and republished in *Un si funeste désir*. Paris: Gallimard, 1962.

Koestler, Arthur. *Darkness at Noon*. London: Vintage, 2005.

Kojève, Alexandre. "Christianisme et communisme." *Critique* 3–4 (1946). Translated as "Christianity and Communism," *Interpretation* 19, no. 2 (winter 1991–92).

———. "Die Geschichtsphilosophie Wladimir Solowjeffs." *Der russische Gedanken* 3 (1930): 305–24.

———. "Entretien avec Gilles Lapouge." *La Quinzaine Litteraire* 1–15 (June 1968).

———. *Essai d'une histoire raisonnée de la philosophie païenne.* 3 vols. Paris: Gallimard (poche), 1997.

———. "Hegel, Marx et le christianisme." *Critique* 3–4 (August–September 1946): 339–66.

———. *Introduction à la lecture de Hegel.* 2d ed. Paris: Gallimard, 1968. Translated, in part, as *Introduction to the Reading of Hegel.* Ithaca, NY: Cornell University Press, 1980.

———. *Kant.* Paris: Gallimard, 1973.

———. *L'Athéisme.* Paris: Gallimard, 1998

———. *L'Idée du déterminisme dans la physique classique et dans la physique moderne* (1932). Paris: Biblio-Essais, 1990.

———. "La métaphysique réligeuse de Vladimir Solovyov." *Revue d'histoire et de philosophie religeuses* XIV, no. 6 (1934): 534–54; and XV, nos. 1–2 (1935): 110–52.

———. *La Notion de l'autorité.* Paris: Gallimard, 2004.

———. "La Philosophie des sciences de M. B. Bavink." *Revue de synthèse* 2, 8, no. 4 (April–October 1934): 234–35.

———. "Le Colonialisme dans une perspective européenne." *Commentaire* 87 (1999). Originally published in German as "Kolonialismus in europäischer Sicht," in *Schmittiana: Beiträge zu Leben und Werke Carl Schmitts,* bd. VI, ed. P. Tommissen. Berlin: Duncker & Humblot, 1998. Translated as "Colonialism from a European Perspective," *Interpretation* 29, no. 1 (fall 2001).

———. *Le Concept, le temps et le discours: Introduction au système du savoir.* Ed. Bernard Hesbois. Paris: Gallimard, 1990.

———. "Note sur Hegel et Heidegger." Ed. B. Hesbois. *Rue Descartes* 7 (1993).

———. *Outline of a Phenomenology of Right.* Lanham, MD: Rowman and Littlefield, 2000.

———. Review of *Archives d'Histoire des Sciences et Techniques [Archiv istorii nauki i techniki], Académie des Sciences de l'URSS. Travaux de l'Institut d'Histoire des Sciences et des Techniques,"* ière série, vols. V/VI (1935). In *Thalès,* X (1935), 237–53.

———, (as Al. Koschewnikoff). *Die religiöse Philosophie Wladimir Solowjews.* PhD, Heidelberg (nr. inv. Ruprecht-Karls Universität Heidelberg: w 3651), 1926.

———, (as Alexandre Kojevnikoff). "La critique de la religion au 17e siècle: Pierre Bayle." In Ecole Pratique des Hautes Etudes, Section des sciences réligieuses, Annuaire 1937–38. Melun: Imprimerie Administrative, 1937.

———, (as Alexandre Kojevnikoff). "La Philosophie des sciences de M. B. Bavink." *Revue de synthèse* 2, 8, no. 4 (April–October 1934): 234–35.

————, (as Alexander Koschewnikoff). "Die Geschichtsphilosophie Wladimir Solowjeffs." *Der russische Gedanken* 3 (1930): 305–24.

————, (as Alexander Koschewnikoff). "Die religiöse Philosophie Wladimir Solowjews." PhD diss., Heidelberg (nr. inv. Ruprecht-Karls Universität Heidelberg: W 3651), 1926.

Koyré, Alexandre. "Bemerkungen zu den Zenonischen Paradoxen." *Jahrbuch für Philosophie und phänomenologische Forschung,* V (1922): 610–13.

————. *De la mystique à la science: Cours, conférences et documents 1922–62.* Ed. Pietro Redondi. Paris: Editions EHESS, 1986.

————. "Die Philosophie Emile Meyersons." *Deutschfranzösische Rundschau* 3 (1931): 197–217.

————. *Etudes d'histoire de la pensée scientifique.* Paris: Gallimard, 1973.

————. *Etudes galiléennes.* Paris: Hermann, 1939.

————. *Etudes newtoniennes.* Paris: Gallimard, 1968. Translated as *Newtonian Studies.* Chicago: University of Chicago Press, 1968.

————. *From the Closed World to the Infinite Universe.* Baltimore, MD: Johns Hopkins University Press, 1957.

————. "Galilée et l'expérience de Pise: À Propos d'une légende." *Etudes d'histoire de la pensée scientifique.* Paris: Gallimard, 1973.

————. "L'évolution philosophique de Martin Heidegger." *Critique* 1 (June 1946): 73–83; *Critique* 2 (July 1946): 161–83.

————. *L'idée de Dieu et les preuves de son existence chez Descartes.* Paris: Bibliothèque de l'Ecole Pratique des Hautes Etudes/Ve section vol. 33, 1922. Translated into German as *Descartes und die Scholastik.* Bonn: Bouvier Vlg, 1923.

————. "Present Trends in French Philosophical Thought." *Journal of the History of Ideas* 59, no. 3 (July 1998): 534.

————. Review of Emile Meyerson, *Du cheminement de la pensée* (1931). *Journal de psychologie normale et pathologique,* nos. 5–6 (1933): 647–55.

————. Review of G. Van der Leeuw, *Phänomenologie der Religion. Recherches philosophiques* V (1935–36): 420–24.

————. Review of Martin Heidegger, *De l'être de la vérité.* Trans. W. Biemel and Al. de Waelhens. *Critique* 23 (1948).

————. Review of N. Hartmann, *Das Problem des geistigen Seins. Recherches philosophiques* IV (1934–35): 407–10.

————. Review of N. Hartmann, *Zur Grundlegung der Ontologie. Recherches philosophiques* V (1935–36): 420–24.

————, (written by Alexandre Kojève). Review of J. Perrin et al., *L'orientation actuelle des sciences,* intro. L. Brunschvicg (Paris: Alcan, 1930). *Revue philosophique,* nos. 9–10 (1932): 315–18.

Kravchenko, Viktor. *I Chose Freedom*. New York: Transaction, 1988.

L'Humanisme et la grâce: Semaine des intellectuels catholiques, 7 au 14 mai 1950. Paris: P. Horay / Centre catholique des intellectuels français, 1950.

Lacoue-Labarthe, Philippe. "A Jacques Derrida: Au nom de." In *L'imitation des modernes: Typographies II*, 229–55. Paris: Galilée, 1986.

———. *La Fiction du politique: Heidegger, l'art et la politique*. Paris: Christian Bourgeois, 1987.

Lacroix, Jean. "Danger de l'humanisme" in "L'Humanisme aujourd'hui: Enquête de l'UNESCO." *Comprendre* 16 (September 1956).

———. *Le Sens de l'athéisme moderne*. Paris/Tournai: Casterman, 1958.

Le Rider, Jacques. *Nietzsche en France*. Paris: PUF, 1999.

Lefebvre, Henri. *L'Existentialisme*. Paris: Sattigaire, 1946.

Lefort, Claude. *Sur une colonne absente*. Paris: Gallimard, 1978.

Lefranc, Jean. *La philosophie en France au XIXe siècle*. Paris: PUF, 1998.

Levinas, Emmanuel. "Comme un consentement à l'horrible." *Le Nouvel Observateur* (January 22, 1988).

———. "De l'évasion." *Recherches philosophiques* V (1935–36): 373–92. Translated by Bettina Bergo as *On Escape*. Stanford: Stanford University Press, 2003.

———. *Difficult Freedom*. Baltimore, MD: Johns Hopkins University Press, 1997.

———. *En découvrant l'existence avec Husserl et Heidegger*. 2d ed. Paris: Vrin, 1967. Translated, in part, as *Discovering Existence with Husserl*. Evanston, IL: Northwestern University Press, 1998.

———. *Humanisme de l'autre homme*. Paris: Fata Morgana, 1994. Translated by Nidra Poller as *Humanism of the Other*. Chicago: University of Illinois Press, 2003.

———. "La vision du poète." *Le Monde nouveau* 98 (1956). Translated by Michael B. Smith as "The Poet's Vision," in *Proper Names*. Stanford: Stanford University Press, 1996.

———. "Martin Heidegger et l'ontologie." *Revue Philosophique* (May–June 1932).

———. *Proper Names*. Stanford: Stanford University Press, 1996.

———. "Reflections on the Philosophy of Hitlerism." Trans. Seán Hand. *Critical Inquiry* 17, no. 1 (fall 1990): 64–71.

———. *Sur Maurice Blanchot*. Paris: Fata Morgana, 1975. Translated in *Proper Names*. Stanford: Stanford University Press, 1996.

———. *Théorie de l'intuition dans la phenomenologie de Husserl*. Paris: Vrin, 1930/1978. Translated by André Orianne as *The Theory of Intuition in Husserl's Phenomenology*. Evanston, IL: Northwestern University Press, 1973.

Levi-Strauss, Claude. "Language and the Analysis of Social Laws." *Structural Anthropology*. New York: Basic Books, 1963.

———. *Le Cru et le cuit*. Paris: Plon, 1964.

———. *The Savage Mind*. Chicago: University of Chicago Press, 1966.

Lévi-Valensi, Jacqueline, and Jeanyves Guérin. "Peut-on être humaniste dans la France des années cinquante?" *Cahiers de Fontenay* 39–40 (September 1985).

Lichtheim, George. *Marxism in Modern France*. New York: Columbia University Press, 1966.

Light, Steven, ed. *Shuzo Kuki and Jean-Paul Sartre: Influence and Counter-Influence in the Early History of Existential Phenomenology*. Carbondale: Southern Illinois University Press, 1987.

Lilla, Mark. "Ménage à Trois." *New York Review of Books* (November 18, 1999).

———. *The Reckless Mind: Intellectuals in Politics*. New York: NYRB, 2001.

———. "What Is Counter-Enlightenment?" In *Isaiah Berlin's Counter-Enlightenment*, ed. Joseph Mali and Robert Wokler. Philadelphia, PA: American Philosophical Society, 2003.

Lindenberg, Daniel. *Les années souterraines*. Paris: Éditions de la découverte, 1990.

Lipgens, Walter, ed. *Documents on the History of European Integration*, vol. 1: *Continental Plans for European Union 1939–1945*. Berlin and New York: Walter de Gruyter, 1985.

Loraux, Nicole. "La guerre civile grecque et la représentation anthropologique du monde à l'envers." *Revue de l'histoire des religions* 212 (1995): 299–326.

Loubet del Bayle, Jean-Louis. *L'illusion politique au XXe siècle*. Paris: Economica, 1999.

———. *Les non-conformistes des années trente: une tentative de renouvellement de la pensée politique française*. Paris: Seuil, 1969.

Lovejoy, Arthur O. *The Great Chain of Being: A Study of the History of an Idea*. Cambridge, MA: Harvard University Press, 1964.

Löwith, Karl. *From Hegel to Nietzsche: The Revolution in Nineteenth-Century Thought*. New York: Columbia University Press, 1991.

———. "Les Implications politiques de la philosophie de l'existence chez Heidegger." *Les Temps modernes* 14 (November 1946): 343–60. Translated as "The Political Implications of Heidegger's Existentialism," in *The Heidegger Controversy*, ed. Richard Wolin, 167–85. Cambridge, MA: MIT Press, 1992.

———. "Reponse à M. de Waelhens." *Les Temps modernes*, no. 35 (August 1948).

Lubac, Henri de. *Catholicisme: les aspects sociaux du dogme*. Paris: Cerf, 1938. Translated as *Catholicism: Christ and the Common Destiny of Man*. San Francisco: Ignatius Press, 1988.

———. *Corpus Mysticum: L'Euchariste et l'Eglise au Moyen-Age*. Paris: Aubier, 1949.

———. *Le Drame de l'humanisme athée*. Paris: Spes, 1945. Translated as *The Dra-*

ma of Atheist Humanism. New York: Sheed and Ward, 1950.

Lyotard, Jean-François. *The Postmodern Condition.* Minneapolis: University of Minnesota Press, 1984.

———. *Signed Malraux.* Minneapolis: University of Minnesota Press, 1999.

Machamer, Peter K., ed. *The Cambridge Companion to Galileo.* Cambridge: Cambridge University Press, 1998.

Macherey, Pierre. "Les Philosophes français de l'après-guerre face à la politique: *Humanisme et terreur* de Merleau-Ponty et *Tyrannie et sagesse* de Kojève." In *Materia Actuosa: Antiquité, Âge Classique, Lumières* (Paris: Honoré Champion, 2000).

Maistre, Joseph de. *Considerations on France.* Montreal: McGill-Queen's University Press, 1974.

Malraux, André. "Is Europe Dead?" *The New Leader* (January 18, 1947).

———. *L'Homme et la culture artistique (Conférence à l'UNESCO, 4 Nov. 1946).* Paris: J.J. Pauvert, 1947.

———. "L'œuvre d'art n'est pas une pierre." In *André Malraux: Cahier de L'Herne,* ed. Michel Cazenave. Paris : L'Herne, 1982.

———. *La Condition humaine.* Paris: Gallimard, 1933. Translated by Haakon M. Chevalier as *Man's Fate.* New York: Vintage, 1990.

———. *Les Noyers de l'Altenbourg.* Paris: Gallimard, 1948. Translated as *The Walnut Trees of Altenburg.* Chicago: University of Chicago Press, 1992.

———. *The Temptation of the West.* Trans. R. Hollander. Chicago: University of Chicago Press, 1992.

de Man, Henri. *L'Idée socialiste, suivi du Plan de travail.* Trans. H. Corbin and A. Kojevnikov. Paris: Bernard Grasset, 1935.

Marcel, Gabriel. *Homo viator.* Paris: Aubier/Montaigne, 1944.

———. *L'Homme problématique.* Paris: Aubier, 1955.

———. *Les Hommes contre l'humain.* Paris: La Colombe, 1951.

Marchand, Suzanne. "Nazism, Orientalism and Humanism." In *Nazi Germany and the Humanities,* ed. Wolfgang Bialas and Anson Rabinbach. Oxford: One World, 2007.

Marion, Jean-Luc. *Being Given: Toward a Phenomenology of Givenness.* Stanford: Stanford University Press, 2002.

———. *Reduction and Givenness: Investigations of Husserl, Heidegger and Phenomenology.* Evanston, IL: Northwestern University Press, 1998.

Maritain, Jacques. *The Collected Works of Jacques Maritain XI: Integral Humanism, Freedom in the Modern World, and A Letter on Independence,* ed. Otto Bird. Notre Dame, IL: University of Notre Dame Press, 1996.

———. *Le docteur angélique.* Paris: Desclée de Brouwer, 1930. Translated by J.F.

Scanlan as *The Angelic Doctor*. New York: Lincoln Mac Veagh / Dial Press, 1931.

Marquard, Odo. *Farewell to Matters of Principle*. Oxford: Oxford University Press [Odeon], 1989.

Marx, Karl. "Introduction to the Critique of Hegel's Philosophy of Right." In Karl Marx and Friedrich Engels, *The Marx-Engels Reader*, ed. Robert C. Tucker. New York: W. W. Norton, 1978.

Masson, André. *Les Années surrealistes*. Paris: Manufacture, 1990.

Masure, Eugène. *L'Humanisme Chrétien*. Paris: Beauchesne, 1937.

Maulnier, Thierry. "*La Condition Humaine* au théâtre." *Preuves* no. 46 (1955).

———. *La Crise est dans l'homme*. Paris: Redier (La Revue Française), 1932.

Mauriac, François. "Un écrivain devant les soviets." *Sept* 15 (March 22, 1935).

Maurras, Charles. "L'homme." In *Oeuvres capitales II*. Paris: Flammarion, 1954.

———. *Pour les mutilés*. Paris: Emile Paul Frères, 1917.

Mazower, Mark. *Dark Continent: Europe's Twentieth Century*. New York: Vintage, 1997.

Mélanges Alexandre Koyré. Vol. 2. Paris: Hermann, 1964.

Merleau-Ponty, Maurice. *Causéries*. Paris: Seuil, 2002. Translated as *The World of Perception*. New York: Routledge, 2004.

———. *Humanism and Terror*. Boston: Beacon Press, 1969.

———. Introduction to Michel Crozier, "*Human Engineering*: Les nouvelles techniques 'humaines' du Big Business Américain." In *Les Temps modernes* 69 (July 1951): 44–48. Republished in *Parcours I: 1935–1951*. Paris: Verdier, 1997.

———. *La Nature: Notes de cours du Collège de France*. Paris: Seuil, 1995.

———. *Les aventures de la dialectique*. Paris: Gallimard, 1955.

———. *Notes de cours, 1958–60*. Paris: Gallimard, 1998.

———. *Parcours I*. Paris: Verdier, 1997.

———. *Parcours II*. Paris: Verdier, 2000.

———. *Phenomenology of Perception*. London: Routledge, 1962.

———. *Sense and Non-Sense*. Trans. Hubert Dreyfus and Patricia Allen Dreyfus. Evanston, IL: Northwestern University Press, 1964.

———. *Signes*. Paris: Gallimard, 1960. Translated as *Signs*. Evanston, IL: Northwestern University Press, 1964.

———. *The Visible and the Invisible*. Evanston, IL: Northwestern University Press, 1968.

Meyerson, Emile. *Identité et réalité*. Paris: Alcan, 1912.

———. *Réel et déterminisme dans la physique quantique*. Paris: Hermann, 1933.

Michaud, Eric. *The Cult of Art in Nazi Germany*. Stanford: Stanford University Press, 2004.

Michel, Henri. *Les Courants de la pensée de la résistance*. Paris: PUF, 1962.

Michel, Henri, and Boris Mirkine-Guetzévitsch. *Les Idées politiques et sociales de la résistance.* Paris: PUF, 1954.

Mieli, Aldo. "Il tricentenario dei *Discorsi* di Galileo Galilei." *Archeion* 21 (1938).

———. "Souvenirs sur Duhem et une lettre inédite de lui." *Archeion* 19 (1937).

Mill, John Stuart. "On Liberty." In *Utilitarianism-On Liberty-Essay on Bentham,* ed. M. Warnock. New York: New American Library, 1974.

Monod, Jacques. *Le hasard et la nécessité.* Paris: Seuil, 1970.

Moyn, Samuel. "On the Intellectual Origins of Furet's Masterpiece." *The Tocqueville Review/La Revue Tocqueville* 29, no. 2 (2008).

Munier, Roger. *Stele Pour Heidegger.* Paris: Arfuyen, 1992.

Murphy, Francis J. *Communists and Catholics in France, 1936–1939: The Politics of the Outstretched Hand.* Gainesville: University of Florida Press, 1989.

Nancy, Jean-Luc. *Being Singular Plural.* Stanford: Stanford University Press, 2000.

———. *Hegel: The Restlessness of the Negative.* Minneapolis: University of Minnesota Press, 2002.

———. *The Inoperative Community.* Minneapolis: University of Minnesota Press, 1991.

———. *L'Oubli de la philosophie.* Paris: Galilée, 1986. Translated in *The Gravity of Thought.* Atlantic Highlands, NJ: Humanities Press, 1997.

———. *La Communauté affrontée.* Paris: Galilée, 2001.

———. *La Déclosion: la déconstruction du christianisme.* Paris: Galilée, 2005.

Nehamas, Alexander. "Foreword" to Alain Renaut, *The Era of the Individual.* Princeton, NJ: Princeton University Press, 1997.

Nietzsche, Friedrich. *Thus Spoke Zarathustra.* Ed. Robert Pippin and Adrian Del Caro. Cambridge: Cambridge University Press, 2007.

———. *Twilight of the Idols and The Anti-Christ.* Trans. R. J. Hollingdale. New York: Penguin, 2003.

Nizan, Paul. *Articles littéraires et politiques.* Vol. 1: 1923–35. Ed. Anne Mathieu. Paris: Joseph K., 2005.

———. *Pour une nouvelle culture.* Paris: Grasset, 1971.

———. Review of Alain's *Propos pour l'education* in *L'Humanité* (December 30, 1932).

———. *The Watchdogs: Philosophers of the Established Order.* New York: Monthly Review, 1971.

Nord, Philip. "Catholic Culture in Interwar France." *French Politics, Culture and Society* 21, no. 3 (fall 2003).

Noth, Ernst Erich. "The Struggle for Gide's Soul." *Yale French Studies* 7 (1951): 12–20.

Ory, Pascal. *La Belle illusion: Culture et politique sous le signe du Front populaire 1935–38.* Paris: Plon, 1994.

Pascal, Blaise. *Pensées.* Trans. A. J. Krailsheimer. London: Penguin Books, 1966.

Pavel, Thomas. *The Feud of Language.* Oxford: Oxford University Press, 1989.

Paxton, Robert O. "France: The Church, the Republic, and the Fascist Temptation, 1922–1945." In *Catholics, the State, and the European Radical Right 1919–1987,* ed. R. J. Wolff and J. K. Hoensch. Boulder, CO: Social Science Monographs, 1987.

———. *Vichy France: Old Guard and New Order 1940–44.* New York: Alfred A. Knopf, 1972.

Pillen, Angelika. *Hegel in Frankreich: Vom unglücklichen Bewusstsein zur Unvernunft.* Munich: Alber, 2003.

Pichot, André. *La Société pure de Darwin à Hitler.* Paris: Flammarion, 2000.

Pinto, Louis. "(Re)traductions: Phénoménologie et 'philosophie allemande' dans les années 1930." *Actes de la recherche en sciences sociales* 145 (December 2002).

Pippin, Robert. *Idealism as Modernism: Hegelian Variations.* Cambridge: Cambridge University Press, 1997.

Pirotte, Dominique, *Alexandre Kojève, un système anthropologique.* Paris: PUF, 2005.

Plotnitsky, Arkady. *The Knowable and the Unknowable: Modern Science, Nonclassical Theory, and the "Two Cultures."* Ann Arbor: University of Michigan Press, 2002.

———. *In the Shadow of Hegel: Complementarity, History, and the Unconscious.* Gainesville: University Press of Florida, 1993.

———. *Reading Bohr: Physics and Philosophy.* Dordrecht, Germany: Springer, 2007.

Ponge, Francis. *Le parti pris des choses.* Paris: Gallimard, 1967.

Poster, Mark. *Existential Marxism in Postwar France: From Sartre to Althusser.* Princeton, NJ: Princeton University Press, 1975.

Pranger, Burcht M. "Politics and Finitude: The Temporal Status of Augustine's *Civitas Permixta.*" In *Political Theologies,* ed. Hent de Vries and Lawrence E. Sullivan. New York: Fordham University Press, 2006.

Préli, Georges. "Le *Très Haut* de Blanchot: Loi, épidémie, et revolution." *34/44, Cahiers de recherché de S. T. D.* 2 (Spring 1977): 67–84.

Prévotat, Jacques. *Les Catholiques et l'Action française.* Paris: Fayard, 2001.

Proudhon, Pierre-Joseph. *Philosohpie de la misère.* Paris: Guillaumin, 1846.

Proust, Marcel. *In Search of Lost Time,* vol. 1. *Swann's Way.* New York: Modern Library Edition, 1998.

Queneau, Raymond. *Journaux 1914–1965.* Paris: Gallimard, 1996.

Rabinbach, Anson. "Communist Crimes and French Intellectuals." *Dissent* (fall 1998).

———. "Legacies of Antifascism." *New German Critique* 67 (winter 1996).

———. *In the Shadow of Catastrophe: German Intellectuals Between Apocalypse and Enlightenment.* Berkeley: University of California Press, 1996.

———. "Totalitarianism Revisited." *Dissent* 53, no. 3 (summer 2006): 77–84.

Rancière, Jacques. "Who Is the Subject of the Rights of Man?" *The South Atlantic Quarterly* 103, nos. 2–3 (spring–summer 2004): 297–310.

Reggiani, Andrés Horacio. *God's Eugenicist: Alexis Carrel and the Sociobiology of Decline.* New York: Berghahn Books, 2007.

Renaut, Alain. *The Era of the Individual.* Princeton, NJ: Princeton University Press, 1997.

Richir, Marc. *Au-delà du renversement copernicien: la question de la phénoménologie et de son fondement.* The Hague: Martinus Nijhoff (Phaenomenologica), 1976.

Ricoeur, Paul. "L'humanité de l'homme: contribution de la philosophie française contemporaine." *Studium Generale* 15 (1962).

———. "Que signifie 'humanisme'?" *Comprendre* #15: "L'Humanisme aujourd'hui: Enquête de l'UNESCO." (March 1956): 84–92.

Roberts, Mary-Louise. *Civilization Without Sexes: Reconstructing Gender in Postwar France, 1917–1927.* Chicago: University of Chicago Press, 1994.

Rockmore, Tom. *Heidegger and French Philosophy: Humanism, Antihumanism, and Being.* London: Routledge, 1995.

Rorty, Richard. *Philosophy and Social Hope.* New York: Penguin, 1999.

Roth, Michael S. *Knowing and History: Appropriations of Hegel in Twentieth-Century France.* Ithaca, NY: Cornell University Press, 1988.

Roudinesco, Elisabeth. *Jacques Lacan.* New York: Columbia University Press, 1997.

———. *La Bataille de cent ans.* 2. vols. Paris: Seuil, 1986.

Rousset, David. *L'Univers concentrationnaire.* Paris: Pavois, 1946.

———. *Les jours de notre mort.* Paris: Pavois, 1947.

Rovan, Joseph. "La remontée au fondement de la métaphysique." *Fontaine* 63 (November 1947): 786–804.

———. *Mémoires d'un Français qui se souvient d'avoir été Allemand.* Paris: Seuil, 1999.

———. "Mon témoignage sur Heidegger." *Le Monde* (December 8, 1987): 2.

Rubenstein, Joshua. *Tangled Loyalties: The Life and Times of Ilya Ehrenburg.* New York: Basic Books, 1996.

Ruyer, Raymond. "'Le Psychologique' et 'le vital.'" *Bulletin de la Société Française de Philosophie* (1938): 183.

Safranski, Rüdiger. *Martin Heidegger: Between Good and Evil.* Cambridge, MA: Harvard University Press, 1998.

Sartre, Jean-Paul. *Being and Nothingness: A Phenomenological Essay on Ontology.* New York: Washington Square Press, 1992.

———. *Cahiers pour une morale.* Paris: Gallimard, 1983.

———. *Carnets de la drôle de guerre.* Paris: Gallimard, 1983.

———. *L'Existentialisme est un humanisme.* Paris: Nagel, 1970.

———. *Search for a Method.* New York: Vintage, 1968.

———. *La Transcendance de l'ego: Esquisse d'une description phénoménologique.* 1965. Paris: Vrin, 2003. Translated as *The Transcendence of the Ego.* New York: Noonday Press, 1957.

———. "Un nouveau mystique." In *Situations I.* Paris: Gallimard, 1947.

———. "Une idée fondamentale de la phenomenologie de Husserl: l'intentionnalité." *Situations I* (January 1939). Paris: Gallimard, 1947.

Schalk, David L. *The Spectrum of Political Engagement: Mounier, Benda, Nizan, Brasillach, Sartre.* Princeton, NJ: Princeton University Press, 1979.

Schrift, Alan D. *Nietzsche's French Legacy: A Genealogy of Post-Structuralism.* New York: Routledge, 1995.

———. *Twentieth-Century French Philosophy: Key Themes and Thinkers.* Oxford: Blackwell, 2006.

Segre, Michael. "The Never-Ending Galileo Story." In *The Cambridge Companion to Galileo*, ed. Peter K. Machamer. Cambridge: Cambridge University Press, 1998.

Seigel, Jerrold. *Marx's Fate.* University Park: Pennsylvania State University Press, 1993.

Sherman, Daniel J. *The Construction of Memory in Interwar France.* Chicago: University of Chicago Press, 1999.

Sirinelli, Jean-François. *Deux intellectuels dans le siècle, Sartre et Aron.* Paris: Fayard, 1995.

———. *Génération intellectuelle: khâgneux et normaliens dans l'entre-deux-guerres.* Paris: PUF (Quadrige), 1994.

Sluga, Hans. *Heidegger's Crisis: Philosophy and Politics in Nazi Germany.* Cambridge, MA: Harvard University Press, 1993.

Solovyov, Vladimir. *Lectures on Divine Humanity.* Trans. B. Jakim. Hudson, NY: Lindisfarne Press, 1995.

———. *Lectures on Godmanhood* (1896). London: D. Dobson, 1948.

Sonnemann, Ulrich. *Negative Anthropologie.* Reinbek bei Hamburg, Germany: Rowohlt, 1969.

Spaier, Albert. Review of Jean Wahl's *Vers le concret. Recherches philosophiques* II (1932–33).

Sternhell, Zeev. *La Droite revolutionnaire 1885–1914: Les origines françaises du fascisme.* Paris: Seuil, 1978.

———. *Les Anti-lumières: du XVIIIe siècle à la guerre froide.* Paris: Fayard, 2006.

———. *Neither Right nor Left: Fascist Ideology in France.* Princeton, NJ: Princeton University Press, 1986.

Stiegler, Bernard. *Technics and Time 1: The Fault of Epimetheus.* Stanford: Stanford University Press, 1998.

Stoekl, Allan. "Introduction: Death at the End of History." In Maurice Blanchot, *The Most High.* Lincoln: University of Nebraska Press, 1996.

———. *Politics, Writing, Mutilation: The Cases of Bataille, Blanchot, Roussel, Leiris, and Ponge.* Minneapolis: University of Minnesota Press, 1985.

———. "Round Dusk: Kojève at 'The End.'" *Postmodern Culture* 5, no. 1 (September 1994).

Stoffel, Jean-François. *Bibliographie d'Alexandre Koyré.* Florence: Leo S. Olschki, 2000.

Strauss, Leo. *On Tyranny.* Revised and expanded edition including the Strauss-Kojève correspondence. Ed. Viktor Gourevich and Michael S. Roth. Chicago: University of Chicago Press, 1991.

Syrotinsky, Michael. "How Is Literature Possible?" In *A New History of French Literature,* ed. Denis Hollier. Cambridge, MA: Harvard University Press, 1989.

Szafraniek, Asja. *Beckett, Derrida, and the Event of Literature.* Stanford: Stanford University Press, 2007.

Taubes, Jakob. *The Political Theology of Paul.* Trans. Dana Hollander. Stanford: Stanford University Press, 2004.

Taylor, Charles. "Engaged Agency and Background." In Charles Guignon, ed., *The Cambridge Companion to Heidegger,* 317–37. Cambridge: Cambridge University Press, 1993.

Teroni, Sandra, and Wolfgang Klein, eds. *Pour la défense de la culture: Les textes du Congrès International des Écrivains, Paris 1935.* Dijon, France: Editions universitaires de Dijon, 2005.

Thao, Tran Duc. *Phenomenology and Dialectical Materialism.* Trans. D. J. Herman and D. V. Morano. Dordrecht, Germany, and Boston: Kluwer, 1986.

Theau, Jean. *La Philosophie française dans la première moitié du XXe siècle.* Ottawa: Editions de l'Université d'Ottawa, 1977.

Thielemons, Henri, S.J. "Existence Tragique: La Metaphysique du Nazisme." *Nouvelle Revue Théologique* 6 (1936): 561–79.

Thomä, Dieter. "The Difficulty of Democracy." In *Nazi Germany and the Humanities,* ed. W. Bialas and A. Rabinbach. London: OneWorld Publications, 2007.

Todd, Olivier. *Malraux: A Life.* New York: Alfred A. Knopf, 2005.

Todorov, Tzvetan. *Hope and Memory: Lessons from the Twentieth Century.* Princeton, NJ: Princeton University Press, 2003.

Tomissen, P., ed. "Der Briefwechsel Kojève-Schmitt." In *Schmittiana VI: Beiträge zu Leben und Werke Carl Schmitts*, bd. VI. Ed. P. Tommissen. Berlin: Duncker & Humblot, 1998.

Tournier, Michel. *The Wind Spirit*. Boston: Beacon, 1988.

Towarnicki, Frédéric de. *À la rencontre de Heidegger: souvenirs d'un messager de la Forêt-Noire*. Paris: Gallimard, 1993.

———. *Martin Heidegger: Souvenirs et Chroniques*. Paris: Rivages, 1999.

———. "Visite à Martin Heidegger." *Les Temps modernes* 4 (January 1946).

Tresize, Thomas. *Into the Breach: Samuel Beckett and the Ends of Literature*. Princeton, NJ: Princeton University Press, 1990.

Ungar, Steven. *Scandal and Aftereffect*. Minneapolis: University of Minnesota Press, 1995.

Vries, Hent de. *Minimal Theologies: Critiques of Secular Reason in Adorno and Levinas*. Baltimore, MD: Johns Hopkins University Press, 2005.

———. *Philosophy and the Turn to Religion*. Baltimore, MD: Johns Hopkins University Press, 1999.

Vries, Hent de, and Lawrence E. Sullivan. *Political Theologies: Public Religions in a Post-Secular World*. New York: Fordham University Press, 2006.

Vuillemin, Jules. *L'Heritage kantien et la révolution copernicienne: Fichte, Cohen, Heidegger*. Paris: Presses Universitaires de France, 1954.

Waelhens, Alphonse de. "Heidegger, Platon, et l'humanisme." *Revue philosophique de Louvain* 46 (1948).

———. "L'existentialisme de Sartre est-il un humanisme?" *Revue philosophique de Louvain* 1946 (44): 291–300.

———. *La Philosophie de Martin Heidegger*. Louvain: Éditions de l'Institut supérieur de philosophie, 1948.

———. "La Philosophie de Heidegger et le Nazisme." *Les Temps modernes* 22 (July 1947).

Waelhens, Alphonse de, and Walter Biemel. *Kant et le problème de metaphysique*. Paris: Gallimard, 1953.

Wahl, Jean. "A propos de l'introduction à la phénoménologie de Hegel par Alexandre Kojève." *Deucalion* 5 (October 1955).

———. *Etudes kierkegaardiennes*. Paris: F. Aubier, 1938.

———. *Existence humaine et transcendance*. Neuchâtel, Switzerland: La Baconnière, 1944.

———. "Existentialism: A Preface." *New Republic* (October 1, 1945).

———. *Introduction à la pensée de Heidegger*. Paris: Librairie Générale Française, 1999.

———. *L'Idée d'Etre chez Heidegger*. Paris: Centre de documentation universitaire, 1951.

———. "Le Problème du choix, l'existence et la transcendance dans la philosophie de Jaspers." *Revue de métaphysique et de morale* (1934): 404–44

———. *Les philosophies pluralistes d'Angleterre et d'Amérique.* Paris: Alcan, 1920. Translated by Fred Rothwell as *The Pluralist Philosophies of England and America.* London: Open Court, 1925.

———. *Petite histoire de l'existentialisme.* Paris: Club Maintenant, 1947.

———. *The Philosopher's Way.* New York: Oxford University Press, 1948.

———. *Poésie, pensée, perception.* Paris: Calmann-Lévy, 1948.

———. "Situation présente de la philosophie française." In *L'activité philosophique en France et aux Etats Unis,* vol. 2, ed. M. Farber. Paris: PUF, 1950.

———. *Vers la fin de l'ontologie: étude sur l'Introduction dans la métaphysique par Heidegger.* Paris: Éditions de l'Enseignement Supérieur, 1956.

———. *Vers le concret: Études d'histoire de la philosophie contemporaine.* Paris: Vrin, 1932.

Waldenfels, Bernhard. *Phänomenologie in Frankreich.* Frankfurt: Suhrkamp Vlg., 1983.

Weber, Elisabeth. "Elijah's Futures." In *Futures: Of Jacques Derrida,* ed. Richard Rand. Stanford: Stanford University Press, 2001.

Weber, Eugen. *Action Française: Royalism and Reaction in Twentieth-Century France.* Stanford: Stanford University Press, 1962.

———. *The Hollow Years.* New York: W. W. Norton, 1994.

Weil, Eric. "Le Cas Heidegger." *Les Temps modernes* 22 (July 1947).

Wernick, Andrew. *Auguste Comte and the Religion of Humanity: The Post-Theistic Program of French Social Theory.* Cambridge: Cambridge University Press, 2001.

Winock, Michel. *Histoire politique de la revue 'Esprit' 1930–1950.* Paris: Seuil, 1975.

———. *Le Siècle des intellectuels.* Paris: Seuil, 1997.

Winter, J. M. *Dreams of Peace and Freedom: Utopian Moments in the Twentieth Century.* New Haven, CT: Yale University Press, 2006.

Wolin, Richard, ed. *The Heidegger Controversy.* Cambridge, MA: MIT Press, 1993.

———. *The Seduction of Unreason.* Princeton, NJ: Princeton University Press, 2004.

Worms, Frédéric, ed. *Droits de l'homme et philosophie.* Paris: Presses Pocket, 1993.

Wright, Gordon. *The Reshaping of French Democracy.* Boston: Beacon Press, 1970.

Wyschogrod, Edith. *Crossover Queries: Dwelling with Negatives, Embodying Philosophy's Others.* New York: Fordham University Press, 2006.

Zhdanov, Andrei, et al. *Problems of Soviet Literature: Reports and Speeches at the First Soviet Writers' Congress.* Ed. H. G. Scott. New York: International Publishers, 1935.

Zimmerman, Andrew. *Anthropology and Antihumanism in Imperial Germany.* Chicago: University of Chicago Press, 2001.

III. JOURNALS

Carrefour, 1946.
Combat, 1944–46.
Critique, 1945–54.
Esprit, 1935–41.
L'Humanité, 1932–37.
Les Temps modernes, 1945–52.
Recherches philosophiques I–VI (Paris: Bovin, 1932–37).
Revue de metaphysique et de morale, 1918–60.
Revue philosophique de la France et de l'étranger, 1918–39.
Zeitschrift für Sozialforschung, 1937.

Index

Cultural Memory | *in the Present*

Hélène Cixous and Jacques Derrida, *Veils*

F. R. Ankersmit, *Historical Representation*

F. R. Ankersmit, *Political Representation*

Elissa Marder, *Dead Time: Temporal Disorders in the Wake of Modernity (Baudelaire and Flaubert)*

Reinhart Koselleck, *The Practice of Conceptual History: Timing History, Spacing Concepts*

Niklas Luhmann, *The Reality of the Mass Media*

Hubert Damisch, *A Childhood Memory by Piero della Francesca*

Hubert Damisch, *A Theory of /Cloud/: Toward a History of Painting*

Jean-Luc Nancy, *The Speculative Remark (One of Hegel's Bons Mots)*

Jean-François Lyotard, *Soundproof Room: Malraux's Anti-Aesthetics*

Jan Patočka, *Plato and Europe*

Hubert Damisch, *Skyline: The Narcissistic City*

Isabel Hoving, *In Praise of New Travelers: Reading Caribbean Migrant Women Writers*

Richard Rand, ed., *Futures: Of Derrida*

William Rasch, *Niklas Luhmann's Modernity: The Paradox of System Differentiation*

Jacques Derrida and Anne Dufourmantelle, *Of Hospitality*

Jean-François Lyotard, *The Confession of Augustine*

Kaja Silverman, *World Spectators*

Samuel Weber, *Institution and Interpretation: Expanded Edition*

Jeffrey S. Librett, *The Rhetoric of Cultural Dialogue: Jews and Germans in the Epoch of Emancipation*

Ulrich Baer, *Remnants of Song: Trauma and the Experience of Modernity in Charles Baudelaire and Paul Celan*

Samuel C. Wheeler III, *Deconstruction as Analytic Philosophy*

David S. Ferris, *Silent Urns: Romanticism, Hellenism, Modernity*

Rodolphe Gasché, *Of Minimal Things: Studies on the Notion of Relation*

Sarah Winter, *Freud and the Institution of Psychoanalytic Knowledge*

Samuel Weber, *The Legend of Freud: Expanded Edition*

Aris Fioretos, ed., *The Solid Letter: Readings of Friedrich Hölderlin*

J. Hillis Miller / Manuel Asensi, *Black Holes / J. Hillis Miller; or, Boustrophedonic Reading*

Miryam Sas, *Fault Lines: Cultural Memory and Japanese Surrealism*

Peter Schwenger, *Fantasm and Fiction: On Textual Envisioning*

Didier Maleuvre, *Museum Memories: History, Technology, Art*

Jacques Derrida, *Monolingualism of the Other; or, The Prosthesis of Origin*

Andrew Baruch Wachtel, *Making a Nation, Breaking a Nation: Literature and Cultural Politics in Yugoslavia*

Niklas Luhmann, *Love as Passion: The Codification of Intimacy*

Mieke Bal, ed., *The Practice of Cultural Analysis: Exposing Interdisciplinary Interpretation*

Jacques Derrida and Gianni Vattimo, eds., *Religion*